THE SELECTED LETTERS OF

Louisa May Alcott

With an Introduction by
MADELEINE B. STERN

Editors
JOEL MYERSON and DANIEL SHEALY

Associate Editor
MADELEINE B. STERN

LITTLE, BROWN AND COMPANY

Boston   Toronto

FIRST EDITION

Library of Congress Cataloging-in-Publication Data
Alcott, Louisa May, 1832–1888.
The selected letters of Louisa May Alcott.
Includes index.
1. Alcott, Louisa May, 1832–1888—Correspondence.
2. Novelists, American—19th century—Correspondence.
I. Myerson, Joel. II. Shealy, Daniel. III. Stern,
Madeleine Bettina, 1912–   . IV. Title.
PS1018.A44   1987   813'.4   [B]   86-27334
ISBN 0-316-59361-3

RRD VA

Designed by Patricia Dunbar

Published simultaneously in Canada
by Little, Brown & Company (Canada) Limited

PRINTED IN THE UNITED STATES OF AMERICA

CONTENTS

LIST OF ILLUSTRATIONS

ACKNOWLEDGMENTS

IN PREPARING THIS edition we have incurred many debts of gratitude. Un-happily, we can thank only in a general way the many librarians who answered our questions about Alcott materials at their institutions. We are also grateful to the following libraries for assistance in using their collections: Barnard College, Boston Public Library, Concord Free Public Library, Fruitlands Museums, Harvard University Libraries (Houghton and Widener), Massachusetts Historical Society, New-York Historical Society, New York Public Library (Henry W. and Albert A. Berg Collection and Manuscripts Division), Orchard House, Schlesinger Library of Radcliffe College, and University of Virginia Library (Louisa May Alcott Collection, Barrett Library).

Alcott's letters are published with the permission of the Estate of Theresa W. Pratt. We are also indebted to Charles M. Ganson, Jr., William F. Kussin, Jr., Charles W. Pratt, Frederick A. Pratt, John W. Pratt, and the Louisa May Alcott Memorial Association for help.

We are grateful to the following institutions for permission to publish materials in their collections: Barnard College Library (Overbury Collection); Trustees of the Boston Public Library; Boston University (Richards Collection and Special Collections); Bowling Green State University; Brigham Young University (Special Collections, Harold B. Lee Library); Brown University Library; Cincinnati Historical Society (Whelpley Collection); Columbia University (Moncure D. Conway Papers, Rare Book and Manuscript Library); Concord Free Public Library; Cornell University Library; Friends Historical Library of Swarthmore College (Elizabeth Powell Bond Collection); Fruitlands Museums; Houghton Library, Harvard University; Historical Society of Pennsylvania; Huntington Library; Iowa State Historical Library; Library of Congress; Lilly Library at Indiana University; Maine Historical Society; Massachusetts Historical Society; Minnesota Historical

Society (Allyn Kellogg Ford Collection of Historical Manuscripts); Morristown National Historic Park; New-York Historical Society; New York Public Library (Astor, Lenox, and Tilden Foundations: Henry W. and Albert A. Berg Collection; R. R. Bowker Papers, Rare Books and Manuscripts Division); New York University (Fales Library); Newberry Library; Pierpont Morgan Library; Princeton University Library (Wilkinson Collection of Mary Mapes Dodge); Schlesinger Library of Radcliffe College; Smith College (Rare Book Room and Sophia Smith Collection); University of Florida (Parkman Dexter Howe Library); University of Michigan Library (Langley Family Papers, Heineman Collection, Department of Rare Books and Special Collections); University of Texas at Austin (Harry Ransom Humanities Research Center); University of Virginia Library (Louisa May Alcott Collection, Barrett Library); Vanderbilt University (Special Collections, Jane and Alexander Heard Library); and Yale University (Collection of American Literature, Beinecke Rare Book and Manuscript Library).

Among the many people who have helped us, we would especially like to thank Judith Strong Albert, Thomas Blanding, Matthew J. Bruccoli, Paul E. Cohen, Rodney G. Dennis, Gary Sue Goodman, Ann D. Gordon, Sidney Ives, Elizabeth Kennedy, Alexandra Krapels, Caroline Langan, A. Dean Larsen, John McAleer, Elizabeth O'Connor, Richard S. Reed, Michael Richman, Justin Schiller, Betsey Shirley, Frederick Wagner, Joyce T. Woodman, and Roberta Zonghi. Armida Gilbert assisted us by diligently tracking down obscure people and events referred to in the letters. Jayne Gordon provided invaluable help by assisting us in contacting Alcott's heirs and by opening Orchard House for our use. Marcia Moss outdid her usual generosity by sharing with us her knowledge of the resources for the study of Concord.

Ann Sleeper first brought this project to Little, Brown, and we are grateful for her help. Christina Ward gave us much help and encouragement in seeing the book through press. We are grateful to Deborah Jacobs for her exemplary copyediting.

Photographic work was done by the staffs of the Concord Free Public Library, Harvard University, University of South Carolina (David Robinson), and University of Virginia.

Finally, each of the editors has individual thanks to offer. Joel Myerson is grateful to the Research and Productive Scholarship Committee of the University of South Carolina, and for her usual patience and support, Greta Little. Daniel Shealy acknowledges the support of the Graduate School of the University of South Carolina, the Southern Regional Education Board, the National Endowment for the Humanities Travel to Collections program, and, at Clemson University, G. W. Koon, Chairman of the Department of

English, and Robert A. Waller, Dean of the College of Liberal Arts. He is also indebted to his parents, Ruby and Ralph Shealy, who have continually offered their kind support and encouragement. Madeleine B. Stern acknowledges the unceasing support of her partner, Dr. Leona Rostenberg, who originally discovered Alcott's pseudonymous works.

ABBREVIATIONS OF
WORKS CITED

Bok. Edward W. Bok, "Louisa May Alcott's Letters to Five Girls," *Ladies' Home Journal* 13, no. 5 (April 1896): 1–2.

Cheney. Ednah Dow Cheney, *Louisa May Alcott: Her Life, Letters, and Journals* (Boston: Roberts Brothers, 1889).

LAFL. Madeleine B. Stern, "Louisa Alcott's Feminist Letters," *Studies in the American Renaissance 1978*, ed. Joel Myerson (Boston: Twayne, 1978), pp. 429–452.

LASC. Madeleine B. Stern, "Louisa Alcott's Self-Criticism," *Studies in the American Renaissance 1985*, ed. Joel Myerson (Charlottesville: University Press of Virginia, 1985), pp. 333–382.

Letters. The Letters of A. Bronson Alcott, ed. Richard L. Herrnstadt (Ames: Iowa State University Press, 1969).

LMA. Madeleine B. Stern, *Louisa May Alcott* (Norman: University of Oklahoma Press, 1950).

Whitman 10. Alfred Whitman, "Miss Alcott's Letters to Her 'Laurie,' " *Ladies' Home Journal* 18, no. 10 (September 1901): 5–6.

Whitman 11. Alfred Whitman, "Miss Alcott's Letters to Her 'Laurie,' " *Ladies' Home Journal* 18, no. 11 (October 1901): 6.

INTRODUCTION

Madeleine B. Stern

IT IS IN A LETTER that the birth of Louisa May Alcott was announced, and it is in letters that much of her productive life is recorded. What a varied history these "monitors," these "comforters"[1] trace — from the childhood, rich in love but poor in worldly goods, that would become a rich literary source to the struggles of youth, the experimentations of the writer, the increasing humanity and warmth of the woman, the extraordinary success that complemented the early disappointments, on to the closing in of age and illness. It is all here, or almost all, despite a few gaps in the pattern. A later writer has said in "The Poet and His Book," "Search the fading letters, finding / Steadfast in the broken binding / All that once was I!"[2] The "I" of Louisa Alcott is here in bright reflection. The letters are mirrors of the self and the life.

On 29 November 1832, Bronson Alcott, teacher, philosopher, idealist, wrote to his father-in-law, Colonel Joseph May:

> It is with great pleasure that I announce to you the *birth of a second daughter.* She was born at half-past 12 this morning, on my birthday (33), and is a very fine healthful child, much more so than Anna was at birth [in March 1831], — has a fine foundation for health and energy of character. . . . Abba inclines to call the babe *Louisa May,* — a name to her full of every association connected with amiable benevolence and exalted worth. I hope *its present possessor* may rise to equal attainment, and deserve a place in the estimation of society.[3]

1. Quotations are from Donald Grant Mitchell ("Ik Marvel"), *Reveries of a Bachelor,* Second Reverie.
2. Edna St. Vincent Millay, *The Poet and His Book,* whose use of the word "letters" has been reinterpreted by the present writer.
3. *Letters,* pp. 19–20.

And so a letter ushers Louisa May Alcott into the world and at the same time encapsulates the family into which she was born. That letter was not only record but prophecy.

Louisa's own epistolary record begins here with another, quite different birthday letter. The brief but poignant note, penned in all likelihood for her mother's birthday on 8 October 1843, reflects the explosive emotions of a troubled, rebellious ten-year-old, who offers her mother a bookmark: "It is not very pretty but it is all I had to give."[4] The rebellion and the giving started early in Alcott's life. Especially interesting is the fact that the letter was written at Fruitlands, the society launched by Bronson Alcott and his English colleague Charles Lane at Harvard, Massachusetts. Indeed, as a New Eden for the Consociate Family, it proved less a kingdom of peace than a realm of denial and dissension. The Alcotts moved there in June 1843. By January of the new year they had departed — not, however, before an observant ten-year-old had participated in a regimen of life that left enduring marks. At Fruitlands (and if there ever was a misnomer, the community at Harvard had found it) linen tunics were the only permissible raiment for a Consociate Family since cotton encouraged slavery and wool deprived the sheep of its natural clothing. The glory of sunrise at breakfast could not compensate for a strict diet of fruits and water for three growing sisters. Conversations about universal brotherhood, Bronson's instructions on the subjugation of body to soul, Charles Lane's lessons on little Louy's vices and virtues conspired less to elevate the family than to spread tension in Eden. On her mother's birthday, besides the note with the bookmark, Louisa Alcott wrote in her diary: "I wish I was rich, I was good, and we were all a happy family this day."[5]

That wish, so early articulated, had been shaped even earlier. Although there are no letters here that stand as witnesses for the first decade of Louisa Alcott's life, that decade can be reconstructed from other sources.[6] Born in Germantown, Pennsylvania, the second daughter of Bronson and Abigail ("Abba") May Alcott, Louisa soon moved with the family to Boston, where her father began his Temple School. While she was never a pupil there, being not quite two when it opened and five when it closed, she had personal experience of her father's "peculiar" and innovative teaching methods.[7] His pedagogy, applied eventually to all four daughters — Anna, Louisa, Elizabeth, and Abby May — stressed "unfoldment" through self-expression,

4. All quotations from Alcott's letters are from the present edition.
5. Cheney, p. 37.
6. For biographical details throughout, see LMA.
7. For Bronson Alcott's pedagogical methods, see Charles Strickland, "A Transcendentalist Father: The Child-Rearing Practices of Bronson Alcott," Perspectives in American History, 3 (1969): 5–73, and a reprinted abridgment in History of Childhood Quarterly 1 (Summer 1973): 4–51.

encouraged conversation and discussion often on sensitive subjects, resorted to allegories and parables, and endorsed the keeping of journals. If Louisa's head was never crammed with facts, she was emotionally charged with the duty of self-denial and the virtue of self-help.

The trials of Christian in his pilgrim's progress were cogitated at home. But abroad in Boston, Louisa could drive her hoop around the Common without stopping, be rescued from a fall into the Frog Pond, and be found by the town crier when she was lost on Long Wharf. The prototype of the tomboy Jo March was already being shaped.

In 1840, when the family moved to the village of Concord, Massachusetts, other influences were at work upon her. Neighbors became friends, and neighbors included the Emersons and the Thoreaus. Henry Thoreau especially guided her to the delights of larks and finches, prunella and cardinal flowers, and it was he who told her that a cobweb was a handkerchief dropped by a fairy. Already stricken with the fever of histrionics, Louisa and her sisters strutted the boards of the corn barn in dramatic exhibitions. For all such delights, intimations of the family's poverty filtered through to her. Yet, despite the poverty, despite her father's incapability of earning a livelihood and her mother's long-suffering fortitude, there is no doubt that Louisa was suffused even then with the love of both parents and the warmth of a truly consociate sisterhood that included one older sister, Anna, and a younger, Elizabeth, born in June 1835. In July 1840 the family was completed with the birth of the youngest sister, Abby May, whose life would be so intimately and tragically interwoven with Louisa's.

In 1841, using the "Alcott-Voyage-fund," for which Ralph Waldo Emerson raised subscriptions, Bronson Alcott sailed for England to visit a school that had been named after him — Alcott House, near Richmond — and the following year he returned to America with his colleagues Charles Lane and Henry Wright, with whom he would establish Fruitlands. Throughout the 1840s Louisa had overheard much and observed much. When she was not rampaging out-of-doors, she was sitting in a corner taking notes. And when the time came for converting those notes into literature, nothing would be forgotten.

Many of the notes she took found their way into her letters. The child who, at twelve or thirteen, was dreaming of the "little room which I suppose I never shall have," who was wading ponds and scribbling "with all her might," had, as she would put it in a letter to her father, fallen "with a crash into girlhood & continued falling over fences, out of trees, up hill & down stairs tumbling from one year to another till . . . the topsey turvey girl shot up into a topsey turvey woman."

Unfortunately, for the period between 1845 and 1853, when the "topsey turvey girl" was "tumbling from one year to another," there is a gap in Louisa's correspondence that must be filled by the researches of the biographer. Those years, between ages thirteen and twenty-one, were of course highly significant. Spent in Concord and in Boston, they saw the planting of many seeds that would later come to flower. Principally, that time was marked by two important developments: the intensity of the family's poverty and the intensity of Louisa's addiction to pen and ink. To alleviate the former, Louisa May Alcott at age nineteen went out to service, becoming a domestic in the household of the Honorable James Richardson of Dedham, Massachusetts. Digging paths through the snow, fetching water from the well, splitting the kindling, and sifting the ashes, she worked for seven weeks and in compensation for her drudgery received four dollars, which the outraged Alcotts promptly returned. Eventually she would convert this humiliating experience into a fairly lighthearted story entitled "How I Went Out to Service,"[8] and the feminist furies that those seven weeks aroused would also be molded to literary ends in the thrillers she would evoke from her inkstand. Now, in the early fifties, she was beginning to publish. Louisa Alcott's first appearance in print occurred in September 1851, when *Peterson's Magazine* ran her poem "Sunlight." This was followed in 1852 by the publication of her first story, "The Rival Painters. A Tale of Rome," which was emblazoned in the *Olive Branch*. The literary life had begun, although those beginnings were not preserved in letters. For the remainder of the decade, however, the gap is filled with a cornucopia of correspondence that illumines the development of the woman and the writer.

Anna Alcott, who had obtained a post as teacher in Syracuse, New York, now became the recipient of an abundance of letters from her younger sister, and those detailed bulletins were augmented by a series of delightfully informative letters to a young flaxen-haired boy from Lawrence, Kansas, named Alfred Whitman. Alf, a pupil at Frank B. Sanborn's school in Concord who boarded with the Pratts, was fifteen to Louisa's twenty-three, but he shared her addiction to the works of Charles Dickens and to the glories of greasepaint. A member of the Concord Dramatic Union's stock company, he soon found his way to her heart and became the Dolphus Tetterby to her Sophia. As Louisa remarked: "I was born with a boys nature & always had more sympathy for & interest in them than in girls, & have fought my fight . . . with a boys spirit under my 'bib & tucker' & a boys wrath when I got 'floored.' " Alf Whitman was one of Louisa's "boys," and when he returned to Kansas he took on the role of epistolary confidant. Later on some of his

8. *Independent* (4 June 1874); reprinted most recently in *Critical Essays on American Transcendentalism*, eds. Philip F. Gura and Joel Myerson (Boston: G. K. Hall, 1982), pp. 128–141.

traits would be incorporated in the character of Laurie, the hero of *Little Women*.

If Alf Whitman was Dolphus to Louisa's Sophia Tetterby, Anna Alcott was the Pythias to her Damon. To her were confided the doings of the "Pathetic Family" of Alcotts and the effects of their economic need upon Louisa. The need runs like a leitmotif through her letters: "I am grubbing away as usual, trying to get money enough to buy Mother a nice warm shawl. I have eleven dollars, all my own earnings." "I have eight cents in the bank at present, $10 owing me, & a fortune in prospect." And to her father Louisa wrote: ". . . mother is in good spirits having just received twenty seven dollars . . . which has paid the rent." Earlier she had asserted to him: "I will make a battering-ram of my head and make a way through this rough-and-tumble world."

The way was made, the pittance earned by sewing sheets, by tutoring, and by writing. A moving letter to the family in Concord sent in 1858 from Boston reports Louisa's despair when she could obtain no employment: "Every one was so busy, & cared so little whether I got work or jumped into the river that I thought seriously of doing the latter. In fact did go over the Mill Dam & look at the water." Louisa Alcott, however, would convert even the temptation at the Mill Dam into a story. Stories bubbled in her brain and were scribbled on paper as she sat in her room in the sky parlor of Mrs. David Reed's boardinghouse on Chauncy Street. From the *Saturday Evening Gazette* she received five dollars for a tale, and in November 1854 the dramatic narrative of "The Rival Prima Donnas" by "Flora Fairfield" appeared in print. A year later the fairy tales she had recounted for Emerson's daughter Ellen were published — *Flower Fables*, the first book by Louisa May Alcott, who, presenting a copy to her mother at Christmas, wrote: "Into your Christmas stocking I have put my 'first-born.'" In 1859 she was still reporting to Alf Whitman: "I have been scribbling foolish stories as usual." Many had found their way into the *Saturday Evening Gazette*, which raised its fees to fifteen or twenty dollars, and two were exalted in the pages of the more distinguished *Atlantic Monthly*, where payment was fifty dollars a tale. By then Louisa had begun work on her first novel, *Moods*.

Throughout the fifties, when she was attempting to please varied readerships at the same time that she (along with concerned friends of the family) was contributing to the Alcott Sinking Fund, Louisa was taking "private notes," poking an "inquisitive nose" and an observant eye "into every crack & corner." As a result, her life and her letters both are rich in images of the people and the world around her. Her understanding of her father shines through a letter that reports: "To Father I shall send . . . some paper; then he will be happy, and can keep on with the beloved diaries though the heavens fall." He looked "serenely at the . . . foolish world" and walked "thro life in quiet sunshine while others groped the dark." Her compassionate perception of her younger sister Abby — later called May — is equally clear: "She is so graceful and pretty and loves beauty so much, it is hard for her to be poor and wear other people's ugly things." When Abby began her studies at the School of Design in Boston, she was "bidding fair to become a second Raphael — She is perfectly wrapped up in drawing skating & dancing & in those three amusements she spends her 'shining hours.' " With as clear an eye and as honed a pen Louisa described the people of Boston, "my beloved old town whose very dirt is interesting to my eyes." In her net of words she captured the men in "Skye terrier whiskers & muffin hats," and back in Concord, when the Hawthornes returned from abroad, Louisa described the arrival of the new neighbors: "Mr. H. is as queer as ever and we catch glimpses of a dark mysterious looking man in a big hat and red slippers darting over the hills or skimming by as if he expected the house of Alcott were about to rush out and clutch him."

The accurate eye, the humorous undertone, the telling word recapture the life of the fifties: Louisa's theatre mania — "I go to the theatre once or twice a week" — alternates with her enthrallment with Dickens. The " 'rain & thunder' arrangements" of the Boston Theatre, its trapdoors and "ghastly fixtures" enchant her. She means "to pervade the theatre," and she does indeed, dramatizing her "Rival Prima Donnas" and writing a farce, *Nat Bachelor's Pleasure Trip*, which is performed in 1860. Her own appearance in private theatricals that feature *The Two Bonnycastles* or *The Rivals*, *The Jacobite*, or *The Morning Call* are climaxed by her rendition of *Mrs. Jarley's Waxworks*, dramatized from Dickens's *Old Curiosity Shop*.

Dreaming of the ten dramatic passions, Louisa still found time to attend Sunday evening receptions of the great Unitarian minister Theodore Parker or to hear the silvery-tongued orator Wendell Phillips. When antislavery senator Charles Sumner was honored in a demonstration that exhilarated antebellum Boston, Louisa was there, seeing the "streets . . . lined with wreaths, flags, & loving people," until, "in a state of rapterous insanity . . . I went home hoarse & worn out."

Two major family events throw into shadow the struggles and lighthearted larks of these germinal years. In 1858 Louisa's younger sister Lizzie, who had contracted scarlet fever some years before, died. "Mr Emerson Henry Thoreau & Frank Sanborn carried her over the threshold of her old home & laid her in the new one at Sleepy Hollow [Cemetery]." Two years later, Louisa's older sister, Anna, was married to John Bridge Pratt. Both events, in their different ways, left Louisa bereft; both are mentioned in the letters, and both would find their way into her masterpiece, *Little Women*.

Meanwhile, events of less private significance were pointing to an ominous future. Between skating and riding excursions, charade parties, husking parties, and masquerade balls, the town of Concord reacted to Harpers Ferry. "We are boiling over with excitement here," Louisa informed Alf Whitman in November 1859, "for many of our people (Anti Slavery I mean) are concerned in it. We have a daily stampede for papers, & a nightly indignation meeting over the wickedness of our country, & the cowardice of the human race." One of the people involved was schoolmaster Frank Sanborn, who was arrested for his friendship with the martyr John Brown.

And so the nation's life, like Louisa's, moved into a new decade whose events would leave a lasting imprint on both. In 1860, Louisa Alcott encapsulated for her correspondents the state of the "Pathetic Family." Father was now superintendent of schools in Concord. The town, however, intending to show that it "has as much muscle as brain," had succumbed to "a Gymnastic fever" spread by Dr. Dio Lewis, and "every one has become a preambulating windmill." The youngest member of the Alcott family "lives for her crayons and dancing," while Mother lives "for the world in general." Anna's world is "composed of John." As for Louisa: "I feel very moral to-day, having done a big wash alone, baked, swept the house, picked the hops, got dinner, and written a chapter in 'Moods.' " She had "two books half done, nine stories simmering, and stacks of fairy stories moulding on the shelf." In short, she was making "a gigantic blot of herself." Before long the "preambulating windmills" of Concord, Massachusetts, would be pursuing more martial exercise, and the writer who dwelled in Concord's Orchard House with the "Pathetic Family" would soon turn soldier in a civil war.

Now, as she informed Alf Whitman after the firing on Fort Sumter,

> every one is boiling over with excitement, & when quiet Concord does get stirred up it is a sight to behold. All the young men & boys drill with all their might, the women & girls sew & prepare for nurses, the old folks settle the fate of the Nation in groves of newspapers, & the children make the streets hideous with distracted drums & fifes. Everyone wears cockades wherever one can be stuck, flags flap over head like parti colored birds of prey, patriotic balmorals, cravats, handkerchief & hats are all the rig, & if we keep on at our present rate everything in heaven & earth will soon be confined to red, white, & blue, & "Hail Columbia" take the place of our Yankee "How are yer?"

As for herself, Louisa sewed blue shirts and scraped lint, studied Dr. William Home on gunshot wounds, and spent some time teaching kindergarten on Boston's Warren Street. In 1862, death claimed Louisa's old friend and neighbor

Henry Thoreau, who "at Mr Emerson's desire . . . was publicly buried from the church, a thing Henry would not have liked but Emerson said his sorrow was so great he wanted all the world to mourn with him."

While death claimed a host of others at the second battle of Bull Run and at Antietam, the Alcott family pursued its usual course, "Father writing & talking," Mother singing "among her pots & pans," feeding and clothing "all the beggars that come along," sewing "for the soldiers" and delivering "lectures on Anti slavery & Peace wherever she goes." In November, Louisa decided to interrupt the pattern by applying for a post as army nurse in Washington, D.C.

It was but six weeks that Louisa Alcott spent in the Union Hotel Hospital, Georgetown, but those weeks left an indelible imprint upon her health and her work. The hospital received the casualties of Fredericksburg, and as army nurse, Louisa applied poultices, handed saws and needles to the surgeon, stuffed bed sacks, read Dickens to her patients, and came to know some of them well. A jolly little nineteen-year-old sergeant, Robert Bane, had lost his right arm at Fredericksburg and was learning to write with his left; John Suhre, a Virginia blacksmith with a wound in his chest, was learning to die. She helped them all, as long as she could, the nurse from Concord in her straight, unruffled skirt and a red rigolette, or scarf, flung round her head. And much that she saw — from the thefts perpetrated by a "sanctified nurse" who prayed while she filched the men's watches and money, to the courage of her stalwart patients — she reported in letters home. Those letters, "written on inverted tin kettles, in my pantry, while waiting for gruel to warm or poultices to cool, for boys to wake and be tormented, on stairs, in window seats & other sequestered spots favorable to literary inspiration," have not survived in their original form. But they did survive long enough to be shaped into a book.

In January 1863 Nurse Alcott succumbed to violent illness variously diagnosed as pneumonia and as typhoid. By 24 January she was back at Concord. "I've been to Washington," she would write to Alf Whitman, "a nursin in the army, got typhoid fever & came bundling home to rave, & ramp, & get my head shaved & almost retire into the tombs in consequence." Indeed, the seizure may have affected her health for years to come; she believed it did. She returned to life with a temporary wig and a renewed determination to extract gold from her inkstand.

Between May and June, revised extracts from the hospital letters she had sent home were run by Frank Sanborn in the *Boston Commonwealth*, and such was the general appreciation of "Nurse Tribulation Periwinkle's" accurate eye, warmth of heart, and telling phrase that two publishers — Roberts Brothers and James Redpath — requested the right to reprint "Hospital Sketches" in book form. The author chose Redpath, a fiery abolitionist to whose beliefs, and contract, she subscribed. The series of letters to the publisher that resulted from this decision provides insight not only into author-publisher relations but into Louisa Alcott's convictions. When asked to yield a percentage of her royalties to charity, she replied: "I too am sure that 'he who giveth to the poor lendeth to the Lord' & on that principle devote time & earnings to the care of my father & mother, for one possesses no gift for money making & the other is now too old to work any longer for those who are happy & able to work for her."

By July 1863, she could declare to a correspondent: "My time is fully occupied with my pen," and the next month *Hospital Sketches* appeared between boards. To her publisher she confided: "I have the satisfaction of seeing my townsfolk buying & reading, laughing & crying over it wherever I go." Although her payment from all editions of the book, including a twenty-five-cent army printing in paper, would amount to only two hundred dollars, her reputation as an accurate reporter of realistic war scenes was established. "I'd rather not offer my green apples when a little time might ripen a few respectable samples," she prudently cautioned Redpath, but yielded when he promptly placed his imprint upon an Alcott fairy story entitled *The Rose Family* and an Alcott collection entitled *On Picket Duty, and Other Tales*.

Meanwhile, even before she had gone to Washington, the author had tried her ink-stained fingers upon another literary experiment — the suspenseful thriller.[9] She had written to Alf Whitman in June 1862:

> I intend to illuminate the Ledger with a blood & thunder tale
> as they are easy to "compoze" & are better paid than moral &
> elaborate works of Shakespeare, so dont be shocked if I send
> you a paper containing a picture of Indians, pirates wolves, bears
> & distressed damsels in a grand tableau over a title like this "The
> Maniac Bride" or "The Bath of Blood. A thrilling tale of passion."

Those thrilling tales punctuated the 1860s. Although the author thought little of them, indeed was secretive about them, publishing them usually anonymously or under the pseudonym of A. M. Barnard, although she considered them "not worth reprinting," they were nonetheless racy narratives employing sharp characterizations and cliff-hanger technique. Moreover, they earned for her not merely the much-needed financial reward of fifty or seventy-

9. For the discovery and analysis of the Alcott thrillers, see Leona Rostenberg, "Some Anonymous and Pseudonymous Thrillers of Louisa M. Alcott," *Papers of the Bibliographical Society of America* 37 (2d Quarter 1943): 131–140; *Behind a Mask: The Unknown Thrillers of Louisa May Alcott*, ed. Madeleine B. Stern (New York: William Morrow, 1975); and *Plots and Counterplots: More Unknown Thrillers of Louisa May Alcott*, ed. Madeleine B. Stern (New York: William Morrow, 1976).

five dollars a story, but an emotional catharsis, for in these blood-and-thunders a powerful, passionate, revengeful heroine tilts with and usually conquers the male lords of creation. Any feminist fury the author may have built up through years of struggle was filtered through these tales. Frank Leslie, the newspaper magnate of New York, published several of them: "Pauline's Passion and Punishment," which won a hundred-dollar prize; "A Whisper in the Dark"; "Taming a Tartar"; and "Perilous Play." Some of them appeared in the gaudy pages of *The Flag of Our Union*, a periodical published in Boston by Elliott, Thomes and Talbot. Their titles are as colorful as their contents: "V. V.: or, Plots and Counterplots," "A Marble Woman: or, The Mysterious Model," "Behind a Mask; or, A Woman's Power," "The Abbot's Ghost: or, Maurice Treherne's Temptation." To these L. M. Alcott added two Ten Cent Novelettes, "The Skeleton in the Closet" and "The Mysterious Key, and What It Opened."

Besides her realistic hospital sketches and her violent thrillers, the experimenting author was working on an autobiographical novel called at this time *Success*, a title that would eventually be changed to *Work*. She was also revising a novel with which she had struggled on and off for six years — *Moods*, a fictional analysis of the "two extremes of love." On the advice of publisher Aaron K. Loring of Boston, Louisa "took out ten chapters in order to shorten it," and at last, on Christmas Day of 1864, her novel was published. "The inspiration of necessity" upon which she had relied in most of her literary endeavors had at last served her well. Fame had begun to smile upon L. M. Alcott, author of *Hospital Sketches* and *Moods*, and fortune upon A. M. Barnard, creator of gruesome, unacknowledged effusions. And now, a few months after Appomattox, another of her childhood wishes — to travel abroad — was about to be granted. She had been invited to sail to Europe, if only as companion to a young invalid.

The merchant prince and shipbuilder William Fletcher Weld headed the fleet that flew the Black Horse Flag to Hong Kong and Melbourne. Having heard that Miss Alcott had been a nurse and wished to travel, he engaged her to chaperon his invalid daughter Anna to the German spas. They sailed aboard the *China* in July 1865, took the Rhine journey and the cure at Schwalbach, and at last arrived at the Pension Victoria in Vevey, Switzerland, framed by Lake Geneva and the Alps of Savoy. There the observant Miss Alcott encountered many birds of strange plumage who would color her stories and sketches. She also met a twenty-year-old Polish boy who had fought in the Insurrection and been forced to leave his country. Louisa found Ladislas Wisniewski as captivating as she had once found Alf Whitman. Like Alf, he would serve as one of the models for the hero of *Little Women*.

After a winter in Nice, the companion, freed from her often onerous duties by the arrival of Anna Weld's uncle, proceeded alone to Paris. There she was greeted by Ladislas, who became her cicerone for an enchanted fortnight. In May, on borrowed money, Louisa journeyed to London, stayed for a while with the Moncure Daniel Conways, enjoyed a Dickens expedition with the literary historian Moses Coit Tyler, and granted the publisher George Routledge the rights to issue *Moods* in return for five pounds. A year after her departure — in July 1866 — the wanderer returned home.

She returned to a family not very different from the one she had left. If Mother looked older and more tired, Father was as serene as before, more serene perhaps, having been elected to the St. Louis Philosophical Society. Anna — her family augmented by two babies, Fred, born in 1863, and John, in 1865 — might be afflicted with increasing deafness, but May was as full of plans, projects, and parties as ever. The family debts had mounted, it was true. The money borrowed to keep Louisa in London must be repaid. The inkstand awaited its genie.

In September 1867, Louisa Alcott received two requests: one, from Horace B. Fuller, to edit a juvenile periodical entitled *Merry's Museum* at a fee of five hundred dollars a year; the other, from Thomas Niles of Roberts Brothers, to write a girls' book. On 28 October she rode into Boston on her load of furniture to set up housekeeping at 6 Hayward Place, a residence she promptly rechristened Gamp's Garret. May joined her to start a drawing class, and the two busiest young women in the Commonwealth of Massachusetts played out their individual roles as Minerva Moody and Raphael.

Converting her European experiences and observations into stories and sketches, cramming the pages of *Merry's Museum* with "incidents, anecdotes & recollections," Louisa now had more offers than she could fill. As she wrote to her mother: "I often think as I go looking round, independent, with more work than I can do, & half a dozen publishers asking for tales, of the old times when I went meekly from door to door peddling my first poor little stories, & feeling *so* rich with a $10." This year, she believed, "I shall make my $1000."

In the spring of 1868, Louisa began work on the book Thomas Niles had suggested, and many of the details concerning that masterpiece in progress were recorded in letters to her publisher. The book that would become *Little Women* was a domestic novel about the four March sisters of Concord, Massachusetts: beautiful Meg, based upon Anna; Amy, striving for artistic elegance in the manner of May; Beth, Jo's conscience, drawn from Lizzie; and Jo — a fictional Louisa. Jo, tall and thin, with sharp gray eyes, long thick hair, and a fiery spirit, was not only the heroine of *Little Women* but the reason for the book's survival. A twentieth-century critic would call Jo "a unique creation: the one young woman in 19th-century fiction who maintains her individual independence, who gives up no part of her autonomy as payment for being born a woman — and who gets away with it."[10]

Louisa took up her pen, but the Marches wrote their own story. In that story there was a place for Laurie, modeled on Alf Whitman and Ladislas Wisniewski (" 'Laurie' is you & my Polish boy 'jintly,' " she confessed to Alf); for Anna's John Pratt, who appeared as John Brooke; for Marmee, staunch defender of human rights. The portrait of Father, with his atypical fads and reforms, was muffled. Her characters were, she wrote to Mrs. Thomas Wentworth Higginson, "drawn from life, which gives them whatever merit they possess; for I find it impossible to invent anything half so true or touching as the simple facts with which every day life supplies me." Many of the incidents too were dredged up from memory: the plays in the barn and the family post office, the sleigh rides and skating frolics. Fact was embedded in fiction. The local was married to the universal. One commentator would capture the quintessential Alcott when he remarked: "She unlatches the door to one house, and . . . all find it is their own house which they enter."[11]

Little Women or, Meg, Jo, Beth and Amy was published on 1 October 1868. Most critics found it sprightly and agreeable, and young readers began to clamor for a sequel. Thomas Niles agreed that the book might have a longer life than he had anticipated, and asked for Part II. Louisa took up the story three years after the curtain had fallen upon Part I. Here were relived Lizzie's (Beth's) death and Anna's (Meg's) wedding. May's drawing classes, Louisa's experiments with sensational stories were all included. But the author adamantly refused to comply with the frequently reiterated request to have Jo marry Laurie. It is artistic Amy who captures the hero, while Jo becomes the wife of the Teutonic, sagacious, authoritative Professor Bhaer. To an admirer Louisa explained: " 'Jo' should have remained a literary spinster but so many enthusiastic young ladies wrote to me clamorously demanding that she should marry Laurie, or somebody, that I didnt dare to refuse & out of perversity went & made a funny match for her. I expect vials of wrath to be poured out upon my head, but rather enjoy the prospect."

On her blue-lined papers Louisa Alcott had depicted the nineteenth-century New England home and countryside. The second part of Little Women was published on 14 April 1869. Some six thousand copies of Part I were now selling, but such a figure soon seemed trifling in light of the sales of the completed work. It appeared that Louisa May Alcott had at last found not only her style but her fortune. Enthusiastic reviews and masses of letters

10. Elizabeth Janeway, "Meg, Jo, Beth, Amy and Louisa," New York Times Book Review (29 September 1968); reprinted in Critical Essays on Louisa May Alcott, ed. Madeleine B. Stern (Boston: G. K. Hall, 1984), pp. 97–98.
11. Cyrus A. Bartol, quoted in LMA, p. [xv].

inundated the author. Lion hunters demanded autographs; sales quickly mounted to thirty-eight thousand. When Bronson Alcott lectured, he was now introduced as the Father of Little Women. The Alcott Sinking Fund overflowed. To keep her place in the public eye, to supply the ever-increasing demand, Louisa immediately composed another "little story about Young America, for Young America" entitled *An Old-Fashioned Girl*. The Little Women series was on its way.

The new book was published on 1 April 1870. The next day the author set sail once again for Europe. The invalid's companion of five years before was now a lion on grand tour. In a sense her life had been divided into two by the publication of *Little Women*. The life that had gone before would permanently influence the life that was to come, but it would never be resumed.

The contrast between those lives is nowhere better discernible than in the plethora of letters the tourist sent home from abroad. "I mean to keep a letter on hand all the time," she wrote to her mother from Morlaix, France, on 14 April, "and send them off as fast as they are done." Traveling with her sister May and a friend, Alice Bartlett, Louisa absorbed and reported to Concord all the colorful sights of the Côtes-du-Nord. Although she was now the observed as well as the observer, no detail of gable or turret, ruin or castle escaped her. Red-nosed priests joined peasant women in wooden shoes to form the dramatis personae of her letters, while the eccentricities of her fellow boarders were regaled for home consumption. "I shall put him in a story" testified to the ever-alert writer's eye. Louisa's sense of humor pervades these travel letters, ranging from a dry, semi-acerbic comment to utter hilarity when a tipsy Frenchman, who claimed to be Victor Hugo's best friend and a child of nature, made advances to Alice Bartlett and was told "it was not allowed in England."

At the same time, two less endearing signs of approaching age crop up in these mementos of the grand tour. An increasing attention to money becomes apparent as Louisa comments upon or complains about the cost of fabric or the expenses of travel, as she demonstrates at once a keen interest in bargains and a reluctance to part with her hard-earned wealth. And along with this trait appears another — a concentrated attention to her bodily ills, to maladies of throat or leg, and to the remedies recommended by doctors: iodine of potash, a variety of pills, opium for sleep. Louisa Alcott is not yet forty years old, but she already suffers from the fatigue engendered by the life that has gone before her great success. Jo March is now an aging Aunt Jo.

By the time the trio of travelers reached Vevey, where Louisa had once met her Polish boy, France and Prussia had declared war. Although Louisa's sympathies were with the latter because Germany had favored the North during the Civil War, she determined that this war she would escape if possible. While refugees flocked into Vevey, revolution seethed in Paris, and Strasbourg was bombarded, the tourists left the happily remembered shores of Lake Geneva for Italy.

Rome offered promise and pleasure to Louisa. With May she visited the artists' studios, and at one of them — George Healy's, on the Via Santa Nicola di Tolentino — she sat for her portrait. Along the Corso and Rome's narrow, intriguing streets the travelers wandered, drinking in the sights and sounds of the Eternal City. Then, in November, the joys of the grand tour were shattered by tragic news from home. John Pratt — "the one young man whom I sincerely honored in my heart" — had died suddenly two days before Louisa's birthday, leaving behind him a widow, Louisa's older sister, Anna, and their two small boys.

The news completely reshaped Louisa's grand tour even as it motivated a characteristic and predictable reaction on her part. Louisa Alcott almost immediately assumed her now-accustomed role of paterfamilias and, so that John's death would not leave his family in want, determined to complete another book. The title *Little Men* would be especially appropriate since the story would be told for John's two boys.

Only a few letters in this collection reflect Louisa's response to John Pratt's death, all written in the winter of 1870 from Rome. One of them — one of the few originally intended for publication — mentions her loss but devotes itself largely to a graphic description of the flood in Rome. The Tiber had overflowed its banks and, to the observant author, the catastrophe provided a picture of "tragedy and comedy, side by side." The comic side even now appealed strongly to Louisa, who enjoyed the sight of "gentlemen paying visits on the backs of stout soldiers, and family dinners being hoisted in at the two-story windows." Despite May's attachment to the arts, Louisa preferred the exigencies of life even in a time of disaster, declaring, "It thrills *me* more to see one live man work like a Trojan to save suffering women and babies, than to sit hours before a Dying Gladiator who has been gasping for centuries in immortal marble."

By the new year, when the flood had abated, Louisa was consumed with her new book. Seated on the balcony of her room at 2 Piazza Barberini, overlooking the Triton in the square, she thought less of Rome than of Boston, less of the present than of the past. Here, in this book, she recapitulated a life long since shed. Based to some extent upon Bronson Alcott's Temple School, the novel refashioned his peculiar pedagogy into the wholesome system of life and learning practiced at Plumfield, the fictional school. This sequel to *Little Women* made use of many of the experiences and observations of Louisa's youth, a youth now consigned permanently to literature.

Little Men was first published in London, where the author spent the last weeks of her journey. Then, leaving May to study art abroad, she boarded the *Malta* for home. At the Boston wharf there was no faithful John Pratt to greet her, but in his stead were Father and Thomas Niles. Their carriage was adorned with a great red placard advertising *Little Men*. The author's grand tour had been framed by two books, both drawn from her earlier life. *An Old-Fashioned Girl* had heralded her departure; *Little Men* would punctuate her return. Changed by time, though never by the miracle of her fame, *the* Miss Alcott had returned to Orchard House, on the Lexington Road.

The Miss Alcott had also returned to the decade that marked her maximum productivity. Between 1870 and 1879 she published the first five volumes of her collected stories, *Aunt Jo's Scrap-Bag*, as well as six of the eight novels in the Little Women series, following *An Old-Fashioned Girl* and *Little Men* with *Eight Cousins*; its sequel, *Rose in Bloom*; and *Under the Lilacs* and *Jack and Jill*. If none of these variations upon the domestic theme of *Little Women* ever equaled that masterpiece, they all in one way or another held her readership enthralled and substantially augmented the Alcott Sinking Fund.

In addition to those six full-length narratives, Louisa contributed more than fifty articles or stories to the periodicals of the seventies: the *Independent* and *Hearth and Home*, the *Woman's Journal*, and especially the *Youth's Companion*.[12] That long-lived weekly, now under the aegis of Daniel Ford, offered to subscribers advertisements of chemical cabinets, electrical equipment, and magic lanterns — along with the tales of Louisa May Alcott. Indeed, so frequently was her work featured by this periodical during the 1870s that she herself might have been called a "Youth's Companion."

Rejections had become a thing of the past. Publishers now outbid each other for Alcott works. With enormous satisfaction Louisa must have written that brief but poignant note of 3 July 1871 to editor James T. Fields, who had once advised her to stick to her teaching since she could not write: "Once upon a time you lent me forty dollars, kindly saying that I might return them when I had made 'a pot of gold'. As the miracle has been unexpectedly wrought I wish to fulfil my part of the bargain, & herewith repay my debt with many thanks."

Not all the Alcott writings of the period were directed to the youth of America. Among her numerous articles were two autobiographical sketches designed, despite their humorous overtones, for the more critical eye of the mature reader: "Transcendental Wild Oats," relating to the consociate dreams and earthly realities of the months at Fruitlands, and "How I Went Out to Service," detailing the writer's humiliating experience as a domestic in Ded-

---

12. See Madeleine B. Stern, "Louisa M. Alcott in Periodicals," *Studies in the American Renaissance 1977*, ed. Joel Myerson (Boston: Twayne, 1978), pp. 369–386.

ham. Similarly, two book-length works of the seventies appealed to adult readers: the autobiographical *Work*, which had once tentatively been entitled *Success*, and the almost Gothic, Faustian novel, *A Modern Mephistopheles*, which was revamped from an earlier, unpublished version. In *Work*, the author is transmuted into a Christie Devon who relives the Alcott lives of servant and actress, companion and seamstress in chapters that recall the struggles of the past. *A Modern Mephistopheles* is in a sense a return to the sensationalism in which the experimenting writer had once indulged, a tale of good contending with evil, narrated in lush words and exotic verbiage. Published by Roberts Brothers in the firm's No Name Series, *A Modern Mephistopheles* appeared anonymously, and public speculation about its authorship titillated the author.

Louisa Alcott's letters of the seventies naturally reflect her extraordinary productivity. Concerned with matters of editing and serialization, copyright and royalties, they offer insights not to be found elsewhere into her relations with publishers, her reactions to her popularity, and especially and most significantly, her attitude toward the craft of writing. In 1877, she writes to a family friend:

> I am thinking of a new book like Old Fashioned Girl, as my publisher tells me that sells better than any other of my immortal tales. So if Miss Alice has any good experiences, funny adventures or interesting incidents in girl-life I shall be very glad to hear of them, & shall calmly put em in & then take all the credit for "those life-like pictures & touching episodes." That's the way books are made, for there is nothing original in the world & the young folks write thier own stories; we only steal & publish them.[13]

Louisa Alcott detested lion hunters —

> I dont believe any one knows how we are bored by company, over a hundred a month, most of them strangers. A whole school came without warning last week & Concord people bring all their company to see us. This may *seem* pleasant, but when kept up a whole season is a great affliction. Mother says we have no home now & no chance to see our own friends. . . . I wish you'd write an article on the rights of authors, & try to make the public see that the books belong to them but not the peace, time, comfort and lives of the writers. It is a new kind of slavery. . . .

---

13. For further discussion of Alcott's dealings with her publishers and the letters from her publishers to her, see Daniel Shealy, "The Author-Publisher Relationships of Louisa May Alcott" (Ph.D. diss., University of South Carolina, 1985).

On the other hand, she valued and welcomed the letters from her youthful fans: "Over a hundred letters from boys & girls," she commented in 1872, "& many from teachers & parents assure me that my little books are read & valued in a way I never dreamed of seeing them. This success is more agreeable to me than money or reputation."

That success of course *was* reputation, and money was — despite the protest — always acceptable to Louisa May Alcott. "My first story," she recalled, "gave me $5.00 & I felt very rich. . . . Now I can ask what I like & get it." "Now I never write a short tale for less than $100. Serials $3000." Her demands were high and her assiduity about receiving her just rewards was intense. To Edward Marston, partner of the English publishers Sampson Low, Marston, she wrote in 1873: ". . . when I am constantly hearing from friends abroad that my books are found every where, especially every railway book-stall in England, & I am frequently recieving letters from English people about them I cannot help feeling that if they sell so well they should be more profitable to me." As for translations of the Alcott oeuvre, for which the author doubtless anticipated remuneration, she happily remarked in 1875: "I shall receive my books in their Dutch dress with pleasure, as I already have them in their French and German attire."

However humbly Louisa Alcott may have regarded her skills as a writer — "the young folks write thier own stories" — she was never modest when it came to the just monetary claims of authorship. The decade of the seventies brought her substantial proof that she had indeed lived to see her youthful wishes come true. She had written at least one good book, she had become famous, she had traveled abroad, and she had earned riches.

Prolific as she was during these years, Louisa did not remain constantly at her desk. She found time for the world outside as well as for her smaller family world, and she found time, too, to write the letters that elucidate her participation in both those worlds. She had once observed the flood of the Tiber in Rome, and now, on 9 November 1872, she observed the fire in Boston — the hand-operated fire engines rushing along moonlit streets, the flames that turned granite to powder, marble to chalk. She watched through the night, and this time converted her impressions not into a story but into a remarkable letter that reanimated for her sister Anna "the red glare, the strange roar, the flying people."

It was during the latter half of these productive seventies that Louisa Alcott began to immerse herself in feminist causes. As late as 1 October 1873 she wrote to Lucy Stone: "I am so busy just now proving 'Woman's Right to Labor' that I have no time to help prove 'Woman's Right to Vote.' " Subsequently, she found — or stole — more time to help the suffrage cause, and by the end of the decade she was working hard to get the timid women of

Concord to register, and she was signing herself, in a letter to the *Woman's Journal*, "Yours for reforms of all kinds." In between, she had expressed her belief in "the same pay for the same good work" and had reacted with dismay and anger to Concord's centennial celebration of its role in the Revolution, a celebration in which hospitalities seemed to be extended only to the men. The village had forgotten the heroines of the present in its desire to exalt the heroes of old, and Louisa was quick to write a candid protest for the *Woman's Journal*.[14]

Not long after the Concord celebration, in the winter of 1875, she took time for a stimulating and exhilarating visit to New York City. Staying at the Bath Hotel, a hydropathic establishment of Dr. Eli Peck Miller on West Twenty-sixth Street, she combined the advantages of Turkish baths with visits to the theatre and receptions for *the* Miss Alcott. Her stay in the city was varied, and if she was occasionally "swamped in a sea of frivolity," she was also ashore on the solid ground of "Speculative Philosophy." Having participated in the glitter of New York literary society, she pursued contrast to its ultimate end by visiting the Newsboys' Lodging House on Duane Street, sending a full description to her little men, Fred and Johnny Pratt. The Alcott itinerary included Christmas Day at Randall's Island — "A New Way to Spend Christmas," as the *Youth's Companion* would entitle her narrative — and a few days later she ventured to New York's Tombs, the grim pile that was the city's Bridewell. New York had unfolded its contrasts to the lion from Concord, contrasts she promptly entrapped in a net of words.

If there had been a newness, an élan in New York, the once-white village of Concord was, in Louisa's eyes, becoming a gray town. Father might continue his "garden ploughing & orchard pruning," his writing, and his plans for a "Socratic Seminary," but there was no evading the fact that "Marmee . . . [was] much changed . . . wears caps & is old & broken sadly." By 1877, when Louisa encapsulated the family for a correspondent, she wrote:

> The Marches . . . are all robust except Marmee who is much broken & is now the cherished "old baby" as she calls herself. Amy is painting away in London & coming home to keep house in March. Meg & the lads are with us here in Boston for the winter. Mr M[arch]. lectures & takes care of his large parish of young men & women. Jo is nurse, housekeeper, scribbler & Papa to the boys.

More and more now, Jo was playing the role of nurse, combining her writing with ministrations to her mother. By 1877 it was clear that Louisa's

14. See *LAFL*, pp. 429–452.

mother, who had lived so many valiant lives in Concord and had become world-famous as the Marmee of *Little Women*, was growing more and more feeble as the days passed. She took pride in the publication of Number 6 in Roberts Brothers' No Name Series, her daughter's anonymous *A Modern Mephistopheles*, and she took pleasure in May's letters with the foreign postmarks that brought happy reports from the wandering artist. Anna's preparations for occupying the Thoreau House on Main Street, to which the Alcotts also planned to move, engaged her interest. But as the summer passed, her illness — diagnosed as dropsy and dyspepsia — became grave. Father was called home from a journey to his native Connecticut, and on 7 September the doctor announced that Mother had reached the beginning of the end. "Stay by, Louy," she murmured, "and help me if I suffer too much."[15] She survived her seventy-seventh birthday, forbade the family to send for May, and insisted that plans for moving into Anna's house be carried out. On 14 November, therefore, the move was made from the Orchard House to the house on Main Street, and, borne upstairs in an armchair, Mother could still smile as she commented, "This is the beginning of my ascension."[16] On 25 November she died.

Out of her sorrow and loss, Louisa wrote a poem, "Transfiguration," and toyed with the idea of writing a memoir of her mother's life. With her father she read the old letters and journals that summoned up long years of cheerless anxiety and dependence, the months at Fruitlands and at Hillside, the later compensations for privation. The memories evoked were too poignant to transfer to print and, although Thomas Niles had agreed to publish the book, she could not continue. Rather, she decided to destroy most of her mother's diaries.

While Father found solace in plans for a Concord School of Philosophy, Louisa now lived vicariously in the letters that arrived from abroad. In February 1878 those letters had brought word that May was engaged to marry a young Swiss whom she had met in her London boardinghouse. Ernest Nieriker, who played chess as well as the violin, was engaged in the banking profession, but as yet his income was extremely modest. Moreover, he was only twenty-two to May's thirty-seven. Despite any silent reservations Louisa may have entertained, she could only rejoice in May's newfound joy. On 22 March they were married, and to the summer child of the Lexington Road — now metamorphosed into Madame Nieriker — Louisa sent a gift of one thousand dollars. The letters that flowed in at the Concord post office reflected nothing but happiness, and in May Louisa described the blissful couple in a letter to a friend: "May *is* very happy, & we get charming letters

15. *LMA*, p. 269.
16. Ibid., p. 270.

from her as she spends her honeymoon in Havre sketching & enjoying fine weather, new sights & a great deal of love. . . . They talk of settling in Paris. . . . May prefers the country, but things are undecided as yet & the pair live in Paradise for a little while. Pity they need ever come out!"

From Paradise the Nierikers moved to Meudon, France, where Louisa hoped to visit them during the autumn. Those hopes were perforce abandoned when her own health seemed unequal to the journey, and later news from abroad simply increased Louisa's regret for this physical incapacity. May expected a child the following November.

While Father was consumed with plans for the Concord School of Philosophy, Louisa completed the fifth volume of *Aunt Jo's Scrap-Bag* and contemplated the changes that had come to Concord. As she put it, "many of the good grey heads are gone & none so excellent have come to fill thier places." Even Emerson, reading a lecture on memory in the vestry of the Trinitarian Church, needed prompting from his daughter lest he mistake a word or misplace a sheet of manuscript. Walden Pond, where Thoreau had once paddled, had been converted into an excursion center. At the Orchard House, philosophers assembled for classes in speculation. Fields once in corn and grass now served as vineyards and orchards. The woods had fallen to the axe. Boston had extended its boundaries, absorbing the white village of Louisa's childhood, transmuting it into a suburb of the metropolis.

Yet for a time all seemed well, and November brought the joyous news that little Louisa May Nieriker had been born on the eighth of the month in Paris. The joy proved short-lived, for word soon followed that May had failed to rally after the birth of her daughter. Sitting helpless in a room on Concord's Main Street, Louisa remembered the golden-haired enthusiast who had sailed away three years before. On the last day of the decade's last year, Emerson appeared at the house on Main Street with a telegram in his hand. It had been sent to him by Ernest Nieriker so that the blow would be softened. May had died, leaving behind a seven-week-old daughter whom she bequeathed as a legacy to Louisa. On 1 January 1880 Louisa wrote to her Aunt Bond: "Dear May is dead. Gone to begin the new year with Mother, in a world where I hope there is no grief like this."

In March, May's box arrived, filled with poignant reminders of the past: the artist's album of Turner copies, her clothes and workbasket, a lock of hair. Then, in the autumn, her baby arrived. On 19 September Louisa waited at the Boston wharf while the passengers disembarked. The captain appeared, holding in his arms a little blonde blue-eyed child dressed in white. Next to him was the companion Louisa had sent abroad, Mrs. Giles, and behind walked Ernest Nieriker's sister Sophie. Louisa held out her arms until

"Miss Alcott's baby" filled them. Father recorded the event in red ink in his diary: *"She Comes!"* [17]

It was a strange new relationship for Louisa Alcott, one that quickened her heart and enriched her days. Now her life was centered on the baby, who came to know her as mother — Lulu's first walk, her little ailments, her outings. "Her love of pictures," Louisa reported, "is a passion. . . . I hope I may live to see May's child as brave & bright & talented as she was, & much happier in her fate." A summer at Nonquitt on Buzzards Bay, where a pair of fat legs tramped through the long hotel piazzas, varied the routine of the Main Street household. There the family, including three servants, played a central role in Miss Alcott's life.

Still she found time to continue taking notes, as she had always done, on life and letters in America. When Walt Whitman came to visit Frank Sanborn in September 1881, Louisa was on hand to watch the poet who had sounded his barbaric yawp over the roofs of the world. While Father discussed Thoreau and Margaret Fuller, Miss Alcott sat in her corner observing the Jove who had descended upon Concord. Later she shared the honors with another poet — the youthful Oscar Wilde — when they were invited to "Jenny June" Croly's glittering New York salon. There the lion hunters could stalk contrasting prey: Oscar Wilde, the mannered Oxonian with sparkling knee buckles and diamond studs, and Aunt Jo, the "youth's companion" dressed in somber black. In the spring of 1882 Louisa lost the god of her early idolatry when, on 27 April, Ralph Waldo Emerson died. Concord, knowing its loss, draped its streets in black, and after the funeral Louisa sat up till midnight, remembering the illustrious neighbor whose library she had so often explored. For the *Youth's Companion* she wrote an article of "Reminiscences," and later planned "to write my recollections of him [Emerson] & all I owe him. They may be interesting some day, for though I am no M. Fuller I have loved my Master all my life, & know that he did more for me than any man except my old papa, & [Theodore] Parker in a way."

Her "old papa," busy with his Mystic Club and his sonnets on immortality, could assuredly "have talked with Plato," and seemed indeed to have discovered the elixir of life. On 24 October 1882, immortality suddenly disowned him. Louisa, staying at Boston's Bellevue Hotel to concentrate on a new book, was summoned home by a telegram announcing that Father had had a paralytic stroke. She found him prostrate, his right side paralyzed, his mind dim, his eyes vacant. Yet he lingered on, and Louisa took time from supervising her two charges to report to friends upon Father's condi-

17. *LMA,* p. 292.

tion. "He likes to hold books & try to read them, & makes letters on a sheet of paper." "He talks now, but brokenly, & seems to have difficulty in expressing even the disconnected thoughts that come & go in his bewildered yet active brain." "His voice is changed, & the old Conn. accent has come back, just now he said, 'Where is my mother?' " One of his first words had been a whispered "Up." "He . . . sits in his chair looking placidly out at the river & the falling leaves."

Between the demands of childhood and of age, Louisa lived. In Boston, at the Bellevue, back in Concord, on Main Street, or at Nonquitt, where in June 1884 she bought a cottage, it was much the same. Her father's slow decline, so painful to watch, formed an obbligato to her life. "I 'trudge in harness,' " she wrote to a correspondent, "& find my burdens heavy & various." And to another, "Freedom was always my longing, but I have never had it."

Louisa Alcott in these later years trudged in a harness shaped not only by her devotion to a growing niece and a declining father but by her own physical ills and the constant demands upon her pen. Her complaints of poor health had for some years punctuated her letters; now, in the mid-1880s, they simply increased. She suffered at intervals from vertigo and rheumatism, writer's cramp and an ache in the back of her head, indigestion and bronchial catarrh. Whether her ills were real or imaginary or both, they plagued her, and in February 1885 she turned to a treatment described as "mind cure," which viewed physical illness as error that could be mentally denied and so healed. As she reported her sensations during treatment, "I feel very still, then very light. I seem floating away on a sea of rest. Once or twice I seemed to have no body, & to come back from another world." Her initial enthusiasm cooled "when thirty treatments left the arm no better and the head much worse," and she returned to the homeopathy and massage from which she had been lured.[18]

Her ills and her sorrows delayed but in the end seldom impeded the work of her pen. The once-compulsive writer had become a compelled writer whose professionalism found ways of supplying public demand. As she had written to her *St. Nicholas* editor Mary Mapes Dodge, " 'Under the Lilacs' was finished by my mother's bedside in her last illness, & this one [*Jack and Jill*] when my heart was full of care & hope & then grief over poor May." Despite her ministrations to a feeble father and a bouncing Lulu, despite her own physical complaints, she managed to dispatch notes on Concord's suffrage attempts to the *Woman's Journal* and to complete her tale of life in Harmony Village, *Jack and Jill*. Her first novel, *Moods*, was revised, with more

18. *LMA*, p. 312.

stress upon the wholesome than upon the morbid, for publication by Roberts Brothers, and Aunt Jo's sixth *Scrap-Bag* of twice-told tales was compiled for avid readers. In answer to a query about her technique, Louisa wrote: "I often have a dozen plots in my head at once and keep them for years." The plots were put to use now as she narrated the *Spinning-Wheel Stories*, "Old-time tales, with a thread running through all from the wheel that enters in the first one." The series appeared first in *St. Nicholas* and then as a book, over the Roberts imprint. In the same way, Louisa began to assemble a collection of stories originally told to Lulu and written down in tiny books tied up in birch-bark covers, a collection to be entitled *Lulu's Library*.

For all her professionalism, for all her productivity, Louisa Alcott found it almost impossible to complete the book that would, as she was well aware, end the saga of the Marches. She began the novel, the sequel to a sequel that would become *Jo's Boys*, in October 1882; it would not be published until four years later. For an author who had produced *Little Women* at the rate of "a chapter a day," [19] and *Little Men* in a few short months, this was slow going indeed. In part this can be attributed to family cares and her own physical ills. She was interrupted almost at the start by news of her father's stroke, and three years later, when she leased the red-brick house at 10 Louisburg Square in Boston, she spent much of her time preparing for the family move. The preparations entailed the sorting of old letters, the burning of many, the rereading of her journals, and adding brief postscripts to the early entries. Such occupations may have delayed the completion of her manuscript.

At one point in her re-creation of that saga, Louisa suffered a violent attack of vertigo and was forbidden to write for six months. To her publisher Thomas Niles she wrote in July 1885: "I ache to fall on some of the ideas that are simmering in my head, but dare not, as my one attempt since the last 'Jo's Boys' break-down cost me a week or two of woe and $30 for the doctor." Writing only an hour a day, later extended to "my two hours pen-work," Louisa Alcott did not complete *Jo's Boys* until July of 1886.

To her physical complaints and family obligations must be added a third explanation for this dilatoriness on the part of a writer who customarily kept to deadlines. Surely she felt a profound reluctance to end a story that in a sense marked the end of her own life. The thread she had dropped at the close of *Little Men* was picked up here in a tale that followed those little men to their maturity. In *Jo's Boys*, Louisa Alcott returned to the past, to a Jo March who had become a literary mentor, to the theatricals at Plumfield, to the reforms she had espoused. She lavished attention upon the character of

19. Cheney, p. 201.

one of Jo's boys, Dan, whose untamed nature reminds the reader of the once-untamed Jo March. The novel was filled with nostalgic reminders — even of what was left unexpressed.

In a brief preface she explained: "To account for the seeming neglect of AMY, let me add that, since the original of that character died, it has been impossible for me to write of her as when she was here to suggest, criticize, and laugh over her namesake. The same excuse applies to MARMEE." The book was dedicated not to any member of the family, but to the author's physician Dr. Conrad Wesselhoeft "by his friend and patient, The Author," and, dispatched to Roberts Brothers, was destined to become yet another Alcott best-seller. As for the weary author, she had been tempted to close her tale with an earthquake that would engulf Plumfield. Instead, having endeavored to suit her readers with several weddings, few deaths, and as much prosperity as the eternal fitness of things permitted, she simply had let the music stop, the lights die out, and the curtain fall forever on the March family.

Louisa Alcott's own epilogue was played out, not in Concord or Boston, but in a nursing home on Dunreath Place in Roxbury. That suburban retreat had been established by Dr. Rhoda Lawrence, homeopathic physician and feminist in whose career Louisa had long been interested; indeed, she had helped raise a loan for the nursing home. Now, suffering from a wide range of complaints — debility and dyspepsia, hoarseness, insomnia, and "nervous prostration"[20] — Louisa felt that management of the large household at 10 Louisburg Square was beyond her. Father and Lulu both required constant attention. She would leave their supervision and the affairs of the household in Anna's hands. Toward the end of 1886, Louisa Alcott exchanged one world for another. The exchange was diminishing.

Now her life — and her letters — consisted primarily of the preoccupations of an invalid and echoed the antiphonal refrain of cure versus ailment. Remedies, homeopathic and botanic, were tried; and an eclectic practitioner, Dr. Milbrey Green, was consulted. Life had become a mixture of gruel and hope. "The life of an invalid," she wrote to Edward W. Bok, "is best left to silence."

Yet there were some variations on the theme of illness. There were visits from Anna and from blooming Lulu; there was a change of the routine with vacations at Melrose, Massachusetts, or at Princeton, Massachusetts, near Mount Wachusett, where she was accompanied by Dr. Lawrence. Finally, there was still the lure of the writing desk, the almost physical need to

20. *LMA*, p. 325.

continue to trace the pattern shaped by a lifetime of writing. Louisa Alcott had lost none of her professionalism, although her strength was utterly diminished. "An hour a day is my limit now, so I accomplish very little, & long to rebel, but dare not." In that hour she accomplished something besides her letters to Lulu or to Mrs. Dodge and Thomas Niles. She could still write brief narratives or adapt stories she had once told to current publishing needs. In that way, a second volume of *Lulu's Library* was readied for the press. Since it consisted largely of reprints from *Flower Fables*, the stories she had once told to Ellen Emerson, she dedicated the book to her "in memory of the happy old times when the stories were told to you & May & Lizzie & some other playmates." A month later, in November 1887, *A Garland for Girls* was published, another compendium of stories suggested by the flowers sent to her at Roxbury. At the same time, the author, still struggling to produce books to satisfy her readership, assembled stories for a third volume of *Lulu's Library*. That volume would be a posthumous one.

It had been, as she wrote to Mrs. Dodge, a "long year of exile from home," and the refuge on Dunreath Place had often resembled a prison. By the new year, when she was fifty-five, she wrote, "I look about 70 — grey & wrinkled & bent & lame. A hard year!" It had been a year dedicated to illness, although Louisa Alcott was unaware that she was dying, in all probability of intestinal cancer. Nonetheless, in her own way, she prepared for death. During the summer of 1887 she completed plans to adopt her nephew John Pratt so that he could apply for renewals of her copyrights if they expired after her death. On 10 July 1887 she signed her will at Princeton, taking care of all the members of her family and leaving to her adopted son, John, her copyrights in trust, the income to be shared by Anna, Fred, Lulu, and himself.

During the early months of 1888 Louisa was drawn to thoughts of the past and of the future. For the *Youth's Companion* she reanimated her memories of her childhood when a boisterous little girl had fallen into the Frog Pond and driven her hoop around the Common. "Recollections of My Childhood" would appear in the periodical in May. In February, nephew Fred Pratt, working for Roberts Brothers, was married to Jessica L. Cate in a ceremony described in minute detail to the Roxbury invalid.

On 1 March, Louisa was able to pay a visit to Father at Louisburg Square. She knelt by his bedside, saying, "Father, here is your Louy, what are you thinking of as you lie here so happily?" He took her hand and pointed above, saying, "I am going *up. Come with me.*" "Oh, I wish I could," she answered. Surely she was aware she would never see him again and, oblivious to her own needs, she forgot her wrap when she returned in the carriage to

Roxbury. Within a short time she complained of a violent headache and sank into unconsciousness. On 4 March 1888 Bronson Alcott died in Louisburg Square. Two days later, Louisa followed him.

Her stories had all been told. Unfulfilled promises must remain unfulfilled. On her table at Roxbury lay scores of letters that would never be answered. Yet throughout her life she had written, to a wide range of correspondents including friends and family, publishers, editors, and aspiring authors, a host of letters that told their own stories and fulfilled many promises. From that grand array of letters of a productive lifetime, such letters as seemed repetitious or insignificant have been pruned. Editorial wisdom has seen fit to hide no secrets nor conceal any pertinent evidence. And what of the letters lost or destroyed by the writer or her correspondents? Since nothing is known of them, nothing can be said of them. They cannot be reconstructed; nor should they be brought, for purposes of reinterpretation of character, to imaginary life.

What letters remain present detailed and abundant evidence of an extraordinary life. Louisa Alcott lived in a nineteenth-century New England that she metamorphosed into literature. The almost unprecedented success that split her life in two with the publication of *Little Women* heightened the drama of her story. That drama — and its foreground and its aftermath — are all reflected in her letters. They embody the warm humanity of the woman and the growing professionalism of the author. They mirror the dimensions of her character and the variety of her experience. They illuminate her time and her place. Here, within the framework of her letters, Louisa Alcott sits for a full-length portrait.

NOTES ON THE TEXT

The Selected Letters of Louisa May Alcott prints in their entirety 271 out of the 649 letters for which we have discovered either the extant manuscript or a printed text.[1] With this edition, 138 of these letters are being published for the first time. The letters we have decided to publish focus on her family life, especially as it relates to her fiction; her relationships with her publishers; her descriptions of people and life in Concord, Boston, New York, and Europe; her comments on contemporary literature; her professional career as an author; her involvement in reform movements; and those personal letters that best show to us the thoughts and beliefs of Louisa May Alcott.

At various times in her career, most noticeably after her mother's death in 1877 and the family's move from Concord to Boston in 1885, Alcott went through her papers and destroyed letters and journals to ensure privacy after her death. Therefore, fewer letters survive from earlier periods in her life than do from later years. Also, individual correspondents often saved her letters, and their correspondence with Alcott often figures disproportionately among the surviving letters (for example, that of Mary Mapes Dodge, Laura Hosmer, Maggie Lukens, and Alfred Whitman). Only because Bronson Alcott copied his daughters' letters from abroad in 1870 do we have a detailed record of that trip. We have not found any letters to Ralph Waldo Emerson, Nathaniel Hawthorne, or Henry David Thoreau; even though Alcott lived close to them in Concord, they must have at least exchanged notes. Because it was traditional in the nineteenth century to return letters after the death of one of the correspondents, it is highly probable that Alcott destroyed these letters.

The publishing history of Alcott's letters is quickly told. Ednah Dow Cheney published approximately eighty letters in her *Louisa May Alcott: Her Life,*

1. We wrote to more than nine hundred American, Canadian, and English libraries for information about their holdings and examined more than three hundred publications by and about Alcott in the hope that they might include letters by her.

Letters, and Journals (1889); many of Alcott's letters to Maggie Lukens and Alfred Whitman were published in 1896 and 1901, respectively; and Madeleine B. Stern published a number of Alcott's letters dealing with her feminist activities and her comments on writing in 1978 and 1985, respectively. Only Stern's texts are accurate and complete. Nearly fifty letters have appeared in various other books and articles.

Alcott's script degenerated after she copied *Work* "three pages at once on impression paper" in 1872[2] and during her final illness. Moreover, she was always careless about spelling, paragraphing, and punctuation. In editing Alcott's letters, we have tried to present a text faithful to the writer yet readable for a modern audience. We have let stand her misspellings (she had particular trouble with "ie" and "ei" words, as in "thier"), contractions such as "dont" and "does n't," punctuation placed outside of closing quotation marks, and the use of an apostrophe to form plurals ("picnic's"). We have silently made the following changes: regularized paragraphing, datelines, salutations, and closings; placed signatures in large and small capitals; and supplied opening or closing paired quotation marks or parentheses, commas in series when the meaning would otherwise be unclear, and missing final punctuation. In addition, when the only available text was a printed one, we have silently turned large and small capitals into capitals and small letters and corrected obvious typographical errors. Alcott's periods and commas are often indeterminate; we have given her the benefit of the doubt according to the context. Incomplete words or confusing abbreviations have been filled out in brackets. Alcott's letters contain few cancellations or insertions; we have printed the final text of the letter, reporting significant revisions in the notes. Alcott reread her letters at a later date and revised or made notes on them; we have mentioned significant later revisions or annotations in our notes. All letters (except those used in our notes) are printed in full, and if ellipses are present, it is because they are there in the original text we used (always a printed one in the absence of a manuscript). Like Emily Dickinson, Alcott wrote many letters as poems directed to friends; we have treated such poems as letters.

We have used the following standard abbreviations in our notes in describing the texts we are using: ALS for autograph letter, signed with name or initial(s); AL for autograph letter, unsigned; and MS for manuscript.

A complete list of all known Alcott letters and their publishing history will appear as "A Calendar of the Letters of Louisa May Alcott" in *Studies in the American Renaissance 1988* (Charlottesville: University Press of Virginia, forthcoming).

2. Journal entry, December 1872, Cheney, p. 268. Later Alcott noted that "the paralysis of my thumb" dated from this time. See also 6 June [1884?] in the present edition.

CHRONOLOGY

1799
29 November   Bronson Alcott is born

1800
8 October   Abigail May is born

1830
23 May   Bronson Alcott and Abby May are married in Boston

1831
16 March   Anna Bronson Alcott is born in Philadelphia

1832
29 November   LMA is born in Germantown, Pennsylvania

1834
September   The Alcotts move to Boston; Bronson begins his
                  Temple School

1835
24 June   Elizabeth Sewall Alcott is born in Boston

1839
23 March   The Temple School closes

1840
26 July   Abby May Alcott is born in Concord

1841
8 May   Bronson sails for England

1842

20 October   Bronson returns to America with Charles Lane and Henry
                       Wright

1843

20 May   Lane buys the Wyman Farm at Prospect Hill in
                       Harvard, Massachusetts

1 June   The Alcotts, Lane, and Wright move to Fruitlands

1844

14 January   Lane leaves Fruitlands; the Alcotts stay with the
                       Lovejoys in Still River

12 November   The Alcotts board with the Hosmers in Concord

1845

January   The Alcotts buy the Cogswell House on Lexington Road
                       in Concord (Hillside)

1 April   The Alcotts move into the Cogswell House

Winter   LMA attends John Hosmer's school in Concord

1846

March   LMA gets her own room for the first time

1848

Winter   LMA writes "The Rival Painters. A Tale of Rome," her
                       first story

17 November   The Alcotts move to Dedham Street, Boston

1849

Summer   The Alcotts move in with Samuel Joseph May, Atkinson
                       Street

19 July   "The Olive Leaf," a family newspaper, is "published"

1850

January   The Alcotts move to Groton Street; Anna opens a school

Summer   The Alcotts contract smallpox

1851

September   LMA's poem "Sunlight," by "Flora Fairfield," is published
                       in *Peterson's Magazine*

Winter	The Alcotts move to 50 High Street; LMA goes out to service in Dedham and earns four dollars for seven weeks, which her family returns
1852	
8 May	"The Rival Painters" is published in the *Olive Branch*
Fall	Hawthorne purchases Hillside and renames it Wayside; the Alcotts move to 20 Pinckney Street, Boston, where LMA and Anna open a school in the parlor
December	LMA hears Theodore Parker preach at the Music Hall
1853	
January–May	LMA keeps a school
Fall	Anna takes a teaching position in Syracuse
October	Bronson begins his first midwestern lecture tour
1854	
February	Bronson returns from lecturing with a dollar profit
Spring	James T. Fields rejects LMA's story about her going out to service
Summer	LMA keeps a school
11 November	"The Rival Prima Donnas" is published in the *Saturday Evening Gazette*
December	*Flower Fables* is published
1855	
June	LMA moves to Walpole, New Hampshire, where she organizes plays by the Walpole Amateur Dramatic Company
July	LMA's family joins her in Walpole
Fall	Anna returns to Syracuse to work in Dr. Wilbur's Asylum
November–December	LMA keeps a school in Boston, staying with cousins Samuel E. Sewall in Melrose or Thomas Sewall in Boston
1856	
Summer	LMA moves to Walpole; Abby and Lizzie contract scarlet fever

October	LMA boards with Mrs. David Reed, 34 Chauncy Street, Boston
December	LMA tutors Alice Lovering, living with the family

1857

Summer	LMA goes to Walpole
September	The Alcotts purchase the John Moore house in Concord (Orchard House)
October	The Alcotts move to Concord
Fall	LMA regularly visits Frank B. Sanborn's school; she begins the Concord Dramatic Union

1858

14 March	Lizzie Alcott dies
March	The Alcotts move into Wayside while Hawthorne is abroad and repairs are being made to Orchard House
7 April	Anna and John Bridge Pratt announce their engagement
July	The Alcotts move into the refurbished Orchard House (called Apple Slump by LMA)
October	LMA moves to Thomas Sewall's house, 98 Chestnut Street, Boston, again tutoring Alice Lovering

1859

April	Bronson is appointed Concord's superintendent of schools; Abby returns to Concord

1860

March	"Love and Self-Love" appears in the *Atlantic*
23 May	Anna and John Pratt are married in Concord
August	LMA writes *Moods* in four weeks
December	Abby goes to work at Dr. Wilbur's Asylum in Syracuse

1861

Early January	LMA begins writing *Success* (later called *Work*)
February	LMA revises *Moods*
July	LMA goes to Gorham, New Hampshire
August	Abby returns to teach in Sanborn's school

1862

January	LMA boards with James T. Fields in Boston; she begins a kindergarten at the Warren Street Chapel
April	LMA gives up her school, returning to Concord while commuting to Boston
6 May	Thoreau dies
June	LMA writes "Pauline's Passion and Punishment" for a hundred-dollar prize offered by *Frank Leslie's Illustrated Newspaper*
November	LMA applies for a nursing position in a Washington hospital
11 December	LMA is accepted by the Union Hotel Hospital
13 December	LMA arrives in Georgetown
Late December	LMA learns that "Pauline's Passion" has won the prize

1863

3 January	"Pauline's Passion" begins serialization (ends 10 January)
7 January	LMA is struck by a serious illness
16 January	Bronson arrives in Georgetown
24 January	LMA and Bronson return to Concord
22 March	LMA is finally able to leave her room
28 March	Anna gives birth to Frederick Alcott Pratt
April	Sanborn asks for "Hospital Sketches"
22 May	"Hospital Sketches" begins serialization in the *Boston Commonwealth* (ends 26 June)
August	*Hospital Sketches* is published
October	Abby announces that she wants to be called May
December	*The Rose Family* and *On Picket Duty, and Other Tales* are published
14 December	LMA's dramatization of *Scenes from Dickens* opens in Boston

1864

February	LMA finishes *Moods*
August	LMA goes to Gloucester with May
December	*Moods* is published

1865

4 February	"V.V.; or, Plots and Counterplots" begins serialization in *The Flag of Our Union* (ends 25 February)
24 June	Anna gives birth to John Sewall Pratt
19 July	LMA leaves for Europe with Anna Weld
November	LMA meets Ladislas Wisniewski in Vevey

1866

19 July	LMA returns home to Boston
August	*Moods* is published in England
3 October	"Behind a Mask; or, A Woman's Power" begins serialization in *The Flag of Our Union* (ends 3 November)

1867

5 January	"The Abbot's Ghost; or, Maurice Treherne's Temptation" begins serialization in *The Flag of Our Union* (ends 26 January)
August	LMA goes to Clarks Island, Massachusetts
September	Thomas Niles asks LMA to write a girl's book; Horace Fuller asks her to edit *Merry's Museum*
October	LMA agrees to edit *Merry's Museum* for five hundred dollars a year
28 October	LMA moves to 6 Hayward Place, Boston

1868

January	The first number of *Merry's Museum* under LMA's editorship appears
1 January	*Morning-Glories, and Other Stories* is published
March–May	LMA moves to Concord
May	LMA begins *Little Women*
15 July	LMA finishes *Little Women*, Part 1
1 October	*Little Women*, Part 1, is published
26 October	LMA moves to Brookline Street, Boston
1 November	LMA begins *Little Women*, Part 2
December	LMA closes Orchard House for the winter; she and May engage rooms at the Bellevue Hotel, Beacon Street, Boston
December	*Little Women*, Part 1, is published in England

1869

1 January	LMA finishes *Little Women*, Part 2
March	LMA moves to Concord
14 April	*Little Women*, Part 2, is published in America
15 May	*Little Women*, Part 2, is published in England
July	LMA visits the Frothinghams at Rivière du Loup, Quebec, on the St. Lawrence
July	*An Old-Fashioned Girl* begins serialization in *Merry's Museum* (ends December)
August	LMA and May go to Mount Desert, Maine
16 August	*Hospital Sketches and Camp and Fireside Stories* is published
October	LMA moves to 14 Pinckney Street, Boston

1870

April	*An Old-Fashioned Girl* is published in America and England
2 April	LMA leaves for Europe with May and Alice Bartlett
27 November	John Bridge Pratt dies

1871

January	LMA begins *Little Men*
15 May	*Little Men* is published in England
June	*Little Men* is published in America
6 June	LMA returns to Boston
October	LMA moves to a boardinghouse at 23 Beacon Street, Boston
19 November	May returns to America

1872

1 January	*Aunt Jo's Scrap-Bag: My Boys* is published
October	LMA moves to Pamelia May's boardinghouse, 7 Allston Street, Boston
November	LMA revises *Success* as *Work*
28 November	*Aunt Jo's Scrap-Bag: Shawl-Straps* is published
18 December	*Work* begins serialization in the *Christian Union* (ends 18 June 1873)

1873

26 April	May returns to London
2 June	*Work* is published in England
10 June	*Work* is published in America
August–October	LMA is in Concord
November	LMA closes Orchard House for the winter and moves to a boardinghouse at 26 East Brookline Street, Boston
December	*Aunt Jo's Scrap-Bag: Cupid and Chow-Chow* is published in America and England

1874

March	May returns from London on a visit
May	LMA moves to Joy Street, Boston
Summer	LMA visits Conway, New Hampshire, with Anna and her children
October	LMA moves with May to the Bellevue Hotel, Boston
5 December	*Eight Cousins* begins serialization in *Good Things* (ends 27 November 1875)

1875

January	*Eight Cousins* begins serialization in *St. Nicholas* (ends October)
February	LMA finishes *Silver Pitchers*
22 February	LMA attends Vassar's tenth anniversary and goes to New York afterward
March	LMA goes to Concord
25 September	*Eight Cousins* is published in America and England
October	LMA moves to Dr. Eli Peck Miller's Bath Hotel, 39 West Twenty-sixth Street, New York

1876

Early January	LMA goes to Philadelphia
February	LMA goes to Boston
June	*Silver Pitchers* is published in America and England
July	LMA starts *Rose in Bloom*
September	LMA finishes *Rose in Bloom*

4 September	May returns to Europe
November	*Rose in Bloom* is published in America and England

1877

January	LMA moves to the Bellevue Hotel, Boston, and writes *A Modern Mephistopheles*
28 April	*A Modern Mephistopheles* is published
May	Anna and LMA purchase the Thoreau House for $4,500 (LMA supplies $2,500)
July	The Alcotts begin moving into the Thoreau House
August	LMA begins *Under the Lilacs*
7 September	Mrs. Alcott's final illness begins
14 November	Orchard House is closed and the Thoreau House is opened
25 November	Mrs. Alcott dies
December	*Under the Lilacs* begins serialization in *St. Nicholas* (ends October 1878)
1 December	*Aunt Jo's Scrap-Bag: My Girls* is published

1878

February	May's engagement to Ernest Nieriker is announced
22 March	May is married in London
June	LMA and Bronson read Mrs. Alcott's letters and diaries
15 October	*Under the Lilacs* is published in America
November	*Under the Lilacs* is published in England

1879

January	LMA moves to the Bellevue Hotel, Boston
Spring	LMA moves to Concord
14 July	The Concord School of Philosophy opens
August	LMA goes to Magnolia, Massachusetts
September	LMA goes to Concord
18 October	*Aunt Jo's Scrap-Bag: Jimmy's Cruise in a Pinafore* is published
8 November	May gives birth to Louisa May Nieriker in Paris
December	*Jack and Jill* begins serialization in *St. Nicholas* (ends October 1880)
29 December	May dies in Paris

1880
April	LMA moves to the Bellevue Hotel, Boston
June	LMA goes to Concord
July–August	LMA goes to New York with Fred and John
August	LMA moves to Concord
19 September	Lulu Nieriker arrives in Boston
9 October	*Jack and Jill* is published
Winter	LMA moves to Elizabeth Sewall Willis Wells's house, 81 Pinckney Street, Boston, on Louisburg Square

1881
Spring	LMA moves to Concord
July	LMA and Lulu go to Nonquitt, Massachusetts

1882
27 April	Emerson dies
Summer	LMA goes to Nonquitt
Autumn	LMA moves to the Bellevue Hotel, Boston, with John; she begins *Jo's Boys*
14 October	*Aunt Jo's Scrap-Bag: An Old-Fashioned Thanksgiving* is published
24 October	Bronson suffers a stroke

1883
March	LMA moves to the Bellevue Hotel, Boston, with Lulu
April	LMA goes to Concord
July	LMA and Lulu go to Nonquitt
10 August	LMA moves to Concord
27 November	LMA moves to Boylston Street, Boston, with Lulu

1884
June	LMA sells Orchard House to W. T. Harris; she buys a cottage at Nonquitt
24 June	LMA goes to Nonquitt with Lulu and John
7 August	LMA moves to Concord
October	LMA moves to the Bellevue Hotel, Boston, with John
November	LMA moves to 31 Chestnut Street, Boston, with John and Fred

8 November	*Spinning-Wheel Stories* is published
December	LMA works to exhaustion on *Jo's Boys* and is forbidden to write for six months
1885	
February	LMA undergoes mind-cure treatments
Summer	LMA goes to Nonquitt; she begins *Lulu's Library*
8 August	LMA moves to Concord
1 October	LMA moves to 10 Louisburg Square, Boston, with Lulu, Anna, John, and Fred
20 November	*Lulu's Library*, Volume 1, is published
1886	
January	LMA begins treatments with Dr. Rhoda Lawrence; she continues work on *Jo's Boys*
Early Summer	LMA goes to Concord
June	LMA goes to Princeton, Massachusetts
4 July	LMA finishes *Jo's Boys*
September	LMA moves to Boston
18 September	*Jo's Boys* is published in England
9 October	*Jo's Boys* is published in America
December	LMA moves to Dr. Lawrence's, Dunreath Place, Roxbury
1887	
June	LMA and the family move to Melrose, Massachusetts; she works on *A Garland for Girls*
July–August	LMA goes to Princeton
10 July	LMA makes and signs her will
1 September	LMA moves to Roxbury
25 October	*Lulu's Library*, Volume 2, is published
November	*A Garland for Girls* is published
1888	
8 February	Fred Pratt marries Jessica L. Cate
1 March	LMA visits Bronson at Louisburg Square
4 March	Bronson dies
6 March	LMA dies

1889
5 October   *Lulu's Library*, Volume 3, and Ednah Dow Cheney's *Louisa May Alcott: Her Life, Letters, and Journals* are published

1893
17 July   Anna Pratt dies
October   *Comic Tragedies* is published

1975
1 July   *Behind a Mask: The Unknown Thrillers of Louisa May Alcott* is published

1976
1 July   *Plots and Counterplots: More Unknown Thrillers of Louisa May Alcott* is published

THE SELECTED LETTERS OF
LOUISA MAY ALCOTT

To Abigail May Alcott

Fruitlands
Sunday
[8? October 1843]

Dearest Mother

I have spent a very pleasant morning and I hardly dare to speak to Annie[1] for fear she should speak unkindly and get me angry. O she is so very very cross I cannot love her it seems as though she did every thing to trouble me but I will try to love her better, I hope you have spent a pleasant morning. Please axcept this book mark from your affectionate daughter.

LOUISA

It is not very pretty but it is all I had to give.

LOUY

ALS: Fruitlands Museums, Harvard, Massachusetts. Undoubtedly written on the occasion of Mrs. Alcott's birthday.
    1. LMA's sister Anna.

To Sophia Gardner

Concord, Tuesday, 23 [September 1845]

Dear Sophia: [1]

I had nothing to do, so I thought I would scribble a few lines to my dear Fire, as Abby still calls you. I have just written a long letter to L——[2] all myself, for mother is too buisy and Anna to lazy. I suppose M——[3] will schold if I call Anna lazy, but she is to lazy to do any thing but drum on the Seraphine[4] till we are all stuned with her noise. I need not tell you we are all alive and kicking, most of our family, that is; Miss F——[5] and

S——[6] are going away, so I shan't have to be fussed any more with them, for Miss F—— is particular and S—— is cross. I have not forgotten the ten matches we lit on a certain night, and my head and bones still shake after the beating they got when I was at Harvard. O, if you had only been with us when we came home! — a stage full of bawling babies and nervous marms to take care of the little dears. I had to be perched on top of the stage, and pitched up and down like butter in a churn. I had a beautiful walk the other day with my governess and the children to a pond called Finch pond,[7] there we found lots of grapes and some lovely flowers; and now, if you won't laugh, I'll tell you something — if you will believe it, Miss F—— and all of us waded across it, a great big pond a mile long and half a mile wide, we went splashing along making the fishes run like mad before our big claws, when we got to the other side we had a funny time getting on our shoes and unmentionables, and we came tumbling home all wet and muddy; but we were happy enough, for we came through the woods bawling and singing like crazy folks. Yesterday we went over a little way from our house into some great big fields full of apple-trees, which we climed, tearing our clothes off our backs (luckly they were old) and breaking our bones, playing tag and all sorts of strange things. We are dreadfull wild people here in Concord, we do all the sinful things you can think of. I have got some hous plants; one of them is called a Crab Cactus, the flower looks like a toad and the leaves look as if they were joined together by a very fine thread. The folks were very much pleased with my fruit, but the grapes were crushed some in tumbling in and out of the cars.[8] I have been pressing coloured leaves, they look very pretty when they are arranged prettly on white paper. I go to school every day to Mr. Lane,[9] but do not have half so good a time as I did at Miss Chase's school;[10] the summer I went there was the happiest summer I ever spent in the country, there was such a lot of jolly girls to play and blab with, and we used to have such good times — though we did used to get mad now and then, it did not last long. I went to court and heard William Whyman acquitted. I hopped right up out of my seat when the foreman said Not Guilty. Poor Mr. Whyman! he cried right out, he was so glad; his trial has lasted three years and the poor man's hair has turned gray, though it was black at first, they have plagued him so.[11] What a silly fool I am to be talking to you about things you do not care about hearing, so I will stop. I shall make you a visit next summer, if you will not come down and see me. Mother said she would pay the postage, so I will scribble with all my might. Our garden looks dreadful shabby, for Father has been gone to New York for a long time[12] and Mr. Lane does not under stand gardening very well. I must say good by now, for I must go and practise for an hour, farewell. Mother sends her love to all the dear folks, and Anny lots to G——; by, by, dear childer,

The lord bless you,
from your affectionate
friend LOUISA.

P.S. If you and M——[13] will come down and see us, I will light ten matches for you, and you shall have a nice big room — if you will only come without delay, for our lives depend upon it, so come with the greatest possible despatch; bring little P——[14] two [i.e., too] for Abby; my respects to Walter,[15] and tell him my finger is better and I hope his is too; hope A——[16] is better, tell her to get well as fast as she can and come with you; I hope Betty G.[17] won't turn her nose up at me the next time I come, for it most broke my heart, it was so affecting; good by, L. M. A.

N.B. Now I have written you a long letter, and you must answer it, M—— must not write a word in it, must be all for me.[18] I pray and beg you will not show this to any body and excuse all mistakes, for I am in a hurry; did you ever see the time when I was not?

L. M. A.

I won't say any more now, my dear S.

MS: Unlocated. Printed: Annie M. L. Clark, *The Alcotts in Harvard* (Lancaster, Mass.: J.C.L. Clark, 1902), pp. 41–43. Tuesday fell on the twenty-third only in September during 1845. Clark says she "followed the original *verbatim et litteratim*, but not quite *punctuatim*."

1. Sophia Gardner Wyman.
2. Frederick Llewellyn Hovey Willis had boarded with the Alcotts at Still River.
3. Probably Marmee, LMA's name for her mother.
4. The seraphine, a small keyboard instrument similar to an organ, was also played by Lizzie (see 27 April 1846, Lizzie's diary, Houghton Library, Harvard University).
5. Sophia Foord (or Ford) stayed with the Alcotts in the summer of 1845 and helped with the children's recreation (see Walter Harding, "Thoreau's Feminine Foe," *PMLA* 69 [March 1954]: 110–116).
6. Possibly Charles Lane, whom LMA called Socrates.
7. LMA is probably referring to Flint's (or Sandy) Pond, about a mile east of Walden Pond.
8. "The little girls no doubt went by stage as far as Littleton, continuing their journey to Concord by the then new and wonderful Fitchburg Railroad" (Clark's note).
9. Charles Lane had returned to the Alcotts' house during the spring or early summer of 1845 and remained there, in charge of the children's reading, until October.
10. Maria Louisa Chase taught the district school at Still River, which LMA and Anna attended in the summer of 1844.
11. "The case against William Wyman for embezzlement grew out of the failure in 1842 of the Phoenix Bank of Charleston, of which Wyman was president. He would appear to have been acquitted of a portion of the charges against him before the Court of Common Pleas

at Concord in June, 1845. The case was finally 'non prossed' at Cambridge the following February" (Clark's note).

12. LMA is probably referring to Bronson's visit to his brother Junius, who was ill.

13. Margaret Gardner.

14. Polly Gardner.

15. Walter Gardner, whom LMA "married" in a childhood ceremony.

16. Possibly Annie Maria Lawrence, a good friend of Lizzie Alcott's.

17. Elizabeth Goodwin.

18. "That is to say, if Margaret wrote, it would be to Anna. The little Alcotts' intimacies were, like most children's, formed through similarity of age; Margaret Gardner 'went with' Anna Alcott; Sophy Gardner with Louisa; to Helen Lovejoy and me Lizzie was our dearest friend; and Louisa conjures Sophy to bring Polly for little Abba May" (Clark's note).

To Abigail May Alcott

[1845]

Dearest Mother

I have tryed to be more contented and I think I have been more so. I have been thinking about my little room which I suppose I never shall have.[1] I should want to be there about all the time and I should go there and sing and think.

> But I'll be contented
> With what I have got
> Of folly repented
> Then sweet is my lot.[2]

from your trying daughter
LOUY

ALS: Houghton Library, Harvard University. Printed: Cheney, pp. 45–46. Addressed "For / Dearest Mother / peace."

1. LMA's wish was granted the following year: "I have at last got the little room I have wanted so long, and am very happy about it. It does me good to be alone" (journal entry, March 1846, Cheney, pp. 47–48).

2. LMA often expressed her thoughts in verse, although she remained modest (and mostly humorous) about her accomplishments, as in a letter to Sophia Foord in which she refers to "this choice collection of poems, which being so exceedingly brilliant will cause to lift your hands in admiration and thus let them tumble into the fire, so that no one may suffer the mortification of not being able to write as finely as your ever loving nonsensical, Louy" ([185–], manuscript copy, Henry W. and Albert A. Berg Collection, New York Public Library, Astor, Lenox, and Tilden Foundations).

To Charlotte Wilkinson

Boston Jan 2d [1853?]

Dearest Lottie[1]

My best wishes for an unlimited number of Merry Christmas's, and Happy New Years, are all I can send you in return for the great bundle of *goodies*, which was recieved with universal joy, and gratitude.

Mother broke down entirely over your letter and *we* like dutiful children followed her example for we felt somewhat forlorn and forgotten among the giving and receiving of presents going on all around us, and it was so cheering to find that though so far away some one had remembered the existence of the "Pathetic Family". Dear Lottie dont wish to be rich, for it cannot make you more kind and generous than you already are, and you would do so much for others, you would leave them no chance to do any thing for you. But I shall get sentimental if I proceed, and I know you will believe without more words how truly grateful we are for your gifts and still more for the kind words and wishes that came with them.

It is universally declared that the food eaten from cousin John's[2] spoons is decidedly sweeter and better than any other and the immense quantity of warmth which proceeds from a certain cloak, is caused we imagine by its having once covered a very warm heart, and it is now duly appreciated by a back which was before somewhat airily clad considering the weather. Lizzie and Abba luxuriate in the aprons, Annie revels in undersleeves and dresses, and I have borne off several little "traps" which I shall treasure as memorials of an excellent little female who *wont* rest till she has given away all she has got and thinks she has not done enough then.

Bonny's long and original letter was deeply interesting and although not "personally acquainted" I hope he will not forget that he has an aunt and four cousins who send him their love and will be most happy to hear from him again if he will do them the honor.

How do you like being a school marm! fascinating amusement is'nt it? I am still struggling with my young ideas which (doubtless owing to the cold weather) dont shoot as I could wish. Annie will probably join Miss Sullivan in her school,[3] and Lizzie is with fear and trembling preparing for the trials of the 'Normal'.[4] Mother has at last retired from public life to the bosom of her family and if she would only repose there it would be highly agreeable, but she *wont* and tires herself most perseveringly.[5] She is at present enjoying the "Mumps", and we keep her toasting like a large muffin and luxuriating in the rest and quiet she is obliged to take.

I suppose you see cousin Sam's letters. If you *dont*, allow me to remark they are perfectly beautiful and it is a matter of great astonishment to us that such lovely thoughts can come from a descendent of a certain *corpulent Deacon.*[6]

I am afraid this jumbled up letter will shock you dreadfully but as I cannot get at you to give you a series of violent hugs I am obliged to offer you this somewhat ra[m]bling epistle and with my quantity of love to Uncle and the brothers believe me dear Lottie ever your affectionate and grateful cousin LOUISA.

ALS: Houghton Library, Harvard University.
    1. Charlotte Coffin May (b. 1833), the only daughter of Mrs. Alcott's brother Samuel Joseph May and Lucretia Flagge Coffin May, married Alfred Wilkinson, a Syracuse, New York, banker and merchant, in 1854.
    2. Charlotte's brother, John Edward May, also called Bonny by the family.
    3. In the fall of 1853, Anna obtained, with the Mays' help, a teaching position in Syracuse.
    4. The normal schools, which high school graduates attended, usually for a two-year course in preparation for a teaching career.
    5. Mrs. Alcott had earlier earned money distributing food and clothing to the poor and by running an intelligence or employment office for people desiring domestic help.
    6. Samuel Sewall Greele's father was deacon of the Federal Street Church in Boston. His mother, Louisa May Greele, was Mrs. Alcott's sister.

To Anna Alcott

Thursday, 27th.
[Spring? 1854]

Dearest Nan, — I was so glad to hear from you, and hear that all were well.

I am grubbing away as usual, trying to get money enough to buy Mother a nice warm shawl. I have eleven dollars, all my own earnings, — five for a story, and four for the pile of sewing I did for the ladies of Dr. Gray's society, to give him as a present.[1]

. . . I got a crimson ribbon for a bonnet for May, and I took my straw and fixed it nicely with some little duds I had. Her old one has haunted me all winter, and I want her to look neat. She is so graceful and pretty and loves beauty so much, it is hard for her to be poor and wear other people's ugly things. You and I have learned not to mind *much;* but when I think of her I long to dash out and buy the finest hat the limited sum of ten dollars can procure. She says so sweetly in one of her letters: "It is hard sometimes

8

to see other people have so many nice things and I so few; but I try not to be envious, but contented with my poor clothes, and cheerful about it." I hope the little dear will like the bonnet and the frills I made her and some bows I fixed over from bright ribbons L. W.[2] threw away. I get half my rarities from her rag-bag, and she does n't know her own rags when fixed over. I hope I shall live to see the dear child in silk and lace, with plenty of pictures and "bottles of cream," Europe, and all she longs for.

For our good little Betty,[3] who is wearing all the old gowns we left, I shall soon be able to buy a new one, and send it with my blessing to the cheerful saint. She writes me the funniest notes, and tries to keep the old folks warm and make the lonely house in the snowbanks cosey and bright.

To Father I shall send new neckties and some paper; then he will be happy, and can keep on with the beloved diaries though the heavens fall.[4]

Don't laugh at my plans; I'll carry them out, if I go to service to do it. Seeing so much money flying about, I long to honestly get a little and make my dear family more comfortable. I feel weak-minded when I think of all they need and the little I can do.

Now about you: Keep the money you have earned by so many tears and sacrifices, and clothe yourself; for it makes me mad to know that my good little lass is going round in shabby things, and being looked down upon by people who are not worthy to touch her patched shoes or the hem of her ragged old gowns. Make yourself tidy, and if any is left over send it to Mother; for there are always many things needed at home, though they won't tell us. I only wish I too by any amount of weeping and homesickness could earn as much. But my mite won't come amiss; and if tears can add to its value, I've shed my quart, — first, over the book not coming out; for that was a sad blow, and I waited so long it was dreadful when my castle in the air came tumbling about my ears.[5] Pride made me laugh in public; but I wailed in private, and no one knew it. The folks at home think I rather enjoyed it, for I wrote a jolly letter. But my visit was spoiled; and now I'm digging away for dear life, that I may not have come entirely in vain. I did n't mean to groan about it; but my lass and I must tell some one our trials, and so it becomes easy to confide in one another. I never let Mother know how unhappy you were in S. till Uncle wrote.[6]

My doings are not much this week. I sent a little tale to the "Gazette," and Clapp[7] asked H. W.[8] if five dollars would be enough. Cousin H. said yes, and gave it to me, with kind words and a nice parcel of paper, saying in his funny way, "Now, Lu, the door is open, go in and win." So I shall try to do it. Then cousin L. W. said Mr. B. had got my play, and told her that if Mrs. B. liked it as well, it must be clever, and if it did n't cost too much, he would bring it out by and by.[9] Say nothing about it yet. Dr. W. tells me

Mr. F. is very sick; so the farce cannot be acted yet.[10] But the Doctor is set on its coming out, and we have fun about it. H. W. takes me often to the theatre when L[izzie]. is done with me. I read to her all the P.M. often, as she is poorly, and in that way I pay my debt to them.

I'm writing another story for Clapp.[11] I want more fives, and mean to have them too.

Uncle wrote that you were Dr. W.'s pet teacher, and every one loved you dearly. But if you are not well, don't stay. Come home, and be cuddled by your old

Lu.

MS: Unlocated. Printed: Cheney, pp. 71–74.
    1. The Reverend Frederick T. Gray of the Bulfinch Place Society in Boston.
    2. LMA's cousin Louisa Willis, the wife of Hamilton Willis, was the daughter of Charles W. Windship (whose first wife was Mrs. Alcott's sister Catherine) and his second wife, Martha Ruggles Windship.
    3. LMA occasionally referred to her sister Lizzie as Betty.
    4. For Bronson's diaries, see note 3 to 16 June [1887].
    5. Possibly *Flower Fables*, which was not published until December.
    6. Samuel Joseph May, with whom Anna stayed in Syracuse.
    7. LMA's first known contribution to the *Saturday Evening Gazette*, edited by William Warland Clapp, Jr., was "The Rival Prima Donnas" in the 11 November 1854 issue, for which she was paid ten dollars ("Notes and Memoranda," Houghton Library, Harvard University).
    8. Hamilton Willis, son of Mrs. Alcott's sister Elizabeth May Willis and Benjamin Willis.
    9. Thomas Barry, manager of the Boston Theatre, was considering LMA's adaptation of "The Rival Prima Donnas." Although he failed to produce it, he did give LMA free tickets at his theatre.
    10. Dr. Charles May Windship, the only child of Mrs. Alcott's sister Catherine, was interested in drama; Joseph M. Field, the prolific dramatist of the Mobile Theatre Company.
    11. LMA's next known contribution to the *Saturday Evening Gazette* was "A New Year's Blessing" in the 5 January 1856 issue.

To Ellen Emerson

[20? December 1854]

Dear Ellen,[1]

Hoping that age has not lessened your love for the *Fairy folk* I have ventured to place your name in my little book, for your interest in their sayings & doings, first called forth these "Flower Fables," most of which were fancied long ago in Concord woods & fields. The pictures are not what I hoped they would be & it is very evident that the designer is not as well acquainted with fairy forms & faces as you & I are, so we must each *imagine* to suit ourselves & I hope if the fairies tell me any more stories, they will let an Elfin artist *illustrate* them. So dear Ellen will you accept the accompanying book, with many wishes for a merry 'Christmas, & a happy New Year,' from your friend,

LOUISA M. ALCOTT. —

ALS: Houghton Library, Harvard University.

1. Ellen Tucker Emerson (b. 1839), second child of Ralph Waldo and Lidian Jackson Emerson. LMA dedicated *Flower Fables* (Boston: George W. Briggs, 1854) to her because she had been the main audience to whom LMA had read earlier versions of the tales in the book. This letter accompanied an inscribed copy of the book (Houghton Library, Harvard University).

On 21 December, Ellen wrote a friend that when she found the book, she "fell down in a swoon." Concerning its history, she said that LMA thought it was Ellen "who made her publish them for I showed the written ones to Mother who liked them so much she advised Louisa to print a book" (*The Letters of Ellen Tucker Emerson*, ed. Edith E. W. Gregg, 2 vols. [Kent, Ohio: Kent State University Press, 1982], 1:82).

To Abigail May Alcott

20 Pinckney Street, Boston, Dec. 25, 1854.

Dear Mother, — Into your Christmas stocking I have put my "first-born," knowing that you will accept it with all its faults (for grandmothers are always kind), and look upon it merely as an earnest of what I may yet do; for, with so much to cheer me on, I hope to pass in time from fairies and fables to men and realities.

Whatever beauty or poetry is to be found in my little book is owing to your interest in and encouragement of all my efforts from the first to the last; and if ever I do anything to be proud of, my greatest happiness will be that I can thank you for that, as I may do for all the good there is in me; and I shall be content to write if it gives you pleasure.

Jo is fussing about;
My lamp is going out.

To dear mother, with many kind wishes for a happy New Year and merry Christmas.

I am your ever loving daughter
LOUY.

MS: Unlocated. Printed: Cheney, pp. 76–77; *LASC*, p. 344 (partial). This letter accompanied a copy of *Flower Fables*, LMA's "first-born."

A partial manuscript copy by Mrs. Alcott reads as follows:

Into your Christmas Stocking I have placed the first fruits of my genius [LMA later canceled "genius" and inserted "little talent"] — knowing that you will accept it with all its faults and look upon it merely as an earnest of what I may yet do, for with so much to cheer me on I hope to pass in time from fairies and folks to men and realities.

What ever beauty or Poetry is to be found in my little book is owing to your interest in, and encouragement of all my efforts from the first to the last. & if ever I do any thing to be proud of, my greatest happiness will be *that*, as I may indeed do, for *all* the good there is in me, and shall be content to write if it *gives you* pleasure. —

I am ever
your loving daughter
LOUISA

(25 December 1854, Houghton Library, Harvard University.)

To Amos Bronson Alcott

[25 December 1854]

For the Attic Philosopher
With wishes for a merry Christmas from his daughter Louisa.[1]

Santa Claus saw while passing thro' Greece
    The sandals Plato had worn
And he thought of a certain philosopher
    Whose feet they would greatly adorn
But feeling the ancient sandals to be
    Out of keeping with modern hose
He changed them into these slippers you see,
    More fitting a land of snows
But still they're adorned on thier surface of green
    With the oak leaves Plato once wore
To remind the good sage when they garnished his feet
    Of the wise man who wore them of yore
The leaves by good rights should have been on the head
    But Santa Claus knew in the street
That both sages & saints wear hats & not crowns
    So the oak leaves were best on the feet
Thus to shield the ten philosophical toes
    From all stubs, slips, stumbles & shocks

And to hide from the eyes of the peeping old world
  The holy Platonic blue socks
The transmagnified slippers good Santa Claus brings
  For the "student & seers" cold feet
The sage thinks so much of all human soles
  His own should most surely be neat,
Then long life & repose to Plato the second
  No matter how empty his *pus*
May he dwell undisturbed with gods poets & saints
  In the green groves of Acade, *mus.*

MS: Houghton Library, Harvard University.
 1. In a later hand, LMA added "with (A Pair of Slippers)."

To Amos Bronson Alcott

Wed Nov 28th [1855]

Dearest Father

 Having no other gift than a heart full of love, to offer you on our joint birthday, I will try & get a letter ready for that day so that the mail may deliver the kiss & affectionate greetings I send to my dear fifty six year old papa. I think it is but right & proper that a thanksgiving feast should be held in the states where we both are, to celebrate the joyful day on which two such blessings as you & I dawned upon the world & I please myself with imagining how differently we looked & acted on making our debut upon the stage where we have been playing our parts so well ever since.

 I know *you* were a serene & placid baby when you began your wise meditations in the quiet little Spindle hill[1] farm house (I believe thats where you decended from on high) looking philosophically out of your cradle at the big world about you & smiling as seriously & affectionately at the young motherly face bent over you, as now when *you* bend over that same kind face, that is motherly still tho no longer young. Fifty six years have passed since then, & that peaceful babys golden head is silver now but the man looks as serenely at the big foolish world & meditates as wisely as he did in his cradle, & nothing but the lines on his face where troubles have been & four tall women at his side, show that years & trials have changed the wise little child into a wiser old man. Surely dear father some good angel or elf dropped a talisman in your cradle that gave you force to walk thro life in

13

quiet sunshine while others groped the dark, I wish you could teach me its magic so that at fifty six I may be as young at heart & full of cheerful courage as this day finds you.

I was a crass crying brown baby, bawling at the disageeable old world where on a dismal November day I found myself, & began my long fight first for a proper quantity of water for my ablutions which was unlawfully withheld from me, then for my rightful food which was denied till I nearly went out of the world I disliked so much, but pork & oysters held me back & supported by these spiritual strengtheners I scrambled up to childhood, out of which after often losing my small self & wandering forlornly thro years of infant troubles & cares, I fell with a crash into girlhood & continued falling over fences, out of trees, up hill & down stairs tumbling from one year to another till strengthened by such violent exercise the topsey turvey girl shot up into a topsey turvey woman who now twenty three years after sits big brown & brave, crying, not because she has come into the world but because she must go out of it before she has done half she wants to, & because its such hard work to keep sunshiney & cheerful when life looks gloomy & full of troubles, but as the brown baby fought through its small trials so the brown woman will fight thro her big ones & come out I hope queen of herself tho not of the world.

I am leading a quiet busy life here, working out my own plans in my own way & trying to keep to the difficult right among many easy *wrongs*, & so far am content with myself for the thought of what you all at home hoped & expected of me makes me careful of my words & actions that you may not be disappointed now as you have often been.

I am sewing busily for friends & am expecting the high honor of making a set of shirts for the Reverend Dr Gannett[2] a present from his worshippers. I shall [try] to put some *life* into them.

Then I am trying to turn my brains into money by stories one of which I hoped to have sent you but cannot. Cousin Hamilton has sent me some books to review for his paper.[3] I dont know what I shall make of them but mean to try for if L[lewellyn] Willis does I fancy I can.

I go to the theatre once or twice a week & tho Forrest[4] does not act Shakespere well the beauty of the play shines thro the badly represented parts, & imagining what I should like to see, I can make up a better Macbeth & Hamlet for myself than Forrest with his gaspings & shoutings can give me. After being on the stage & seeing more nearly the tinsel & brass of actor life, (much as I should love to be a great star *if* I could,) I have come to the conclusion that its not worth trying for at the expense of health & peace of mind, & I shall try to be contented with the small part already given me &

acting that well try to mix the tragedy & comedy of life so wisely that when the curtain falls I can jump up as briskly as the stage dead always do, & cheered by the applause of my little audience here, go away to learn & act a new & better part in the Lords theatre where all *good* actors are *stars*.

I went the other day to see the statuary at the Atheneum,[5] there is a very fine full length statue of Beethoven which I liked best of all, his face is beautiful & his deep eyes tho only of bronze seem *looking* music as powerful & sweet as his hand ever wrote. A large cloak falls round him & in his hand is a manuscript covered with partly written notes taken from some of his real music. I wish you could see it. The one of Judge Story is of marble & he is a quiet handsome old judge with his gown on laying down the law with a wise outstretched finger & a Solomon expression of countenance. My beautiful Orpheus has had both his legs broken but they are stuck on again & he still looks earnestly into Hell for his lost wife like a faithful spouse as he is. Your Diana is still striding on with her long limbs like her human sister who is more warmly dressed but who would enjoy a bare legged run with a fat little stag, as the marble lady is.

Thebe & Ganymede is a new one. Thebe very sad & crushed in her feelings has given up the cup & holds the urn to Ganymede the new waiter who looks up into her face with a half laughing half pitying expression & wont take the urn from her. I liked it much. Also two little figures of children one dancing with hair & clothes blown back, so natural that the small marble feet seem as if they must make a sound in falling, as they keep time to a flute in the hands of the little dancer. The other is a child with a broken tambourine, so very sorrowful that marble tears seem tumbling out of its eyes, but I have filled my paper & cannot describe more. When you come we will go together & see our stone relations. Can you not write to me & send some of your quiet in a letter? Good bye God bless you dearest father & let you spend many more happy birthdays with or near your ever loving child LOUISA

ALS: Houghton Library, Harvard University.

1. Bronson was born on 29 November 1799 in Wolcott, Connecticut. The hill on which his great-grandfather John Alcocke settled, and on which he was born, was called Spindle Hill because of the household crafts associated with it. Bronson's mother pulled flax and his father made plows, rakes, boxes, baskets, and brooms for local sale.

2. Ezra Stiles Gannett succeeded William Ellery Channing as pastor of the Federal Street Church in Boston.

3. Hamilton Willis edited a financial gazetteer for the Boston *Saturday Evening Gazette* and *Boston Journal*; we are uncertain to which paper LMA is referring.

4. Edwin Forrest, the famous American Shakespearean actor, was engaged for a long run at the Boston Theatre, which included a number of performances of Shakespeare.

5. LMA is probably referring to John Frazee's bust of Judge Joseph Story and to the

following sculptures by Thomas Crawford, all on display at the Boston Athenaeum: "Orpheus," "Hebe and Ganymede," and "Two Statues of Children." No full-length statue of Beethoven or statue of Diana seems to have been exhibited during this period.

To Miss Seymour

Walpole   Sept 21st [1856]

Dear Miss Seymour[1]

Mother forgot to send my message in her letter so I make bold to do it myself knowing you will excuse me for trespassing on your time & troubling you with my concerns.

Will you be so kind as to ask Mr Norris of the "Olive Branch,"[2] or Mrs Jennison of the "Ladies Enterprise",[3] if they would take some stories from me. I am writing for the "Gazette" & "Sunday News" but neither of them pay very well, & as money is the principle object of my life just now I want to add another string or two to my bow, & feel a great desire to write for the "Olive Branch" as it pays well I believe.

Mr Norris may remember a story I wrote for him some years ago, & may have seen some of my later ones in the Gazette which have been so kindly noticed & commented upon[4] that I feel encouraged to offer my wares to any one who will lend a helping hand to a struggling fellow mortal who wishes to earn her living by her pen.

Now dear Miss Seymour dont trouble yourself about this but if in some of your pilgrimages about town you happen near State St will you make this enquiry for me & tell Mr N how glad I should be to write a story or two for him, & thereby confer a great favor on my "umble" self.

We are all well & blooming & enjoying this lovely Autumn weather up here among the hills.

Father left last week on a lecturing tour to New York Philadelphia Boston & elsewhere, to be gone all winter probably.[5]

Abby is coming to town with me to take lessons in crayon heads of Mrs Hildreth if that lady does not join her spouse in New York.[6] It will be a fine opportunity for Abby who has great taste & love for that sort of thing.

Annie & Lizzie will remain with mother & a nice stupid winter they will have for lectures & meetings are among the "lost arts" in this place.

Mother wants to add a line so I will come to a "focum". Ever yours, L M ALCOTT

ALS: Louisa May Alcott Collection, Barrett Library, University of Virginia Library. A half-page letter from Mrs. Alcott is on the last page. The Alcotts had moved to Walpole, New Hampshire, in July 1855, where Benjamin Willis, whose deceased wife was Mrs. Alcott's sister, allowed them to live rent-free in one of his houses.

1. Possibly the "Miss Seymore" who was May's teacher in Boston in 1852 (7 December 1852, May's diary, Houghton Library, Harvard University). The only teacher by that name listed in contemporary Boston directories is Almira Seymour.

2. Thomas F. Norris published the *Olive Branch*, a paper devoted to Christianity, polite literature, general intelligence, agriculture, and the arts. LMA's "The Rival Painters" appeared there on 8 May 1852, but there is no record of anything else by her in it.

3. Mrs. Jennison, probably an editor of the *Ladies' Enterprise: A Journal of Literature and Art*, published in Worcester between 1853 and 1856.

4. LMA had published five stories and a number of poems in the *Saturday Evening Gazette* through September 1856.

5. Bronson left in September to visit his mother in Connecticut and to deliver a number of lectures, or "conversations." While in New York, he met Walt Whitman; see *The Journals of Bronson Alcott*, ed. Odell Shepard (Boston: Little, Brown, 1938), pp. 286–287, 289–291.

6. Richard Hildreth, historian and philosopher, and his wife, Caroline Neagus Hildreth. He had moved to New York in 1854. Mrs. Hildreth's portrait of Bronson, done in 1857, appealed to Mrs. Alcott, who wrote the artist, "You have converted my long, sharp, somewhat angular spouse into a peerless prophet and seer" (26 February 1857, diary, copy by Bronson, Houghton Library, Harvard University). The portrait appears following p. 138.

To William Warland Clapp, Jr.

Walpole Oct 9th / 56

Mr Clapp

I am anxious to know if the popularity of my contributions to the Gazette will warrent you to engage with me for a story each month for the coming six at fifteen or twenty dollars each as the length or excellence may vary.

I have had other offers in advance of this but am not sure of their reliability & prefer the Gazette as it circulates among a class of readers with whom I have other agreeable connexions than those of a literary character

Please let me hear from you at your earliest convenience, & shall be glad of the usual compensation for the last two stories.[1]

Respectfully
L. M. ALCOTT.

ALS: Houghton Library, Harvard University.

1. LMA had received ten dollars apiece for "Mabel's May Day" and "The Lady and the Woman" in the 24 May and 4 October issues of the *Saturday Evening Gazette* ("Notes and Memorandum," Houghton Library, Harvard University).

To William Warland Clapp, Jr.

Walpole Oct 27th / 56

Mr Clapp

I recieved your letter containing $20 on Saturday,[1] & thank you for your criticisms on my stories. I find it difficult to make them interesting & yet short enough to suit your paper. But hope to improve in both points.

Respectfully
L M ALCOTT

ALS: Houghton Library, Harvard University.

    1. "Ruth's Secret" appeared in the 6 December 1856 *Saturday Evening Gazette.* Mrs. Alcott wrote Bronson the next day that LMA would use the money for "repairing her wardrobe" and to pay "her way to Boston" (28 [October 1856], Houghton Library, Harvard University).

To Anna Alcott

(Copy)
[2] Nov 1856.

Sunday morn.

No 1

Beloved lass,

I reached town unbroken & met Fidelia[1] in the parlor, she welcomed me very kindly & introduced me to my future room mate a crumpled looking girl with a knob of light hair & a suprised eye. They were just going to dinner so I said I'd warm my feet & wait till by & by, but Mrs Reed[2] came up from the table & embraced me like a Ma, urged me to come & eat, & when I was afeared & said "No", took me to my room.

> "The way into my parlor is up a winding stair,
> But its a very cosy place when once you're safely there."

It is "situate" at the top of the big house a queer pie shaped room, but nicely carpeted, with two bureau's (for which I gave praise) a dormer window with a table & rocking chair in it for my private benefit. A head bumping closet rich in shelves & pegs holds my reserved resources, & just outside the door (there being no "chimbly" inside) is a Tophet stove[3] which warms all out doors & freezes me. It would'nt be in character to be too comfortable so as

18

I can *look* at a stove I must'nt expect to feel it, or it might make me too luxurious, which perhaps is a merciful dispensation.

Well, after joking about a little while the boarders ate & departed, I went down to the empty dining room & "partook copiously" of everything while chatting with Mrs Reed. Then she had to go out & I did likewise, refreshing myself with a grand sweep thro my beloved old town whose very dirt is interesting to my eyes. I went to the U. S. Hotel. Ham was affable & Lu "flew at me like a wasp" set me down before her & poured the following news into my willing ear.[4]

Ham is so glad to have some one to escort Lu about that he will give us tickets [to] anything we want to see & (hear oh my people!) he is going to get a "Pass" from Barry so that I can go in to the Theatre with them when I like & for nothing as Barry owes me something for my play.[5] Lu & I can pop in of afternoons & Ham can come for us when we go in the eve so I cried Hurra! & kissed her on the spot. We are going to the Opera this week, Forrest is coming. Lu has got a Merchantile ticket for us, also tickets for the Lowell course by Mr Gjana an Italian, on the "Italian Reformers" so fun beameth in the distance for this "umble" worm.[6] Tomorrow there is to be a grand reception of Charles Sumner & we are going to the State House to behold the same.[7]

I spent the rest of the P.M. gabbling & laying plans with Lu, went down to tea at the great table & was introduced to a party of her friends who had read my "works" & deigned to look upon me as a rare & worthy specimen of humanity. After [manuscript breaks off]

Lu gave me the scarlet crape shawl for theatre goings & as it is a very fine affair I feel illuminated to a great extent when I get it on. Molly Sewall was delighted with her things & seemed glad to see me.[8] Auntie is expecting Ab & spoke of her taking music lessons with Sophy which will be grand.[9] Mary May has been sick but is robust & "digressing" again.[10] Mrs Kilborn wants me to study German but having tried ninetynine times I've no faith that I shall succede the hundredth.[11]

Boston is nicer & noisier than ever. Cars go rumbling about, the sidewalks are perfect rainbows in point of color Fremont flags[12] are flapping like birds of prey over a lady's head & crowds of people are swarming up & down in a state of bustle very agreeable to behold after the still life of Walpole. I feel "uplifted" to a great extent as to my prospects for fun if not for work. Whipple, Emerson, Beecher, Ike Marvel,[13] & other worthy folks are to lecture & I have tickets, then the theatre *pass* for afternoons, walks with Lu which are always pleasant for we go to see pictures, get books, shop or eat goodies, my quiet garret to write & dream in, & some pleasant fellow boarders to make home comfortable.

The weather is perfect, warm & brihlike spring, & I think it a good omen that all the way down it grew clearer & clearer till I reached Boston in broad sunshine without a cloud in the sky which was so full of them when I started. I am looking about me in all directions, Clapp will take a story a month[14] which gives me ten dollars & nearly pays my board then by sewing I can easily make up the other two even if Mrs Lovering dont want her governess again.[15] Clothes are expected to rain down from heaven, or the fashions to change to one comforter & a pair of boots which are easy to get. I feel hopeful in my mind & more determined than ever to try my experiment & be independant of every one but my own two hands & busy head. It seems rather queer sometimes to be in a city full of very rich relations & yet feel as if I dared not ask them for any help even to find work, for when I do they are so busy about their own affairs that my concerns seem a bother & I go away thinking I will never ask again.

Lu & Molly are my firm stand by's & tho neither of them have anything for me to do but a little sewing sometimes they give me something better than work or money, in thier good will & sympathy, & the sisterly interest they take in my success.

Now dearest Nan I've spun my spin & rather a long one for a three days experience — so good by & a kiss, your ever

loving LOU.

ALS: Houghton Library, Harvard University (partial).
    1. Probably a domestic.
    2. LMA moved in October 1856 to Mrs. Mary Ann Reed's boardinghouse at 34 Chauncy Street, which she later depicted as Mrs. Kirke's house in *Little Women*, where "Jo's Garret" was located. Her husband, David Reed, published the *Christian Register*.
    3. That is, a furnacelike or hellish stove.
    4. LMA's cousins Hamilton and Louisa Willis.
    5. Probably a reference to "The Rival Prima Donnas," which Thomas Barry had considered two years earlier.
    6. Professor Guglielmo Gajani of the University of Bologna began delivering a series of six lectures entitled "The Early Italian Reformers" at the Lowell Institute on 5 November.
    7. Charles Sumner, U.S. senator from Massachusetts, returned to Boston after his caning on the floor of the Senate by Preston S. Brooks of South Carolina. The next day, LMA "saw him pass up Beacon Street, pale and feeble, but smiling and bowing" (journal entry, 3 November, Cheney, p. 86).
    8. Molly Sewall was the daughter or wife of Thomas Sewall.
    9. Louisa Caroline Greenwood May, adopted daughter of Joseph May, became the second wife of George William Bond in 1843. Sophia Elizabeth Bond was the daughter of May's first wife and was born in 1841, a month before her mother's death.
    10. LMA's great-aunt, Mary Goddard May, wife of Samuel May and associated with temperance and antislavery reforms.
    11. Possibly Mary E. Kilbourn (see 19 May 1861).
    12. John Charles Frémont, nominated for president by the newly formed Republican Party in June 1856, was defeated by James Buchanan.

13. The critic Edwin Percy Whipple; Donald Grant Mitchell, who as "Ik Marvel" wrote the popular novels *Reveries of a Bachelor* (1850) and *Dream Life* (1851); and the well-known preacher Henry Ward Beecher.

14. "Ruth's Secret."

15. LMA was indeed hired to tutor Alice Lovering during the winter of 1856–57.

To Anna Alcott

No 2

November [1856].

Thursday 6th

No 2

My Dearest Nan.

I *must* begin my letter or I never shall get it done I have so much to tell my lass about the jovial times I'm having in this Vanity Fair. To begin journal fashion.

Sunday — I wrote to you, & in the eve went with Hamilton & Lu to Parker's. There I found Mr Sherbe (of course) Garrison Phillips, John P. Hale, Sanborn, some Germans, of whom I only knew Mr. Kriesman the singer, Mrs Howe, a straw colored supercillious lady with pale eyes & a green gown in which she looked like a faded lettuce.[1] Young Canner & his wife, (Miss Torn[?],) also graced the scene, he with fine eyes & she in very dirty gloves but as full of admiration for her spouse as "Mrs Macawber." Sherbe asked me every imaginable question proper & improper, Sanborn bowed like a well-sweep & talked about books as usual, Phillips made me a happy girl by a five minutes chat, & Mr Parker said "How is your worthy father," which was very agreeable to my feelings — Mrs P[arker]. & Miss [Hannah] Stevenson were very kind, introduced many folks to me, & asked me to come often. I stared, blushed, & sat a mass of enjoyment the whole evening, looking at the good, wise faces round me & secretly resolving to go every Sunday it was so pleasant.

Monday — Wrote all the morning copying "Ruth."[2] After dinner I went out to see the Sumner demonstration,[3] & having missed Lu Willis went to Beacon St. & there saw one of my idols very finely. Eight hundred gentlemen on hors[e]back escorted him & formed a line up Beacon St. through which he rode smiling & bowing, he looked pale but otherwise as usual. I suppose you have seen an account of it, but it was better to see the real thing, so I shall tell you about it. The only time Sumner rose along the route was when he passed the Orphan Asylum & saw all the little blue aproned

21

girls waving their hands to him. I thought it was very sweet in him to do that honor to the fatherless & motherless children. A little child was carried out to give him a great bouquet, which he took & kissed the baby bearer. The streets were lined with wreaths, flags, & loving people to welcome the good man back, & as he rode up Beacon St. where many of the houses were shut I thought of the time when Daniel Webster a great, gloomy, disappointed man passed that way & found them all open, with flowers & handsome women & shouting gentlemen to comfort him as he went by,[4] & tho I was only a "love lorn" governess I waved my cotton handkerchief like a meek banner to *my* hero with honorable wounds on his head & love of little children in his heart. Hurra!!

I could not hear the speeches at the State House so I tore down Hancock St. & got a place opposite his house. I saw him go in, & soon after the cheers of the horsemen & crowd brought him smiling to the window, he only bowed, but when the leader of the cavelcade cried out "Three cheers for the *mother* of Charles Sumner!" he stepped back & soon appeared leading an old lady who nodded, waved her hand, put down the curtain, & then with a few dozzen more cheers the crowd dispersed.

I was so excited I pitched about like a mad woman, shouted, waved, hung onto fences, rushed thro crowds, & swarmed about in a state [of] rapterous insanity till it was all over & then I went home hoarse & worn out.

I was very sorry I didnt go with Lu for she was with Parker's party & had a fine time. They were in Tremont St. almost alone (for everyone scrambled across the Common to see the State House fun) & when Sumner passed, Parker burst out with three great cheers all by himself, the ladies clapped, & Sumner laughed like a boy as he waved his hat to his best friend. Was'nt it funny & like Parker?

Tuesday — I wrote till Lu came, & we had a fine walk while she did some shopping, after I got home & was in my room one of the girls came up with a great square box directed to me from "L Willis". I opened it & there was a lovely Talma,[5] large & soft & warm, just what I needed but never thought of buying — I had a dance of joy in it & blessed my little relative who played Providence so kindly for this old "shorn sheep." So now you needn't imagine me suffering in the faded cloak for I take my walks abroad like any lady in the land with my smart Talma & new gloves, (my one expense since I came.) Mrs Kilborn informed Lu, whom she knows a little, that she was "very glad Miss Alcott had come for it made the house gayer she was such a funny, good natured girl." I dont wish to be a "peacock" but I *do* wish you to know that I've done my best to be agreeable & not "show my angles" too much. Mrs K. is rather sentimental I think, for she embraced me the other night & begged me to love her, for she was "dying for the want of affection."

22

I was rather taken aback for she seems very cheerful & unwidow like. But Miss Reed says she is very unhappy for she lost her husband & little boy in one year, & has suffered a great deal. So I got up a sensation upon the subject & resolved to be very friendly if I could do her any good. She is rather pretty & seems amiable, tho fond of flirting & not very careful of other peoples feelings, but I may be wrong.[6]

Wednesday — I finished "Ruth's Secret" & took it to Molly who liked it, & then sent it to Clapp. Fanny looks miserably & wont live long I think. Write to her but dont mention what I say. At one o clock Ham called for me to go & see Mr Barry who wished to be introduced to the rash being who wrote "The Rival Prima Donna's," so, arrayed in my best attire I was borne to the sacred pile.[7] Barry was out, & I was glad of it, for it gave us time to look about, which I assure you I did. Into every crack & corner I poked my inquisitive nose & glanced my well opened eye, I promenaded about the stage which is immense, went up & saw the "rain & thunder" arrangements, the dressing rooms paint rooms, & heavenly bodies generally, then down into the bowels of the earth among trap doors & ghostly fixtures very strange to behold, after which I sat in a corner & heard the Opera people rehearsing up stairs, & such scolding, swearing, moaning & jabbering I never heard, but being in Italian it was interesting tho profane.

We went at last to Barry's office, & there in a bower of plays sat a stout, grey-headed gentleman with a clever face & an English voice, who was very polite to me, & while I took private notes talked with Ham about plays & actors, which was just what I liked. Mr B. said he never would advise anyone to choose that profession it was such a hard life & so few succeded, he told two things which I send for your benefit, Nan.[8] A pretty talanted girl of seventeen was brought to him by her brother who said she was stage struck & wanted to try her powers. Mr B asked what line she played, she had known Fanny Kemble[9] & had a fancy to play "Lady Macbeth" & that sort of thing. She was very small & utterly unfit for it, so Mr B thought the only way to cure her was to show her the folly of her wish, which he did till she got into a passion, wept, & bemoaned herself, vowed she *would* play, & went off at last in great woe. But the next day sent a note thanking him for his advice & deciding to do nothing about the matter. So *she* was cured. The other story was of a young man who was rampant to act but had no talant so Barry undertook to cure *him* also. He was engaged to play a few nights & lest his friends should applaud his bad acting out of kindness & so do him harm, Mr B. put some persons before the curtain to hiss, which they did & the young man was so mortified at his failure, & so tired of the whole concern that he played but two nights & then went & did as Papa wished him to, viz became a minister. I told Mr B. I had a stage-struck sister whom I

23

would bring to *Dr* Barry to be cured, & he said "perhaps I may fail if she has the genius Mr Willis thinks she has." There is news for "Mrs Prig"[10] thinks I, & Ham spun away some time about our plays. Then the Pass question came up, & Barry said that Passes were no longer allowed, but whenever I wished to go to the Theatre if I would write him a note in the morning or come myself I should always have two seats whenever I liked. At which I sang for joy, metephorically speaking. This he said would give me a chance to see things, & would be of use to me in any future plays I might write, for if the "R[ival]. P[rima]. D[onnas]'s" succeded it was a foundation for others. He didn't speak of altering the play as I thought he would, & I wondered what I was taken there for, till after we came out, when Ham told me that Barry merely wished to *see* & talk with me, for he liked the play, & had given it to Mr Oakes to read, if *he* approved, it would go, for Oakes is a good judge & Barry's right hand man in these things. I laughed in my sleeve at the fuss but was contented as long as I could go to the Theatre as often as I liked. Just think of the "richness?" Mrs Barrow wants to act the play, so does Mrs Wood,[11] & between them I suppose it will end in smoke; tho Ham predicts a blaze of glory — I'm resigned to either, tho the more I think of it the flatter it seems.

I spent the P.M. fixing for the eve & after supper went with Ham & Lu to the Opera. La Grange was "Norma", & for the first time in my life I understood how one could go crazy over Operas. La Grange was a fine "Norma", a classic looking woman, & acted as beautifully as she sang,[12] such tones & gestures I never heard or saw before. I cried & *enjoyed* my soul almost out of my body with the music. It was her Benefit, & she was presented by Mr Barry with a diamond eagle pin. Ham showed it to us before it was given, for he spends his time behind the curtain while we sit before it. Everyone rose & waved & shouted & it was great. Next week Forrest comes, & I shall take Barry at his word, for I mean to pervade the theatre promiscuous like[13] & make theatrical hay while the sun shines.

I have written this today because I was boiling over & must find a "went". Other people are so kind in taking me about for *my* amusement that I feel I can afford paper & postage for *yours*. After this I shall write every Sunday & expect punctual & copious answers.

Dear Nan, I'm going to make some calls to day & shall ask every one to have an eye out for you. I *must* get something to do here so come to enjoy the fun with me. Tell Betty her gingerbread has been the staff of my life, & keep Mother warm,

so bless you & good by from "old Lou."

24

ALS: Concord Free Public Library. LMA later crossed out the names of people in this letter; we have restored her original readings, reporting significant revisions in the notes.

1. Emmanuel Scherb, German refugee writer and lecturer; the reformers William Lloyd Garrison, Wendell Phillips, and John Parker Hale; Franklin Benjamin Sanborn taught school in Concord from 1855 to 1863; A. or H. Kriessman, both listed as music teachers in contemporary Boston directories; Julia Ward Howe, wife of Parker's friend Samuel Gridley Howe and later author of "The Battle Hymn of the Republic."

2. "Ruth's Secret."

3. For the Sumner demonstration, see 2 November 1856.

4. Daniel Webster, statesman and politician, had many triumphs in Boston before being attacked for his support of the Compromise of 1850 and the Fugitive Slave Law.

5. A talma is a long, irregular cape that sometimes has a shoulder cape or hood.

6. This paragraph has three long vertical lines drawn through it in a different color ink than that used in the letter.

7. LMA later inserted "Boston Theatre" here.

8. LMA later inserted "A. & I were stage struck then" above this sentence at the top of the page.

9. Fanny Kemble, a famous British actress LMA had met at Walpole the previous July (journal entry, Cheney, p. 82).

10. In their theatricals, LMA played Sairey Gamp to Anna's Betsey Prig, both being characters from Dickens's *Martin Chuzzlewit* (1844).

11. Mrs. Julia Bennett Barrow, an English actress then playing in *John Gilbert and His Daughter*; Mrs. John Wood, a regular performer at the Boston Theatre.

12. When LMA saw Anna Caroline de la Grange performing in *Norma* on 5 November, she was quite "stage-struck" (journal entry, Cheney, p. 86).

13. LMA later canceled "promiscuous like" and inserted "faithfully."

To Amos Bronson Alcott

Boston, Nov. 29, 1856.

Dearest Father, — Your little parcel was very welcome to me as I sat alone in my room, with snow falling fast outside, and a few tears in (for birthdays are dismal times to me); and the fine letter, the pretty gift, and, most of all, the loving thought so kindly taken for your old absent daughter, made the cold, dark day as warm and bright as summer to me.

And now, with the birthday pin upon my bosom, many thanks on my lips, and a whole heart full of love for its giver, I will tell you a little about my doings, stupid as they will seem after your own grand proceedings. How I wish I could be with you, enjoying what I have always longed for, — fine people, fine amusements, and fine books. But as I can't, I am glad you are; for I love to see your name first among the lecturers, to hear it kindly spoken of in papers and inquired about by good people here, — to say nothing of the delight and pride I take in seeing you at last filling the place you are so fitted for, and which you have waited for so long and patiently. If the New Yorkers raise a statue to the modern Plato, it will be a wise and highly creditable action.

. . . .

I am very well and very happy. Things go smoothly, and I think I shall come out right, and prove that though an *Alcott* I *can* support myself. I like the independent feeling; and though not an easy life, it is a free one, and I enjoy it. I can't do much with my hands; so I will make a battering-ram of my head and make a way through this rough-and-tumble world. I have very pleasant lectures to amuse my evenings, — Professor Gajani on "Italian Reformers," the Mercantile Library course, Whipple, Beecher, and others, and, best of all, a free pass at the Boston Theatre. I saw Mr. Barry, and he gave it to me with many kind speeches, and promises to bring out the play very soon. I hope he will.

My farce is in the hands of Mrs. W. H. Smith, who acts at Laura Keene's theatre in New York.[1] She took it, saying she would bring it out there. If you see or hear anything about it, let me know. I want something doing. My mornings are spent in writing. C. takes me one a month, and I am to see Mr. B., who may take some of my wares.[2]

In the afternoons I walk and visit my hundred relations, who are all kind and friendly, and seem interested in our various successes.

Sunday evenings I go to Parker's parlor, and there meet Phillips, Garrison, Scherb, Sanborn, and many other pleasant people. All talk, and I sit in a corner listening, and wishing a certain placid gray-haired gentleman was there talking too. Mrs. Parker calls on me, reads my stories, and is very good to me. Theodore asks Louisa "how her worthy parents do," and is otherwise very friendly to the large, bashful girl who adorns his parlor steadily.

Abby is preparing for a busy and, I hope, a profitable winter. She has music lessons already, French and drawing in store, and, if her eyes hold out, will keep her word and become what none of us can be, "an accomplished Alcott." Now, dear Father, I shall hope to hear from you occasionally, and will gladly answer all epistles from the Plato whose parlor parish is becoming quite famous. I got the "Tribune," but not the letter, and shall look it up.[3] I have been meaning to write, but did not know where you were.

Good-by, and a happy birthday from your ever loving child,

LOUISA.

MS: Unlocated. Printed: Cheney, pp. 88–90; Marjorie Worthington, *Miss Alcott of Concord* (Garden City, N.Y.: Doubleday, 1958), pp. 82–84. Cheney says this was written at Mrs. Reed's boardinghouse.

1. Mrs. William H. Smith, wife of the stage manager of the Boston Museum, performed LMA's *Nat Bachelor's Pleasure Trip* as an after-piece to her benefit performance of *The Romance of a Poor Young Man* at the Howard Athenaeum in Boston on 4 May 1860. Laura Keene's Theatre in New York, built for the famous actress, seated twenty-five hundred and opened 18 November 1856.

2. William Warland Clapp, Jr.; Robert Bonner, editor of the *New York Ledger*, which did not carry any works by LMA during this period.

3. LMA may be referring to one of these items in the *New York Daily Tribune*: "The Lecture Season," which lists Bronson as one of the "popular Lecturers" available (20 November 1856, p. 5); "Woman's Rights Convention," which announces that Bronson has been elected one of seven vice-presidents (26 November 1856, p. 5); or "Woman's Rights Convention," which prints a letter from Horace Greeley supporting the cause (27 November 1856, pp. 6–7).

To Anna Alcott

No 10

The Boston Bulletin
A second edition will be issued on Tuesday next.
No 10.
[28–31] December [1856].

Sunday 11 A.M.

Dearest Pythias.

I will begin in an orderly manner & grapple with the various subjects as they come which is the only way to preserve these great events to an admiring posterity.

Monday. Sent you a parcel by C Titus, taught my babe, & recieved a blow in this wise. My N Year's Tale was sent back with these remarks from Clapp "My Dear Miss Alcott. I dont think the publication of this story would add to your literary reputation, & tho I dislike to say so I must tell you that I think it inferior to anything you have written. Pardon this freedom & believe me, Yrs Truly W. W. Clapp."

I was very much taken aback, not knowing that I had any "literary reputation" to sustain, & not caring much for his opinion for he didnt like "Lady & Woman"[1] & Parker did, so though rather disturbed at seeing my $10 vanish I "possessed my soul in patience" & thought I'd send the story some where else & let Clapp ask for another before I sent it. I know he will for Ham. says he likes my wares, & now he may wait for them. Dont be alarmed, I've three stories ready to be disposed of & Lovering for a mainstay, my wits are getting sharpened, & I can sew like a steam engine while I plan my works of art.

27

Tuesday. Sewed, taught Alice, & failing to draw a ticket took courage & under shelter of my Pa's friendship wrote to Mr Giles for one.[2] A very polite note with the ticket came back & I went with Lu & the Holbrooks to the first lecture of a course on Shakespeare which I want very much to hear.

Wednesday was a very busy day, see if it was'nt. At nine I went out with Lu on a shopping excurtion, & while in at Warrens she told me to look at cottons, & went off to another part of the store.[3] I thought she might be going to get me some thing but never dreamed of the grandeur in store for me.

She said nothing when she came back & at twelve I rushed to Loverings, taught & walked my two hours, then to Mary's for a book Ab wanted, next to Mr Bonds in Milk St. to send it to her, & then home to dinner. In the P.M. I walked to South Boston to give Ann Gates her Christmas present from Lu. Got home cold, tired & low in my mind, & the first thing I saw was a box from home. I clutched it, swept up stairs, & startled the family by dancing a hornpipe with it in my arms, then like a young whirlwind swarmed to my garret, ripped it open & plunged in, laughing, crying, munching the gingerbread, putting on the flannel cap, flapping the yellow butterfly holder & sprinkling salt water over letters & presents in a perfectly rapterous & imbecile manner. You dear good souls to think of me in the midst of your hustle! If you'd sent diamonds & side saddles you couldn't have pleased me more; it seemed so homelike & dear to see the little things come tumbling out as I burrowed, even the old tin box was touching to my feelings for it reminded me of the cockroachy cupboard where my family daily "dish thier tea." The picture hangs on one side of my table, the fragmentary[4] on the other, the cushion reposes on the bureau, & the gingerbread is stored away in my closet a perfect mine of riches, which I visit often & gloat over in a state of high crunch,[5] the letters pervade the town in my pocket, & the thought of you all fixing the box for me keeps me happy & brave at heart, even though Clapp's do turn up their noses & boots wear out faster than could be desired.

After brooding over my goodies forgetful of my tea, I went with Lu to see Joe & had a pleasant time of it, for we had a carriage & jingled through the bright busy streets, stopping at jewellers, flower stores & confectioners. We found Joe reposing in a luxurious room with Mrs Roper in the everlasting brown gloves, reading "The Wide Wide World" to him.[6] She retired at once & we made our call, Lu gave him a gold pencil & some flowers. He looks miserably & seems very lazy elegant & lofty minded.

After our call we drove home & spent the eve trimming Lu's rooms with Christmas green. At parting she gave me a small box saying "A little present & a merry Christmas, dear," & I scrambled home expecting to find a set of muslins, but lo & behold, it was a handsome silk gown the first I ever had. Mrs K. says it is a very nice one & will last a long time, it is one stripe bronze & black & one of silvery grey. Lu says she is going to have it made for me in great style; so now she has got me fixed up like a christian & I feel made. Isn't she good?

Thursday. At the Drs for my Christmas dinner & had three more presents, Mrs Reed gave me a set of laces, Mrs Windship a pair of light gloves, Mary Barker a bottle of perfume, & Sam a pretty handkerchief.[7] I spent the P.M. helping them fix for the evening, & after a standing tea "the party came in." Abby[8] arrived with the Bonds looking very pale & lofty in her meek gown & as I sat in a corner I enjoyed the remarks her relations made about her for they seemed astonished that an Alcott should dance & talk like other people, & thought her a very pretty graceful girl, "as she is sez I." She behaved beautifully, & I was proud of "little Huldah." There were about five & twenty young beings there & refreshments "fair & free". I drank a cup of divine coffee which I thought was very foolish till it appeared to be the best thing I could have done for at 11 Lu had a severe attack of asthma & I came into town & took care of her all night. My coffee kept me wide awake tho I was very tired & so I could be useful. I wish Cousin Lizzie could have seen Lu then for she thinks Lu plays sick when she is'nt, but I dont think people sit bolt upright gasping all night if they could go to sleep, however bats is bats & "brickbadges" is "brickbadges".[9] At 8 Ham went off & we went to bed sleeping till 11 then I had breakfast & spent the day waiting on my "little mother". In the eve as she felt like sleeping I went with the Holbrooks to Giles & heard a fine lecture on the "Men of Shakespeare," next time it is the "Women" then Tragedy & Comedy & lastly a general glorification of the divine "Will." I enjoy them very much for the wise humpback is as feirce & eloquent as ever & darts about like a crooked flash of lightening. He is married to a young lady who fell in love with his genius & wrote to him often before they met, at last she married him, he dont drink now, & is a better & happier little man.

Saturday. Slept till 10, wrote an hour, then went to Alice, who was sick. Dined at Molly's & as Uncle Sam sent me a ticket for the Anti Slavery Fair I went & had a pleasant time seeing Ade & all the Mays besides hosts of other relations & friends.

Now I will meander & "digress" — How fine about dear old father![10] I told S. Sewall[11] & he was surprised to hear of the three hundred earned & more coming & I was delighted that the stupid world waked up & paid him for his wise sayings. I had letters from him yesterful[12] full of courage & good news. If he comes down ask him to bring my Fairy Book for Mr Lovering wants to see it. "Flower Fables" is a great favorite with the childred, & they seem fonder than ever of "Oclow". I always see two or three heads at the window watching for me & general rush takes place as I go in. Alice is better behaved, Anna lives in my lap, while the twins walk over me, & Charly presents sweetmeats & talks sagely about his "youth" when I took care of him.[13] I hope the performances will prove as profitable as they are agreeable.

About leaving Walpole. I'll do my best to forward it, & begin looking about for a house at once. Lu would like to live with us & I should like to do anything for her she does so much for me. Let me know your plans & I'll help them on. My answer to your pathetic appeal on the subject of letters is a promise to write eight pages a week, God willing, I *am* very busy but hope never to be too much so to write to my "Innermost," who shall have her scribble "brought regular & drawed mild." You ask about funds &c. I have eight cents in the bank at present, $10 owing me, & a fortune in prospect. I shall this week dispose of another story, & ask Jewett about a book of collected tales.[14] Mr Lovering *may* be in earnest about printing the "Christmas Elves,"[15] the play *may* come out & I *may* become a woman of wealth in a few months, but "life is a strife" to say nothing of a "bubble" & no suspicion of a "dream" at least to me, so I shall keep a "flummin" & may come home with my "pickin dish"[16] full. Dont be troubled about me I'm well & chirk,[17] & if I pay my board, in a great state of comfort as far as self is concerned, but I want to send something home & it frets me because I cant, but I live in hopes & that is the cheering idea which "inweigles" me on. So keep up your heart & we'll yet "walk in silk attire & siller hae to spare."[18]

Wednesday morn — Having written so *short* a letter I will add a little more before it goes. Coming from lecture last eve I found your parcel in the empty parlor & revelled in it while I toasted my toes. You say "Rouse yourself Pillicoddy",[19] & I am roused, but I am also homesick & wish to be, not for the place (dern it) but for you & tho happy as a grig in many ways[20] am haunted with the thoughts of you freezing within & without, hang like mill stones about my neck & keep me from enjoying that perfect repose so pleasing to a human worm. The fact is I feel so old, so very "anxious about many things," beside other girls that I dont care for their sort of fun & am contented to sit by like a placid grandma & watch thier gambols. I dont know why it is unless the various pummelings I've had make me afraid to skip & revel lest I smash my being[21] & get brought up with a crash as usual. People tell me I'm very silent & reserved, looking much but saying little, to which I respond "that is a good thing in a woman," which is a slight dab at Mrs K who gobbles all day like a milk clapper.

My week will be a gay one if it ends as it began & all comes to pass that promises. Monday at the Fair, Tuesday Giles' lecture, Wed (today) a Hop here being New Year's Eve. Thursday a party at Madam Bond's also the

Greele's, when the new gown will appear, Friday the Festival at Faniuel Hall Sat to "Ravels" with the Loverings, & Sunday eve to my Parkers best of all. I wish you were here.

I wish I could send you something better than this *brief* note & the picture of our saintly Pa whom Mrs H[ildreth] has endowed with a swelled cheek & a crumpled bib. Kiss them all for me keep from freezing & be what you always have been "The Angel In The House." Good bye, write soon to your faithful "Damon."[22]

ALS: Concord Free Public Library. LMA revised this letter at a later date; significant revisions are reported in the notes below.

    1. "The Lady and the Woman."

    2. Henry Giles began a series of six lectures entitled "Human Life in Shakespeare" at the Lowell Institute on 23 December.

    3. G. W. Warren & Co., dry goods merchants at 192 Washington Street.

    4. LMA later canceled "fragmentary" and inserted "catch-all."

    5. LMA later canceled "gloat over in a high state of crunch" and inserted "munch at all hours."

    6. Susan Warner's best-selling novel *The Wide, Wide World* (1852), published under the name Elizabeth Wetherell.

    7. Dr. Charles May Windship's wife Susan's maiden name was Barker, and these may be her relations.

    8. LMA later canceled "Abby" and inserted "May."

    9. LMA later canceled this sentence.

    10. LMA is probably referring to the profits from a series of Conversations Bronson was giving in New York.

    11. LMA's cousin Samuel E. Sewall, lawyer, antislavery and woman's rights activist, and trusted financial adviser of the Alcotts; see Nina Moore Tiffany, *Samuel E. Sewall: A Memoir* (Boston: Houghton, Mifflin, 1898), for details of his life.

    12. LMA originally wrote "yesterful full" and in a later hand revised it to "yesterday full."

    13. Possibly the Loverings' children.

    14. John P. Jewett, a Boston publisher.

    15. LMA wrote another children's book, *Christmas Elves*, which May illustrated but which was never published. It had earlier been submitted by Bronson to Phillips, Sampson of Boston (7 May, "Diary for 1856," p. 358, Houghton Library, Harvard University).

    16. LMA later canceled "a 'flummin' " and "pickin dish" and inserted "on grubbing" and "pocket."

    17. LMA later canceled "chirk" and inserted "rosy."

    18. That is (from the Scots), "silver have to spare." In a later hand, LMA wrote "20 years later we did" here.

    19. A reference to John Maddison Morton's one-act farce *Poor Pillicoddy*.

    20. In a later hand, LMA wrote "Nanny & I" here.

    21. LMA later canceled "smash my being" and inserted "forget my duty."

    22. LMA signs herself "Damon" to Anna's "Pythias" in reference to the youths whose friendship became immortalized in Greek legend.

To Amos Bronson Alcott

[1 January 1858]

Dearest Father,

As Annie has told you all the news I can only wish you a very "Happy New Year" & a kiss which I send here![1] We have spent a quiet pleasant day, & mother is in good spirits having just received twenty seven dollars from Mr Wigglesworth which has paid the rent so that is settled.

She thinks of going to Boston tomorrow to do some little jobs & see Dr Giest[2] about Lizzie's cough which is a great trouble to her.

Your letters are a great pleasure & we now & then show them to Mr Emerson who inquires often about you & your success.[3]

Abby is to fill up this page so good by

Ever your loving demon
LOUISA.

ALS: Houghton Library, Harvard University. Postscript to Anna's letter to her father of 1 January 1858.

    1. A drawing of lips pursed for a kiss appears here.

    2. Dr. Christian Geist of Boston attended Lizzie in her last illness.

    3. Bronson would return on 23 January from more than two months of giving lectures in New York and Ohio.

To Eliza Wells

Concord Mar 19th [1858]

Dear Eliza[1]

I write to you supposing your mother is in Boston where she will have already learned what I have to tell you, that our Lizzie is *well* at last, not in this world but another where I hope she will find nothing but rest from her long suffering.

She has been failing slowly all winter though Dr Gheist[2] told us she was better. We went on with our plays because he said we must keep her cheerful, & she loved to see us getting ready. But two sadder girls never acted than Annie & I for the thought of the patient shadow sitting at home was always before us.

She has sewed constantly till the last week, then her "needle felt heavy"

32

she said & she put away her work neatly & carefully never to take it up again.

Last Friday night after suffering much all day, she asked to lie in Father's arms & called us all about her holding our hands & smiling at us as she silently seemed to bid us good bye. We thought her going then but she lingered all through Saturday in great pain begging us to help & stretching her poor thin hands for the ether which had lost its effect upon her.

At midnight she said "Now I'm comfortable & so happy," & soon after became unconscious. We sat beside her while she quietly breathed her life away, opening her eyes to give us one beautiful look before they closed forever.

She was buried on Monday. Dr Huntington[3] read the Church Service & we sang her favorite hymn. Mr Emerson Henry Thoreau & Frank Sanborn carried her over the threshold of her old home & laid her in the new one at Sleepy Hollow.

We asked no one to the funeral & sent no word to Boston for we wished to be alone, & fathers friends did all we needed more beautifully & acceptably than any we could have asked & everything was simple & quiet as she would have liked it.

It was very grateful to us all to see their sympathy for father & the tender respect they paid his child tho' they have never seen her since we came back to Concord.

We longed for dear Uncle Sam or Mr Parker who loved Lizzie & always missed her face when she was not at church. But Uncle was too far away & Parker sick. Dr Huntington read very beautifully & spoke of Lizzie as if he had known & loved her. Mr Emerson had told him what a good unselfish patient child she was, & she made friends even in her death.

For two years she has suffered & we cannot wish her back, but the house is very strange & poor Mother sits in the empty chamber trying to believe that she shall never hear Lizzie's voice again or see her dear face on the pillow.

We shall go to our new home soon where she can be more truly what we often called her "Our Angel In the House".[4]

We hope to see your mother while in town for Lizzie often spoke of her & of Walpole, which we all have reason to remember sadly for her sake.

Dear Eliza perhaps if I ask you now you may be able to forgive & forget whatever unk[ind]ness you may *believe* me guilty off, & I hope you may sometime learn to know me as I really am, *& have been,*

Your grateful & loving cousin
LOUISA.

We all send much love to you & the children, Uncle Edwin & all kind Walpole friends.

Tell Hattie Annie will write soon tho' we should still like the promised letter from her. A heart full of love from us both to our "dear Dorr."[5]

L. M. A.

ALS: Concord Free Public Library.
    1. Eliza May Wells, oldest child of Thomas Goodwin Wells and Elizabeth Sewall Willis Wells.
    2. However, Dr. Geist had visited the Alcotts on 9 January and, after examining Lizzie, had told them, "I cannot give you much hope" (Anna Alcott to Bronson, 9 January 1858, Houghton Library, Harvard University).
    3. The Reverend Frederic Dan Huntington.
    4. LMA had earlier called Anna this (see [28–31] December [1856]). She also wrote a poem with this title about Lizzie (see Cheney, p. 97).
    5. Hatty Dorr, a former schoolmate of Mrs. Alcott's.

To the Alcott Family

Boston Sunday eve.
[October 1858]

Dear People

You will laugh when you hear what I have been doing. Laugh, but hear, unless you prefer to cry, & hear.

Last week was a busy, anxious time, & my courage most gave out, for every one was so busy, & cared so little whether I got work or jumped into the river that I thought seriously of doing the latter. In fact did go over the Mill Dam & look at the water. But it seemed so mean to turn & run away before the battle was over that I went home, set my teeth & vowed I'd *make* things work in spite of the world, the flesh & the devil.

Lovering sent no answer about Alice,[1] & nothing else could I find. I waited till Friday, then rushed out & clamored for work. Called on Mrs Lovering, she was out. Tore across the Common to Mrs Reed. She had no sewing but would remember me if she had. Asked Mr. Sargent,[2] had nothing for me to do. Then I said "Damn!" & after [a te]mpestuous night got up, went [stra]ight to Mr Parker's & demanded him.[3] [Yo]u may judge what desperate earnest [I] was in to go to people I knew so little. Mr P. was out also Miss L. But Mrs P. was in,[4] & I boldly [went?] up. I dont know what she thought of me for I was muddy & shabby, pale & red-eyed, grim one minute & choky the

34

next. Altogether a nice young person to come bouncing in & demanding work like a reckless highway woman.

I told her in a few words that we were poor, I *must* support myself, & was willing to do anything honest; sew, teach write, house work, nurse, &c.

She was very kind, said she would confer with Theodore & Hannah; [5] & I came away feeling better, for, though she gave me no work a little sympathy was worth its weight in gold just then, & no one else offered me a bit.

To day went to church, heard a sermon on "Good is set against evil". Tried to apply it, but did n't do it very well. At noon Hannah H. called & offered me a place as seamstress at the Reform School Winchester. Sew 10 hours a day, making & mending for 30 girls. Pay small at first, but it is a beginning & honest work.

Miss H. evidently thought I wouldn't take it for she said, "Mrs P. told me of your visit, was it in earnest or only a passing idea?" "I was in desperate earnest, & shall be glad of any thing, no matter how hard or humble," said I in my tragic way. "May I depend [on] you, & do you like sewing?" "You may depend on me if my health holds out with the 10 hours work. As for liking, it was not what I *want* but what I can *get* that I must take & be grateful for." She seemed satisfied, gave me a ticket, said, "Try it a week," & told me to go on Monday.

So I shall go & try my best, though it will be hard to sit patching & darning day after day with a dozen stories bubbling in my brain & "knocking proudly on the lid demanding to be taken out & sold." Knocking about is good for me I suppose. I get so much of it, I shall grow mellow & fit to eat in the fullness of time, though I think peacefully growing on the parent tree with plenty of sun an easier way.

Monday eve.

Now what *do* you think? Last eve when my mind was all made up to go out to W. in comes a note from Lovering saying that on talking it over they concluded to have me come & governess Alice for the winter.

I skipped for joy, & dear Molly said "Stay here & sew for me & that will pay your board, you help so much in many ways & make it so lively." I agreed at once, & there I am. Allyluyer! I went & told Hannah H & she was glad & said, "I knew it was n't the thing for you & only offered it as a little test of your earnestness, meaning to get you something better in time." Mr P. said "The girl has got true grit," & "we were all pleased with you." So that is right, & the ten hours will dwindle to four, with walking, play & lessons to vary the time. [6]

It has been a hard week but it is all right now, & I guess the text will prove true in the end, for my despair found me friends, & duty was made easier when I had accepted the hardest. Amen.

I begin tomorrow & am in fine spirits again. "Here we go up up up —
And here we go down down downy" is a good song for me.

With love your tragic comic

Lu.

ALS: Houghton Library, Harvard University. The manuscript is torn; missing words or letters
are supplied in brackets.
    1. LMA had tutored Alice Lovering in 1858.
    2. James T. Sargent, who, with his wife, Mary Fiske Sargent, would later found the
Radical Club, meetings of which LMA attended.
    3. The famous preacher Theodore Parker lived at 1 Exeter Street in Boston. LMA later
portrayed him as Mr. Power in *Work.*
    4. Mrs. Lydia Cabot Parker, Theodore Parker's wife.
    5. Hannah Stevenson, a close friend of the Parkers. We do not know why LMA refers
to her as Hannah H. later in the letter.
    6. In a later hand, LMA wrote "& fair wages for my work" here.

To Alfred Whitman

Boston Oct 27th [1858]

My Dearest Dolphus.[1]

I've been hoping to get a minutes peace to write to my boy for ever
so long but such a fussing & mussing as I've had to keep up ever since I
came that I'm most tired out & begin to despair of ever getting any quiet.

Carrie[2] may have told you that I've gone to seek my "fortin" & found it in
the shape of a demonic little girl who *dont* digest her food & *does* rave & tear
& scold & screech like an insane cherubim.[3] For the sum of two hundred &
fifty dollars a year I am expected to keep the sweet angel happy & instil into
her youthful mind such knowledge as her dyspepsia will permit. Her Ma is
a kind soul & provides funds for her amusement in the most liberal manner
so I go riding about the country in thier carriage or cars & buss'es to see the
various works of art & nature which abound in these parts. I like it as well
as I do any work & pile as much fun into my evenings as possible.

Lectures abound & very fine ones too. The Theatres are getting underway
& private plays flourish famously. I am going to one tomorrow night where
they will perform "Somebody Else" & "The Unprotected Female" one of Mrs
Woods parts.[4]

We are to have "Dombey & Son" when I am expected to do "Edith Granger" a vast tragic style of female which I shall murder most cheerfully.[5]

My family are robust. Mother & Annie dozing along at home with Carrie

& John by way of enliveners. Abby is getting her plumage in order ready for a flight to town where the longed talked of drawing lessons will come off. She is very well & in great spirits about her winters work & play — has many engagements for skating dancing & "larking" parties already made & intends to do & enjoy more this winter than any young woman ever did before.

I have been hoping to hear from my Dolphus though I was base enough to neglect answering his last letter. What have you been doing & how do plays prosper? I always love to get letters & to answer them too if not "drove mad" by a press of work.

Your picture travels about with me in my desk & I often long to see my "yellow haired laddie" & have a little fun or a confabulation about the state of the world in general our part of it in particular — I'm old in years but as much of a girl as ever about some things, & one of them is a strong liking for people who dont think much of themselves. Such people being rare birds now a days ought to be made much of & thought lots of by other people — So dont think I'm demented if I "much"[6] you & call you *my boy* for I have a very sincere love & respect for you dear Alf, not as a boy only but for many excellent & noble qualities which will make you a good & happy man I hope — So dont be desponding or blue for it dont pay & though I cant always follow my own preaching I believe it all the more & hate to see any one afflicted in a like manner. Carrie says you are blue & we all set about thinking what we could do to drive away the indigo devils, a pack of letters was voted a good cure & so I add my mite in the way of "daubage" —

Write to me again & I'll always answer & if you come to Boston let me know at 98 Chestnut St[7] & we'll do something great.

Good bye dear Alf & believe me ever

your loving friend LOUISA —

We shall all come down in a body & carry you back to Concord if you dont have a joyful mind & be a merry Tetterby —[8]

Tell Carrie to send you the "Lament for the cock tailed pussy." Its mighty funny.

L. M. A.

ALS: Houghton Library, Harvard University. Printed: Whitman 10, 6 (partial).

1. For information about sixteen-year-old Alfred Whitman, who had moved from Concord to Kansas with his father that autumn, see Elizabeth Bancroft Schlesinger, "The Alcotts Through Thirty Years: Letters to Alfred Whitman," *Harvard Library Bulletin* 11 (Autumn 1957): 363–385.

2. Caroline ("Carrie") Hayden Pratt, daughter of Minot Pratt of Concord and sister of Anna's future husband, John Pratt.

3. Alice Lovering.

4. James Robinson Planché's *Somebody Else* and Joseph Stirling Coyne's *A Scene in the Life of an Unprotected Female*, both one-act farces.

5. Edith Granger, second wife of Paul Dombey in Dickens's *Dombey and Son* (1848).

6. Whitman, in his article, said that LMA used "much" in the same way someone else might use the verb "pet."

7. Although LMA may have stayed briefly with the family of Thomas Sewall at 98 Chestnut Street when she returned to Boston in October 1858 looking for work, she eventually located at Mrs. Reed's boardinghouse.

8. Sophy and Dolphus Tetterby are characters from *The Haunted Man* (probably LMA's adaptation of Charles Dickens's story of that title), a play performed in Concord. After that play, LMA, who played Sophy, called Alfred Whitman Dolphus, from the part he played. This is explained in *My Boys*, the first volume of *Aunt Jo's Scrap-Bag* (Boston: Roberts Brothers, 1872), pp. 15–16.

To Anna Alcott

Boston Bulletin, — Ninth Issue.

Sunday Eve, November, 1858.

My Blessed Nan, — Having finished my story, I can refresh my soul by a scribble to you, though I have nothing to tell of much interest.

Mrs. L[overing]. is to pay me my "celery" each month, as she likes to settle all bills in that way; so yesterday she put $20.85 into my willing hands, and gave me Saturday P.M. for a holiday. This unexpected $20, with the $10 for my story (if I get it) and $5 for sewing, will give me the immense sum of $35. I shall get a second-hand carpet for the little parlor, a bonnet for you, and some shoes and stockings for myself, as three times round the Common in cold weather conduces to chilblains, owing to stockings with a profusion of toe, but no heel, and shoes with plenty of heel, but a paucity of toe. The prejudices of society demand that my feet be covered in the houses of the rich and great; so I shall hose and shoe myself, and if any of my fortune is left, will invest it in the Alcott Sinking Fund, the Micawber R. R., and the Skimpole three per cents.

Tell me how much carpet you need, and T[homas]. S[ewall]. will find me a good one. In December I shall have another $20;[1] so let me know what is wanting, and don't live on "five pounds of rice and a couple of quarts of split peas" all winter, I beg.

How did you like "Mark Field's Mistake"? I don't know whether it is good or bad; but it will keep the pot boiling, and I ask no more. I wanted to go and see if "Hope's Treasures"[2] was accepted, but was afeared. M. and H. both appeared; but one fell asleep, and the other forgot to remember; so I still wait like Patience on a hard chair, smiling at an inkstand. Miss K. asked

38

me to go to see Booth[3] for the last time on Saturday. Upon that ravishing thought I brooded all the week very merrily, and I danced, sang, and clashed my cymbals daily. Saturday A.M. Miss K. sent word she could n't go, and from my pinnacle of joy I was precipated into an abyss of woe. While in said abyss Mrs. L. put the $20 into my hands. That was a moment of awful trial. Every one of those dollars cried aloud, "What, ho! Come hither, and be happy!" But eight cold feet on a straw carpet marched to and fro so pathetically that I locked up the tempting fiend, and fell to sewing, as a Saturday treat!

But, lo! virtue was rewarded. Mrs. H. came flying in, and took me to the Museum to see "Gold" and "Lend Me Five Shillings."[4] Warren,[5] in an orange tie, red coat, white satin vest, and scarlet ribbons on his ankles, was the funniest creature you ever saw; and I laughed till I cried, — which was better for me than the melancholy Dane, I dare say.

I'm disgusted with this letter; for I always begin trying to be proper and neat; but my pen will not keep in order, and ink has a tendency to splash when used copiously and with rapidity. I have to be so moral and so dignified nowadays that the jocosity of my nature will gush out when it gets a chance, and the consequences are, as you see, rubbish. But you like it; so let's be merry while we may, for to-morrow is Monday, and the weekly grind begins again.

MS: Unlocated. Printed: Cheney, pp. 107–109; Marjorie Worthington, *Miss Alcott of Concord* (Garden City, N.Y.: Doubleday, 1958), pp. 100–102.

    1. LMA's "Notes and Memoranda" (Houghton Library, Harvard University) shows she received twenty dollars for "Mark Field," which could be either "Mark Field's Mistake" or "Mark Field's Success" in, respectively, the 12 March and 16 April 1859 issues of the *Saturday Evening Gazette*.

    2. LMA's "Notes and Memoranda" (Houghton Library, Harvard University) shows she received twelve dollars in 1858 for "Hope's Treasures," but there is no record of a story by this title being published.

    3. Edwin T. Booth, whom LMA saw in *Hamlet* (see Cheney, p. 102).

    4. The Boston Museum; Charles Reade's five-act melodrama, *Gold;* John Maddison Morton's *Lend Me Five Shillings*, a one-act farce.

    5. William Warren, the actor.

To Alfred Whitman

Concord Dec 26th [1858]

Dearest Alf.

    I was mightily pleased to hear from my boy & to learn that he was so well & happy in his new home.

I am spending my Christmas in Concord to help with some little jollifications got up to please Thedy,[1] & what do you think they gave me to act but that blessed part of "Major Murray."[2] I should have refused any one else but to make poor Thedy's last Christmas pleasant I would have played Falstaff or Julius Caesar.

The anguish of soul that fell upon me when I came to play it was fearful. I think there must be something in the part peculiarly repugnant to the human mind, for I never could get through the first long speech to save my life, & utterly routed Carrie's idea's by informing her that my false name was "Charles Antwerp a merchant of Vardeck &c."[3] My raiment was not of an explosive nature for which remembering your afflictions I was truly grateful.

We played in the Pratt parlor after a nice little tree full of gifts & goodies had been stripped, & had no stage or properties but rambled about among the audience in a perfectly vague manner quite as confusing to them as it was bewildering to us.

John Duck[4] got under the table for a chest & the Major with a wooden sword pried up the table cloth & dragged him out. Franky Hall was the Corporal & bore us to prison with appalling fierceness.

Mr Pratt read the part of the villianous "Sir Richard" with angelic meekness. Carrie darted in & out of Mrs Pottle's & Lady S's clothes with amazing rapidity, & Annie & John did the "lovyers" to the life.[5]

Thedy seemed to enjoy it very much & we were applauded copiously by a large & brilliant audience of fifteen.

How you spent your holiday time I hope to hear in the course of ages. You were the best of boys to go & write me a nice letter before I'd written to you. I had been thinking of it & only delayed because Carrie wanted to make a bundle to go all at once — Now she is so busy I shall not wait for her but send off our budget hoping you'll get it by the New Year.

Abby & I are fussing about in Boston. Abby is at the "School Of Design"[6] & is getting on splendidly bidding fair to become a second Raphael — She is perfectly wrapped up in drawing skating & dancing & in those three amusements she spends her "shining hours".

I still struggle with my dyspeptic cherubim who I flattered myself was getting christianized under my mild care, when she suddenly took to convulsions & has been as cross as an invalid angel & has worn me to a thread paper with the "worret" of it. She still remembers "Bobby Shaftoes"[7] his "yellow hair."

I shall want to know what you think of things in Kansas when you have seen more for we are all interested in the doings there — Only dont go & get "kilt" in any rows, though I suppose such things are getting old stories now. Have you ever read a story called "Herman" "Or Modern Knighthood"?[8] Its a very clever story & much in it about Kansas.

Boston Jan 2ond 1859 — My Dear Boy — I left my note unfinished, Christmas day being interrupted by the advent of John & Carrie & the exodus of a large oyster pie which so absorbed me soul & body that the claims of friendship were forgotten till it was too late to send my epistle from Concord as we planned.

Now having made my excuse I'll say adux & wishing my dear boy a Merry Christmas & a Happy New Year close my remarks —

Ever your loving friend,
Lou "jintly" with
"Sophy"

Abby desires her best love to "Mr Tetterby." Write again soon wont you? They are to have the "Jacobite" & the "Rough Diamond"[9] at Sanborns this week — Lets go. —

Please send me your directions, & write to your old girl once a month at least — S. T.

ALS: Houghton Library, Harvard University.

    1. Theodore Parker Pratt, John and Carrie Pratt's brother, was severely ill at this time and died in 1859.

    2. Major Murray was a character from James Robinson Planché's *The Jacobite*, a comic drama often performed by the drama groups in Walpole and Concord in which LMA participated.

    3. LMA should have said "Charles Vardeck, a merchant of Antwerp."

    4. John Duck, a character in *The Jacobite*.

    5. Since this play was performed at the Pratt house, Minot Pratt probably read Sir Richard's part; Widow Pottle and Lady Somerfield are other characters in *The Jacobite*.

    6. In December, May began to study under Salisbury Tuckerman at the School of Design in Boston.

    7. When Whitman visited LMA at the Loverings' in 1858 before leaving for Kansas, Alice "jumped upon him," calling him "Bobby Shafto [and] combing down his yellow hair quite to [LMA's] confusion" (31 October 1858, Mrs. Alcott's diary, Houghton Library, Harvard University).

    8. Sarah H. Palfrey, writing as E. Foxton, published *Herman, or Young Knighthood* in two volumes in 1866 with a preface stating that the "story was written in the years eighteen hundred and fifty-seven and fifty-eight" (Boston: Lee and Shepard). We have been unable to find an earlier printing; the pasted-up printer's copy for the book does indicate an earlier newspaper format (Houghton Library, Harvard University).

    9. John Baldwin Buckstone's *The Rough Diamond*, a comic one-act drama.

To Alfred Whitman

Feb 13th [1859]

My Dearest "Dolphus".

Your letter found me in the exciting whirl of a mass of Plays & I read it with one eye while I hammered red heels onto my shoes with other (or rather over saw that delicate bit of carpentry). You were a true Tetterby not to forget the existance of your "little woman" who often thinks of her "little man" & wishes she could see his face a coming in at the door to have a little chat & a great "muching".

We did want you at the plays for men of sense (theatrical & common) were wanting. John B Pratt was our main stay & a host in himself, but it is & always will be a mystery to me how anything decent was concocted out of the chaos which existed —

Mr Sargent the father of Abbys friend Kitty took it into his head to have some grand doings at his house while Ab was staying there, so we rummaged up two gents & with the four Sargents,[1] John Ab & I, we got up some startling things I assure you — Lord forgive me I forgot to say that the great Geo B[2] was there also — We got up some fine scenes & the rooms being very large & full of fine things we made a great spread in the way of gold & damask chairs draperies &c.

We had a play you *may* have heard of called the "Jacobite" — John as "Duck" I the "Widder," Kitty as "Patty." Edward Adams Johns cousin as "Sir Richard" Geo Cabot (Parkers nephew) the famous "Major" & a nice one he was too,[3] having got a real dress from the theatre in which he made a great lash. Ab was "Lady Sowerford" & made her first appearance quite "a success" really putting a deal of life & spirit into that flat young womans character —

After the "Jacobite" the great G. B. & the greater L. M. A. *did* the "Morning Call"[4] in a very unique manner, Sir Edward being got up in a red velvet hunting suit & a surprising wig, to say nothing of top boots & an emerald pin as large as a warming pan. "Mrs Chilling[s]tone" was troubled with a violent desire to grasp him by the wig, to pluck him by the nose & otherwise pummel & maltreat him he looked & acted so like a fool —

Old "Marm Jarley"[5] exhibited her wax "stattoas," & the evening wound up with a magnifique spread, banquet, or collation, at which we imbibed copiously of every thing & revelled in ice creams oysters chicken salad & other abominations, finishing off at twelve P.M. by a general warble & flourish. The Sargents were so pleased they mean to have plays every month.

The grand Masonic Ball[6] comes off this week & Abby is in woe being invited there by Cabot & to another here by E Adams. I think between the two stools she will come to the ground, for she is'nt fit to go anywhere after exhausting herself with "Lady Sowerford" — Do you remember the fun we had at that last Ball when we sat till three in the morning staring our eyes out at the people "bobbing around" down below?

Since my education is completed by learning the "Lancers"[7] I feel it my duty to frequent places of public resort & indulge in the "mazy" with great energy & liberality so if you were here we'd go to the ball & do something great.

Annie & John are "Darby & Joaning" over the fire & evidently wish there were but *two* people present so like a dutiful younger sister I must stop my writing & gently subside.[8]

Wed eve Feb 15th[9]

Finding myself a love lorn creeter all the folks having gone to "lecter",[10] I will resume my blotting to you — I am rather stupid in my mind having been up till twelve last night making a ball dress for Miss Ab, who is now rejoicing in its splendors at a ball to which she was invited by Edward Adams who came in style & bore her away to her first ball —

The Masonic Rout is to night & tho "Major" Cabot wanted Lady Summerford to go up she preferred "Sir Richard's" "Swarry" — Nan is there in the little gallery watching Louis Pratt's bow legs Geo Prescotts sylph like figger & the airy graces of the Miss'es Staples Bowers & Billings — Dont you wish *we* were there?[11]

What funny doings you are having in Kansas with your wandering Legislature, wolf hunts, & summer weather — You must tell me about the flowers there when they come for I'd like to see & know about the posies where with you will regale your blessed nose in the spring —

My dear old Ma has been very sick but didnt make up her mind to be "kilt" this time whereat we rejoice & "sound the loud timbrel o'er Egypts dark sea" — Mother Pratt has a weakness of the bones which allows her to sit down but on no account will consent to her getting up — which is rather trying to an active old lady like her — Thedy is better & strange as it seems is quite comfortable — Carrie is jocose & topsey turvey as ever & John the "dearest boy in the world" barring *my* private boy who shant be plagued with any more rubbish from his loving old woman SOPHY.

My letter is full of scrabbles but folks *will* talk & read so I kept putting in wrong words which makes confugion & daubiners. Pray excuse it. —

The girls send thier love —

1. John T. Sargent, his wife, Mary, and their children, Kitty and Arthur.
2. George Bartlett, son of Dr. Josiah Bartlett of Concord, had participated in LMA's theatricals.

3. Edward Adams, John Pratt's cousin, and George Cabot, Theodore Parker's nephew.

4. Charles Dance's *A Morning Call*, a one-act comedietta, featured Mrs. Chillingstone as a character.

5. *Mrs. Jarley's Waxworks*, a monologue inspired by readings from Charles Dickens and one of LMA's favorites.

6. The Grand Masonic and Civic Ball for the benefit of the Corinthian Lodge, featuring music by the ten-piece Germania band, was held on 16 February (program, Concord Free Public Library).

7. A set of quadrilles.

8. As LMA described the scene in a letter to her father, "Annie came too late to act but was a great help & enjoyed seeing 'her lad' admired as only much tender hearted souls can — She seems happy to be with him again after a long separation of a fortnight — John is working away like a man, very cheerful & so kind & good to us all that I *cant help* loving him & respecting him more & more. He is so honest simple & sincere that he seems a different creature from the other young men I see — If he could only get some good business I should be quite resigned to having Annie settled, for she is'nt much to anybody now but John" (13 February [1859], Houghton Library, Harvard University).

9. LMA is confused: Wednesday would have been the sixteenth.

10. Possibly the lecture by Samuel Johnson of Salem, delivered on Thursday, 17 February, before the Concord Lyceum. Since all other Lyceum lectures during this period were on a Wednesday, Johnson may have missed his original date and come a day later, thus accounting for LMA's entry.

11. George L. Prescott, later the leader of Concord's Civil War regiment; Abby Staples, daughter of Samuel Staples, who had jailed Thoreau in 1846 for nonpayment of taxes; either Maria Augusta or Lydia Bowers.

To Alfred Whitman

Boston April 17th [1859]

My Dearest Dolphus.

I recieved your illustrated letter & Ab & I on reading it were moved to put a night cap in our pockets & come to see "our boy" full speed — but on second thoughts resolved to write as soon as time allowed — We are as busy as ever gadding about to lectures & "high fun see's" of all kinds — Emerson & E. P. Whipple are giving splendid courses just now[1] & we enjoy them amazingly though it takes three evenings every week & with the other jauntings about leaves but little time for collecting a bodys ideas & writing letters, so yours has not been answered you see.

Dont berate yourself so fiercely about letter writing but keep on & become a perfect being in that respect. *I* like your letters & hope you wont give up sending them to me as my other boy has for I have'nt heard from Willy Bellows for a year or two & am afraid he has dis remembered his old Ma, so dont you go & do likewise —

44

You must'nt be a lonely sorrowful Tetterby either — I cant have it & whenever you feel home sick & solitary sit down & write to me feeling sure that I like it, that I can sympathize in your feelings & am always proud of any ones confidence & affection.

I have been through all that sorrowful loneliness & distaste for things & places & know how hard it is to bear, but believe me dear Alf its good for us & if we take it patiently & bear it bravely it will make us better & stronger though we may not feel so at the time. It will teach us to find happiness in ourselves & make us independent of others for our real pleasures — Things will brighten by & by, something will come to make life full of interest & then you will see that the hard or disagreeable past with its troubles & disappointments has been a good school for you.

Work is an excellent medicine for all kinds of mental maladies & I am glad you take it so cheerfully, though its not so pleasant as the study & fun of a school boys life. You are a school boy still though not under Sanborns teaching — your lessons I know are, & will be hard & your play times may be short, but never cave for that study faithfully & earn *some* prizes for yourself for good behaviour & patient application at least, if not for fine talents & brilliant accomplishments — Graduate a *good man* & your Master will ask nothing more.

You *can* be what you *will* to be, so dont think ill of yourself my dear — for those who know & love you see much to respect, much to exteem in your character & nature — A kind honest heart, a humble idea of self & a sincere desire to find & do the right — I know you are all this for if so good a man as John loves & respects you I am sure you are worthy his regard — Keep so, & be as like him as you can & in time you may find as great a blessing as he has in his "Lass" — & I cant wish you any better happier fortune than that — I didnt mean to deliver a lecture but it "kind of came" & is lovingly meant from your old friend.

The weather here is perfectly absurd & trying to the last degree — It either rains "guns" or blows them & often both together to the utter despair of the human race. Boston is a Nile of mud & Aggassiz[2] must be in his element for the inhabitants are turtleized in water proof shells & waddle about like the real article, dodging & splashing in the most natural & lively manner —

Ab & I go out on aquatic expeditions called shopping never sure that we may not find watery graves & be borne home mere "dem damp moist unpleasant bodies." India rubber mud scows called boots are our shipping accomodations, & the female portion of the community present the appearance of a flock of ostriches promenading in old fashioned fire buckets — the male portion in their "strait jacket" style of coat Skye terrier whiskers & muffin hats look like dandyfied bucanniers in jack boots & eye glasses — A boating club would flourish now.

Carrie is visiting her Aunt Ann & leaves a card upon her friends occasionally — We are going up there to a tea fight with John on Thursday, & I wish I was to see my "yellow haired laddie" there too. —

I am done with my "little treasure" now & am a gentleman at large & in want of a "sittewation" so if any one in Laurence wants a governess companion or man of all work I will come "for a consideration" — I came near going to Europe this spring but those perverse old baggages the Fates were against me & I still pine for a "furrin" trip as I have done for the last ten years — Lets you & I go as sailors & work our passage over, then travel on boat like "Consuelo" & "Joseph Hayden"[3] all over Europe having a nice time — Will you go?

We have had a very brilliant theatrical season & wound up with some plays before the "Fraternity" as Mr Parkers young people are called — It was like our town ball doings only not so good — & after it was over we recieved a written note of thanks from the President & a pressing invitation to join the society as ornaments thereof. We have'nt yet but mean to for they are a nice gay set & have grand times with their balls plays & picnic's —

The "Oyster Pie" is one of those poetic gems which deserve to be set in an imperishable crown for my "early brow" as you remarked to your son "Johnny" alluding to his infant sister "Sally" — I will forward my next when it comes.

Annie was going to send you a story by "Mrs Bluggage"[4] but as I believe she has not I will honor you with copies of the two parts — Mr Whipple read the first & demanded a sequel[5] which I got the old lady to write & which he was pleased to consider good — I send corrected editions of this great work that you may have the perfect whole.

Ripley Bartletts[6] poems are truely Emersonian in depth & splendor — "We have a great man among us" — Have you seen them?

Abby sends a note written a few ages ago but too valuable to be lost — She is coming on finely & will be an immense artist one of these days.

My letter has been written amidst the "confugion" of company & the dying agonies of an old pussy who was so ugly she decided to die & I hope she will carry out her good intention. Good bye my dearest Dolphus, write soon to your loving friend LOUY A.

ALS: Houghton Library, Harvard University.
      1. Emerson delivered a series of six lectures at Freeman Place Chapel in Boston between 23 March and 26 April; Edwin Percy Whipple began a series of twelve lectures entitled "The Literature of the Age of Elizabeth" at the Lowell Institute on 15 March.
      2. Jean Louis Rodolphe Agassiz, professor of geology and zoology at Harvard College.

3. Consuelo and Joseph Haydn, characters in George Sand's *Consuelo* (1842–1843).

4. LMA gave an original monologue for friends as "Oronthy Bluggage," inspired by her readings in Dickens (see Whitman 10, 5).

5. Possibly a reference to the two "Mark Field" stories.

6. Ripley Bartlett, George Bartlett's younger brother.

To Alfred Whitman

Concord Nov 8th [1859]

My Dearest Dolphus,

I have just received your letter & leaving my dinner "to waste its sweetness on the desert air" I sit down to answer it in a burst of virtuous repentance. I shant make a bit of an excuse for it would be a lie but leaving my sins in all their blackness I will begin to be good "right away quick," & trust to you for forgiveness for my seeming neglect which was an aggravated case of chronic procrastination.

You are a dear boy to think of me so far away & write me such a good long letter, & I'll do my best to answer it by spinning a long yarn about everything I can collect. Annie has left her ancestral hall to seek the object of her affections, that is she has gone to Boston to make a long visit so that she may see John oftener & take a sip of the enjoyments of Boston. They have been going to see Booth & keep writing rapturous accounts which harrow up my very soul & fill me with rage that I cant go to[o].

Mother took a little flight also last week, to meet her brother S. J. May, just returned from Europe,[1] so Abby & I are desolate "widders". We have been putting father & ourselves through a course of rice pudding, I having rashly baked a gigantic delicacy of that pleasing substance. We none of us like it but from a sense of duty have devoted our energies to its distruction, manfully attacking it morning noon & night & cheering each other on with jokes & fun of all kinds, but the crowning moment came this morning when after two days assault we gave in, I was heaving the remnants in triumph to pussys plate & she was in such an excited state that she scaled my back in doing which she distracted my attention & pitching over the poker I fell prostrate pudding puss & all. Abby set up a cry of victory & danced about the mournful ruins while kitty fell upon her prey & I gathered myself up with the consolation that whatever bones were broken the dreadful pudding had suffered worse damage & had at last disappeared from the face of the earth. Father arrived at this critical moment with your letter & in that I found a balm for every wound.

The moral of this tale is — Never make your puddings too large, & never shout till you are out of the wood.

Concord is as dull as ever though we make fitful efforts to enliven it. We had a Charade party the other day & great fun thereat. We had Franklin Benjamin Sandborn for the first — Father in an old fashioned suit on a pedestal in the exact attitude of the Franklin statue for the first word, & very finely he looked with his white hair cocked hat knee buckles & frills. A scene from the Buzzards [2] with a great deal of "Brother Benjamaning" in it for the second. I was "Mr. Buzzard" Abby "sister Lucretia" & it was intended to be very splendid but we got to laughing at the falling off of my wig, so Ab forgot her part which upset me & all I could do was to wink energetically for her to "go on", & keep dabbing at the shaving cup in my hands. I got my lather into a fine state but Abby stuck fast, & after a general shriek of prompting from behind she ended by going off with a loud "Brother *Benjamin*" which threw some light upon our seemingly insane procedings.

"Sanborn" was brought in in a conversation between Carrie & I. She wanted a school for her child & I recommended in a series of personal remarks, the Sanborn Seminary where my own nine darlings were imbibing knowledge copiously. The whole was the great creature himself. As the audience was composed of his pupils it was recieved with "great applause."

Ham-let & Mar-rage (marriage) were the others & we wound up with a dance.

We missed Tetterby very much for the new boys though clever & polite have no ideas about our kind of doings so we had to fall back upon Horace Mann's son & his tutor Arthur Serle [3] who has a room here &, is a charming little man very musical & jolly.

Carrie means to have a husking party in a few days with pumpkin pies, gingerbread & cider, dancing red ears of corn &c. Wont you come?

You are bewailing your seventeen years think of my anguish in a few weeks when I decend into the "sere & yellow leaf" of twenty seven. Its awful, but I dont feel more than ten so thats a comfort. Carrie is twenty three tomorrow so you see we are all getting into the vale of years & must make the most of our fun.

Dont go & be a man before I see you again for I like my little Tetterby better than I shall "Mr Whitman."

You speak of the weather — it *has* been cold enough to nip a bodys nose off, & the Indian summer is a myth. Abby got out her skates weeks ago, has half a dozzen hackeys[?] under consideration, & many engagements for "Goose Pond." [4] The "dark man" is flourishing in a great state of moustache & whisker which effort seems to have exhausted his mind. Sanborn has a fresh crop of

six foot boys fierce boatmen horsemen & dancers, & several very pretty girls —
Fanny Mansfield, "Major" as we call her is the best, she is Abbys firm ally,
rows rides shoots & dances like a trump.

Riding is all the rage now, & we have had several fine trips going in parties
of eight & ten riding all abreast through town in a very martial & astonishing
manner. Abby gets on the craziest horses & goes full tilt any where firmly
persuaded that nothing can possibly happen & that horses are her natural
element. I hang on & follow after *as* fully persuaded that my doom is near
but determined to enjoy the fun to the last gasp.

What are your ideas on the Harpers Ferry matter?[5] If you are *my* Dolphus
you are full of admiration for old Brow[n]s courage & pity for his probable
end. We are boiling over with excitement here for many of our people (Anti
Slavery I mean) are concerned in it. We have a daily stampede for papers,
& a nightly indignation meeting over the wickedness of our country, & the
cowardice of the human race. I'm afraid mother will die of spontaneous
combustion if things are not set right soon.

Abby intends to drop a line so I wont waste any more time for you — I
have been scribbling foolish stories as usual & if I had one by me I'd send it
to my old man with all my heart, for I remember the Tetterby sereen & his
fondness of the literature of his native land — I'll send you the very next —
one that is worth a cent's postage — It may be The Atlantic will have one
but I dont know yet.[6] Good bye my dear "Dolphus" write when you can to
your ever loving "SOPHY" —

I'm heartily glad you have recovered from the "Blues" which is a worse
disease than the "Shakes." Keep well & happy & good & God bless you my
dear lad.

MS: Unlocated; photostatic copy at Houghton Library, Harvard University.
    1. Mrs. Alcott went to Boston on 5 November to greet her brother, who had been in
Europe for the previous ten months (Bronson's "Diary for 1859," p. 615, Houghton Library,
Harvard University).
    2. John Maddison Morton's *The Two Buzzards*, a farce.
    3. Both Horace Mann, Jr., and Benjamin Pickman Mann, sons of the educator and
president of Antioch College Horace Mann, attended Sanborn's school, but on 15 September
1859, Sanborn wrote that "Mrs. Mann has concluded to send me her youngest son," making
Benjamin the more likely candidate for the reference here (*Young Reporter of Concord*, ed. Kenneth
Walter Cameron [Hartford, Conn.: Transcendental Books, 1978], p. 19); Arthur Searle, an
1856 graduate of Harvard College.
    4. Goose Pond, somewhat between Walden and Flint's (or Sandy) ponds.
    5. John Brown attacked the federal arsenal at Harpers Ferry, Virginia, on 16 October
and held it for two days before being captured. He was tried and convicted of treason, and
hanged on 2 December.
    6. Probably "Love and Self-Love," which appeared in the March 1860 *Atlantic Monthly
Magazine*.

To Alfred Whitman

Sat March 2ond [1860]

Dearest Of Dolphuses.

I should have seized my "dauber" the moment I recieved your last letter & written a reply "immeadiate" if I had not been in a vortex of costumes for a grand Masquerade Ball[1] at the Town House given by the Dominie[2] & his scholars, nineteen of whom came coolly one after the other to me for ideas or dresses till I was nearly distracted.

It came off last eve & was a fine affair, but would have been finer to me if a certain blond gentlem[an] & lady from Iowa & Syracuse had been there, being partial to the two. Everyone had done their best to be splendid & splendid they were, for many of the gentlemen hired their dresses of Costumers & so were all as smart as you please in velvet cloaks, plumy hats, slashed doublets, & big boots. The ladies were queens, vivandiere's, Swiss girls, & the usual pretty & unmeaning chara[c]ters. Frank Stearnes was Alcibiades in a real Greek dress gorgeous to behold. Eddy E a Zouave, Harry Stearnes Don Giovanni, (just imagine it!) Ward Rob Roy, Ned Bartlett Robin Hood, Rip B the Knave of Diamonds, Geo B a "Turkey Buzzard" as he elegantly discribed a Turkish dress, Frank Wheeler a Spaniard in a black slouched hat, feathers & big cloak, as fierce as his black whiskers could make him, Nan Pratt was an old lady from Maine & made a deal of fun with her "umbrel bag & spec's", Sophy Tetterby went as "Lady Teazle"[3] in crimson & white brocade with pearls promiscuous & white plumes in her classic pate, feeling like a jack daw all fun & feathers & looking like Vashti or any other fabulous old being given to dress & the vanities of the flesh. Carrie was an Indian girl & looked it to the life, with real paint & a grand costume. Miss Wilson was Shakespeare's "Beatrice", Annie Bartlett a fat shepardess, Grace Mitchell a Scotts lassie, & Russel "Friar Waterproof," Lizzie Bartlett the Union & little Simmons Gen Scott, Joe Thayer was '76 & Mrs Barker Queen Victoria.[4]

There were seventy five or a hundred in masks besides a gallery full of spectators & band of five tooters & scrapers & Johnny to call, with his one eye more askew than ever with the excitement of the thing.

I couldnt find any one out & very few guessed who I was thinking Annie was me not knowing she had come.

I rushed madly into all kinds of dances & came out right side up to my own great amazement not knowing any thing but the Lancers. I danced with "Richard the Third" a Mr Fiske from Boston (unbeknown) "A Court Fool" (young James) Don Pedro (Frank) Charles the Second (Geo Brooks) Don

Caezor de Bazon (Hersey Goodwin) & Figaro (a Collegian name forgotten) beside a skip with my precious Bogs a jovial little "Tar" for the occasion, who danced double shuffles & sailors hornpipes like a born "salt."[5] Maggie[6] as "Child Of The Regiment" held her court & danced into "the hearts of her countrymen" in a manner interesting to behold with her three inch boots & red cap set at each & all of them.

The fun lasted till 11, then by order of the higher powers they broke up & peace fell upon the town which has been in a stir for the last week, for which I give praise & sing "hally luyer."

Hire your building & in May when my works of art are done, I will come & turn Matron of the "Minerva Institu[t]e" established by A. W. Whitman for the relief of the mental famine in Iowa, & carried on by Mr & Mrs Adolphus Tetterby late of Concord, Mass. I will bring a load of sponges, crash towels & a portable soap factory, & go into the rudiments of an English education with vigor, writing over the door of the Wash house "Cleanliness is next to Godliness". I suppose the surrounding districts would be depopulated at once & you & I regarded as Goths & Vandals.

It seems so funny to think of "Alf" as a teacher that my mind refuses to do it & I exult in the cap & coat that keep you "Alf" still for I hate to have my boys grow up & expect a "Mr" & a handshake, instead of a "Bellus" or "Dolphus" & a maternal grab no matter when nor where. How old are you? & do you prefer to have me be Miss Alcott prim & proper or topsey turvey "Sophy" who loves you dearly & would fly out of the front windows if she should see you "droppin in" some day? I'm eight & twenty but as young as ever & look upon myself as a kind of Phoenix continually a rising spick & span from ashes & fire, so dont you go to growing *old* as you grow *up* but be "my boy" at heart all your days if you dont get tired of it, no fear that I shall.

You say the last year or two have been hard unhappy ones to you & I dont doubt it, but you know in every ones life there comes a waking up time & its well for them if it comes at the beginning & not at the end when it is too late to mend the past. These times are private revivals & do more good than any public ones as I know yours has for the line "now thank Heaven I've waked up & mean to stay waked up," was better than a dozen Camp meetings, a bushel of prayers & a years "experiencing of religion." Stand to that & whether the world ever hears of you or not you will be a successful man in the best sense of the word.

There was always something very brave & beautiful to me in the sight of a boy when he first "wakes up" & seeing the worth of life takes it up with a stout heart & resolves to carry it nobly to the end through all disappointments & seeming defeats. I was born with a boys nature & always had more sympathy for & interest in them than in girls, & have fought my fight for nearly fifteen [years] with a boys spirit under my "bib & tucker" & a boys wrath when I got "floored," so I'm not preaching like a prim spinster but freeing my mind like one of "our fellows," & as such I wish you all success, a cheerful heart, an honest tongue & a patient temper to help you through the world for its rough going & up hill work much of the way.

Dont forswear the Eves but remember Adam was'nt happy alone even in Paradise, so find a little better half by & by who dont wear "mittens" & through the power of a genuine woman's love regain & keep your Eden green through a long & happy life. So hopes your loving old friend, LOU, otherwise your "Sophy Tetterby."

ALS: Houghton Library, Harvard University. Printed: Whitman 10, 6 (partial), where it is incorrectly dated 1861.

1. About the preparations for the masquerade ball, see LMA's journal entry for March 1860 in Cheney, p. 120.

2. Dominie, the young people's name for Sanborn.

3. LMA's repertory included the character of Lady Teazle, the heroine of Richard Sheridan's *The School for Scandal*.

4. The Concordians include Frank Preston Stearns, Ralph Waldo Emerson's son Edward Waldo Emerson (b. 1844), Thomas Ward, Edward R. (Ned) Bartlett, Ripley Bartlett, Frank Wheeler, Anna W. Pratt, Annie Bartlett, Grace Mitchell, Elizabeth Bartlett, and William Simmons. Mrs. Barker may be the woman of that name who opened a "sewing school" in 1861 (see Sanborn, *Young Reporter of Concord*, ed. Kenneth Walter Cameron [Hartford, Conn.: Transcendental Books, 1978], p. 31).

5. Hersey Bradford Goodwin, son of the late Concord minister of that name; George Brooks, a Concord lawyer; Bogs was LMA's name for Seymour Severence (see 22 June [1862]).

6. Maggie Plumly of Springfield, Massachusetts, an occasional visitor to Concord, whom Sanborn describes on 21 November 1861 as "the bright star of the evening" at a party (*Young Reporter of Concord*, p. 34).

To Alfred Whitman

April 5th Fast Day [1860]

My Beloved "Tetterby".

I never forget my Dolphus but I have been the busiest old Sophy alive for my "works of art" are in such demand that I shall be one great blot soon. Do you know that your topsey turvey friend has got into the "Atlantic" & recieves fifty dollars a story?[1] Well its a fact, & I still live. Mr Redpath wrote the other day for a bit of poetry on "John Brown" also my autograph, which was such a rich joke we have'nt done laughing at it yet.[2] I send my last

Gazette infliction,[3] I should have sent more but I never thought you'd care for such rubbish so I spared you but you are heartily welcome to anything of mine that can give you pleasure my dear Alf.

We have just been riding horseback & my hand is so shaky I cant write with my usual elegance for the pen like "Cousin Fenix's"[4] legs goes off in unexpected directions & is not as calm as could be desired.

I forget what was going on when I wrote last but on Tuesday night we had a new sort of amusement called kidnapping.[5] Ab will tell you about it for I am so full of wrath I dont dare to unbottle myself for fear of the explosive consequences. I was not on the spot & could not free myself by joining in the fray but I am to be one of a Vigilance Committee so I shall have my share in future combats.

Annie Whiting[6] immortalized her self by getting into the kidnapper's carriage so that they could not put the long legged martyr in. One of the rascals grabbed her & said "Get out." "I wont" said Annie. "I'll tear your clothes." "Well tear away." "I'll whip up the horses & make them run away if you dont get out." "Let them run to the devil but I shant stir." & the smart little woman didnt till the riot was over. Young Warren[7] charged at the foe with a rake & Sanborn's boys rushed about like hero's.

Dont you wish you & I had been here? Then there would have been a regular Waterloo, & two Wellingtons in the field.

Annie & John may be married in June[8] so we are full of work & I am full of woe for I think its a very "tryin" thing to have men come & fetch away a body's relations in this sort of way.

Father is Superintendant of the schools & had a great time the other day, with all the schools in the Town Hall & speeches presents singing &c. I was deluded into perpetrating a song & send you a copy of it & the doings generally for if you still love this smart old place you may care to hear of its progress in all directions.[9]

My paper is at a "focum" & my wits were there a long time ago, so accept a deal of love dearest of Dolphus'es & dont forget your old SOPHY.

ALS: Houghton Library, Harvard University. Printed: Whitman 10, 6 (partial).

1. LMA received fifty dollars for "Love and Self-Love" (journal entry, November 1859, Cheney, pp. 104–105).

2. James Redpath published LMA's "With a Rose, That Bloomed on the Day of John Brown's Martyrdom," a poem that had first appeared in the 20 January 1860 *Liberator,* in his *Echoes of Harper's Ferry* (1860). Along with the poem, he printed a facsimile of her signature.

3. LMA's most recent stories in the *Saturday Evening Gazette* were "Mark Field's Mistake" and "Mark Field's Success."

4. Cousin Fenix, a superannuated and confused nobleman in Charles Dickens's *Dombey and Son* (1848).

5. For a description of Sanborn's arrest on 3 April in conjunction with a U.S. Senate

hearing about his role in the John Brown affair, see his *Recollections of Seventy Years*, 2 vols. (Boston: Richard G. Badger, 1909), 2:208–212, and "Mr. Sanborn's Account of His Own Arrest," *New York Daily Tribune*, 10 April 1860, p. 6.

6. Daughter of Colonel William Whiting of Concord.

7. Henry Warren.

8. In a later hand, LMA has written "were married in May" here. The marriage took place on 23 May.

9. LMA's "Children's Song" contained descriptions of her Concord neighbors, including Thoreau as "the Hermit of blue Walden" and Emerson as the "Poet of the pines" (see Bronson to his mother, 12 April 1860, *Letters*, p. 311. A copy of the broadside printing of the poem is in Mrs. Alcott's diary, April 1860, Houghton Library, Harvard University; it is also printed in Cheney, pp. 110–111).

To Anna Alcott Pratt

Sunday Morn, [27? May] 1860.

Mrs. Pratt:

My Dear Madam, — The news of the town is as follows, and I present it in the usual journalesque style of correspondence. After the bridal train had departed,[1] the mourners withdrew to their respective homes; and the bereaved family solaced their woe by washing dishes for two hours and bolting the remains of the funeral baked meats. At four, having got settled down, we were all routed up by the appearance of a long procession of children filing down our lane, headed by the Misses H. and R.[2] Father rushed into the cellar, and appeared with a large basket of apples, which went the rounds with much effect. The light infantry formed in a semi-circle, and was watered by the matron and maids. It was really a pretty sight, these seventy children loaded with wreaths and flowers, standing under the elm in the sunshine, singing in full chorus the song I wrote for them. It was a neat little compliment to the superintendent and his daughter, who was glad to find that her "pome" was a favorite among the "lads and lasses" who sang it "with cheery voices, like robins on the tree."

Father put the finishing stroke to the spectacle by going off at full speed, hoppity-skip, and all the babes followed in a whirl of rapture at the idea. He led them up and down and round and round till they were tired; then they fell into order, and with a farewell song marched away, seventy of the happiest little ones I ever wish to see. We subsided, and fell into our beds with the new thought "Annie is married and gone" for a lullaby, which was not very effective in its results with all parties.

Thursday we set our house in order, and at two the rush began. It had gone abroad that Mr. M. and Mrs. Captain Brown[3] were to adorn the scene,

54

so many people coolly came who were not invited, and who had no business here. People sewed and jabbered till Mrs. Brown, with Watson Brown's widow and baby came;[4] then a levee took place. The two pale women sat silent and serene through the clatter; and the bright-eyed, handsome baby received the homage of the multitude like a little king, bearing the kisses and praises with the utmost dignity. He is named Frederick Watson Brown, after his murdered uncle and father, and is a fair, heroic-looking baby, with a fine head, and serious eyes that look about him as if saying, "I am a Brown! Are these friends or enemies?" I wanted to cry once at the little scene the unconscious baby made. Some one caught and kissed him rudely; he did n't cry, but looked troubled, and rolled his great eyes anxiously about for some familiar face to reassure him with its smile. His mother was not there; but though many hands were stretched to him, he turned to Grandma Bridge,[5] and putting out his little arms to her as if she was a refuge, laughed and crowed as he had not done before when she danced him on her knee. The old lady looked delighted; and Freddy patted the kind face, and cooed like a lawful descendant of that pair of ancient turtle doves.

When he was safe back in the study, playing alone at his mother's feet, C. and I went and worshipped in our own way at the shrine of John Brown's grandson, kissing him as if he were a little saint, and feeling highly honored when he sucked our fingers, or walked on us with his honest little red shoes, much the worse for wear.

Well, the baby fascinated me so that I forgot a raging headache and forty gabbling women all in full clack. Mrs. Brown, Sen., is a tall, stout woman, plain, but with a strong, good face, and a natural dignity that showed she was something better than a "lady," though she *did* drink out of her saucer and used the plainest speech.

The younger woman had such a patient, heart-broken face, it was a whole Harper's Ferry tragedy in a look. When we got your letter, Mother and I ran into the study to read it. Mother read aloud; for there were only C., A.,[6] I, and Mrs. Brown, Jr., in the room. As she read the words that were a poem in their simplicity and happiness, the poor young widow sat with tears rolling down her face; for I suppose it brought back her own wedding-day, not two years ago, and all the while she cried the baby laughed and crowed at her feet as if there was no trouble in the world.

The preparations had been made for twenty at the utmost; so when forty souls with the usual complement of bodies appeared, we grew desperate, and our neat little supper turned out a regular "tea fight." A., C., B.,[7] and I rushed like comets to and fro trying to fill the multitude that would eat fast and drink like sponges. I filled a big plate with all I could lay hands on, and with two cups of tea, strong enough for a dozen, charged upon Mr. E. and

Uncle S.,[8] telling them to eat, drink, and be merry, for a famine was at hand. They cuddled into a corner; and then, feeling that my mission was accomplished, I let the hungry *wait* and the thirsty *moan* for tea, while I picked out and helped the regular Antislavery set.

We got through it; but it was an awful hour; and Mother wandered in her mind, utterly lost in a grove of teapots; while B. prevaded the neighborhood demanding hot water, and we girls sowed cake broadcast through the land.

When the plates were empty and the teapots dry, people wiped their mouths and confessed at last that they had done. A conversation followed, in which Grandpa B. and E. P. P.[9] held forth, and Uncle and Father mildly upset the world, and made a new one in which every one desired to take a place. Dr. B[artlett]., Mr. B., T[horeau?]., etc., appeared, and the rattle continued till nine, when some Solomon suggested that the Alcotts must be tired, and every one departed but C. and S. We had a polka by Mother and Uncle, the lancers by C. and B., and an *étude* by S., after which scrabblings of feast appeared, and we "drained the dregs of every cup," all cakes and pies we gobbled up, etc.; then peace fell upon us, and our remains were interred decently.

MS: Unlocated. Printed: Cheney, pp. 132–135.

1. Anna Alcott married John Bridge Pratt, son of the former Brook Farmer Minot Pratt, on 23 May, the same date as Abigail and Bronson's marriage. In attendance were the Alcotts and Pratts, Lidian and Ralph Waldo Emerson, Sanborn, Henry David Thoreau, Elizabeth Palmer Peabody (Boston reformer and longtime acquaintance of the Emersons), and the bridegroom's grandparents and his aunt and uncle, John and Lydia Williams. The marriage was performed by Samuel Joseph May, assisted by Ephraim Bull, since May was not a licensed minister in Middlesex County (Carrie Pratt to Alfred Whitman, 19 June [1860], Houghton Library, Harvard University). The marriage certificate is at Orchard House.

2. Probably Elizabeth Hoar, engaged to marry Emerson's brother Charles, who died in 1836; either Elizabeth Bradford Ripley or Phebe Bliss Ripley, both Emerson's cousins.

3. Probably Samuel May; Mary Ann Day Brown, the martyred John Brown's second wife.

4. Belle Brown, widow of John Brown's son Watson, who died of wounds received in the Harpers Ferry raid, and her baby, Frederick Watson Brown.

5. John Pratt's grandmother Rebecca Beals Bridge.

6. Probably Carrie Pratt and Abby (May) Alcott.

7. Possibly Bonny, the family nickname for Samual May's son, John Edward May.

8. Ralph Waldo Emerson and Samuel May.

9. John Pratt's grandfather John Bridge; Elizabeth Palmer Peabody.

To Adeline May

[July? 1860?]

Dear Ade: [1]

I should have answered your note before . . . We are all blooming and just now full of the Hawthornes[2] whose arrival gives us new neighbors and something to talk about besides Parker, Sumner and Sanborn. Mr. H. is as queer as ever and we catch glimpses of a dark mysterious looking man in a big hat and red slippers darting over the hills or skimming by as if he expected the house of Alcott were about to rush out and clutch him. Mrs. H. is as sentimental and muffing as of old, wears crimson silk jackets, a rosary from Jerusalem, fire-flies in her hair and dirty white skirts with the sacred mud of London still extant thereon.

Una is a stout English looking sixteen year older with the most ardent hair and eyebrows, Monte Bene airs and graces and no accomplishments but riding which was put an end to this morning by a somerset from her horse in the grand square of this vast town. She was not hurt but her Byronic papa forbid her to distinguish herself in any manner again and she is in a high state of wrath and woe.

Julian is a worthy boy full of pictures, fishing rods and fun and Rose a little bud of a child with scarlet hair and no particular raiment, which is cool and artistic but somewhat startling to the common herd.

Annie is making us a visit and is as blithe a bride as one need wish to see. The world is composed of John and John is composed of all the virtues ever known, which amiable delusion I admire and wonder at from the darkness of my benighted spinsterhood. Abby lives for her crayons and dancing, father for his garden, mother for the world in general and I for my pens and ink, and there you have a brief account of the "pathetic family" for the time being.

Love to your circle all around . . . This note is written with a room full of people all in full gab and with a pen inflicted with the rickets so you will doubtless be able to join your father in his opinion regarding the handwriting . . . I should love to go to Leicester but have a glimmering hope of Conway [New Hampshire] and am waiting.

MS: Unlocated. Printed: Marjorie Worthington, *Miss Alcott of Concord* (Garden City, N.Y.: Doubleday, 1958), pp. 109–110.

1. Adeline May, daughter of Samuel Joseph May's cousin Samuel May.

2. The Hawthornes arrived in Boston from Liverpool, England, where Nathaniel had served as the American consul, on 28 June 1860, and then went immediately to Concord. Their

children, referred to further on in the letter, are Una (b. 1844), Julian (b. 1846), and Rose (b. 1851).

To Anna Alcott Pratt

[ca. August? 1860?]

My Lass, — This must be a frivolous and dressy letter, because you always want to know about our clothes, and we have been at it lately. May's bonnet is a sight for gods and men. Black and white outside, with a great cockade boiling over the front to meet a red ditto surging from the interior, where a red rainbow darts across the brow, and a surf of white lace foams up on each side. I expect to hear that you and John fell flat in the dust with horror on beholding it.

My bonnet has nearly been the death of me; for, thinking some angel might make it possible for me to go to the mountains, I felt a wish for a tidy hat, after wearing an old one till it fell in tatters from my brow. Mrs. P.[1] promised a bit of gray silk, and I built on that; but when I went for it I found my hat was founded on sand; for she let me down with a crash, saying she wanted the silk herself, and kindly offering me a flannel petticoat instead. I was in woe for a spell, having one dollar in the world, and scorning debt even for that prop of life, a "bonnet." Then I roused myself, flew to Dodge,[2] demanded her cheapest bonnet, found one for a dollar, took it, and went home wondering if the sky would open and drop me a trimming. I am simple in my tastes, but a naked straw bonnet is a little too severely chaste even for me. Sky did not open; so I went to the "Widow Cruise's oil bottle" — my ribbon box — which, by the way, is the eighth wonder of the world, for nothing is ever put in, yet I always find some old dud when all other hopes fail. From this salvation bin I extracted the remains of the old white ribbon (used up, as I thought, two years ago), and the bits of black lace that have adorned a long line of departed hats. Of the lace I made a dish, on which I thriftily served up bows of ribbon, like meat on toast. Inside put the lace bow, which adorns my form anywhere when needed. A white flower A. H. gave me sat airily on the brim, — fearfully unbecoming, but pretty in itself, and in keeping. Strings are yet to be evolved from chaos. I feel that they await me somewhere in the dim future. Green ones pro tem. hold this wonder of the age upon my gifted brow, and I survey my hat with respectful awe. I trust you will also, and see in it another great example of the power of mind over matter, and the convenience of a colos-

58

sal brain in the primeval wrestle with the unruly atoms which have harassed the feminine soul ever since Eve clapped on a modest fig-leaf and did up her hair with a thorn for a hairpin.

I feel very moral to-day, having done a big wash alone, baked, swept the house, picked the hops, got dinner, and written a chapter in "Moods."[3] May gets exhausted with work, though she walks six miles without a murmur.

It is dreadfully dull, and I work so that I may not "brood." Nothing stirring but the wind; nothing to see but dust; no one comes but rose-bugs; so I grub and scold at the "A." because it takes a poor fellow's tales and keeps 'em years without paying for 'em.[4] If I think of my woes I fall into a vortex of debts, dishpans, and despondency awful to see. So I say, "every path has its puddle," and try to play gayly with the tadpoles in *my* puddle, while I wait for the Lord to give me a lift, or some gallant Raleigh to spread his velvet cloak and fetch me over dry shod.

L[ouisa]. W[illis]. adds to my woe by writing of the splendors of Gorham, and says, "When tired, run right up here and find rest among these everlasting hills." All very aggravating to a young woman with one dollar, no bonnet, half a gown, and a discontented mind. It's a mercy the mountains are everlasting, for it will be a century before *I* get there. Oh, me, such is life!

Now I've done my Jeremiad, and I will go on twanging my harp in the "willow tree."

You ask what I am writing. Well, two books half done, nine stories simmering, and stacks of fairy stories moulding on the shelf. I can't do much, as I have no time to get into a real good vortex. It unfits me for work, worries Ma to see me look pale, eat nothing, and ply by night. These extinguishers keep genius from burning as I could wish, and I give up ever hoping to do anything unless luck turns for your

Lu.

MS: Unlocated. Printed: Cheney, pp. 167–169.
    1. Possibly Mrs. Theodore Parker.
    2. Dodge Brothers, dry goods merchants at 39 Franklin Street in Boston.
    3. LMA began *Moods* in August 1860.
    4. According to LMA's journal, she sent "A Modern Cinderella" to the *Atlantic* in April 1860, when it was accepted, but she does not record the seventy-five-dollar payment for it until September (Cheney, pp. 121, 122).

To Louisa Caroline Greenwood Bond

Apple Slump Sept 17th [1860]

Dear Auntie[1]

I consider this a practical illustration of one of mother's naughtily amended sayings, "Cast your bread upon the waters & after many days it will return buttered." & this "rule of three" dont "puzzle me" as the other did for my venerable raiment went away with one, if not two feet, in the grave & came back in the guise of three stout angels having been resurrectionized by the spirit who lives on the other side of a Charles River "Jordan". Thank you very much, & be sure the dreams I dream in them will be pleasant ones for whether you sewed them or not I know they bring some of the Auntie influence in their strength softness & warmth, & though a Vandal I think any prayers I may say in them will be the better for the affectionate recollections that will clothe me with the putting on of these friendly gowns, while my belief in both heavenly & earthly Providences will be amazingly strengthened by the knowledge of some lines here whose beauty renders it impossible to doubt the existence of the life hereafter.

We were very glad to hear that "the Papa" was better,[2] for when paternal "Richard's" aint "themselves" everybody knows the anxious state of the domestic realms. I hope Georgie[3] (last name dis remembered) has recovered from the anguish of discontented teeth & berry seeds, & that "the Mama" was as much benefitted by the trip as the other parties were, barring the horse perhaps.

This amiable town is convulsed just now with a Gymnastic fever[4] which shows itself with great violence in all the schools & young societies generally. Dr Lewis has inoculated us for the disease & "its taken finely" for every one has become a preambulating windmill with all four sails going as if a gale had set in, & the most virulent cases present the phenomena of black eyes & excoriation of the knobby parts of the frame to say nothing of sprains & breakage of "wessels" looming in the future.

The "city fathers" approve of it & the city sons & daughters intend to show that Concord has as much muscle as brain, & be ready for another Concord fight if Louis Napoleon sees fit to covet this famous land of Emerson Hawthorne Thoreau Alcott & Co. Abby & I are among the pioneers & the delicate vegetable productions clash their cymbals in private when the beef eating young ladies faint away & become superflous dumb belle's.

Saturday we had J. G. Whittier, Charlotte Cushman, Miss Stebbins the sculpteress & Mr Stuart Conductor of the Underground Railroad of this charming free country,[5] so you see our umble place of abode is perking up

60

& when the great authoress & artist are fairly out of the shell we shall be "an honor to our country & a terror to the foe," provided good fortune dont addle or bad fortune smash us.

Father continues to stir up the schools like a wild pudding stick, mother to sing "Hebron"[6] among her pots & pans, Annie & the Prince Consort to bill & coo in the little Dove-cote, Oranthy Bluggage to launch ships on the "Atlantic" & make a gigantic blot of herself in working the wessel, Abby to teach the Fine Arts & play propriety for the family, & the old house to put its best foot foremost & hoot at the idea of ever returning to the Chaos from which it came.

This is a condensed history of the "pathetic family" which is also a "happy family" owing to the prevelence of friends & lots of kindness in the "original packages" which are always arriving when the "Widow Cruise's oil bottle" begins to give out. You know I never *could* do any thing in a neat & proper manner so you will recieve this topsey turvey note as you do its writer, & with love to all from all believe her dear Auntie

ever lovingly yours L. M. A.

ALS: Special Collections, Jean and Alexander Heard Library, Vanderbilt University. Printed: Cheney, pp. 112–114.

    1. Louisa Caroline Greenwood May Bond, Mrs. Alcott's sister through adoption and wife of George William Bond.

    2. George Bond's first son by his first wife (Sophia A. May) married Rebecca Calhoun Huidekoper on 22 August 1859, and their first child, Louisa Van Buren Davis Huidekoper, was born on 8 July 1860. This may be the event to which LMA is referring.

    3. In a later hand, LMA has written "von Hersline" here.

    4. For Dr. Dio Lewis, who turned Concord into a "vast gymnasium" in which everyone "donned a gray tunic and tossed bean bags," see LMA, p. 102.

    5. John Greenleaf Whittier, the poet and abolitionist; Charlotte Cushman, the actress; Emma Stebbins, portrait artist and monument sculptor; Captain Charles Stewart, described by Sanborn as "an Englishman who is engaged in aiding slaves to escape from Missouri Kansas into Iowa" (16–18 September 1860, *Young Reporter of Concord*, ed. Kenneth Walter Cameron [Hartford, Conn.: Transcendental Books, 1978], p. 27). Whittier's account of this event is in *The Letters of John Greenleaf Whittier*, ed. John B. Pickard, 3 vols. (Cambridge: Harvard University Press, 1975), 2:471.

    6. "Hebron," a song by Laura Rush (see T. Comer, *The Boston Musical Institute's Collection of Church Music* [Boston: Otis, Broaders, 1840], p. 204).

To Anna Alcott Pratt

[after 17 December 1860]

Abby's letter was a blow. What shall I do without her?[1] I'm very glad that she is so much liked, & so fortunate in all her plans, but her room is *so* empty, the house so old & still without our lively girl, & her little things are really pathetic to me as I fix them up to send her. I cant bear to think that our "Baby" is really a woman, seeking her fortune at last, & may never come back little Ab any more. Mother groans as her last bird hops out of the nest, & I bedew my stitches with tears; yet we both think it best for her to stay, & when she sends me her money I shall comfort myself with filling a trunk with new & old things all in order to send her.[2]

Then I'll come down & see you & John. Is n't it odd that Ab likes teaching in an idiot Asylum & you didn't . Such a gay creature in such a sad place. I hate to think of it, yet she will get on better than you, tender-hearted thing. Its a comfort to know you are safe & happy with your John & not to tug & worry out in the world alone any more. Bless you!

Write to A. often & tell her how to make life easier than you found it. Your experience will help her. Knocking round comes hard at first.

AL: Houghton Library, Harvard University (partial). LMA revised this letter at a later date, including changing "Abby" to "May."

  1. After May had finished her art lessons in Boston, she was invited to accept a position as drawing teacher and pianist in Dr. Hervey B. Wilbur's asylum in Syracuse, New York. She left Concord on 17 December.

  2. LMA continued in this plaintive vein to Alfred Whitman: "Mrs Ab has gone off to Syracuse to teach music & drawing, & is having great times with six horses in the stables, balls, frozen lakes for skating & no prim sisters to quench her youthful ardor. Dr Wilber her employer likes her very much & may want her to stay all summer, if she does I shall go into sack cloth & ashes as permanant wear, for if I cant have *one* sister at home where is the use of having any at all?" (25 January [1861], Houghton Library, Harvard University).

To Anna Alcott Pratt

School Festival.[1]

———

Concord Mar. 8th
[i.e., 18? March 1861]

Dearest Nan.

I have waited to tell you of the fine school festival which came off this p.m. & was very charming. I send a Programme & most everything was excellent. Some of the dialogues were acted, & Pilgrim's Progress was told by the children popping up one after the other with thier parts, ending very prettily by a little girl saying solemnly, "And behold, it was all a dweem!"

Emerson spoke, & my song was sung after a little flurry before hand. It has one verse in it about John Brown, Philips & Co. & some of the old fogies thought it better be left out.[2] But Mr Emerson said, "No, no, that is the best. It must be sung, & not only sung but read. *I* will read it," & he did, to my great surprise & pride. Concord never will dare to say a word now. What a queer narrow minded set many of the people are.[3]

Dear old Papa looked like a mild shepherd with his flock, & never knew the surprise in store for him as a reward for all the time & help he has so freely given the schools.

When all was done F. B. S[anborn]. asked people to stay for a little scene set down on the hill. People paused & Father was invited to the stage. Looking rather bewildered he went, to be met by a tall, handsome boy, Fred Harlow, who stood looking straight up in the old man's face as he made his little speech & presented a fine Pilgrim's Progress & Herbert's Poems full of the best illustrations, "from the scholars of all the schools as a token of thier grateful love & respect." Father was quite overcome; he blushed like a boy, his eyes were full, & hugging his dear books he thanked them so prettily it was a sight to see, as all the children clapped & shouted at the success of the great secret.[4]

It was a lovely occasion, & has stirred up the town[5] immensely. Father deserves all (& more) of the praise he gets, for he has worked as no Superintendant has yet in C., & the schools are in better order than they ever were before.

AL: Houghton Library, Harvard University (possibly a draft); partial manuscript copy by Anna Alcott Pratt at Houghton Library, Harvard University. A two-page fragment from LMA's diary, also describing the occasion, is at Houghton Library, Harvard University. The date of 8 March is obviously in error; the school festival took place on the eighteenth.

1. Descriptions of the school festival are in LMA's journal (Cheney, pp. 126–127) and in Bronson's *Superintendent's Report of the Concord Schools . . . for the Year 1860–61* (Concord: Benjamin H. Tolman, 1861), Supplement, pp. 1–11.

2. LMA's "Song" contained the lines "Here is our New World . . . / Here are our future men, / Here our John Browns again; / Here are young Philipses eyeing our blunders."

3. Anna's manuscript copy has a more detailed description of the proposed deletion of the John Brown verses: "Father was aghast, for it was the pride of his life since Emerson pronounced it 'excellent very excellent.' Mother was rabid, & denounced the whole town, & I sternly said 'They shall sing every word, or nary song shall they have.' Well we went to the meeting, Mr. [John Shepard] Keyes came & said 'Thank you Miss Alcott for y'r fine song Miss Alcott the *second* verse especially.'" She continues: "Sanborn said 'Stand to y'r principles Miss Alcott & let them get the credit of a good thing in spite of themselves.' & when father asked Mr. Emerson's advice about giving it up he said 'No, No, it shall be sung, & not only sung but read first & I will read it,' & to my amazement he did it in the face of the whole town. Lord! I felt so grand. . . ." (21 March 1861, diary, Houghton Library, Harvard University).

4. Anna's manuscript copy contains this description of the event: "Mr. Sanborn rose to announce a recess, but instead of so doing he said he was requested to pause a moment for the playing of a little scene not set down in the programme. He beckoned father onto the stage, up went the unsuspecting old dear, & a tall pretty boy stepping out from a herd of children, went to him, & looking up straight into his face made a nice simple speech asking him to accept 'Pilgrim's Progress & Herbert's Poems from the scholars of all the schools as a token of

their gratitude, affection & respect, & thanking him for his wise mild & untiring care of them.'
I thought father w'd have lost his head, he blushed, his eyes were full of tears, & hugging his
books he thanked them for his present so prettily it was a sight to behold. . . ." (21 March
1861, diary, Houghton Library, Harvard University).

5. LMA had written "stupid" before "town," then canceled it.

To Alfred Whitman

Concord May 19th [1861]

Dear Alf.

If I had not been sewing violently on patriotic blue shirts for the last
month I should have written to my "Dolphus" most assuredly, & having at
last done my share of the five hundred azure envelopes I lay down my needle
& take up my pen with great inward contentment, the first article being my
abomination & the last my delight.

Of course the town is a high state of topsey turveyness, for every one is
boiling over with excitement & when quiet Concord does get stirred up it is
a sight to behold. All the young men & boys drill with all their might, the
women & girls sew & prepare for nurses, the old folks settle the fate of the
Nation in groves of newspapers, & the children make the streets hideous
with distracted drums & fifes. Everyone wears cockades wherever one can be
stuck, flags flap over head like parti colored birds of prey, patriotic balmor-
als, cravats, handkerchiefs & hats are all the rig, & if we keep on at our
present rate everything in heaven & earth will soon be confined to red,
white, & blue, & "Hail Columbia" take the place of our Yankee "How are
yer?"

Edward Emerson has a company of "Concord Cadets" who poke each
others eyes out, bang their heads & blow themselves up with gunpowder
most valiantly & will do good service by & by I've no doubt if there is
anything left of them when ordered to the field.[1]

We have the "East Quarter Home Guard" consisting of one Captain, one
drummer, one flag bearer, & one private, & when the regiment is on parade
the effect is superb. They always halt before each house & give several shrill
little hurra's for every member of the family after which they march away in
a state of breathless enthusiasm.

The regular Concord Company are in Washington[2] & we have long letters from George Prescott, the interesting Messer & the heroic butcher Dean.[3]
Capt Barrett[4] backed out at the last minute & Prescott took his place. We

had both merry & sad times before they went but now it is all over & an old story as everything is in America a week after it happens.

Are you going to have a dab at the saucy Southerners? I long to fly at some body & free my mind on several points, but there is no opening for me at present so I study Dr Home on "Gun shot wounds,"[5] & get my highly connected self ready to go as a nurse when the slow coaches at Washington begin to lay about them & get their fellow men into a comfortably smashed condition.

I suppose you have heard from Carrie of her turning teacher in East, no, South Boston, also of Sam Hall's being taken Vi-et-armis, & married by the famous Widow Kilborn to the great wrath of his family & the imme[n]se satisfaction of hers.[6] If you have'nt heard of these all absorbing facts you will soon, so I'll leave her to elaborate upon the subject.

We are all robust both at Pickle Roost & Apple Slump the latter place is exulting in the speedy return of its younger member who will soon be done in Syracuse & is coming back home to turn drawing teacher in Sanborn's school as Miss Hammatt[7] leaves in July. Abby says "I have nice manly letters from Alf & he seems to have improved mightily in all respects. I wish he would come East again dont you?"

Yes, very much, but not to be shot or otherwise maltreated in the present scrimmage. Write to us as often as you can & tho this is a short letter its a hearty one dear Alf, from

your loving old "SOPHY".

ALS: Houghton Library, Harvard University. Printed: Whitman 10, 6 (partial).

1. Edward Waldo Emerson worked with the Concord "drill club." As reported by his sister Ellen, Edward "said the drill club meets every morning at 6 o'clock and drills till 7.30" (10 May 1861, *The Letters of Ellen Tucker Emerson*, ed. Edith E. W. Gregg, 2 vols. [Kent, Ohio: Kent State University Press, 1982], 1:250).

2. The Concord Artillery of the State Regiment, Massachusetts Volunteer Militia, was ordered to Washington immediately after the shelling of Fort Sumter on 12 April 1861. They departed Concord on 19 April (see Townsend Scudder, *Concord: American Town* [Boston: Little, Brown, 1947], pp. 227–228, and the Concord town report for 1862).

3. Privates George E. Messer and Joseph G. Dean.

4. Captain Richard Barrett, for twenty years commander of the Concord regiment, refused to lead his troops, arguing that there was no one he could trust to run his heavily mortgaged farm and that his work in the Middlesex Fire Insurance office was too vital. Instead, Lieutenant George Prescott volunteered to lead the regiment; he was later officially elected captain (Scudder, *Concord*, pp. 228–229).

5. Dr. William Home's "Report on Various Cases of Gunshot Wounds Received in Actions in Upper Canada in 1838" appeared in the July 1840 *Edinburgh Medical and Surgical Journal*.

6. Samuel Hall, Jr., was married to Mary E. Kilbourn in Boston by James Freeman Clarke on 2 May (*Boston Evening Transcript*, 8 May 1861, p. 3).

To Alfred Whitman

Alpine House Gorham N.H.

Sunday Aug 4th [1861]

My Dear Alf.

The direction above will in part account for my long delay in answering your last letters, for the getting ready for this trip was a work of time & it took a fortnight to get my wits steady after I got here as I've never seen the White Mountains before & had my hands & eyes full I assure you.

I was planning to write to you about the plays when father injured his back very much & kept me busy for a week with housekeeping. I told Carrie to let me know what ones she sent that I might not send duplicates, she was a long time doing so & when she did Mr Sanborn told me you had fixed upon your bill & wanted a prologue by him. Our plays are scattered far & wide & the few that remain are not good ones so I let the whole thing alone after hearing that you were supplied, & am sorry you could not have them after all.

Your last letter I brought up here with me & a rainy Sunday makes the answering of it just the employment I like, for the house is still, the Mts have their night caps of cloud on & the wind whistles like November, so I settle myself in my room & spin a little to my Dolphus in spite of wind or weather.

Our Fourth was celebrated by the usual Regatta, & a house full of cousins. Neddy Conner got knocked into a cocked hat by the wad of a cannon & Mr Wheeldon had some fine fire works in the eve.[1] Sanborns boys won the races & set off for a camping out spree on Monadnoc as soon as vacation arrived. E Emerson Tom Ward & several others entered College in good style.[2] Will enter when it begins I mean but passed excellent examinations.

I suppose Carrie has told you about the Concord Company's return from the War with five men missing either killed or captured in the fight at Bulls Run.[3] I dont know all their names but Cyrus Hosmer & Sydney Rice are among them.[4] Dont you go & be smashed. Gen Scott is an old goose to make such a move against his own judgment[5] & I think they are making a mess of it at Washington. We cant spare our private & particular boys to be cut up & tormented by the chivalrous Southern rowdies, so stay at home my

66

lad till they get going nicely & then fire away with a will & if you get broken cry out out "Sophy!" & I'll come & mend you thro thick & thin.

You speak of Ellesworth & Winthrop & tho I never saw either I mourned over their loss as if they were my own brothers, & Winthrops articles are the best things the Atlantic has had this long time.[6]

Speaking of that slow coach Magazine[7] reminds to answer your question relative to my gems of fancy. They have had a story most a year & Uncle S. J. May went last week to stir them up or get it. They said it was accepted but others had to come first & "Debby's Début" was soon to appear,[8] so being sure of my $75 or 100 I fold my hands & wait, thinking meantime as you will do when you read it that it dont take much brains to satisfy the Atlantic critics. They like that flat sort of tale so I send it as I should a blood & thunder one if they ordered it for money is my end & aim just now & I thank my stars it can be got with no little trouble.

When I go back I will have a "picter" taken for my Dolphus & as I always take very dark & hunched up you will be gratified with an image of a stout mulatto lady with a crooked nose, sleepy eyes & a tempestuous gown.

Now I'll tell you a little about my doings here. I am with Mr & Mrs Willis in a big Hotel[9] which looks as if it rained out of the sky & lit in this valley of the Androscoggin with Mountains all round it & a little village near by. The landlord owns a great farm keeps 40 cows, 60 horses, 100 servants men & women & small beasts innumerable. The Grand Trunk Railroad passes the door so twice a day flocks of travellers come & go for no other railway comes so far & stages take people to all points from here. It is very gay about the house yet if you wish to be quiet in five minutes you can be in perfect solitude & an hours walk will bring you to the most splendid view of Washington, Adams Madison & Jefferson the great guns of the range, beside hundreds of smaller mountains many of which were never trodden by human feet & one as much unknown as when the world began.

Last week we ascended Mt Washington the highest of all, being 6285 feet above the level of the sea. The road up is the most wonderful thing I ever saw for it is wide & smooth & winds so that you dont realize what an immense height you are climbing till you see it apparently below you in some parts which you have passed & above in others you have yet to reach. It goes over chasms that make one dizzy to see, round sharp turns where it seems like a hanging balcony as you look down great precepices in some places two miles deep, often full of snow or blasted trees white & bare as skeletons. The views were astonishing & when at the Tip Top House it seemed as if I could see the whole world laid out like a map before me, for trains were like flocks of sheep in the green intervales, rivers, lakes & ponds shone everywhere & the clouds floated below as in a very curious way, while the air from the snow drifts below made one forget that it was midsummer. Nothing grows so high & the stones look as if they were piled there by the Flood.

The mountain horses skip from rock to rock like goats & look very funny with their heads down sliding & climbing with ladies in old hats, mens coats & no hoops, on their backs, for the fashions are of no account up there & every one tumbles about in a full & easy style that just suited me.

The drive down was a thing to remember, for we rattled & banged full trot along a road with all eternity the other side a low wall in a way that disturbed my heroic mind, & when the trace broke so demented was my state that I offered a stout green garter to mend the fracture, & immortalized that humble article of dress by assisting in the perilous dicent Mt Washington.[10] I wish you & Carrie Nan & John had been there for it was a day & a scene to remember all ones life.

From my window I see Mt Carter, Moriah, Hayes & Suprise, beside the Imp & its ugly human profile. Mr Willis has had a gap cut so we see the blue peak of Madison & all round us line above line of hazy hills rise & melt into the horizon.

The evenings here are jolly for there is music, dancing, singing, flirting, & high doings generally. A party of young Collegians were here a day or two ago & kept us all up till after midnight with their College songs & spirited dancing.[11] No one waits for introductions but all fly up & dance or sing as if at home & then disappear to be no more seen.

I am enjoying it highly but Ab returns on Tuesday & I'd rather see her than the whole Wt Mt range so I shall march off on Friday, therefore your next may be sent to Concord as usual & you may follow in person as soon as you can.

Good by my dear Alf ever your loving friend Lu.

The Jarley Scene is at home but I'll send it when I go, & you must make a "hit" in it.

ALS: Houghton Library, Harvard University. Printed: Whitman 10, 6 (partial).

1. Edward Connor, age twelve; probably William Willder Weildon, editor of the *Bunker Hill Aurora*.

2. Both Edward Waldo Emerson and Thomas Ward were graduated from Harvard College in 1866. They roomed together in 1863 (see Sanborn, *Young Reporter of Concord*, ed. Kenneth Walter Cameron [Hartford, Conn.: Transcendental Books, 1978], p. 39).

3. The Concord regiment fought at the first battle of Bull Run, on 21 July 1861. For information on their return to Concord, see Townsend Scudder, *Concord: American Town* (Boston: Little, Brown, 1947), pp. 237–238, and the Concord town report for 1862 (p. 14).

4. According to the Concord town report for 1861, Third Sergeant Cyrus Hosmer, First Sergeant William Sidney Rice, and Privates Henry L. Wheeler, Edward S. Wheeler, and William C. Bates had been taken prisoner; other soldiers had been killed (see also 22 June [1862]).

5. General Winfield Scott had urged a cautious approach toward training his green

recruits but allowed himself to be persuaded by the press and politicians to mount an attack on Richmond, Virginia, before he was fully satisfied with his troops. As a result, some thirty thousand troops under General Irvin McDowell were defeated and sent on an ungainly retreat to Washington.

6. Ephraim Elmer Ellsworth, originator of a regiment of firemen from New York, was shot on 24 May 1861 as he removed a Confederate flag from a hotel in Alexandria, Virginia; Theodore Winthrop, contributor of articles describing his unit's march to Washington in the *Atlantic,* died on 10 June 1861.

7. The *Atlantic,* which had been slow paying LMA for her work.

8. "Debby's Début" appeared in the August 1863 *Atlantic Monthly Magazine.*

9. LMA stayed with Hamilton and Louisa Willis at the Alpine House in Gorham, New Hampshire. She described her visit in four letters to the *Boston Commonwealth* in 1863, for which she was paid either twenty or thirty dollars (see LMA's "Notes and Memoranda" and Mrs. Alcott to Samuel Joseph May, 30 August 1863, both Houghton Library, Harvard University). The letters are reprinted in Joel Myerson and Daniel Shealy, "'Louisa May Alcott on Vacation: Four Uncollected Letters," *Resources for American Literary Study* 14 (Spring-Autumn 1984): 113–141.

10. LMA's account of fixing the harness with her garter is in the 7 August 1863 *Boston Commonwealth.*

11. In her account published in the 31 July 1863 *Boston Commonwealth,* LMA talks of being awakened at midnight by the sounds of furniture being put up the chimney and the "Wedding March" being performed on the walls with boots.

To Abigail May Alcott

Oct 8th 1861

Dearest Marmee,

It has troubled me for a long while to see such an old brush on the toilette table of the lady who possessed the handsomest head of hair in the house, so here is a new one with loving wishes for many more happier brighter birthdays than this which is rainy without & busy within.

Ever your loving Lu.

ALS: Houghton Library, Harvard University.

To Alfred Whitman

Concord Nov 12th [1861]

My dear old boy.

Your pathetic demand for speedy answers to your letters shall not be disregarded by Sophy Tetterby while she has the use of her right hand though she has precious little in the way of news to tell. I have just taken your letter from the P. O. & though an uncut gown hovers before my minds eye I let it hover & attend to you first.

Abby wrote you a long scribble about a fortnight ago have'nt you recieved it? & are your mails trustworthy & regular institutions? I hope so, for what a loss to the literature of our age it would be should our correspondence come to grief. Carrie is a good correspondant I believe, I *mean* to be, but Nan & John are beyond hope.

Now let me see what bits of news I can rake up. Concord is quiet now after two very jolly months, for the city folks are gone, the parties done, mild weather over, & F. B. S.s scholars studying like bees to make up for the lost time. A series of dances at the hall were very jovial for only "our set" went & we felt free & easy. They were got up by Shepard,[1] the Barretts, the Bartletts, & Hersey Goodwin & were exceedingly merry & nice for the young men were bound to have them go & spared no pains to gain their point. Abby danced herself sick & I pegged away till the natives must have begun to fear my reason was touched in my old age, but I couldnt resist the great smooth floor & the twankling of Balls harp, so skipped like a lively ostrich & enjoyed myself amazingly.

Sanborn has no very pleasant new scholars so we dont see much prospect of fun in that direction for they are mostly young & there are only about thirty in all. Abby teaches drawing there & gets her class along very successfully. Edward Emerson who went to College all so fine has been sick & still is so delicate & consumptiveish his father has taken him away for a year & he is to travel to the West Indies or Californie, & loaf about getting strong.[2] He looks like a young ghost now & his many admirers are in a great state of woe lest the handsome boy should go & die.

I am planning to pass the winter in Boston if the Fates will allow, being tired of two Concord winters. Miss Peabody has opened a "Kinder Garten" Childs Garden, or play & school "jined" after the German plan, & it is making a "great hit."[3] She has more babes than she wants & her idea is for me to teach on one side of the Common while she does on the other, for the pupils are all little West Enders & too small to go far. I like that style of teaching better than any other, & as its hard times for story writers shall be glad to lay hold of a few hundred in this way. Miss P expects to make $2000 this year & if I can pick up a quarter of that I shall be contented.

Ab will keep house & stir up the town, Father will keep the schools straight, & mother "much" her race generally, & that comprises the history of the Alcott family. The Pratt branch are busy & clever as usual. Annie cosying along in her nest at E Boston, & John vibrating between his ledgers & his spouse like a well behaved & affectionate pendulum.

He had a funny time the other day which for want of more exciting news I will mention. He & Nan came up to pass a Sunday, Nan decided to stay longer so John walked to Lexington as usual, there to take the cars into town, he likes the trip & they come so often it makes it cheaper to walk part way. Arriving at Lexington too soon for the cars he strolled on to take the West Cambridge car rather then wait, & meeting a man who offered him a ride there he accepted & perched on butter boxes rumbled into Cambridge, when he got down he found both his legs asleep & after walking a few steps feeling very queerly he suddenly fainted away & tumbled flat in the road. The man had driven off another road, the car was a mile away & tho the last thing he saw was a woman coming towards him she didnt stop to help but probably thinking him tipsey went by on the other side & left him to the Lord. How long he lay he dont know but got his wits about him at last & after a while managed to hop to the cars & get home with a sprained ancle & a dizzy head. At night we got a letter recounting the mishap & begging Nan to come home. We were as much disturbed at the idea of our private & particular John lying in the dirt & being thought a drunken stroller as if it had been Fremont or Louis Napoleon & the fate of a nation depended upon his keeping on his blessed legs. Nan went off like a rifled cannon twenty miles at one shot, & has been cosseting up "her lad" ever since. He strained or cramped the cords of his leg by sitting in a bad position & in getting down put something out of order in his internal machinery, but he is right again now & will shun butter boxes next time I hope.

Two subjects in your letter remain to be discussed namely picters & tales. As for our likenesses[4] I can testify that mine was taken for you last Aug, but falling into Abs clutches she made a solemn vow never to finish her picture of Mother if I sent mine away before another was taken for they think this the best ever "took" & are afraid I never shall be amiable enough to go & make a peacock of myself again, so I am only waiting to go to town & have a good wide awake picture taken for you, when I shall leave Ab the dozy one as pay for her perverse meddling in my affairs. I doubt if she ever has one of herself though she has promised a dozen people copies of her figure head, for she thinks herself a fright in spite of looking glasses & many assurances to the contrary from others outside her partial family. She is'nt a "Wenis" I allow but the new fashion of blue ribbons round the head & short curls in front is very becoming & N.Y. dress makers have done wonders in the way of pretty gowns & bonnets. So we want her to be "took in her early bloom" while she is rosy plump & becomingly arrayed, but as yet the prayers of family, friends & sweethearts have proved unavailing. As the French heroines say "I swear to you mon ami" that the next time I go to town I will be done off & forward my self to you if my days are spared.

The story problem remains unsolved. Ticknor took the tale[5] paid $50 for it & as it dont appear I imagine its lost, for when Mr Lowell gave up the editorship he left the papers in great confusion & Mr Hawthorne has waited

71

a year for one of his articles. As I have my money *I* dont care two straws if old "Debby" never makes her "Début" except that I cant send another till she is well out of the way. Mr Field[6] says he has Mss enough on hand for a dozen numbers & has to choose war stories if he can, to suit the times. I will write "great guns" Hail Columbia & Concord fight, if he'll only take it for money is the staff of life & without one falls flat no matter how much genius he may carry. Aint I a good Sophy to be so prompt? Do thou the same & bless you — Ever your "little woman."

Did you know that Carrie is very much out of health & they are afraid it is her heart like Thedy.[7] Dont tell her I spoke of it but write as often as you can for she is very blue & needs all we can do to keep her up. She still teaches for the Drs say she must not brood over her state as it will only make it worse, & they hope to mend her up. I pray they will tho she rather likes the idea of being past help. L. M. A.

ALS: Houghton Library, Harvard University. Printed: Whitman 11, 6 (partial).

    1. Edward O. Shepard, a high school teacher.

    2. Edward Waldo Emerson left for California on 12 May 1862. His trip took him through Omaha; Fort Kearney, Nebraska; Fort Laramie, Wyoming; Salt Lake City; Sacramento; San Francisco; Panama; and New York before he returned to Concord on 6 October (*The Letters of Ralph Waldo Emerson*, ed. Ralph L. Rusk, 6 vols. [New York: Columbia University Press, 1939], 5:256–257).

    3. Peabody's school, based on the ideals of the Swiss educator Johann Heinrich Pestalozzi, was at 20 Pinckney Street in Boston. LMA stayed with James T. and Annie Fields while teaching. On 22 December 1861, Mrs. Alcott wrote Samuel Joseph May that Elizabeth Palmer Peabody's school was so successful, with forty students at ten dollars a quarter, that another one "for a humbler sort of persons" at six dollars a quarter was wanted (Houghton Library, Harvard University).

    4. A picture that is identified as taken in 1862 is reproduced in Cheney, p. 140.

    5. "Debby's Début."

    6. James T. Fields, publisher of the *Atlantic Monthly Magazine.*

    7. Theodore Parker Pratt, John's brother, had died at age sixteen in 1859; Carrie Pratt died in 1866 at the age of twenty-nine.

To Alfred Whitman

April 6th [1862]

My Dear Old Boy.

    If you had been keeping a Kinder Garten all winter & visiting about at the same time you would'nt have found much leisure for letter writing or anything else, but tho I didnt write I heard of you through Carrie & May & always said "Give Dolphus my love", but of course they forgot it & I cant blame them.

    I have been as busy as a bee with my dozen babes at Warren St Chapel in Boston teaching on the new plan.[1] Miss Peabody & Mr Barnard[2] got it up & if it was'nt hard times it would do very well. I visited about at J. T. Fields the great publishers where I saw Mrs Stowe, Fanny Kemble, Holmes, Longfellow, & all the fine folks besides living in style in a very smart house with very clever people who have filled it with books, pictures, statues & beautiful things picked up in their travels.[3]

During a three weeks visit at Mr Sargents[4] we had a Masqu[e]rade & while at Roxbury I helped in three evenings of plays. Then in Concord (as I suppose Carrie has told you) we had a grand Masque in March when 400 people appeared in fine costumes & had a merry time.

May was the Goddess of Dancing & looked lovely in crimson sandals, white & gold dress & a curly head a la Greek. She is quite famous for her graceful dancing & Sanborn proposed the character which was much admired. Carrie was News from the war, all papers & a little telegraph on her head. I was a Monk & no one knew me even after we unmasked for a black beard & cowl changed me into a jolly friar & made great fun. The boys called me "sir" pushed me round in the dressing room, & asked me to tie & pin them up supposing I was a man, & the girls flirted in earnest till I took off my beard when they shouted. Nan didnt take a dress & John did not come up. The costumes were very fine, Shepard was splendid as Hamlet & Frank as the Duke of Buckingham was quite gorgeous.[5] I wish you had been here.

Concord is in a state of intense excitement just now for the great F. B. S. is engaged to one of his teachers Miss Leavett.[6] She is his cousin, looks enough like him to be his twin sister & is as cool & sharp as he, a pair of lemons they will be & sugar will be needed to sweeten the compound. They are to be married in July & go on with the school which is very easy as she is now his only teacher & wont need any salery when she is Mrs S. Carrie is raging & few like it as Miss L is not a favourite with any one in town or school.

This is all the news except that a newspaper is to be set up here called the Moniter & Rip B is coming down this evening to unfold the grand plan & secure the services of "the first female writer of the age". I will send you a copy if it ever comes to anything.[7]

May says "Thank Alf for the letter & accounts of the Tableaux & tell him I'll write soon." Concord is very gay & as she is in everything letters have to wait as I know to my sorrow. Write when you can dear Alf to your

loving old woman SOPHY.

I am at home now for a month & go up & down to my school every day & shall do so till June when Nan & John are coming & my vacation will leave me free to enjoy my native sphere & their good company. Cant you run over & make us a call? Are you really going to be a lawyer? I'll have a lawsuit at once.

I sent you a long thing about Jarley last winter, didnt you get it?

ALS: Houghton Library, Harvard University. Printed: Whitman 11, 6 (partial).

    1. LMA's kindergarten at the Warren Street Chapel in Boston failed to bring in sufficient funds for her board. After working in it from January to April, LMA turned the school over to May for a month and wrote a story that "made more than all my months of teaching" (journal entry, April 1862, Cheney, p. 131). Her mother's comment was: "a failure — Swindle of her Time and her money" (26 December 1861, diary, Houghton Library, Harvard University).

    2. Reverend Charles Francis Barnard, minister of the Warren Street Chapel from 1837 to 1866.

    3. LMA stayed with the Fieldses while in Boston, enjoying their literary salon, which played host to the major writers of the time.

    4. John T. and Mary Sargent's house at 18 Chestnut Street in Boston.

    5. Probably Frank Wheeler.

    6. Sanborn married his cousin Louisa Augusta Leavitt on 16 August 1862.

    7. Ripley Bartlett's weekly paper, the *Monitor*, published LMA's "The King of Clubs and the Queen of Hearts" between 19 April (its first issue) and 7 June 1862; its last issue was on 21 June 1862.

To Sophia Foord

Concord May 11th [1862]

Dear Miss Ford

As I promised to write you when Henry died[1] I send these few lines to fulfil that promise though I suppose you have seen notices of the event in the papers.

Father saw him the day before he died[2] lying patiently & cheerfully on the bed he would never leave again alive. He was very weak but suffered nothing & talked in his old pleasant way saying "it took Nature a long time to do her work but he was most out of the world." On Tuesday at eight in the morning he asked to be lifted, tried to help do it but was too weak & lying down again passed quietly & painlessly out of the old world into the new.

On Friday at Mr Emerson's desire he was publicly buried from the church, a thing Henry would not have liked but Emerson said his sorrow was so great he wanted all the world to mourn with him. Many friends came from Boston & Worcester, Emerson read an address good in itself but not appropriate to the time or place, the last few sentences were these & very true.[3]

"In the Tyrol there grows a flower on the most inaccessible peaks of the mountains, called "Adelvezia" or "noble purity," it is so much loved by the maidens that their lovers risk their lives in seeking it & are often found dead at the foot of the precipices with the flower in their hands. I think our friend's life was a search for this rare flower, & I know that could we see him now we should find him adorned with profuse garlands of it for none could more fittly wear them."

Mr Channing wrote the Stanzas[4] & they were very sweetly sung, Father read selections from Henry's own books, for many people said he was an infidel & as he never went to church when living he ought not to be carried there dead. If ever a man was a real Christian it was Henry, & I think his own wise & pious thoughts read by one who loved him & whose own life was a beautiful example of religious faith, convinced many & touched the hearts of all.

It was a lovely day clear, & calm, & spring like, & as we all walked after Henry's coffin with its fall of flowers, carried by six of his townsmen who had grown up with him, it seemed as if Nature wore her most benignant aspect to welcome her dutiful & loving son to his long sleep in her arms. As we entered the church yard birds were singing, early violets blooming in the grass & the pines singing their softest lullaby, & there between his father & his brother we left him, feeling that though his life seemed too short, it would blossom & bear fruit for as long after he was gone, & that perhaps we should know a closer friendship now than even while he lived.

I never can mourn for such men because they never seem lost to me but nearer & dearer for the solemn change. I hope you have this consolation, & if these few words of mine can give you anything you have not already learned I am very glad, & can only add much love from us all & a heart full from your

Lou.

Come & see us when you can, after this week we shall be clean & in order, & always ready.

I enclose a little sprig of "andromeda" his favourite plant a wreath of which *we* put on his coffin.

ALS: Pierpont Morgan Library. Printed: Walter Harding, "Thoreau's Feminine Foe," *PMLA* 69 (March 1954): 115 (partial); *A Sprig of Andromeda: A Letter from Louisa May Alcott on the Death of Henry David Thoreau* (New York: Pierpont Morgan Library, 1962), with facsimile of the manuscript.

1. Thoreau died on 6 May 1862 and his funeral was held on the ninth; for a description of the ceremonies, see Walter Harding, *The Days of Henry Thoreau* (New York: Alfred A. Knopf, 1965), pp. 466–468.

2. When he saw Thoreau on 4 May, Bronson found him "confined to his bed and has

not many days of his mortality to give us" (*The Journals of Bronson Alcott*, ed. Odell Shepard [Boston: Little, Brown, 1938], p. 346).

3. For this passage in the published essay, see Joel Myerson, "Emerson's 'Thoreau': A New Edition from Manuscript," *Studies in the American Renaissance 1979*, ed. Joel Myerson (Boston: Twayne, 1979), p. 54.

4. Ellery Channing, poet and Thoreau's first biographer; for his poem on Thoreau's death, see Kenneth Walter Cameron, "Channing's Hymn at Thoreau's Funeral," *Emerson Society Quarterly* no. 2 (1st Quarter 1956): 16–17.

To Alfred Whitman

Concord May 11th [1862]

Dearest Dolphus

This is rather a tumbled bit of paper but I feel drawn towards it because of the fat little horse trotting on the crown above there, which by the way looks more like a muffin than a crown, & more like a cloud of dust than either.[1]

If I'm not prompt this time it will be the fault of the mail not the female, for your letter came last eve & I answer it this morning with my head in a blauze for fear of accidents or company which might prevent this important epistle from going tonight. I send you the first two numbers of our Concord paper,[2] & if you or any of your friends like to subscribe we shall be glad for we want the Monitor to succede though Rip Bartlett did start it. Sanborn writes for it also Dr Charles Jackson,[3] & several Boston men, also Carrie, Ab & I so "you see what a mass of talent is secured & if only patronized how vast an influence this modest sheet may exert over the two hemispheres." Thats a quotation from Rip who is so wrapped up in the thing I expect to hear that he is a "lunacy" any day. I get ten dollars a page for my foolish little story for being very local it takes & makes the paper sell, & as money is the end & aim of my mercenary existence I scribble away & pocket the cash with a thankful heart. There are two more numbers out which I'll send if I can find them, & if you subscribe they will all be furnished that your numbers may be complete. I think its safe to subscribe for six months as it will certainly live till then if not longer. Uncle May of Syracuse has subscribed for a year & many others. I thought it might interest you as a Concord affair. I have given all the authors names that I know for a deep mystery shrouds some of the writers & its just as well perhaps as no one is very anxious to know who they are.

Edward Emerson starts on an overland trip to California tomorrow,[4] with a party who are going to hunt buffaloes, camp out & get scalped by the Indians as a neat finish to the expidition. Julian Hawthorne & Tom Ward wanted to go but their Ma's courage gave out before the time came & the boys were in a great state of woe & cursed their hard fate tragically.

Henry Thoreau died on Tuesday & was publiclly buried from the church on Friday. Mr Channing wrote an Ode, Mr Emerson made an address, & Father read selections from Henry's own books proving that though he didnt go to church he was a better christian than many who did. A party of great people from Boston came up, the church was full & though he was'nt made much of while living, he was honored at his death.

You say you have been blue this spring. Why? Dont allow it my Dolphus, for while you keep your good spirits you can do most any thing & Satan cant get you. As to my thinking you aint a boy, bless you I dont expect you to wear flat irons on your head & stop growing. I dont care if you are six feet ten, with a beard down to your waist, a wife & fourteen children, if you are only "a boy at heart" & dont forget your old Sophy.

About the pictures, I own we are a shabby set, but May has had hers done & will send you one the latter part of the week when they come home, & if I like the style I shall have some taken of my own "queen like figger," & dispatch one as soon as I lay hands upon it.

About the paper you are to edit let me know what sort of thing you want & I'll do it though I aint pious a bit & my line is fun. I'll over haul my rubbish & see if I can find anything suitable.

I did not write "My Garden" but a funny Miss Dodge[5] & I think its very jolly dont you? My garden is very much in her style for I poke down seeds every spring, think they are weeds, pull them up & wait & wonder all summer why they dont come up & bloom.

"The South Breaker" is better than Prescotts usually are, being more natural & simple, with less blood & thunder & very little *jewelry* which last is her pet hobby. I read "Sir Rohan's Ghost" & thought it had great merits & great faults.[6]

Carrie did not go to Port Royal[7] for they would neither have young or unmarried women, so as she couldnt be forty in a minute, & no young man was handy to marry, she gave it up though I doubt if she would have gone as she has no health, & a girl with an incurable heart complaint is better at home than in a place like that. Miss Buttrick[8] & myself were chosen to go from Concord before the word came that unmarried women were forbidden, & we were getting our ideas settled about it but nothing came of it except the sending of Seymour Severence[9] who was a grand person being sensible, kind & interested in the thing. There is to be a school in Washington for the blacks & if I am asked I shall go as I like the plan.

I have'nt seen Davidson[10] as he has been sick with mumps ever since he came. Did you get the last Jarley? Have "A Word" by all means & glorify the "Wax Werks" as much as possible.

Now my dear old lad good by for a few weeks, & when next I write I hope to send you a "speaking likeness" of your loving friend "SOPHY".

ALS: Houghton Library, Harvard University. Printed: Whitman 11, 6 (partial).

    1. LMA refers to an embossed seal in the shape of a horse on top of a crown at the upper left corner of the first page.

    2. Ripley Bartlett's *Monitor.*

    3. Dr. Charles Thomas Jackson, Lidian Emerson's brother.

    4. For Edward Waldo Emerson's trip to California, see 12 November 1861.

    5. "My Garden," by Mary Abigail Dodge, whose pen name was Gail Hamilton, appeared in the May 1862 *Atlantic Monthly Magazine.*

    6. "The South Breaker," by the noted short-story writer Harriet E. Prescott (later Mrs. Spofford), appeared in the May and June 1862 issues of the *Atlantic Monthly Magazine,* her novel, *Sir Rohan's Ghost,* had been published in 1860.

    7. LMA considered going to Port Royal, South Carolina, to teach "contrabands," the black slaves who escaped to or were brought within Union lines (journal entry, October 1863, Cheney, p. 154).

    8. Adeline E. Buttrick.

    9. Seymour Severence, an excellent gymnast, boarded at Orchard House in 1860. He served as the model for the gymnast in "The King of Clubs and the Queen of Hearts."

    10. Possibly Frank S. Davidson, a student in Sanborn's school and a cadet at West Point.

To Alfred Whitman

Concord June 22ond [1862]

Dear Dolphus.

Looking over the card rack just now to find a direction I discovered a note from you which I never saw before, & upon inquiring found that Ab got it from the P. O. read it, put it in the rack & forgot to tell me of it, so I never knew I owed you a letter, & after a good scolding all round sit down to pay my debts "immeadiate."

The one news is that "our boys" have returned after a years imprisonment in various places, (they were taken at Bulls Run[1] you know) of course the town got up a row banged drums, fired cannon, tooted & bawled, gave banners to the breeze, dinners eaten, odes sung, speeches made & a grand hurrah-boys generally. "Our gallant fellow citizens" who ran away & very justly got caught, look fat, brown, & lazy, & loaf about making a large spittoon of the Mill-Dam as they spin yarns & condecendingly regard their friends as if the nation was under everlasting obligations to them & all should fall down & adore.

There were five, Sidney Rice, Cyrus Hosmer, to whom I pledged my young affections at the mature age of nine, two Wheelers & Adams.[2]

Ab's picture is pretty good but darker than she is & rather hunched up for she had no one to arrange her. She thinks it is awful & has a fit if any one asks for a sight. Hers is so unsatisfactory I am afraid to try for I shall be awful, so possess your soul in patience till I can screw my courage up & "be took."

Upon the subject of Chores I sympathize, having had them to do all my days & never being able to conquer my prejudices regarding them. They are good for me I've no doubt but after many years constant taking I think the dose might be lessened with out harm. If I lived alone I should make the beds once a week, clean house every ten years, & never cook at all which would simplify things grandly.

You ask about the Monitor & I reply it does still exist but is failing fast & I expect to be invited to the funeral soon. Rip is as crazy about it as ever & believes it to be the main support of the nation. My story is done & half paid for, till it is wholly so I shant write any more. If I had the other copies I'd send them but they are all given away but one set which are stuck in my book, or rather the story is. Console yourself its not worth reading. Maggie has jilted Bogs & he is at Port Royal.[3]

I intend to illuminate the Ledger[4] with a blood & thunder tale as they are easy to "compoze" & are better paid than moral & elaborate works of Shake-speare, so dont be shocked if I send you a paper containing a picture of Indians, pirates wolves, bears & distressed damsels in a grand tableau over a title like this "The Maniac Bride" or "The Bath of Blood. A thrilling tale of passion," &c.

Ab & I have been watching a family of owls who live in our elm while we wrote our letters which will account for their stupidity, for the two young owls are just waking up & their mother with one eye open is urging them to fly with maternal hoots of encouragement, & they resist with little squeaks, goggling about as if tipsey, & we long to go & get all three but being Sunday we abstain & try to write.

Bless you & Amen.

Your SOPHY.

ALS: Houghton Library, Harvard University.

1. For the Concord regiment's participation in the battle of Bull Run, see 4 August [1861]. Bates, Hosmer, Rice, and the two Wheelers had been captured on 21 July 1861 and imprisoned at Richmond, Virginia; New Orleans; and Salisbury, North Carolina, before being

released in June 1862 (see Edwin S. Barrett, *What I Saw at Bull Run* [Boston: Beacon, 1886], and especially pp. 31–32, where he describes their capture).

2. Cyrus Hosmer, a year younger than LMA, lived next door to the Alcotts when they moved to Concord in 1840, and the two became good friends. For the Wheelers, see 4 August [1861]. The only Adams listed among the Concord units is James C. Adams, but his regiment did not go into action until August 1862.

3. Bogs is the character based upon Seymour Severence in "The King of Clubs and the Queen of Hearts"; Maggie Plumly was engaged to marry Severence.

4. Possibly the *New York Ledger*, though no contribution by LMA during this period has been found there. Her first sensational tale was "Pauline's Passion and Punishment" in the 3 January and 10 January 1863 issues of *Frank Leslie's Illustrated Newspaper*.

To Mrs. Joseph Chatfield Alcox

[early December 1862]

My Dear Grandma.[1]

When I got home from Boston on my birthday the first thing I saw was your picture, it seemed almost as good as finding the dear old lady herself & it was very kind of you to send what we shall all value so much. Father always keeps the little picture Uncle Junius[2] did of you hanging up in his room, so now we have put the new one in ours & there is Grandma looking just as she looked when she used to sit in her corner as busy as a whole hive of bees over her "little mess of works" as she called it.

We are all going on much as usual, Father writing & talking, taking care of the schools & keeping his topsy turvy family in order. Mother sings away among her pots & pans, feeds & [c]lothes all the beggars that come along, sews for the soldiers & [d]elivers lectures on Anti slavery & Peace wherever she goes. Annie & her good man John are keeping house in Chelsea & in the spring hope to have a little Lu to add to their treasures. I write stories, help keep house & now & then scold every body as I used to do you know. Abby teaches drawing & music, goes to parties, rides horseback, rows boats, has beaux & is a very gay & pretty girl, the youngest member of the family is a big pussy who is my baby & a very agreeable person to have in the house. Do you hate cats as much as Father does?

I am getting ready to go to Washington[3] as an army nurse in one of the Hospitals & expect to have a hard winter if I do but I like it & want to help if I can. Have any of our peopl[e] gone to the War? Four or five Mays have gone & if I was only a boy I'd march off tomorrow.

Tell Cousin Dwight that his letter was given to Annie to answer because she had seen him & was the oldest of us, but having a husband & a house to take care of she do[nt] do her duty by other people, so I the old maid will write him a letter as soon as I get out of this hurry up work for I may be sent for any day & must be ready.

I have always wanted to see & know my Alcott aunts, uncle[s] & cousins & wonder if I shall ever do so. Father & I have planned a visit out West ever so many times but either there is no money when we have time or no time when we have money, & if the war goes on we shall be so poor we shall have to dress in newspapers & live on potatoes I'm afra[id.]

Whenever I make a fortune one of the first things I do will be to go & get Grandma & keep her so comfortab[le] that she will never want to leave us but just grow youn[g] & jolly & knit stockings for her children & grand children till she is a hundred years old. Give my love to all about you & keep the biggest piece for yourself from your loving grand child LOUISA

ALS: Houghton Library, Harvard University. The manuscript is torn; missing words or letters are supplied in brackets. LMA's letter is a postscript to one from Mrs. Alcott, the end of which is at the top of the first page of LMA's letter.

1. Mrs. Joseph Chatfield Alcox, Bronson's mother. The spelling of the family name had been changed in about 1820.

2. The deranged Junius Alcott had committed suicide in 1852 by throwing himself into a machine.

3. On 11 December, she received a note from Hannah Stevenson ordering her to go not to Armory Square in Washington but to the Union Hotel Hospital in Georgetown.

To Edward J. Bartlett and Garth Wilkinson James

Concord Dec 4th 1862

Dear Old Boys[1]

At the last minute we hear of the box about to be sent for your jolli-fication & comfort, & though in a great fume to do no end of things for you, we have only time to fly up garret & fill a pair of bags with nuts & apples & all good wishes for our private & particular boys. Ned! your sisters say you like apple sauce so I beg you'll have as many messes as you like out of the apples that grew in the old trees by the straw-berry bed where Wilkie stood one day with his hands in his pockets while we fed him with berries till he was moved to remark with a luxurious condescenion, "hell this is rather a nice way of eating fruit is'nt it?". You dont have time for that sort of amuse-ment now, do you Sergeant?

The nuts are a sort of edible contraband, black, hard to take care of &

not much in them in the end, but if the President cracks his nuts as thoroughly as I suspect you will these, we shall soon have you home again to play whist & sing, "Pop, pop, pop"! We miss you very much and are dreadfully reduced in the gentleman line, school parties are an aggravation to the female mind. Lint Picks languish, Game parties are a myth & forlorn damsels ride & walk with never a peg-top or muffiny cap to bear them company.

Something must be done soon for even the Town School is deprived of its Shepard & Stone & a venerable Fulsom with a pair of daughters takes the place of the departed Dominies.[2]

Abby & I play beau to the best of our ability but its not the genuine thing you see, & we sadly bewail the loss of the "Slashers & Crashers" who have deserted us for "the tented field" the only sort of desertion they will ever be guilty of as every one knows.

Now boys, if you intend to be smashed in any way just put it off till I get to Washington to mend you up, for I have enlisted & am only waiting for my commission to appear as nurse at the "Armory" Something Hospital so be sure you are taken there, if your arms or legs fly away, some day (which the Lord forbid!) & we will have good times in spite of breakages & come out jolly under creditable circumstances like Dickens "Mark Taply."[3]

Is there anything the old ladies can send you in the next box? Do give it a name if there is & let us help feed, clothe or assure the Defenders of the Faith if we cant take a hand in the fighting.

Father, mother, Abby and the great grey cat all send regards & love & would rejoice to receive a line from either of you, if any odd minutes occur when home letters are done or duty dont call.

Bless your buttons & long may you wave is the parting sentiment of your

affectionate old friend
L. M. ALCOTT.

MS: Unlocated; manuscript copy with a red gothic A at the top of the first page (incorrectly identified as LMA's original) at Houghton Library, Harvard University. Printed: Gladys E. Hosmer, "Louisa May Alcott: War Nurse," *Trained Nurse* 89 (August 1932): 145–146.

1. Edward J. Bartlett was in the Forty-fourth Regiment of the Massachusetts Volunteers; for Garth Wilkinson James, see September [1863].

2. Edward O. Shepard and G. A. Stone were replaced by Nathaniel S. Folsom, who taught high school in Concord from 1862 to 1866.

3. Mark Tapley, a perennially cheerful character in Dickens's *Martin Chuzzlewit*.

To Anna Alcott Pratt

Monday P.M.
[30 March 1863]

Dearest little "Mother,"[1]

Allow me to ask who was a true prophet? Also to demand *"Where* is my *niece* Louisa Caroline?" No matter, I forgive you & propose three cheers for our *nephew.* Hurrah! Hurrah! Hurrah!

I wish you could have seen the performances on Sat. eve. We were sitting deep in a novel & had given up expecting father owing to the snow, when the door burst open & in he came all wet & white, waving his bag & calling out, "Good news! Anna has a fine boy." With one accord we three opened our mouths & screamed for about two minutes; then mother began to cry, I to laugh, & May to pour out questions, while Papa beamed upon us all shiny, red & damp yet the image of a proud, old Grandpa.

Such a funny eve as we had, for Marmee kept breaking down, & each time she emerged from her handkerchief she said solemnly "I *must* go right down & see that baby." Father had told every one he met from Emerson to the coach driver & went about saying, "Anna's boy, yes, yes, Anna's boy," in a mild state of intoxication. May & I racked our brains at once for a name, & decided on Amos, Minot Bridge Bronson May Sewell Alcott Pratt, so that all the families would be pleased.

I was so anxious to hear that I toddled up to town this morning (my first walk[2]) & found John's note. Grand ma & pa P. came up to hear the great news; but we could only inform them of the one tremendous fact that Pratt Jr. had condescended to arrive. Now tell us his weight, inches, color &c.

I know I shall fall down & adore when I see the mite, yet it sends my soul to think of "L. C." on the pin-cushion, & all the plans I'd made for "my niece". I demand a twin at once; & I shall call him "Thomas Pib" to the end of his days we had such fun over the name.

Now get up quickly, & be a happy Mamma. Of course John is much annoyed at the whole affair & does *not* consider Tom Pib *the* most amazing product of the 19th century.

Bless the baby!

Ever your admiring
Rack a bones
Lu.

ALS: Houghton Library, Harvard University. Printed: Cheney, pp. 149–150.
    1. Frederick Alcott Pratt, born 28 March.

2. Soon after LMA reported to the Union Hotel Hospital on 14 December 1862, she fell severely ill with fever. Bronson arrived there to attend her on 16 January, found her with a delirious fever (later diagnosed as typhoid), and took her home to Concord on 24 January. Her head was shaved at doctor's orders, and she wore a wig for some time. It was not until 22 March that she was able to leave her room.

To Annie Adams Fields

Concord June 24th [1863]

Dear Cousin Annie.[1]

Thanks for the Conway thought[2] & the "Flute's" promotion.[3] Kindly critisism never offends but to me is often more flattering than praise for if any one takes the trouble to critisize it seems to prove that the thing is worth mending.

Poetry is not my forte & the lines were never meant to go beyond my scrap book. Perhaps the place in which they were composed may be partly account for the halting rhyme; they jingled into my sleepy brain during a night watch beside the bed of a one-legged lad dying of wound fever in the Hospital last Dec; were forgotten till father found them among my papers,[4] read them like a partial parent as he is, to neighbor Hawthorne, who asked for them the other day & without telling me their destination sent them to sit in high places where they hardly belong.

I am immensely busy just now getting up some Scenes from Dickens[5] for the benefit of the Fifty fifth colored regiment, & enriching the Commonwealth with my valuable contributions,[6] but I will set my wits to work on the "forlorn" line & see if I can better it. How will this do?

"Spring mourns as for untimely frost,
The genius of the wood is lost."[7]

Or is the r in frost as objectionable as in lorn? If my little ship is to be launched in the Atlantic I must attend to her build & rigging & see that she does not founder for want of proper ballast as an honorable flag is flying at the mast head.

If you come to Concord shall we not see you at the Gables? mou[n]tains we cannot offer but poets & philosophers with very little snow upon their heads & the country pleasures we enjoy in this our "Happy Valley."

With the best regards to Mr Fields I am

very truly yours
L. M. ALCOTT.

ALS: Huntington Library. Printed: Nan Cooke Carpenter, "Louisa May Alcott and 'Thoreau's Flute': Two Letters," *Huntington Library Quarterly* 24 (November 1960): 72; *Fields of the Atlantic Monthly*, ed. James C. Austin (San Marino, Calif.: Huntington Library, 1953), pp. 316–317.

1. Annie Adams Fields, whose husband James T. Fields was a prominent publisher and author, was a writer herself. She was the daughter of Zabdiel Boylston Adams and Sarah May Holland Adams; her grandmother was the sister of Mrs. Alcott's father.

2. During the Civil War years, the Fieldses often vacationed at Campton Village, New Hampshire.

3. "Thoreau's Flute" appeared in the September 1863 *Atlantic Monthly Magazine*. It had been sent to Annie Fields by Sophia Hawthorne (journal entry, May 1863, Cheney, p. 151).

4. When Sophia Hawthorne sent the poem to Annie Fields on 14 June 1863, she said of its composition: "She never wrote it down till after recovering from her severe illness, it being an inspiration one Midnight at Georgetown" (Francis Dedmond, "Sophia Hawthorne and Louisa May Alcott's 'Thoreau's Flute,' " *Concord Saunterer* 16, no. 1 [Spring 1981]: 25).

5. *Scenes from Dickens*, one of LMA's favorite dramatic performances, originally consisted of "Copperfield," "Cricket on the Heath," "Haunted Man," "Sir Humphrey's Clock," "The Chimes," "Pickwick Papers," and a prologue, "Old Yule & Young Christmas" (25 December 1857, May's diary, Houghton Library, Harvard University).

6. "Hospital Sketches" began appearing in the *Boston Commonwealth* on 22 May 1863.

7. These lines were printed in the *Atlantic*, but with "genius" capitalized. The original readings were "Spring came to us in guise forlorn / The Genius of the wood is gone" (*LMA*, p. 124).

To Miss Russel

Boston July 13th [1863?]

My Dear Miss Russel.

Had your proposal come to me a year ago I should very gladly have availed myself of it if we had suited each other. But now my time is fully occupied with my pen & I find story writing not only pleasanter than teaching but far more profitable, so I am glad to change the work which I have done for fifteen years for more congenial employment.[1]

Hoping that you may succeed in your search I am

Very truly yours
L. M. ALCOTT.

ALS: Louisa May Alcott Collection, Barrett Library, University of Virginia Library.

1. In her journal for October 1863, LMA wrote: "A year ago I had no publisher, and went begging with my wares; now *three* have asked me for something, several papers are ready to print my contributions, and F. B. S[anborn]. says 'any publisher this side of Baltimore would be glad to get a book' " (Cheney, p. 154).

To James Redpath

Mr Redpath.

Being lamentably stupid about business of all sorts I'm very much afraid I'm not very clear about the compact.[1] But I believe stating it woman-fashion it means — I have five cents on each copy, you have ten to do what you like with & I'm not to meddle. Out of the ten you pay for the cost of the book & give something to the charity to which I heartily wish I could add my share.[2] Is that right? If so I agree with perfect confidence in "my publisher" & all good wishes for his success in the small venture as well as my own.

Father thinks Mr S. E. Sewall would be a good person to arrange the matter as he understands such things, is a friend to both sides, & if he approves I am satisfied.

I have just reread the Memorandum & it seems all right. I dont wish to be grasping but I do wish to have my Hospital attempt pay its own expenses in the way of doctor's bills &c as it was under taken against the advice of many persons & considered a disastrous failure in one respect.

I send the few notices I have kept, but as I do not see many papers I have not much to offer in the way of vanities, though I often hear others speak of notices they have seen.

I also enclose some of the letters from which extracts can be made if desirable, they at least will give some idea of the various opinions expressed upon this mighty matter.

Will you be kind enough to preserve & return them all when you have made such use of them as you think best as I value some of them very much.

Father wishes me to add that his letter is at your service.

Respectfully yours
"T. P."[3]

ALS: New-York Historical Society. Printed: *LASC*, pp. 359–360.

1. This letter is written in response to Redpath's letter of 29 June 1863, in which he states the terms of the "compact." For each copy in cloth sold at fifty cents, the "orphan fund" would receive ten cents and LMA four; for each paperbound copy for Army reading, the orphans would receive five cents and LMA two (Louisa May Alcott Collection, Barrett Library, University of Virginia Library).

2. According to the "Publisher's Advertisement" in *Hospital Sketches* (Boston: James Redpath, 1863), "besides paying the Author the usual copyright, the publisher has resolved to devote at least five cents for every copy sold to the support of orphans made fatherless or homeless by the war." LMA originally wrote "wish I could give all my share," then canceled "give all" and inserted "add."

3. Nurse Tribulation Periwinkle was the name given herself by the author in her hospital letters.

To James Redpath

[July? 1863]

Mr Redpath.

I return your Contract signed, & am sure it is all right. About the dreadful percentage, over which I have puzzled my stupid head till I believe I understand it, I can only say that I too am sure that "he who giveth to the poor lendeth to the Lord" & on that principle devote time & earnings to the care of my father & mother, for one possesses no gift for money making & the other is now too old to work any longer for those who are happy & able to work for her. On this account I often have to deny myself the little I could do for other charities, & seem ungenerous that I may be just. All that is rightly mine I prefer to use for them much as I should like to help the orphans, yet wish that you should first entirely repay yourself for all outlays of time, trouble & money in getting up the book.

You ask about any other story I may have. Mr Sanborn[1] spoke to me some time ago on the same subject & advised me to prepare one written several years ago, that you might examine & pronounce judgment. I have partially done so & send the first six chapters for to you [i.e., you to] read if you like. As all my things go by contraries this may come to something as I dont like it myself. Another one which I do like, & for that very reason dont offer though I think it better written & more interesting. This one was begun with the design of putting some [of] my own experiences into a story illustrating the trials of young women who want employment & find it hard to get. From time to time I see articles on the same subject & various people have begged me to finish "Success" as I at first christened the book.[2]

The story is made up of various essays this girl makes, her failures & succeses told in chapters merry or sad, & various characters all more or less from life are introduced to help or hinder her.

Some of the incidents are old now but perhaps may as well stand as the story is the better for them, & slavery troubles are not easily forgotten. These scenes however are at the end of the book & it will be time enough to change them when it is accepted.

I dont know that so small a part is of any use except as a sample, but if you approve I can send more as I rewrite & shorten it, for now it spun out too much.

If this is not a saleable thing, Mother thinks a volume of my best, or rather most popular stories (for the best never are popular) might do better, & could easily be arranged as I have printed copies of most all of them. There is one Mr Parker liked, another Mr Emerson praised, & several that have been copied into papers & magazines. This has often been suggested to me but I never cared to do it as so many better books were waiting to be read.

We like the extracts from the letters, & I wait to see my second book in its go abroad gown. Respectfully Yrs L. M. A.

I should like to keep the copy right of the book myself.

ALS: New-York Historical Society. Printed: *LASC*, pp. 360–361.

1. Sanborn had published "Hospital Sketches" in the *Boston Commonwealth*, of which he was editor, from 22 May to 26 June 1863 before Redpath's publication in book form. LMA received forty dollars for her contribution (Mrs. Alcott to Samuel Joseph May, 30 August 1863, Houghton Library, Harvard University).

2. LMA labored for years upon her autobiographical novel, at one time called *Success* and renamed *Work: A Story of Experience*, published in 1873 by Roberts Brothers.

To James Redpath

Friday Aug 28th [1863]

Mr Redpath.

I have delayed writing both because of company, & that I might collect my wits a little, for such a burst of new plans & projects rather made my head spin.

Firstly, we all like the book very much, & I have the satisfaction of seeing my towns folk buying, reading, laughing & crying over it wherever I go.[1] One rash youth bought eight copies at a blow, & my dozen would have gone rapidly if I had not locked them up & solemnly signed your paper after inserting the number 12 in the blank you left, so I shall come for no more, & as yet have given away but three to my soldier boys, "Baby B"[2] among them.

I had a visit from an army surgeon the other day who considered my mules striking likenesses, & the book "one to do no end of good both in & out of the army &c." I didn't quite see how but haven't the least objection to its revolutionizing the globe if it can. All is pleasant & looks promising. I hope such a powerful work wont distract the mind of the nation from more useful matters.

I send ten stories & have two more if I can only get them.[3] Leslie printed one but never sent me a copy or told me the date of its appearance.[4] Is there any place where news[pa]pers of that sort are filed? No one takes it here & though I've asked the lazy Frank I get no answer & should like to add it, also one which Fields has to look at "My Contraband".[5] It would be a good one to open with if it comes out in time. I suppose I have a right to republish these things without asking leave have n't I? There are many other tales of the "thrilling" style but they are not worth reprinting.

It will take some time to prepare "Success" as I cannot work very steadily without my poor old head beginning to ache & my family to predict relapses. If you wish I can go on with it while the tales are coming out (if they come) & be ready in case a discerning public demand further gems from my illustrious pen.

My sister will call on Monday & take the first chapters out of your way if you decide on the tales appearing first, as I like to refer to them now & then while going on with others. Ellery Channing asked her last evening at a party why her sister did not collect & republish her stories, which remark has been made by several others before. Whether they will "go" is another thing. I dont think much of them being hastily written & to suit purchasers. But here they are & some of them has done well in humbler walks of life.

The editorial plan was so like an old dream coming true, that my family shouted over it, as we have had several domestic newspapers[6] conducted by "T. P." I can only say, I know nothing about the real thing nor the requirements needed,[7] but if there is any thing in the way of selections, reading MSS, or noticing common books I might perhaps do that, the latter work I have done, & enjoy fussing over papers very much. I asked a wise body about salaries, or whatever that sort of wages are called, & was told that they varied from five hundred a year to three or four thousand according to the amount of work done & the ability of the individual. I could not give all my time to it, & had planned to go to Port Royal this winter, but am not positively engaged to do so.[8]

Mother wants me to tell you that Conway & our Consul at Venice shouted over the Sketches in some palace in that mouldy city, & the Consul sent his compliments to "Nurse P."[9]

I do *not* inherit the paternal fussiness in this respect, & a thing once in the printer's hands is such a good riddance I never care to aggravate myself or him with any but the simplest corrections.

If the stories need any other arranging I can do it at once. I merely put them hastily together for you to look at.

L. M. A.

ALS: New-York Historical Society. Printed: *LASC*, pp. 361–362 (partial).

1. Alcott wrote in her journal of August 1863: "On the 25th my first morning-glory bloomed in my room, — a hopeful blue, — and at night up came my book in its new dress. I had added several chapters to it, and it was quite a neat little affair. An edition of one thousand, and I to have five cents on each copy" (Cheney, p. 153).

2. Sergeant Robert Bane, also called Baby B., one of Alcott's hospital patients (see journal entry, July 1863, Cheney, p. 152).

3. *On Picket Duty, and Other Tales*, published by James Redpath in December 1863, contained only one reprinted work, "The King of Clubs and the Queen of Hearts," among its four stories.

4. LMA must be referring to "A Whisper in the Dark," which appeared in the 6 June and 13 June 1863 issues of *Frank Leslie's Illustrated Newspaper*. Her only other contribution to *Leslie's* at this time was "Pauline's Passion and Punishment," which was one of those "tales of the 'thrilling' style" she said were "not worth reprinting."

5. "The Brothers" appeared in the November 1863 *Atlantic Monthly Magazine* and was retitled "My Contraband; or, The Brothers" when LMA reprinted it in *Hospital Sketches and Camp and Fireside Stories* (Boston: Roberts Brothers, 1869).

6. One of the domestic newspapers was entitled "The Olive Leaf" (see *LMA*, p. 62). A manuscript of "The Olive Leaf," dated 19 July 1849, is at Houghton Library, Harvard University.

7. In her journal entry of September 1863, LMA wrote: "Received $40 from Redpath for 'Sketches,' — first edition; wanted me to be editor of a paper; was afraid to try, and let it go" (Cheney, p. 154).

8. For her unfulfilled plans about Port Royal, see 12 November [1863].

9. Moncure Daniel Conway, reformer and co-editor with Sanborn of the *Boston Commonwealth*, wrote of *Hospital Sketches*: "The series . . . showed every variety of ability, and excited much attention" (*Autobiography, Memories and Experiences*, 2 vols. [Boston: Houghton, Mifflin, 1904], 1:369). William Dean Howells served as American consul in Venice from 1861 to 1865.

To James Redpath

[early September 1863]

Mr Redpath

I dont wish to be obstinate about the stories but I still feel that I'd rather have "Success" come first. Several family friends agree with me & unless you send a Sheriff after me I shall decline sending them to market *yet*.

"Success" you shall have as soon as I can finish it — if you still desire it — but I cannot feel that because one book goes well, happening to be on a matter in which all are interested just now, another will do the same, & therefore in spite of friendly prophesies at home & abroad I'm rather slow to rush into print except in the small way I have followed so long.

Miss Prescott has just got out a book of Tales[1] & I dont care to follow her example in act any more than in style. I'd rather not offer *my* green apples when a little time might ripen a few respectable samples.

Sanborn spoke of sundry small changes to be made in another edition of "H. S's." — if another is to come cannot the covers be *dark* green or drab? *I* saw no fault in its getting up, but fussy people say the margin should be wider & the cover darker. Having a maternal interest in the clothes my offspring wear & the impression they make I mention these things though I dare say you knew them already.

As soon as I have finished a piece of work long waiting for an end I will prepare "Christie" for the public eye.

Respectfully Yours —
L. M. ALCOTT.

The N.Y. gentleman is a man of sense, not only to like our book & cry over it, but to own that he did, for a few tears wrung from a man are better than a gallon of the feminine "briny," I think, because harder to get & usually the genuine article.

P.S. No 2 — Fields has accepted "My Contraband" pronounced it "Capital," & paid fifty dollars for it before hand, which is amiable of him & agreeable to me. I shall go on writing for *him* with an eye to *our* future collection of Tales, & when a good variety has stood the Atlantic test (which by the way I dont value two straws except as far as others are influenced) we can produce the "Social Sketches" & be glad we waited. Dont you think so?

L. M. A.

ALS: New-York Historical Society.
 1. Harriet Prescott Spofford's *The Amber Gods and Other Stories* was published in early September 1863.

To Alfred Whitman

Concord Sept [1863]

My dear old Dolphus.

Carrie sent me word the other day that you felt badly because we none of us wrote, & you wanted to hear. Of course all the times I'd planned to write you & didn't, immediately rose up before me & in a great state of remorse I rush at my pen here at six oclock in the morning & scribble a line to my beloved Tetterby.

My only excuse is I've been to Washington a nursin in the army, got typhoid fever & came bundling home to rave, & ramp, & get my head shaved

& almost retire into the tombs in consequence, not to mention picking up again, & appearing before the eyes of my grateful country in a wig & no particular flesh on my bones, also the writing some Hospital Sketches & when folks said put em in a book, doing the same & being drove wild with proof, & printers, & such matters, besides keeping house, seeing company, adoring my nephew, & furnishing literary gems for sundry papers —— Thus you see I have not been idle though I've seemed to neglect my old boy.

How do you come on? What are you doing? & when are you coming East to be clutched at & kissed by all the "girls you left behind you"? Annie says Carrie showed her a fine picture of your father & self & writes me that Dolphus has gone & growed up in the most appalling manner. Now I wish to know what you mean by that? I'm not changed a bit, barring the wig, & I dont wish my boys to be men folks in this rapid manner. Wilkie James has gone & been made Adjutant in the 54th, got smashed at Fort Wagner & blossomed into a hero; his brother, a sixteen year older, has put on a Lieutenant's shoulder straps & pranced off with the 55th.[1] Julian Hawthorne has set up a manly whisker & got into college,[2] so all my boys are gone & I'm a love lorn old Sophy.

Among my hospital fellows was a jolly little Sergeant who had lost his right arm at Fredricksburg — he learned to write with his left hand & sends me the funniest letters you ever saw. He has got a false arm, shouldered his rifle & is going back to his regiment for "another dig at those thundering rebs" as he says.

Dont you feel inclined to give them a slap? or are [you] helping in the peaceful & perhaps more sensible ways?

Carrie probably has told all the news about her family so I will mention what my own is up to just now, though we go on pretty much as usual. Father writes & sees to his schools; mother sings "Glory Hallelujah" over the papers & makes berry pies; Ab has been at Clarke's Island with a party of young people from New York & Concord.[3] Rowing, dancing, sailing, flirting & singing are the amusements in which they spend their shining hours. She says she is as brown as a berry & as plump as a partridge, so her trip has done her good. Annie & her John brood over the infant Freddy who is the one perfect & divine brat in the world though his nose turns straight up & he has n't half a dozen hairs on his head.

I live in my inkstand scribble, scribble from morning till night & am more peckish than ever if disturbed.

There we are & I hope you recognize the picture.

Our Concord company is to return tonight[4] & the town is in as wild a state of excitement as it is possible for such a dozy old place to be without dying of brain fever. Flags are flapping every where, wreaths & "Welcome home" are stuck on every stickable place & our drum corps, consisting of eight small boys with eight large drums, keep a continual rub-a-dubbing.

Now my son drop me a line & send me one of your new "picters" that I may behold your manly charms. I have no photographs now & must wait till my plumage is renewed when I will return the favor as I believe that is ettiquette.

Bless your buttons & "adoo". Yours Ever SOPHY TETTERBY.

ALS: Houghton Library, Harvard University.

   1. Lieutenant Garth Wilkinson James, wounded with Colonel Robert Gould Shaw's all-black regiment at the battle for Fort Wagner in Charleston Harbor; Lieutenant Robertson James fought in the Union Army's southern campaigns. They were sons of Henry James, Sr., and brothers of the novelist Henry James, Jr. (Leon Edel, *Henry James: The Untried Years* [Philadelphia: J. B. Lippincott, 1953], pp. 184–187).

   2. Julian Hawthorne entered Harvard College in 1863 but proved to be such a desultory student that he was asked to leave at the beginning of his senior year because of his poor academic standing and many absences.

   3. May had gone to Clarks Island, near Plymouth, Massachusetts, with the Sanborns and other friends on 1 August (Mrs. Alcott's diary, Houghton Library, Harvard University).

   4. The company was returning from the battle at Gettysburg. According to Julian Hawthorne, on such occasions "we all set out to work, and . . . lemonade enough had been made to flavor Walden Pond. . . . The Alcott girls and a score more of the prettiest in the village stood in white frocks to serve out the drinks. Louisa, in her hospital costume, conducted the ceremonies" ("The Woman Who Wrote Little Women," *Ladies' Home Journal* 39 [October 1922]: 121).

To James Redpath

Sept 29th [1863]

Mr Redpath.

   I send you copies of paragraphs from two letters lately recieved, one from Wasson to father, the other to myself from Serjeant James, one of the Wagner heroes & son of Henry James.[1] Use them if you like. I am expecting a letter from one of my boys to whom I sent the book, & from Chas Sumner who told father he was intending to write.

   I was afraid the price would hurt the sale of the book & think the plan you suggest a good one.[2] About selling the copyright I'm unable to decide knowing so little of such matters, but will inquire & let you know as soon as may be.

   If I go to Port Royal "Success" will have to wait, but letters or "Sketches" from there will make a better because truer book &, I think, one that would sell more rapidly than a common romance.

I've written to Mr Judd[3] for information & shall soon know how my winter is to be employed. I've another story for Fields nearly done[4] & when the "Contraband" (or "Brothers" as he insists on naming it) is out next month I'll hand him this & continue doing so till we get enough for our book of Tales.

I should like to tell the Congregationalist some of the pious doings I saw at the Union; the sanctified nurse who sung hymns & prayed violently while stealing the men's watches & money; the much esteemed lady whose devout countenance was abominated by the boys though the Chaplain approved of her till it was found that her exhortations ceased when the patients had made their wills in her favor; & sundry other samples of humbug which so disgusted "Nurse P" that she resolved to put her religion into her work rather than her words & save souls in ways of her own, that seemed to suceed though not of [a] kind to bear telling in a newspaper.

Respectfully Yrs
L. M. A.

Send the check on Sat if you will be so kind.

ALS: New-York Historical Society. Printed: *LASC*, pp. 362–363.
  1. David Atwood Wasson, writer of radical religious works, and Garth Wilkinson James. The clipped paragraphs she copied on the last page of the letter were: from Wasson, "Let me tell you what extreme pleasure I have taken in reading 'Hospital Sketches.' Written with such extraordinary wit & felicity of style, & showing such power to portray character! Surely she has a brilliant literary future before her"; from James, "Your wonderful little book was recieved while suffering much from my wounds. Greatly am I indebted to you for it; it has whiled away several otherwise weary hours & I have enjoyed it exceedingly."
  2. Mrs. Alcott wrote Samuel Joseph May on 10 September that because " 'the *Trade*' think it costly," the next printing of the book would "be got up cheaper" (Houghton Library, Harvard University). As a result, a paperbound printing was published the following year and priced at twenty-five cents.
  3. Orange Judd, publisher of *Hearth and Home*; LMA's first publication in this magazine did not appear until 1872.
  4. No other Alcott story appeared subsequently in the *Atlantic*.

To Mary Elizabeth Waterman

Concord, Nov. 6th / 63

My Dear Miss Waterman.[1]

I was very glad to hear from you although it always fills me with anguish of spirit to see your beautiful handwriting because my own then looks more like turkey tracks than ever. However I forgive you & return thanks for the distinguished approbation with which you have honored my "umble" works of art.[2]

"Hospital Sketches" still continues a great joke to me, & a sort of perpetual surprise-party, for to this day I cannot see why people like a few extracts from topsey turvey letters written on inverted tin kettles, in my pantry, while waiting for gruel to warm or poultices to cool, for boys to wake and be tormented, on stairs, in window seats & other sequestered spots favorable to literary inspiration. People are very kind & very easily pleased & I'm much obliged, but I dont understand it at all & probably never shall.

I should like to see you mightily & spin a hospital spin if you fancy such things, for it was a most interesting experience & I never tire of thinking and talking about "my boys." Several have written to me, "Baby B" is not married but has gone to Oberlin College & is as jolly as ever. Another "boy" of five & thirty has come back with his one leg to his old place at Mr Balls where he resigns himself to pounding gold as he can no longer pound Rebs, & has five infant cats of an Ethiopian complexion for his contrabands.

I wish to state that T. Periwinkle no longer wears a wig (I should say an old frisette once owned by the mother of Dr Bellows) but appears on all occasions with a fine flowing crop like the youngest Miss Pecksniff.[3] I would advise all *young* ladies of thirty to shave their brows, pass a few months in the deepest seclusion & then find themselves back in their teens, as far as appearance goes, both a convenient & artistic arrangement. "Brother Tom" should have been "neighbor Thorn."

May is still doing pictures, making clay pies & casting Saint Pauls, Anne Pages,[4] "One more unfortunate" & other bursts of genius; beside taking lessons in Anatomy once a week in Boston, & filling up her leisure hours with French, flirtation, Bazig[5] & boating. Father placidly meditates among his apple barrels & says — "Fine eyes!" when Miss Waterman's name is mentioned. Mother pets her family, knits army socks, sings "Siloam"[6] and delivers home lectures. "Mrs Coobidy" is wrapt up in little Darby,[7] & old "Trib" sits in her room trying to write two novels,[8] several tales & a book of Christmas songs all at once, beside answering letters & wrestling with three publishers — All send love & I am as ever yours affectionately, T. P.

ALS: Miscellaneous Manuscripts, Newberry Library.

1. Waterman had attended Agassiz's school in Cambridge before going as a teacher in the early 1860s to Sanborn's school in Concord. She first met the Alcotts soon after Lizzie's death, in March 1858, and thereafter was a frequent visitor to their home (see her reminiscences of LMA, Fruitlands Museums, Harvard, Massachusetts).

2. In her reminiscences of LMA, Waterman recalls that Hospital Sketches had been sent

to her "from Fortress Munroe by one of the young men that [LMA] used to call her boys" (Fruitlands Museums, Harvard, Massachusetts).

3. Mercy Pecksniff, in Dickens's *Martin Chuzzlewit*, has hair described as a "loosely flowing crop."

4. Possibly the Ann Page who taught the Alcott children at Fruitlands.

5. A card game resembling pinochle.

6. A variant of the song "Shiloh."

7. Anna Pratt and her son, Fred. John Pratt played Darby to Anna's Joan in the family theatricals.

8. *Success* and *Moods* (Boston: A. K. Loring, 1865).

To Thomas Wentworth Higginson

Conord Nov 12th [1863]

My Dear Mr Higginson.[1]

To receive a letter with Beaufort[2] at the beginning & "Higginson" at the end was both a surprise & honor for which I thank you, as for the commendation & the criticism.

I knew that my contraband did not talk as he should, for even in Washington I had no time to study the genuine dialect, & when the story was written here I had no one to tell me how it should be.

The hospital ship & the "row of dusky faces" were taken from a letter of Mrs Gage's, describing her visit & interview with the Wagner heroes in Hilton Head Harbor.[3] Perhaps she was mistaken, in the locality, women often are inaccurate when their sympathies are at work.

I should like of all things to go South & help the blacks as I am no longer allowed to nurse the whites. The former seems the greater work, & would be most interesting to me. I offered to go as teacher on one of the Islands but Mr Philbrey objected because I had no natural protector to go with me, so I was obliged to give that up.[4]

Fields spoke of engaging some letters for his Magazine if I did go, & I was much disappointed as I was willing to rough it anywhere for a time both for the sake of the help it would be to me in many ways, & the hope that I might be of use to others.

Dont you want a cook, nurse, or somewhat venerable "Child" for your regiment? I am willing to enlist in any capacity for the blood of old Col. May asserts itself in his granddaughter in these martial times & she is very anxious to be busied in some more loyal labor than sitting quietly at home spinning fictions when such fine facts are waiting for all of us to profit by & celebrate.

Father & mother desire to be remembered.

Very Truly Yours
L. M. ALCOTT.

My regards to the "Apollers."

ALS: Special Collections, Harold B. Lee Library, Brigham Young University. Printed: *LASC*, p. 344.

1. "My Contraband," a story of race relations that probes into problems of miscegenation, "called forth a letter of commendation and frank criticism from T. W. Higginson, which was very encouraging to the young writer." This letter to the reformer, soldier, and author Thomas Wentworth Higginson is obviously LMA's reply to that "letter of commendation" (see Cheney, pp. 139, 153, 154).

2. Beaufort, South Carolina, where Higginson was encamped. He was colonel of the first Negro regiment in the Union Army (First South Carolina Volunteers) between November 1862 and May 1864.

3. Frances Dana Barker Gage, reformer and abolitionist, went to the Sea Islands of South Carolina in October 1862.

4. According to her journal, in October 1863, LMA "thought much about going to Port Royal to teach contrabands" (Cheney, p. 154).

To James Redpath

Concord Dec 2nd [1863]

Mr Redpath.

I prefer not to part with H. S's. But will gladly help on the "Camp Fire" series by letting you have as many of my stories as you like.[1] Two or three suitable for such purpose might be put in a small book. I have one "On Picket Duty" which the Atlantic wouldn't take, & other warlike matters simmering in my head. "A Hospital Christmas" is one & if Ticknor would let us have the brothers these three would do as a beginning perhaps if you want them.[2]

As soon as the Sanitary plays are over[3] I'll work with all my might at Success & let you have it as soon as possible, for I want that to come first.

My time seems likely to be pretty fully occupied if I accept all the offers made me. Leslie asks for several more tales, Fields wants another in "the Brothers" style, & Richardson the unknown makes a proposal which I send for you to see,[4] & if you will be so kind, to give me your opinion of the enterprize. Are they clever people? & is it worth my while to accept?

I suppose if my stories are printed in the "dime set"[5] they can still be gathered into one volume at some time with others, if we think best?

Respectfully & illegibly L. M. A.

ALS: New-York Historical Society. Printed: *LASC*, p. 364.

    1. Redpath planned to make *On Picket Duty, and Other Tales* the first number of his *Books for Camp Fire* series, also called *Books for Camp and Home*.

    2. Neither "A Hospital Christmas," which appeared in the 8 January and 15 January 1864 issues of the *Boston Commonwealth*, nor "My Contraband; or, The Brothers" was collected in *On Picket Duty*.

    3. LMA dramatized *Scenes from Dickens* for the Sanitary Commission Fair in Boston on 14 December, raising $2,500 for the cause.

    4. Frank Leslie of *Frank Leslie's Illustrated Newspaper;* Charles B. Richardson of the *United States Service Magazine*.

    5. Writing to LMA on 1 December 1863, Redpath called the *Books for Camp Fire* series his "dime set" (Louisa May Alcott Collection, Barrett Library, University of Virginia Library).

To James Redpath

Tuesday eve.
[after 2 December 1863]

Mr Redpath.

My only objection to your plan is that I dont see *where* the double pay comes in. The old stories were never *well* paid for & I thought some time I'd make a book of them as you suggested — but if I tag one of the best onto a new one I get nothing for it, it is lost to the book & done with for ever. The one you speak of is the best perhaps of the old batch, & I had already laid it by to go with the other good ones as they come. If you have made arrangements to get out the first book with "Picket Duty" & an old one, I will give up "King Of Clubs & Queen of Hearts," or you can have "Cross On The Church Tower," though I dont think either will go very well with "Picket Duty."[1]

If you can let me have ten or twenty dollars it would be a great favor, for having engaged in the plays I cannot give out, sundry expenses must be incurred & I rather depended on "my works" to supply the necessary funds. Please give May the Ms of "C. H."[2] for I'm going to try Harper for the fun of it, & let James T. [Fields] rest a little — As ever

L. M. A.

ALS: New-York Historical Society.
    1. "The Cross on the Old Church Tower" appeared in *On Picket Duty, and Other Tales*.
    2. Probably "A Hospital Christmas."

To Alfred Whitman

Jan 2ond 1864.

My Dear Alf.

I wish you a happy New Year to begin with, & add many thanks for the picture which you so kindly sent your apparently neglectful Sophy. Your father I never saw, but mother thinks he looks very like his brother whom she used to know. You have grown & altered so much I can see hardly any trace of the Dolphus I used to know. But the new aspect seems to assure us that "our Alf" is every inch a man & one we should like to see among us again. Is n't he ever coming?

I have thought so often of you, & some letter which I've an idea I never answered, that my courage grew less & less every time I prepared to write & was interrupted, that at last as I got busier & busier I gave it up in despair, though I never forgot & always asked Carrie when & what she heard from you.

My only excuse is that when publishers once get hold of a body they give that body no peace & keep them at work like "negro mulatto slaves" all day & every day, & are never satisfied. James Redpath is my present overseer & a sweet time I have of it, but as money is rather a necessary of life & he hands it over with a charming ease I cleave unto him, & devote my energies to the earning of filthy lucre.

Then my correspondents multiply & several of my Hospital friends & "boys" keep writing & asking for answers, besides business letters which arrive at the rate of two a day if not more. So you see I *do* the necessary & *think about* doing the agreeable.

Just of late we have been busy having plays at the Tremont Theatre for the Sanitary while the great Fair was held in the Music Hall near by. We Concord people got up some Scenes from Dickens as we did ages ago you remember. I wished I had my old company as the new one was made up of busy men & incapable women, with a few blessed exceptions. I dare say Carrie may have told you something about it though she was not able to go. We did as well as we could & after endless disappointments, mishaps & "flare ups" we managed to have "Trotwood & David," "Camp & Prig", & "Mrs Jarley's Waxwork," & people were good enough to be pleased. [1]

If you are of a forgiving nature you will write me a nice letter some rainy day & tell me all about your late doings & beings in the military line, for since I went to the war I've grown very martial in my tastes, & like to hear of the things in which I can take no part.

Carrie is very ill although she wont leave her school & go home yet; she will soon be obliged to go I am afraid & will never return again. Her Dr says he can do [no] more for her & she looks wretchedly. In writing to her please dont mention that I have spoken to you about her health as she is very queer upon that point. As she is & has been so unhappy for many years I cannot regret the end for her, though I shall miss her very much, & have always loved her for the noble qualities which she possesses.

All send love to you dear Alf, & I am as ever

your "SOPHY".

ALS: Houghton Library, Harvard University. Printed: Whitman 11, 6 (partial).
    1. Writing to James Redpath about the theatricals, LMA commented: "You missed very little in not seeing the Dickens Scenes for so many people seceded that they were very poorly played & the whole thing was a scramble. Manager Bartlett would not let us off so we did what we could, but it was acting under difficulties" (23 December [1863], New-York Historical Society).

To James Redpath

Jan 24th / 64

Mr Redpath.

The little green backs[1] were *very* welcome & I hardly knew my own scribbles in their new dress. I never liked "Picket Duty" very well for Yankee talk is my abomination, though as the great James professed to like it I thought I'd try to suit him; I did n't, nor myself either. "The King of Clubs" suits me better & the "Cross on the Church Tower" is pious enough to please any one I hope. It was written so long ago I'd forgotten the whole family.

You ask about errors, there are none of any consequence except in "Picket Duty" where poor Flint is made to talk something that is not even down east Yankee.

On page 21 he swallows a "tub" instead of a "nub" — page 23 needs another *b* in "shabby", the word "loopin" is "loafin" — page 26 — *stoxe* is *store*, & *keell* is kill — also omit the "per" in the sentence "offered permotion on the field" — there is an l omitted on page 11 in the 10th line — & Flag substituted for sore on the 30th page — which would do very well if the Rebs did not think as much of their flag as we & fight for it more pluckily —

Page 36 poor dear Wilhelmina Carolina Amelia Skeggs suffers the same amputation of a letter as before, & I begin to think no one has ever read the Vicar of Wakefield. The two Dicks are bad, but I suppose it cannot be helped now unless in the new edition if there is one.

I should like Billings for the Fairy Tales,[2] though Miss Green[3] has a delicate fancy & if she would let me see her designs before engraved I could tell her how to make them suit me better. Several people have urged me to get out "Beach Bubbles"[4] or Songs for the seaside — which were printed but never paid for some years ago — They came out in the Gazette & were copy righted in my name by Mr Clapp so they have never been reprinted & were much liked. There are a dozen I believe, & perhaps if prettily illustrated would make a good summer book.

Respectfully L. M. ALCOTT.

"Success" is just where I left it for though I have tried a dozen times I cannot get on with it, so must wait for inspiration. Writing books is too hard work for one who likes to finish soon.

ALS: New-York Historical Society. Printed: *LASC*, pp. 365–366.

　　1. *On Picket Duty, and Other Tales* was sold in green paper wrappers; for the book's publication and contents, see 2 December [1863] and [after 2 December 1863]. Henry James, Sr., had written of his pleasure in LMA's "charming pictures of hospital service" (clipping, Alcott Papers, Houghton Library, Harvard University).

　　2. Redpath published LMA's *The Rose Family. A Fairy Tale* in 1864, but the volume of "fairy tales" was never published as such; for the strange history of the manuscript, see *Louisa's Wonder Book — An Unknown Alcott Juvenile*, ed. Madeleine B. Stern (Mount Pleasant: Central Michigan University, 1975), pp. 10–12.

　　3. Hammatt Billings, who probably illustrated the second volume of *Little Women*; Elizabeth B. Greene, illustrator of LMA's *Morning-Glories, and Other Stories* (Boston: Horace B. Fuller, 1868).

　　4. The poems entitled "Beach Bubbles" had appeared between 21 June and 23 August 1856 in the *Saturday Evening Gazette*, Quarto Series.

To James Redpath

Jan 29th [1864]

Mr Redpath.

　　It strikes me that S. R. Bartlett is making a "coil" about a very small matter, & I know nothing to be done, on my part, except to repeat what I wrote on sending you the story. It was never wholly paid for though Atlantic prices were promised, or rather more than that as we were to have $5.00 a column. I recieved $30, & no one else anything as I was told by several of my fellow contributors.[1]

As the paper died in a little while & was not much known nor read while it lasted I fancied my "King of Clubs" was rather wasted on the desert air, & that there would be no harm in republishing it, as I said to Bartlett when I gave it to him that I wished to be at liberty to do so by & by if I chose. He may [i.e., made] no objection & as I did not know that the Monitor was copyrighted I never thought of asking his leave to print my own story.

It seems neither neighborly nor necessary to make objections now, & it does not appear to me that we have either of us done anything unlawful or unjust. I never asked for the rest of the money due me as I knew the Monitor was going down & did not want to add another fret to the many borne by its commander.

Respectfully L. M. ALCOTT.

ALS: New-York Historical Society. Printed: LASC, p. 365.
1. "The King of Clubs and the Queen of Hearts," published by Ripley Bartlett in the 19 April–7 June 1862 issues of the *Monitor*, was reprinted both in *On Picket Duty, and Other Tales* and *Hospital Sketches and Camp and Fireside Stories*, despite Bartlett's "coil."

To James Redpath

[February? 1864?]

Mr Redpath.

Your letter has quite settled my mind on several points, & now I can comfortably attend to my own affairs without half a dozen plans bewildering my wits.

Thank you for so clearly & kindly enlightening me, & be assured I have no intention of changing "my publisher" if by doing so I seem in any way to imply distrust, dissatisfaction or a desire to better myself at his cost. I think the literary laws *are* just & shall abide [by] them, hoping that your "faith in my ability" may be rewarded, & future books may prove a good investment for us both.

I had a sort of feeling that it was n't quite fair for Fields to offer an engagement after another manager had run all the risks of bringing the new debutante out. He wont have "Moods," unless you get tired of your bargain

& send me adrift. I'm not sure that I dont take a little naughty satisfaction in being able to say No — when he asks me, for between him & Ticknor things dont go as freely as I like, & the Atlantic is dreadfully afraid of certain words & ideas which such a big ocean ou[gh]t to be glad to carry into a safe harbor.

Speaking of the Atlantic reminds me of another thing I want to ask you about. F likes my stories & pays promptly & well for them, but if I go on writing for him wont he expect to print them if I ever want them in a book?[1] He *has had* the best, & even those you saw may not be mine to give you, at least three or four. Father thinks he would make a fuss if I did it, what do you say? Would not any paper or Magazine do the same?

Now about "Moods" — it is a big thing, thirty chapters long — rather odd, sentimental, & tragical — written for my own amusement at various spare times during the last three years. My family laugh & cry over it, & think it fine — they are no judges — neither am I — Mr Emerson offered to read & give his opinion long ago but I hadn't the courage to let him.

It is done except the last Chap — do you care to see it? If so let me know & I will send half by May next Wed — It is such a vast Ms that I'm afraid it will appal you, though I've taken out ever so many pages & simmered it down almost as much as I can. One or two things might be omitted if you think best. I should very much value your criticism even if you bundled the book home with "Rubbish" written on the cover.[2]

I'll try not to be "spoilt," & think ten or fifteen years of snubbing rather good training for an ambitious body; but people mustn't talk about "genius" — for I drove that idea away years ago & dont want it back again. The inspiration of necessity is all I've had, & it is a safer help than any other.

I have not seen the Traveler[3] & dont know when the notice, or whatever it was, appeared. Some one said one paper wished I'd write a novel, that is all I know, & I think I'll gratify them.

Very truly yours
L. M. ALCOTT.

ALS: New-York Historical Society. Printed: *LASC*, pp. 363–364 (partial).

1. James T. Fields of Ticknor and Fields, publishers of the *Atlantic Monthly*, accepted the following Alcott stories for that periodical: "Love and Self-Love," "A Modern Cinderella; or, The Little Old Shoe" (October 1860), "Debby's Début," and "The Brothers." Of these, "A Modern Cinderella" and "The Brothers" were reprinted in *Hospital Sketches and Camp and Fireside Stories*.

2. *Moods*, to which LMA refers, was not published until December 1864. James T. Fields and Redpath were both at one time interested in it (see Cheney, pp. 154, 156).

3. The *Boston Traveller* for 29 January 1864 called *On Picket Duty, and Other Tales* "thoroughly readable" (p. 1).

To James Redpath

Concord   Feb 2d [1864]

Mr Redpath.

I have written to my amiable townsman S. R. Bartlett & hope he will feel satisfied. One thing has escaped your memory I find, & that is that I told you in one of my notes about the stories that "King of Clubs" had been printed in the Monitor but not paid for &c. I did not mention copyrights because I did not know anything about them. Its of no consequence probably, but I am quite sure I told you that much.[1]

I dont know what to say about "H[ospital] S[ketches]'s," my wise friends say "Dont sell it," so I hold on as I'm bid, though I cannot see any great wisdom in it. The high price killed the sale of it, one literary party said, & many have complained. But *I* think it is done with now so why bewail any mistake at the outset?

Suppose you make me an offer for it, & then we will see.

I send a corrected copy of "P[icket]. D[uty]," the first story contains about all the mistakes I believe.

I should like to see what the Post & Traveller say if its worth the trouble of slipping into a note sometime.[2] I dont agree with J. T. [Fields?] & never shall. I hate Yankees. Leslie & Richardson still send for stories & "Success" still remains in a muddle. L. M. A.

I have nothing but the Fairy Tales. If you want to do any thing about them for next Christmas you can have them. I have added a new one.

ALS: New-York Historical Society. Printed: *LASC*, pp. 366–367.
    1. For "The King of Clubs and the Queen of Hearts," see 29 January [1864].
    2. The *Boston Post* for 29 January 1864 called *On Picket Duty, and Other Tales* "a capital story" (p. 1).

To James Redpath

Redpath Rooms   Friday morn.
[Spring? 1864]

Mr Redpath.

I recieved a note from Roberts Brothers this morning enclosing one from you to them. They say — "If you (meaning me) are under any engagement to Mr Redpath which we are obliged to purchase we cannot think of making any proposals with reference to publishing. We also decline to purchase his plates."

I had no intention of doing anything with "Rose Family" which is your property, but I *did* wish to have the Brothers to get up my book of fairy tales, & think they are still mine to do as I like with as you told me when I saw you some time ago that you did not feel able to get them up in the expensive way they should be done, also that such books were not very profitable, & let the whole thing rest after I had hurried to get them ready as you said it took a good while for illustrations.

I have signed no contract about them & as you have no new books or tales of mine in hand, or any still unsettled for I believe I am at liberty to dispose of the fairy tales to whom so ever will do them to suit me.

I desired father to enquire if the Bros. got out fairy books, & he entered into the matter more than I meant he should till I had seen you. I wish to be honorable & right in my dealings all round, & as I find my things will go elsewhere to do the best I can. You spoke of not publishing any more for a time[1] — "Camp-Fire" books at least — & as I am not able to write new stories I want to make the old ones profitable & think a Christmas book might do well if finely gotten up.

I shall do nothing further till I hear from you as I still have the fear of some dreadful breach of etiquette before my eyes, tho I *dont* fear any Bartlett transactions this time I assure you.

I came in from Medford where I was going when I last saw you, & shall be in town till tomorrow P.M. so any message or letter from you I will call for tomorrow morning when father will be in town.

I was sorry to hear that you were ill, & send the sympatting regards of a fellow sufferer to your typhoid son.

Respectfully yours
L. M. ALCOTT.

ALS: New-York Historical Society. Printed: *LASC*, p. 367.
    1. Redpath's last advertisement appeared in the 15 April 1864 *American Publishers' Circular*, ending his brief career as a publisher.

To James T. Fields

Concord May 28th [1864]

My Dear Mr Fields.
    Many thanks for the green "Maine Woods,"[1] through which I have been delightfully wandering in spite of rainy weather, feeling the while as if

Thoreau were walking with me again, so entirely does he seem to have put himself into his book.

Mrs Hawthorne frequently expresses her satisfaction in & gratitude for the fitting & friendly cares bestowed upon her & hers during the sad yet beautiful Monday which will not soon be forgotten.[2] Mr Hawthorne is gone, but [she] still finds herself patiently, hopefully awaiting his return. Many of us will have the same feeling, I fancy, because he was one of those who are felt not seen, & we shall not really miss him till we turn the last leaf of his story without an end.

Father & mother desire to be remembered, & with love to Cousin Annie I am

Very truly yours
L. M. ALCOTT.

ALS: Huntington Library. Printed: Nan Cooke Carpenter, "Louisa May Alcott and 'Thoreau's Flute': Two Letters," *Huntington Library Quarterly* 24 (November 1960): 74.

1. Thoreau's *The Maine Woods*, published on 28 May 1864.

2. Nathaniel Hawthorne, who had died on 19 May, was buried in Concord on Monday, 23 May. LMA's poem to Hawthorne, written in November 1862, nicely describes her feelings about him; see Rita K. Gollin, "Louisa May Alcott's 'Hawthorne,'" *Essex Institute Historical Collections* 118 (January 1982): 42–48.

To Abigail May Alcott

[25 December 1864]

I am happy, very happy tonight for my five years work is done, and whether it succeeds or not, I shall be the richer and better for it, because the labor, love, disappointment, hope and purpose, that have gone into it, are a useful experience that I shall never forget. Now if it makes a little money and opens the way for more, I shall be satisfied, and you in some measure repaid for all the sympathy help and love that have done so much for me in these hard years. I hope Success will sweeten me and make me what I long to become more than a great writer — a good daughter. And so God bless you, dear mother, and send us all a Happy New Year.

MS: Unlocated; manuscript copy by Bronson at Houghton Library, Harvard University. Printed: *The Journals of Bronson Alcott*, ed. Odell Shepard (Boston: Little, Brown, 1938), p. 367; *LMA*, p. 142. Bronson notes that this was sent to his wife with a copy of *Moods*, which was published on Christmas Day.

To Annie Maria Lawrence

My Dear Miss Lawrence.

I have a vague recollection of some little girl who was Lizzie's friend in the old Still River days,[1] but do not recal the name though very glad to welcome any one who knew & loved our Lizzie.

Those *were* jolly times, & I never think of them without a laugh. The Gardeners were our mates then, & I remember being married to Walter by Alfred Haskell with a white apron for a veil & the old wood shed for a church. We slapped one another soon after & parted, finding that our tempers didn't agree. I rather think my prejudices in favor of spinsterhood are founded upon that brief but tragical experience.

I am glad if my scribbles amuse you & thank my friend "Mrs Podgers"[2] for bringing me another expression of good will. "Moods" wont suit you so well I suspect, for in it I've freed my mind upon a subject that always makes trouble, namely, Love. But being founded upon fact, & the characters drawn from life it may be of use as all experiences are & serve as a warning at least.

I also have been a schoolmarm for ten years, but I dont like it & prefer pen & ink to birch & book, for my imaginary children are much easier to manage than living responsibilities.

My little nephew, Annie's son, is calling "Aunty Wee-wee" to come & take him for his daily constitutional, & the young lord of the house must be obeyed. Please remember me to the Gardeners, & believe me

Very truly your friend
L. M. ALCOTT.

Concord Feb 3rd / 65.

ALS: Fruitlands Museums, Harvard, Massachusetts. Printed (in facsimile): Annie M. L. Clark, *The Alcotts in Harvard* (Lancaster, Mass.: J. C. L. Clark, 1902), between pp. 38 and 41.

    1. For Still River, see LMA to Sophia Gardner, 23 [September 1845].
    2. "Mrs. Podgers' Teapot" appeared in the 24 December 1864 *Saturday Evening Gazette*.

To Moncure Daniel Conway

My Dear Mr Conway.

Mr Sanborn offers me a place in his parcel & I want to do myself the pleasure of sending you a copy of my little book because you were so kindly interested in the other one.[1]

"Moods" is not what I meant to have it, for I followed bad advice & took out many things which explained my idea & made the characters more natural & consistent. I see my mistake now for I find myself accused of Spiritualism, Free Love, Affinities & all sorts of horrors that I know very little about & dont believe in.

Perhaps I was over bold to try the experiment of treating an old theme in a new way. But out of my own observation & experience I ventured to say what I thought to the young people whom I see so often making blunders that mar their whole lives, & then blaming God or fate, & becoming dismal martyrs when they should be cheerful workers.

Self abnegation is a noble thing but I think there is a limit to it; & though in a few rare cases it may work well yet half the misery of the world seems to come from unmated pairs trying to live their lie decorously to the end, & bringing children into the world to inherit the unhappiness & discord out of which they were born. There is discipline enough in the most perfect marriage & I dont agree to the doctrine of "marry in haste & repent at leisure" which seems to prevail. I onor it too much not to want to see it all it should be & to try to help others to prepare for it that they may find it life's best lesson not its heaviest burden.

The book has been sharply criticised & I am glad of it, though I wish I had done better justice to my own idea.[2] I heartily believe it, am willing to be blamed for it, & am not sorry I wrote it, for it has not only cleared & fixed many things in my own mind, but brought me thanks & good wishes from many whom I find I have served better than I knew.

Pardon my egotistical note, but I did want to set myself right before you if I could, as it is too late to do it here before others, & with all its imperfections "Moods" is an honest, well meaning, little book.

Please remember me to Mrs Conway, & with affectionate regards from us all believe me

Very truly yours
L. M. ALCOTT.

Concord Feb 18 / 65.

ALS: Henry W. and Albert A. Berg Collection, New York Public Library, Astor, Lenox, and Tilden Foundations.

1. Before leaving for Europe in the spring of 1863, Conway had suggested that LMA "arrange my letters ["Hospital Sketches"] in a printable shape, and put them in the 'Commonwealth' " (journal entry, April 1863, Cheney, p. 150).

2. Although the reviewer in Harper's Weekly for 21 January 1865 discovered in Moods "great power and absorbing interest" (9:35), Henry James, Jr., writing in the September 1865 North American Review, felt that the "two most striking facts" of the book were "the author's ignorance of human nature, and her self-confidence in spite of this ignorance" (101:280).

To Mr. Ayer

Mr Ayer.

    I do not usually reply to the letters of strangers, having barely time to answer my friends, but you so entirely misunderstand Moods that I am anxious to set you right as far as I can in a hasty letter.

    Your first question concerns the relations between Sylvia, Moor & Warwark [i.e., Warwick]. I know them to be *possible* as I have seen seen them more than once; they are *natural* though not common, for peculiar minds demonstrate their thoughts & feelings in peculiar ways; they are *desirable* only so far as they help men & women to understand themselves & each other.

    You think that Moods teaches that marriage should be founded on some indefinable feeling or attraction not upon respect or esteem. Now if there is any thing that I heartily detest it is the theory of Affinities, also Spiritualism & Free Love, though I am grieved to find myself accused of all three. I honor marriage so highly that I long to see it what it should be life's best lesson not its heaviest cross. It has so great an influence upon us all that it should be held in greater reverence, prepared for carefully entered upon solemnly, & kept holy by being kept true. Respect & esteem must be the foundation, but above & beyond must be an abiding love that makes all things possible & without which no marriage is a true one, no household a home.

    Half the misery of our time arises from unmated pairs trying to live their legal lie decorously to the end at any cost. Better a few cases of open infidelity that warn & shock than many hidden tragedies that doom the innocent children as well as guilty parents.

    If you read carefully the 17th & 18th Chapters you will see that Sylvia did try to be all she should to Moor, did give up love for duty, & resist temptation, trying to do right through all delusions & mistakes although it cost her life. Warwick has been pronounced an impossible character, but as he was drawn from life he must stand for what he is worth. Not a base nor treacherous man, but one possessing great faults as well as virtues & like better men most inconsistent, unwise & blind when in love. He too makes his mistakes, endeavors to amend them, & is true to his belief of what is right in defiance of the world's opinion. He asked Sylvia to be true to herself & not decieve Moor, & in time she saw the worth of this advice, found Warwick upright even when most tempted to claim her after Moor knew all, & was helped to see her way out of the dark by his plain dealing.

    These latter chapters were more carefully written than any others, & as the book has been underway for six years there has been no occasion for haste any where. In justice to myself I want to say that by the advice of my publisher I took out ten chapters in order to shorten it; this I find was very unwise for these chapters explained much that now is obscure & made the whole story more natural & consistent. I shall know better another time, & do not blame my critics for failing to understand what I have not fully explained.

The design of Moods was to show the effect of a moody person's moods upon their life, & Sylvia, being a mixed & peculiar character, makes peculiar blunders & tries to remedy them in an uncommon manner. I had no desire to settle or unsettle any question, to convince or convert any one to any theory whatever, but wrote straight out of my own observation, experience & instinct.

Others beside yourself have made the same mistakes regarding my purpose, & perhaps it is well for me that they have as it will teach me that even a little romance has some influence for good or evil & make me careful in what I write hereafter. I think Moods will do no harm to the pure hearted & for them alone was it written. That it has done some good I already have proofs in the letters I receive from good women who have tried to do their duty & become meek martyrs instead of happy workers in God's world; young girls thank me for the warning I have unconsciously given them, & more than one minister has assured me that with all its faults the book has has taught a lesson that many needed to learn.

Pardon my seeming egotism, but when thoughtful men or women honor me with sincere praise or blame I desire to show that I am grateful for both by an equal sincerity on my part.

Respectfully Yours
L. M. ALCOTT.

Concord Mar. 19th / 65.

ALS: Concord Free Public Library. LMA later added much additional punctuation to this letter; we have restored her original readings.

To Amos Bronson Alcott

Monday 31. July [1865].[1]

At dawn left for London, and after going through a long tunnel as dark as Egypt and as Gassy as the Pit, we emerged into sunshine and a gallery of lovely pictures.**** We had a carriage to ourselves holding six, and like a small 'bus cushioned every where and carpeted, with racks for bags &c, gas for the dark tunnels which were many, and every thing so cosy that it was hard to believe we were in a car. A burly guard with badges all over him looking like a horse in a silverplated harness locked and unlocked the door at the stations, and our baggage went on the top of our car as if we went in a private carriage. I mention this lest you should think that we larked in public car, 'a la Americans'. May would have been wild to stop and sketch the pretty sceneries that came on either side. Every thing was so unyankee, so quiet and well kept. Each field seemed to have been newly weeded, each road freshly rolled, each garden just put in order, and each house newly scrubbed from garret to cellar. The farmhouses were my delight, with low thatched roofs, ivy up to the eaves, flowers all about the latticed windows, and buxom women or rosy children at the doors. Long low barns with hay ricks near by, trim hedges, fat cattle, green and yellow fields all about. Such perfect shades of color, delighted one's eyes, for grass was never so green, wheat so deeply golden, woods so dark, or rivers bluer than those, I saw under an April like sky, grey and misty one hour, serene and sunny the next; or black with a sweeping shower. Nothing was abrupt, nobody in a hurry, and nowhere did you see the desperately go ahead style of life that we have. The very cows in America look fast, and the hens seem to cackle fiercely over their rights like strong minded old ladies; but here the plump cattle stood up to their knees in clover, with a reposeful air that is very soothing, and the fowls cluck contentedly as if their well disciplined minds accepted the inevitable spit with calm resignation, and the very engine instead of a shrill devil-may care yell, like ours, did its duty in one gruff snort, like a beefy giant with a cold in his head. This slow going nation are very interesting, and I find things extremely soothing to my nerves, so I've nothing to do but fold my hands and let myself be made comfortable.

Wednesday, 2d Aug. London.

To Westminster Abbey. A gloomy old place with tombs and statues, and chapels and stained windows, and old vespers[?] in black gowns. A. was soon tired, but I managed to see most all I wanted, Spencer's tomb, Milton's, Ben Johnson's, Goldsmith's and many other old friends. I picked and pressed a leaf of ivy for mother, and am making a little book of flowers from every place Ive stopped at. One cannot describe the Abbey, it is too vast but one does not forget it and feels the richer all his live, for having seen it. We passed palaces statues, and interesting things all the way and I longed to stop and look &c.

MS: Unlocated; manuscript copy by Bronson at Houghton Library, Harvard University.

1. LMA accompanied Anna Weld and her half brother George on a European trip that lasted from 19 July 1865 to 19 July 1866.

To Ellen Conway

Nice April 15th [1866]

My Dear Mrs Conway.

Many thanks for so kindly & promptly answering my letter. Dr Weld is here & matters are getting settled. I wanted to be off at once but my patient begs for one more week so I shall not be in England till the first week in May as I want a few days in Paris.

I think the room near you at Wimbledon will be the best to begin with, & if it doesn't suit I can look up another. The one near Mrs Taylor[1] I should like very well only I dont need but one room & plate &c is only a bother. I'm very simple in my habits & only want a bed & three meals in some respectable house within walking distance of you & not too far from the sights of London.

If you will engage a room or make some arrangement about my coming the first week in May to the place near you, or any other that seems right to you, at any sum not exceeding a pound a week, I shall be satisfied & thank you very much.

I hate hotels & should like to feel that I could go at once to some little place where it was clean & quiet & within reach of a friendly face or two.

A line addressed to me here for *this* week, or to the care of Madame Dyne 148 Rue de Rivoli Paris, if you write *next* week will inform me where I am to go on reaching London.

I fear I'm troubling you but hope to have it in my power to return the kindness some time.

With best regards to Mr Conway

I am yours truly
L. M. ALCOTT.

P.S.

As I am not "written all over with money, talent or beauty" I may not be able to get at any English hearts,[2] but they cant shut me out of their parks, ruins, castles & streets so I shall get something, & enjoy larks if I cant see poets, & babies & buttercups at Wimbledon if the Queen wont let me in at Windsor.

Our old landlady was French Governess to the Princesses for fourteen years & wishes to give me some letters to her friends at Court so I may get peeps at Royalty if I wish it, which I *dont* particularly. I'd rather see Dickens, Browning & Carlyle than her Majesty & the nine royal children in a row.

L. M. A.

ALS: Brown University Library.

1. The wife of Peter Alfred Taylor of Aubrey House, England, at which LMA stayed while there. LMA did spend "a fortnight at a lovely old place on Wimbledon Common with the Conways" in May (journal entry, Cheney, p. 182).

2. While in England, LMA negotiated for the publication of *Moods*: "I suppose Routledge will send me a copy of 'Moods' when its out. I didn't ask him but think he ought. Did I tell you he had paid me my $25! As Paradise Lost went for £10 I ought to be satisfied with £5 for my *great* work. Oh, the vanity of authors!" (to Mrs. Ellen Conway, [early July 1866], Moncure D. Conway Papers, Rare Book and Manuscript Library, Columbia University).

To Abigail May Alcott

[1?] Jan 1868

A Happy New Year dear Marmee.

Things look promising for the new year. Ford paid $20 for the little tales & wants two every month.[1] Gazette $25 for the "Bells."[2] Loring $100 for the two Proverb stories.[3] Leslie takes all I'll send[4] & Fuller seems satisfied.[5]

So my plan will work well & I shall make my $1000 this year in spite of sickness & worry.[6] Praise the Lord & keep busy, sez I.

I asked Putnam if he wanted a story, & he at once said "yes". So I sent him "The Blue & Grey."[7] He pays $7.00 a page, so there is another iron in the fire. Allyluyer!

I am pretty well & keep so busy I have n't time to be sick. Every one is very clever to me, & I often think as I go looking round, independent, with more work than I can do, & half a dozen publishers asking for tales, of the old times when I went meekly from door to door peddling my first poor little stories, & feeling *so* rich with a $10.

Its clear that Minerva Moody[8] is getting on in spite of many downfalls, & by the time she is a used up old lady of 70 or so she may finish her job & see her family well off. A little late to enjoy much may be, but I guess I shall turn in for my last long sleep with more content, in spite of the mortal weariness, than if I had folded my hands & been supported in elegant idleness, or gone to the devil in fits of despair because things moved so slowly.

Keep all the money I send; pay up every bill, get comforts & enjoy your selves. Let's be merry while we may. And lay up a bit for a rainy day. With which gem from Aristotle I am, in the good old fashioned style, honored madam, your dutiful & affectionate daughter

L. M. ALCOTT.

Regards to Plato. Dont he want new socks? Are his clothes getting shiney?

113

ALS: Houghton Library, Harvard University. Printed: Cheney, pp. 187–188.

1. Daniel Sharp Ford, editor of the *Youth's Companion*, published these stories to which LMA may be referring: "Our Little Newsboy" (18 June 1868; reprinted from the April 1868 *Merry's Museum*), "My Polish Boy" (26 November and 3 December 1868), and "What Fanny Heard" (13 May 1869).

2. "What the Bells Saw and Said" appeared in the 21 December 1867 *Saturday Evening Gazette*.

3. A. K. Loring of Boston published *Kitty's Class Day* in mid-April 1868 and both *Aunt Kipp* and *Psyche's Art* in mid-May. They were collected as *Louisa M. Alcott's Proverb Stories* and published by Loring in mid-May. LMA is probably referring to the last two titles; her journal for 25 February 1868 indicates that she has just written *Kitty's Class Day* (Cheney, p. 198).

4. Both "Taming a Tartar" and "The Baron's Gloves" appeared in four weekly installments, beginning on 30 November 1867 and 20 June 1868, respectively, in *Frank Leslie's Chimney Corner*.

5. Horace B. Fuller, publisher of *Merry's Museum*, which LMA edited from 1868 to 1870.

6. LMA's "Notes and Memoranda" shows her 1868 earnings as $1,573 (Houghton Library, Harvard University).

7. "The Blue and the Gray" appeared in the June 1868 *Putnam's Magazine*, published by George Palmer Putnam.

8. LMA is referring to herself (see Cheney, p. 129).

To Moses Coit Tyler

Boston Jan 5th 1868.

My Dear Mr Tyler.[1]

On my return yesterday from a holiday "lark" I was agreeably surprised to find your letter. It is very good of you not to mind being called a cherub & put in print "jintly" with an irrepressable spinster on the rampage.

But I did have such a good time that day, thanks to my prince of guides,[2] that when I was ordered to write a Sketch I couldn't resist trying to tell the fun of that expedition.[3] As you perceive the last part is an addition, for you & I didn't eat "weal pie" &c, nor visit the Monument. But *I* did with Mr Raets, one of Mrs Travers'[4] young bachelors, & though that trip was like the play of Hamlet minus the Prince, I thought it would make a proper finale for the Dickens Day, & availing myself of the literary license I up & did it.

If Mr Johnson[5] asks for any more I'll give him No 2 of the same sort, for I think the world would enjoy an account of the Professor tapping away at Milton's chimney for a bit of the original brick, & eating gingerbread out of a paper bag in Smithfield, not to mention insinuating himself & *party* into *Charter* House & sundry other famous places by the persuasive power of "the cherubic countenance".

Tell Mrs Gage not to get prophetic for L. M. A. is a chronic spinster, & knew that the Professor was already appropriated, so she could enjoy London with a free mind & find balm for her solitary soul in that memorable mixture of shrines & shillings, history & happiness, mud & metaphysics.

I still cherish the dream of returning for another revel in dear, dirty, delightful London, for I enjoyed myself there more than any where else, & felt at home. Before sailing I'll drop you a line suggesting that you put your University in one pocket, your family in the other, & come too.

I have had several very pleasant letters from Mrs Taylor & the Conways, & from time to time have enjoyed your articles in the Independent.[6] Especially the House of Commons letter, for I wanted it shown up & couldn't do it myself, because, being stowed in the cage, my "vision was limited."

Which remark reminds me that I've heard Dickens read again & though I enjoyed it very much I couldn't set up again the idol who fell with a crash last year in London.[7] Why *will* he wear two rivers of watch guard meandering over his vest, a diamond ring on each hand, curl his grey hair, & come upon the stage with a youthful skip? Oh, why?

I am spending the winter in Boston & having a capital time. If you ever come this way call at "Gamp's Garret" No 6 Hayward Place & "try the cowcumber." With regards to your wife & "the orphans" I am yours truly, in a corner — L. M. ALCOTT.[8]

I'll certainly come on the [manuscript torn] of June next, thank yo[manuscript torn]

ALS: Cornell University Library. Printed: Jessica Tyler Austin, *Moses Coit Tyler* (Garden City, N.Y.: Doubleday, Page, 1911), pp. 31–33 (without postscript).

1. Moses Coit Tyler, who had been in England promoting Dr. Dio Lewis's health regimen, returned to America to become professor of rhetoric and literature at the University of Michigan.

2. Tyler had served as LMA's guide in London, especially to those locales associated with Dickens. Writing to his wife on 15 September 1866, he commented upon LMA's "enthusiasm and appreciation of drollery," and described her as "a jolly Yankee girl, full of the old Nick [the devil] and thoroughly posted on English literature, so that it is great fun to take her about, as she appreciates all the literary associations" (Austin, *Moses Coit Tyler*, p. 31).

3. "A Dickens Day" appeared in the 26 December 1867 *Independent*.

4. After leaving the Taylors', LMA stayed at Mrs. Travers's in Westbourne Grove.

5. Oliver Johnson, managing editor of the *Independent*.

6. Tyler's unsigned "A Phase of the Labor Question in England" appeared in the 2 January 1868 *Independent*.

7. LMA was very disappointed when she heard Dickens read at St. James's Hall, considering him a fake. She writes, in an untitled note in the 21 September 1867 *Boston Commonwealth*, that "youth and comeliness were gone, but the foppishness remained; and the red-faced man, with false teeth, and the voice of a worn-out actor, had his scanty grey hair curled" (p. 1).

8. This closing is crammed into the margin, or corner, of the last page.

To Thomas Niles

Mr Niles

I think "Little Women," had better be the title for No 1. "Young Women," or something of that sort, for No 2, *if* there is a No 2.

Twenty chapters are all that I planned to have & there are but eight more. I dont see how it can be spun out to make twenty four chapters & give you your 400 pages.[1] I will do my best however. I liked the looks of the page which you sent.

We are enjoying the books[2] which accompanied the blocks. "The Earthly Paradise" I particularly like.[3] Sainte Beuve also is very interesting,[4] but I can see how people who know little of the personal history of his celebrated women might feel disappointed at finding portraits & not lives. Jean Ingelow's stories have begun to circulate among my young friends,[5] & the "Black Polyanthus" is the favorite with them all.[6]

With many thanks I am

yours respectfully

L. M. ALCOTT

My sister is at work on "Meg in Vanity Fair" —[7]

ALS: Collection of American Literature, the Beinecke Rare Book and Manuscript Library, Yale University.

1. The first edition of the first volume (Boston: Roberts Brothers, 1868) contained 341 pages and twenty-three chapters. LMA's journal for 15 July 1868 indicates that her manuscript had 402 pages (Cheney, p. 199).

2. All the books LMA refers to were published by Roberts Brothers.

3. *The Earthly Paradise* (1868–1870), a poem by William Morris.

4. Charles-Augustin Sainte-Beuve, *Portraits of Celebrated Women* (1868).

5. *A Sister's Bye-House* (1868), by the English poetess and children's writer Jean Ingelow. LMA had earlier written a blurb for her poetry, praising its "warmth and grace, which goes straight to one's heart, while the music of many of her lines causes them to go singing through one's memory long after the book is closed" (Ingelow, *The High Tide with Notices of Her Poetry* [Boston: Roberts Brothers, 1863], supplement, p. 4).

6. "The Black Polyanthus," a story in Ingelow's *A Sister's Bye-House.*

7. For this illustration, see [mid-July? 1868].

To Thomas Niles

[mid-July? 1868]

Mr Niles.

I send the proof, corrected, also "Meg at Vanity Fair," admiring herself in the glass.[1] I like it, but the engraver may see many faults, & will please point out such as my sister can mend. I hope whoever engraves the blocks wont spoil the pictures & make Meg cross-eyed, Beth with no nose, or Jo with a double chin. They ruined some of Miss Green's lovely designs & much afflicted me.[2]

I send ten more chapters, making the story 402 pages long. Not having the first half by me was rather a disadvantage, as I dont remember it very well, so may have missed some of the threads. Please "make note on if so be."

I don't care for a Preface, but on one of the first pages, as a sort of motto, we fancy having the lines I send, as they give some clue to the plan of the story.[3]

Yours truly
L. M. ALCOTT.

ALS: Fruitlands Museums, Harvard, Massachusetts.
    1. This somewhat freakish illustration, which one hopes is the result of the engraver's poor sense of human anatomy, is in the first volume of *Little Women*, facing p. 135.
    2. Elizabeth B. Greene illustrated LMA's *Morning-Glories, and Other Stories*. In later years, however, LMA's loyalty to Greene wavered, as she wrote Mary Mapes Dodge on 8 October [1874?]: "I like Mrs Innis's drawing better than Miss Greene's. . . . Her children are altogether charming, thier little fat legs captivate me entirely." But, LMA added, "I love E. B. G. & dont mind her infants dropsical heads very much" (Special Collections, Harold B. Lee Library, Brigham Young University).
    3. The lines, starting "Go then, my little book," appear at the beginning of *Little Women*.

To Mary E. Channing Higginson

Concord Oct. 18th [1868]

My Dear Mrs Higginson.

I certainly *will* "write you a few lines" to express my thanks for the friendly letter with which you & Col. Higginson lately honored me, & to tell you how encouraging such expressions of interest are from persons whose commendation is of such value.

I am glad my "Little Women" please you,[1] for the book was very hastily written to order & I had many doubts about the success of my first attempt at a girl's book. The characters were drawn from life, which gives them whatever merit they possess; for I find it impossible to invent anything half so true or touching as the simple facts with which every day life supplies me.

I should very gladly write this sort of story altogether, but, unfortunately, it does n't pay as well as rubbish, a mercenary consideration which has weight with persons who write not from the inspiration of genius but of necessity.

Your husband gave me the praise which I value most highly when he said the little story was "good, & American." Please give him my hearty thanks for the compliment; also for the many helpful & encouraging words which his busy & gifted pen finds time to write so kindly to the young beginners who sit on the lowest seats in the great school where he is one of the best & friendliest teachers.

Should I ever come to Newport I shall try to present to you the bashful, but grateful individual who is

Very truly yours
L. M. ALCOTT.

Your husband asks if American children say "no end". They are learning it from English books & college slang. Laurie, who says it, was lived abroad.

Like "Amy" I am often troubled by my parts of speech, especially *whiches* & *thats* for they never *will* get into thier proper places.

ALS: Henry W. and Albert A. Berg Collection, New York Public Library, Astor, Lenox, and Tilden Foundations.

1. The first volume of *Little Women* was published in early October.

To Thomas Niles

[early 1869]

Mr Niles.

I can only think of the following titles. "Little Women Act Second". "Leaving the Nest. Sequel to Little Women".

Either you like. A jocose friend suggests "Wedding *Marches*" as there is so much pairing off, but I dont approve.

Suggestions gratefully received.[1]

yrs truly

L. M. A.

ALS: Houghton Library, Harvard University. Printed: *LASC*, p. 376.

    1. Niles himself had suggested the title *Little Women* for the first volume (letter to LMA, 16 June 1868, Houghton Library, Harvard University).

To Lucy Larcom

53 Chauncy St.[1]

[January? February? 1869]

My Dear Miss Larcom.[2]

    Lizzie Greene tells me that two of my twice-lost stories have turned up again in spite of Mr Fields' assurance that the house had been searched in vain.[3]

There were twelve, I think, some in verse & some in prose beside four lovely sketches on wood by E. B. G.

Four years ago the first Ms was lost, I rewrote it & the reprehensible Ticknor proceded at once to lose the second Ms, like wise the blocks. Where at Mr Fields made me the princely offer of resigning all claims to the poor little stories, & leaving me free to re write & dispose of of them as I liked.

I should be glad to do so as these small affairs command good prices now, & if the Mss. turn up I should like to reclaim them as I have no copies & but little leisure to do the work for the third time.

I have Mr Fields leave to reclaim them & will do so if you will tell me when I can call or send for them.

May I ask the favour of you to save any other waifs of mine which may be found among the ruins of the Ticknorian dynasty? I shall be very grateful for the kindness as my own researches only end in wrath & vexation of spirit.

Respectfully yours

L. M. ALCOTT.

ALS: Overbury Collection, Barnard College Library.

    1. LMA was staying in a boardinghouse at 53 Chauncy Street, Boston, at this time.

    2. Lucy Larcom, co-editor of *Our Young Folks*, published by Fields, Osgood.

3. Probably a reference to *Jamie's Wonder Book* [*Will's Wonder Book*] (see *Louisa's Wonder Book — An Unknown Alcott Juvenile*, ed. Madeleine B. Stern (Mount Pleasant: Central Michigan University, 1975), pp. 11–12.

To Alfred Whitman

Boston Jan. 6th / 69

Dear Alf.

I have planned to write to you dozens of times but work prevented, now I really *will*, though piles of Mss. lie waiting for my editorial eye. Dont you ever think old Sophy forgets her Dolphus, why bless your heart I put you into my story as one of the best & dearest lads I ever knew! "Laurie" is you & my Polish boy[1] "jintly". You are the sober half & my Ladislas (whom I met abroad) is the gay whirligig half, he was a perfect dear.

All my little girl-friends are madly in love with Laurie & insist on a sequel, so I've written one which will make you laugh, especially the pairing off part. But I didn't know how to settle my family any other way & I wanted to disappoint the young gossips[2] who vowed that Laurie & Jo *should* marry. Authors take dreadful liberties, but you wont mind being a happy spouse & a proud papa, will you?

I am such a busy old bee I find no time for pleasure not even for writing letters, so every one is neglected & I am burdened with a perpetual sense of guilt. But publishers come roaring after me if I dont do my work, & money tempts my mercenary mind, so I scratch away hoping a time of rest will come in the course of ages.

I am so glad to hear how happy you are, & should dearly love to see you in your own home. I cant realize that my boy is married[3] & has a little Tetterby, I can only think of you as sober Alf who used to come & have confidences on the couch, a la Laurie, & be very fascinating without knowing it. If any thing in those old times does you good & makes thier memory sweet I am truly glad, for it gives an added charm to have to go halves in it with some one who has n't got any, & I should very much like to find another Alf to fill the empty place there, if that was possible.

I'm fond of boys, as you may have discovered, & always want one some where handy, so, as you say you haven't grown up (which is a great comfort to me) I wish you'd come East & be our Alf again, if Mrs Mary dont object.

How jolly it would be to have a good old-time gossip all together. I wonder if we *could* go back & be Dolphus, Sophy, Anthony William & Tilly

Slow boy again. I'm afraid, your baby, John's big boys, Nan's ear trumpet & my venerable face would destroy the illusion. Never mind, hearts dont grow old & we'd "be friendly" just the same. Good by, my dear boy, write to me & you shall truly get an answer from your ever loving old SOPHY.

ALS: Houghton Library, Harvard University. Printed (with partial facsimile of the manuscript): Whitman 11, 6 (partial).

    1. Ladislas Wisniewski, whom she had met in November 1865 at the Pension Victoria in Vevey, Switzerland.

    2. LMA originally wrote "little dears" before canceling it and inserting "young gossips."

    3. Whitman had married Mary Brown, whose father, John S. Brown, had been at Brook Farm, in April 1867.

To Samuel Joseph May

Boston Jan 22ond [1869]

Dear Uncle.[1]

Thank you for your note & kind thought of me. I shall be very grateful for any thing from Grandpa's book. There is a constant demand for short articles & I particularly like to dip [in]to other people's memories [for] incidents, anecdotes & [re]collections. I've used up [al]l the stories you gave me [&] long to pick your mind of more, do save up all the plums you get for they have the right flavor.

Fuller says your subscription for last year's "Merry" is not paid, but dont mind such a small thing, let the "Editor" send you a copy & play its all right.

Merry is not what I wish it was, but little Fuller does his best on a small capital & hopes to improve. If you know of any one who wields a sprightly & sensible pen pray ask them to drop us a line now & then, for Fuller mildly suggests th[at] I should write the wh[ole] magazine, which was not in the bargain, & [I] cant afford it being mercen[ary.]

I am getting on ver[y] well for a "shiftless Alcott" & after paying up the debts was able to give S. E. S. two hundred out of the three that Roberts gave me for the first 3000 of "Little Women".[2] The fifth thousand is underway I believe,[3] & he says as it goes so well there is no reason why it should not run to ten thousand. It is selling in England,[4] & though I get no copy right it helps to make "my works" known.

The sequel is in press,[5] & I often have letters asking [w]hen it will be out. Some [pr]etty little letters from [ch]ildren please me very much, for they are the best critics of such things. I [d]ont like sequels, & dont think No 2 will be as popular as No 1, but publishers are very *perverse* & wont let authors

121

have thier way so my little women must grow up & be married off in a very stupid style.

Father is enjoying the success of his book,[6] & also of his conversations which have done well,[7] so it really seems as if the dear man's serene patience was to be rewarded after thirty years of neglect.

Mother is happy in the turtle dove's nest, & May busy with her pupils, [I] scribble all I dare, & w[e] all indulge in the hope th[at] the "Pathetic family" is comi[ng] out right side up after all.

I saw your Joe[8] at the Radical Club[9] yesterday looking very well. Tom Greele & wife are on & cousin Lizzie better.[10]

With love to all I am, dear Uncle ever yours afffectionately Lu.

ALS: Houghton Library, Harvard University. The manuscript is torn; missing words or letters are supplied in brackets.

1. Samuel Joseph May, Mrs. Alcott's brother.

2. Bronson was notorious for not caring where funds for the subsistence of his family came from, often cheerfully accepting "gifts" from his father-in-law and Emerson. In her journal for January 1869, LMA wrote: "Paid up all the debts, thank the Lord! — every penny that money can pay, — and now I feel as if I could die in peace" (Cheney, p. 202).

3. The Roberts Brothers cost books show that 4,500 copies of the first volume of *Little Women* had been printed by the end of 1868. LMA is perhaps referring to the sixth printing of 1,000 copies done in February.

4. Sampson Low of London published the first volume of *Little Women* in early December 1868.

5. In her journal for January 1869, LMA noted: "Sent the sequel of 'L.W.' to Roberts on New Year's Day" (Cheney, p. 202).

6. Bronson's *Tablets*, also published by Roberts Brothers, was issued in September 1868.

7. Bronson wrote to William Torrey Harris on 15 January 1869: "My friends say the Conversations have been a great success" (*Letters*, p. 458).

8. Probably Joseph Edward May, LMA's uncle's son.

9. The Radical Club, founded by the Sargents in Boston, brought the leading people of the times together between 1867 and 1880 for discussions of literature and religion (see Mary F. Sargent, *Sketches and Reminiscences of the Radical Club* [Boston: James R. Osgood, 1880]).

10. Cousin Lizzie is probably Elizabeth Sewall Willis Wells.

To Ellen Conway

Boston Feb 9th [1869]

My Dear Mrs Conway.

I have been thinking I'd write for some time, but work or illness has prevented & it has been put off too long. A very kind letter from Mrs Taylor lately received reminded me of my negligence. I virtuously set about repairing it.

I have heard of you frequently through the Sanborns who always have pleasant news to tell us of your doings, especially little Milly whom I long to see. I suppose Eustace is "growed out of knowledge" & Dana isn't afraid of people now.[1]

I was glad to hear from Mrs T. that you were settled at Notting Hill with your father & mother & the Smallys near by.[2] I remember Mrs S. as Phebe Garnaut, Mrs Phillips' adopted daughter.[3] I hope Mrs Travers still flourishes for I recommended my friend, Kitty Sargent, to go there for a while till she looks about her. She is a nice quiet soul, plays finely, paints, & enjoys our sort of people. Mr Conway will remember John T. Sargent who lost his church by exchanging with Parker in the old days.[4] Kitty is his eldest daughter & goes to London to study painting &c.

May & I are having a jolly winter boarding in Boston, she teaching drawing & studying the same with Wm Hunt,[5] I writing, editing & poking about in my usual style. Father & mother are with Anna who is keeping house just out of town. Apple Slump is left to its fate till spring & father is getting weaned from his rustic fences, his Emerson & his apple-bin. He has been talking, preaching, publishing & disporting himself gaily in the public eye which, after ignoring him for thirty years, suddenly beams graciously upon him.

I still live in hopes of leaving & having larks again on English ground, but must bide my time. The rainy day rambles about London were pleasantly recalled this winter by meeting Mr Tyler, who was as jolly & "cherubic" as ever. His mother & sister in law are in Boston & I see a good deal of them. He likewise introduced me to Theodore Tilton,[6] who dont seem to be grown up yet. After one call he, T. T., came strolling in one rainy slippery Sunday eve about nine o clock saying he was home sick, hungry & blue, would I come out for a walk & then take supper at the Parker House? It struck me as rather funny, but I went, & after coasting about the streets under an umbrella as deliberately as if it was a balmy summer's eve, we turned into Parkers & had a friendly dish o tea. Theodore talked in a steady stream all the time about every thing under the sun — Muller[7] Madonnas, beer, religion, prize-fighters, his children & eternal damnation. It was as good as a play & I enjoyed it all the more because John Dwight & Henry Denny[8] at thier tables were evidently wondering — "What the deuce Louisa Alcott was doing drinking wine with a gay young party in a public house at ten o clock on a Sunday night."

We left before eleven & I dont know as Henry Denny has finished his supper yet. He camped out with us last summer & took only 72 different articles for use & comfort during four days of roughing it in the bush. One was a bootjack to drain on after bathing. Was n't that romantic & characteristic? He was much afflicted last Oct by the marriage of my cousin Carrie May[9] who has been one of his flames for years. He didn't wish to marry her himself but he didn't want any one else to do it, & the poor dog in the manger took to a velocipede I believe as the only solace for his woe. Is n't he funny?

I hope you like gossip for I've filled my letter with it, & hope for some in return.

Remember me most kindly to Mr Conway, present my respectful regards to the boys, & if you can make up your mind to it kiss little Milly for yours affectionately

L. M. ALCOTT

I was going to send you my "Little Women" but F. B. S. did so & I thought it would look peacocky in me & I didn't. May desires to be remembered to you all.

ALS: Moncure D. Conway Papers, Rare Book and Manuscript Library, Columbia University.
    1. Mildred Conway, her daughter, and Eustace and Dana Conway, her sons.
    2. Notting Hill Square in London, where the Conways had a house; George W. Smalley, English writer and friend of the Conways.
    3. Phoebe Garnaut, adopted as their daughter by Wendell Phillips and his wife in 1849, married Smalley in 1860.
    4. In 1844, when exchanges with the radical preacher Theodore Parker were banned by the Unitarian establishment, James T. Sargent invited him into his pulpit, causing the Executive Committee of the Unitarian Association to force Sargent's resignation.
    5. William Morris Hunt, the artist, under whom May Alcott studied in Boston.
    6. Theodore Tilton, editor of the *Independent*.
    7. Charles Louis Müller, a French artist under whom May had studied.
    8. John Sullivan Dwight, a former Brook Farmer and editor of *Dwight's Journal of Music*; Henry Gardiner Denny, a lawyer friend of Conway's since their college days.
    9. Caroline May married Alexander Henry Davis in October 1868.

To Elizabeth Powell

Concord Mar. 20th [1869]

Dear Miss Powell. [1]

I feel highly honored that my stupid "Little Women" have been admitted to your College, & hope they will behave themselves in such learned society for the poor things have had few advantages & are rather bashful, like thier Ma. Pray make them useful for the cure of head aches or any other ill which they can lighten, that being the best use that can be made of the little book.

A sequel will be out early in April, & like all sequels will probably disappoint or disgust most readers, for publishers wont let authors finish up as they like but insist on having people married off in a wholesale manner which much afflicts me. "Jo" should have remained a literary spinster but so many enthusiastic young ladies wrote to me clamorously demanding that she should marry Laurie, *or* somebody, that I didnt dare to refuse & out of perversity went & made a funny match for her. I expect vials of wrath to be poured out upon my head, but rather enjoy the prospect.

If you ever come this way remember Concord & pay us a visit. We are all to be at home in the summer, having spent the winter in Boston, & all will be glad to see you, especially father, who considers Miss Powell one of his "fine maids," as he calls his favorites.

With thanks for your kind reception of my daughters I am

yrs truly
L. M. ALCOTT.

ALS: Elizabeth Powell Bond Collection, Friends Historical Library of Swarthmore College.

    1. Elizabeth Powell, who later became the dean of Swarthmore College, was from 1866 to 1870 an instructor in calisthenics at Vassar College. She had, according to Ellen Emerson, come to Concord in the spring of 1865 "to lead the Gymnasium" (*The Letters of Ellen Tucker Emerson*, ed. Edith E. W. Gregg, 2 vols. [Kent, Ohio: Kent State University Press, 1982], 1:320).

To Elizabeth B. Greene

Concord April first [1869].

Dear Little Measles.

I've been sitting in the lap of luxury at Watertown for a week, eating strawberries, picking "ot-ouse" flowers & drinking wine in the most abandoned manner. I had a little box of goodies done up for you & was coming for a social revel on your bed, but it rained so I was afeared to go in the cars & the Adamses[1] couldn't send me in as they had only nine horses eating thier heads off in the stable. I was mad but smiled sweetly & said "Damn!" in private.

When I got home I found your jolly epistle & was glad, for I always like to see your saucy letters a curling up thier tails & prancing just as you do. There never was such a wandering owl as you are! I never know on which perch I shall find you next. But as long as you can roll your eyes at me & go larks it dont matter. I'm proper glad you have got out of your vortex & are coming round so well. "Mind your eye," is the most appropriate piece of slang I can think of just now. Dont go to Imping too soon. I'll see if the "bugs & birds & beastises" will furnish something woodsy & fine enough for the jolly little picters.

Oh, Betsey! such trials as I have had with that Billings no mortal creter knows! He went & drew Amy a fat girl with a pug of hair, sitting among weedy shrubbery with a light-house under her nose, & a mile or two off a scrubby little boy on his stomach in the grass looking cross, towzly, & about 14 years old! It was a blow, for that picture was to be the gem of the lot. I bundled it right back & blew Niles up to such an extent that I thought he'd never come down again. But he did, oh bless you, yes, as brisk & bland as ever, & set Billings to work again. You will shout when you see the new one for the man followed my directions & made (or tried to) Laurie "a mixture of Apollo, Byron, Tito & Will Greene."[2] Such a baa lamb! hair parted in the middle, big eyes, sweet nose, lovely moustache & cunning hands; straight out of a bandbox & no more like the real Teddy than Ben Franklin. I wailed but let go for the girls are clamoring & the book cant be delayed. Amy is pretty & the scenery good but — my Teddy, oh my Teddy!

Mrs Parker is a dear old soul — & I'll certainly go & see her if the snow *ever* melts & the sun *ever* shines. We can go flummin on runners by July perhaps. Play we do? I'm very well barring a deaf ear, no voice, newralagy in my legs, & a small Vesuvius in full irruption on each thumb. But my brains will work & I can hold a pen so Oh be joyful! Drop a line now & then its so relishing.

Ever yours
ALCOTT.

ALS: Louisa May Alcott Collection, Barrett Library, University of Virginia Library. Printed: Carroll A. Wilson, *Thirteen Author Collections of the Nineteenth Century*, eds. Jean C. S. Wilson and David A. Randall, 2 vols. (New York: Scribners, 1950), 1:8–9.
    1. The merchant Alvin Adams and his wife were friends of the Alcott family.
    2. Possibly Tito Melema, a character in George Eliot's *Romola* (1863), and William Batchelder Greene, who had attended Bronson's Conversations.

To the Springfield Republican

Latest News From Concord

Nurse Periwinkle Frees Her Mind.
To the Editor of The Republican: —
"The Titan minds his own affair."
Emerson

As it has become the fashion to make a yearly report of the condition of Concord and its inhabitants, and as no gossip concerning this immortal town seems to be considered too trivial for the public ear, we feel it our duty to add to said yearly report lately published, the last rumor afloat.

It is said that a new hotel is about to be established, called "The Sphinx's Head,"[1] where pilgrims to this modern Mecca can be entertained in the most hospitable and appropriate style. Walden water, aesthetic tea, and "wine that never grew in the belly of the grape"[2] will constantly be on tap for the refreshment of thirsty guests. Wild apples by the bushel, orphic acorns by the peck, and Hawthorne's pumpkins, in the shape of pies, will be furnished at philosophic prices. The house will be filled with Alcott's rustic furniture, the beds made of Thoreau's pine boughs, and the sacred fires fed from the Emersonian wood-pile. Boats for the week on the Concord River will always be in readiness to waft the eager pilgrim over the reposeful stream, whose proper name is Mosquitoquid.[3] Telescopes will be provided for the gifted eyes which desire to watch the soarings of the Oversoul, when visible, and lassoes with which the expert may catch untamed hermits, or poets on the wing. Samples of Autumn Tints, Mosses from the Manse, Rhodora, and herbs from the Garden, will be supplied gratis;[4] also photographs of the faces divine which have conferred immortality upon one of the dullest little towns in Massachusetts.

Guides will be in attendance to show the most famous portions of the glorified sand-bank, and a daily bulletin will appear telling the most favorable hours for beholding the various lions — something in this style, perhaps: —

"Emerson will walk at 4 p.m.

"Alcott will converse from 8 a.m. till 11 p.m.

"Channing may be seen with the naked eye at sunset.

"The new Hermit will grind his meal at noon, precisely.

"The ladies of Concord will not be exhibited on Saturdays."

The need of an establishment like this has been long and deeply felt, especially since each spring brings, with the robins, a flock of reporters, who like the brisk and inquisitive birds, roost upon Concordian fences, chirp on Concordian door-steps, and hop over Concordian hills and fields, scratching vigorously, as if hoping to unearth a new specimen from what is popularly believed to be the hot-bed of genius. If these early birds get no worms, it is not their fault, as the inhabitants of this much-enduring village will testify; the feminine portion, especially, for to them the words "private life," "sanctity of home," "domestic seclusion," are a hollow mockery during six months of the year.

Having been taught that home is a woman's proper sphere, and that publicity should be abhorrent to her delicate soul, the trials of these delicate ladies may be imagined, when they find themselves living in a lantern, as it were, illuminated by the radiance of their lords, and held up for the inspection of the public eye. There seems to be no mode of escape for them, no matter how willingly they would relinquish even the faintest ray of the reflected lustre, for they get booked whether they will or no. The servant of the public, or the ardent admirer, demands an interview with Jove or Hermes, lingers to see the god feed, and Juno *must* appear, regardless of inefficient Ganymedes, washing day, and crying babies. Diana steps into the garden *en deshabille* to pick peas, and is startled by the appearance of a bland young gentleman, who, while asking his way to Norridge, takes mental notes and produces a pen and ink photograph of her, curl-papers and all.

Or Psyche, repairing to her rural bower, finds, not her Cupid, but an artistic stranger who tranquilly announces that he has "come to sketch the abode of genius," and proceeds to do it.

No spot is safe, no hour is sacred, and fame is beginning to be considered an expensive luxury by the Concordians. Their plaints are pathetic, though many of the performances behind the scenes are decidedly comic; for, following the examples of the Great Tormented, some of these haunted ones step out of the back window when the hunter enters the front door; others take refuge in the garret, while the more timid flee into the wilderness and do not emerge until a bell is rung to inform them that the peril is past. It is whispered that one irascible spinster, driven to frenzy by twenty-eight visitors in a week, proposed to get a garden engine and "play away" whenever a suspicious stranger was seen entering her gates. This bold idea was not accepted however, hospitality being one of the ruling passions of the Marthas[5] who are in danger of sinking under the accumulated horrors of spring cleaning and spring visitors.

The plan of setting up a new hotel originated with these amiable ladies, and their first exercise of the elective franchise, will be to vote which of the philosophers shall open "The Sphinx's Head." We heartily wish them success, though we much fear that their patronage will exceed their profits.

Tribulation Periwinkle

Concord, May 4, 1869.

MS: Unlocated. Printed: *Springfield Republican*, 5 May 1869, p. 2; Joel Myerson, "Louisa May Alcott on Concord: A New 'Tribulation Periwinkle' Letter," *Concord Saunterer* 17, no. 1 (March 1984): 42–43.

1. Named after Emerson's poem "The Sphinx" (1841).
2. "Bring me wine, but wine which never grew / in the belly of the grape," the first two lines of Emerson's poem "Bacchus" (1847).
3. A pun on the insect-infested Musketaquid River.

4. References to Thoreau's "Autumnal Tints" (1862), Hawthorne's *Mosses from an Old Manse* (1846), and Emerson's poems "The Rhodora" (1839) and "Days" (1857), especially the seventh and ninth lines of the last.

5. Martha was the patron saint of housewives.

To Roberts Brothers

Messrs. Roberts Brothers, Gentlemen: Many thanks for the check which made my Christmas an unusually merry one.[1]

After toiling so many years along the up-hill road, always a hard one to women writers, it is peculiarly grateful to me to find the way growing easier at last; with pleasant little surprises blossoming on either side, and the rough places made smooth by the courtesy and kindness of those who have proved themselves "friends" as well as "publishers."

With best wishes for the coming year,

I am, yours truly,

L. M. ALCOTT.

Boston, Dec. 28th, 1869.

MS: Unlocated. Printed: "Miss Alcott and Her Publishers," *Boston Daily Evening Transcript*, 29 December 1869, p. 2; Cheney, pp. 202–203.

1. Roberts Brothers sent LMA $2,500 in royalties with its letter of 25 December 1869 (Houghton Library, Harvard University).

To Abigail May Alcott

Morlaix April 14th 1870.

Dearest Marmee,

Having got our "poise" a bit by a day and night on land, I begin at once to scribble to you, as I mean to keep a letter on hand all the time, and send them off as fast as they are done.

We had a twelve day's passage owing to a double screw which they were trying and which delayed us, though it is safer than one. The weather was cold and rainy, and the sea rough, so I only went up once or twice, and kept warm in my den most of the time. After the first two days, I didn't feel sick, except my head as usual. I slept, ate, ruminated and counted the hours.

May poked about more, and was liked by all. There were no beaux except fast N.Y. men, so she had no flirtations. Alice was not sick at all and very kind to us, as were the Howes.[1]

We got to Brest about noon Wednesday. Alice and I got our trunks through the Custom House, and after some squabbling with the men got all aboard for Morlaix[2] which is a curious old place worth seeing. It was a lovely day, warm as our June, and we had a charming trip of three hours through a country already green and flowery. We reached our Hotel all right, and after a nice dinner had baths and went to bed. May's room being some way from mine, she came and bunked in with me in my little bed and we slept.

To-day is lovely, warm, and I am sitting at an open window looking on the square, enjoying the queer sights and sounds, for the air resounds with the rattle of many wooden shoes on the stones. Market women sit all about selling queer things, among which are snails: they buy them by the pint, pick them out with a pin like nuts and seem to relish them mightily.

We went out this A.M. after breakfast and took a stroll over the queer town. May was in heaven and kept having raptures over the gables, the turrets with storks on them, the fountains, people and churches. She is now sketching the tower of St. Melanie, with a crowd of small boys round her enjoying the sight and criticising the work. It don't seem very new to me, but I enjoy it, and feel pretty well. My bones only ache at night, and then not badly. May is very well, and Alice kind and pleasant. We are to study French every day when we settle, and I am to do the mending &c. for Alice, who is to talk for us, and make our bargains. So far we go well together, and I think shall have no trouble, for A. is [a] true lady, and my other A. was not.[3]

Tomorrow we go onto Lamballe where we take the diligence to Dinan[4] fourteen miles further, and there settle for some weeks. — I wish the boys could see the funny children here in little wooden shoes like boats, the girls in blue cloth caps, aprons, and shawls just like the women, and the boys in funny hats and sheepskin jackets.

Now I must go and get May who can't speak a word of French, and has a panic if any one speaks to her. The beggars afflict her, and she wants to give them money on all occassions.

This P.M. we go for a drive to see all there is, as neither Alice nor I are great walkers. "Adoo" till by and by. I wish I could send you this balmy day.

MS: Unlocated; manuscript copy by Bronson at Houghton Library, Harvard University. Printed: Cheney, pp. 212–214.

1. LMA, May Alcott, and Alice Bartlett had left New York aboard the French steamer *Lafayette* on 2 April 1870 and had arrived in Brest, France, on 14 April. May had agreed to

accompany twenty-four-year-old Alice only if LMA could go also. Dr. Estes Howe was treasurer of the Cambridge Gas Light Company.

2. Morlaix, France, is about four miles from the English Channel.

3. Alice Bartlett and Anna Weld.

4. Dinan, France, an ancient town on the left bank of the Rance.

To Abigail May Alcott(?)

Dinan, Sunday, 17th April [1870].

Here we are all settled at our first neat stopping place and are in clover as you will see when I tell you how plummy and lovely it is.

We left Morlaix Friday at 8 A.M. and were so amazed at the small bill presented us that we could'nt praise the town enough. You can judge of the cheapness of things when I say that my share of the expenses from Brest here, including two days at a Hotel, car, 'bus, and diligence fare, fees and every thing, was $8.00. The day was divine, and we had a fine little journey to Lamballe where the fun began; for instead of a big Diligence, we found only a queer ramshackle thing, like an insane carry all, with a wooden boot and queer perch for the driver. Our four trunks were piled on behind and tied on with old ropes, our bags stowed in a wooden box on top, and ourselves inside with a fat Frenchman. The humpbacked driver, "ya hooped" to the horses, and away we clattered at a wild pace, all feeling dead sure that something would happen, for the old thing bounced and swayed awfully, the trunks were in danger of tumbling off, and to our dismay we soon discovered that the big Frenchman was tipsy. He gabbled to Alice as only a tipsy Frenchman could, quoted Poetry, said he was Victor Hugo's best friend, and a child of nature, that English Ladies were all divine, but too cold, for when he pressed Alice's hand, she told him it was not allowed in England, and he was overwhelmed with remorse, bowed, sighed, rolled his eyes, and told her that he drank much ale, because it flew to his head and gave him "Commercial Ideas." I never saw any thing so perfectly absurd, as it was, and after we got used to it we laughed ourselves sick over the lark. You ought to have seen us and our turnout, tearing over the road at a break-neck pace, pitching, creaking, and rattling. The funny driver, hooting at the horses, who had their tails done up in chignons, blue harness and strings of bells. The drunken man warbling, exhorting, and lanquishing at us all by turns, while Alice headed him off with great skill. I sat a mass of English dignity and coolness suffering alternate agonies of anxiety and amusement, and May, who tied her head up in a bundle, and looked like a wooden image. It was rich, and when we took up, first a peasant woman in wooden shoes and a fly-away cap, and then a red-nosed priest smoking a long pipe, we were a supurb spectacle. In this style, we banged into Dinan, stopped at the gate, and were dumped, bag and baggage in the Square. Finding Madame Coste's[1] man was not for us we hired a man to bring our trunks up for us. To our great amazement an oldish woman, who was greasing the wheels of a diligence, came, and catching up our big trunks, whisked them into two broad carts, and taking one trotted down the street at a fine pace followed by the man with the other. That was the finishing touch, and we went laughing after them through the great arched gate into the quaintest, prettiest, most romantic town I ever saw. Narrow streets with overhanging gables, distracting roofs, windows and porches, carved beams, and every sort of richness. The strong old lady beat the man, and finally landed us close by another old gate at a charming house fronting the south, overlooking a lovely green valley, full of gardens, blooming plum and peach trees, windmills, and a ruined castle, at sight of which we all skipped. Madame Costé recieved us with rapture, for Alice brought a letter from Mrs Lodge who stayed here, and was the joy of the old lady's soul. We were in great luck, for being early in the season, she had three rooms left, and we nabbed them at once. A salon with old oak walls and wardrobes, blue damask furniture, a fireplace, sunny windows and quaint furniture. A little room out of it for Alice, and upstairs a larger room for May and me, with two beds draped in green chintz, and carved big wardrobe &c. and best of all, a sunny window toward the valley. For these rooms and our board we each pay $1.00 a day, and I call that cheap. It would be worth that to get the sun and air alone, for it is like June, and we sit about with open windows, flowers in the fields, birds singing, and every thing lovely and spring like.

We took possession at once and dressed for dinner at six. We were then presented to our fellow boarders, Madame Forney a buxom widow, her son Gaston, a handsome Frenchy youth of 23, and her daughter, a homely girl of 20, who is to be married here on the 3rd May.[2] After a great bowing and scraping, we had a funny fish dinner, it being Good Friday. When they found we did'nt speak French, they were "desolated," and begged us to learn at once, which we solemnly vowed to do. Gaston knew English, so May at once began to teach him more, and the ice being broken we got gay and friendly at once. I could understand them pretty well, but cant talk, and Alice told them that I was forbidden to say much on account of my throat. This will give me a chance to get a fair start. May pegs away at her grammar, and with that and the elegant Gaston, she will soon begin to "parley-voo."

After dinner, we were borne to the great salon, where a fire, lights and a piano appeared. Every one sat round and gabbled except the Alcotts, who looked and laughed. Madamoiselle Forney played, and then May convulsed them by singing some "Chants Amerique" which they thought very lively and droll. They were all attention and devotion to Madame Coste, a tall old lady with whiskers, [who] kept embracing Alice and beaming at us in her great content at being friends of "Chere Madame Lodge". Alice told them that I was a celebrated authoress, and May a very fine artist, and we were beamed at more than ever. — Being tired, we turned in early, after a jolly time in our own little salon, eating chocolate and laying plans.

Saturday, we had coffee in bed at 8, walked on the ramparts and in the Park under the old tavern till 10 when we had breakfast; then till dinner at 6, we rampaged about having raptures about every thing. I can't tell you how lovely it is! The climate *must* cure me, for they say throat and lung invalids always get well here. The air is dry and soft, the town lies high, and we are in the sunny country part. Shall live cheaply, learn French, enjoy my life, and grow fat and strong. D. V.[3]

Private

I think this is to be one of our lucky years, and this trip a success if things go on as well as they have begun, for not a single hitch have we had from the time we left Boston. It don't seem possible that a fortnight could do so much, and put us in such an entirely new scene.

May is in a state of unutterable like bliss, and keeps flying out with her big sketch book, and coming back in despair, for every thing is so pictur-esque she don't know where to begin. This is a good chance for her in every way. No one speaks English in the house but Alice, and she threatens to talk only French to us, which will be awful but useful. Two pleasant half English ladies live near, and I shall rush to them when I'm exhausted by "the baby talk," as I call French.

Our house is on the walk close to the great tower of Anne of Brittanny, and the public walk which is made on what used to be the moat. Ask some one to lend you a "Murry's Guide" and you can read all about the place. There are a good many English here, and we shall come to know some of them, I don't doubt, which will complete our task and give a relish. To-morrow Gaston is to escort us to the mineral waters on donkeys, and we shall be an imposing sight as you may suppose.

Direct your letters to me, "Care of Mademoiselle Coste, place St. Louis, Dinan," for the present. It will save a postage, and we shall stay a month at least.

Good bye, God bless you all, May sends lots of love, and so does

Your Lu.

MS: Unlocated; manuscript copy by Bronson at Houghton Library, Harvard University. Printed: Cheney, pp. 214–217 (partial).

1. Madame Coste owned the pension on the Place St. Louis in Dinan, where the three stayed.

2. Bronson originally wrote "pretty" and then canceled it and inserted "homely." About Madame Forney and her family, LMA wrote to Mary Sewall on 24 April 1870 that "their ways amuse us mightily": "The girl is to be married next week to a man whom she has seen twice, and never talked to but an hour [in] her life. She writes to him what her mother dictates and says she should be ashamed to love him before they were married. Her wedding clothes absorb her entire mind and her Jules will get a pretty doll when he takes [her] . . . to wife. Gaston, the son, puts on blazé airs, though only 22, and languishes at May, for they can't talk as he don't know English, nor she French." Jules Clomadoc, Alice Forney's fiancé, was described by LMA in a letter to her family of 24–27 April 1870: "[he] . . . amuses us very much. He is a tiny man in uniform with a red face, big moustache and blue eyes. He thinks he talks English, and makes such very funny mistakes. He asked us if we had been to 'promenade on monkeys,' meaning donkeys, and called the Casino 'the establishment of dance.' He addresses all his attentions to the Ma, and only bows to his future wife who admires her diamonds and is contented." A long description of the wedding is in LMA's letter to her family of 6 May 1870 (manuscript copies by Bronson at Houghton Library, Harvard University).

3. *Deo volente*, God willing.

To the Alcott Family

May 13th[–14, 1870] Dinan.

Dearest folks,

No letters yet, and as I get letters from T[homas]. N[iles]. and Baker,[1] I don't see where yours are. I think the direction has puzzled some of the stupid Postmasters, and that you had better direct to Munroe and Co. no. 7, Rue Scribe, Paris, for all the letters so directed come right. I *know* you have written, and it breaks my heart to think of my letters stowed away somewhere. I'd rather pay lots of extra postage than not have my lawful letters.

I have but two bits of news: one is I've got a new dress, gray silk, costing 90 cts per yard, thick, silvery, and very pretty in the piece. Alice and I got ours together in a very nice way. Finding that there was a Paris dressmaker here, and that we could send to a Paris house for patterns and get silks cheap, we did so. And having selected our dresses they were sent us Express free, and are to be made up next week in walking suits all so fine. I wish I could send you and Nan each one like it.

My other bit of news is, that I have got a Dr. My poor old leg was so bad, I couldn't bear it any longer. After two weeks of misery, and hearing and hearing there was an excellent English Dr. here, I rushed off to him one day, and asked for something to make me sleep. I found Dr. Kane[2] a hand-some hearty grayheaded Englishman who was very sensible in his ideas, and gave me some good advice about diet, wine &c. He said as the Drs. have done that it was rhuematism of the membrane next the bone, and that it was more painful than dangerous. He gave me quieting pill, and some Iodine of Potash, recommended sleep and mattress, a little wine, and lots of sleep. Not to walk at all, but to drive a good deal, and get up my strength without medicine, if possible. This is a good healthy plan, he says, and we like it, so I guess we shall stay another month. Dr. K. is very kind and jolly, and said when he found I'd been a army nurse, that he should esteem it an honor to cure me. He is a rich bachelor and the girls call him my beau, and plague me about him. Madlle Coste knows him and his niece, and has asked them here to breakfast next week.

But the point of the joke is that I'm much better. My leg lets me sleep, and I eat and feel quite chipper again. The weather has been cold, and I tried to walk too much, and so had a bad time. Now I drive and, as Alice goes halves, it is cheap for us both.

We drove to Guildo[3] yesterday to see if we should like it for July. It is a queer little town on the sea shore, with ruins near by, bright houses and lots of boats. Rooms a franc a day, and food very cheap. The man of the house, a big brown Peggotty sailor, has a sloop and promised the girls as much sailing as they liked. We may go, but our plans are very vague, and one day we say we will go to one place, and the next to another, and shall probably end by staying where we are.

We are all growing fat, and Alice sasses me about it. She is much better, and her deaf ear is well. May sleeps like a boa constrictor, and is in clover generally. We laugh so much, we ought to [be] plump as porpoises.

I had a letter from P. Baker saying he was to be married the 9th May, and go at once to Germany. He said he had written to John about the photographs but got no reply. If there is any fuss, or it is not profitable, just stop the whole thing and let Allen howl.

Niles is devoted in sending me notices and bits of news about my works.[4] If people knew how O. F. G. was written, in what a hurry and pain and woe, they would wonder that there was any grammar at all. I'll get M. R. Sewall to read the next M.S. and then every morsel will be right.

I havn't written a thing as yet and don't feel as if I ever should.[5] Ive got so lazy and sozzle round all day and don't do a thing. If that is what I need, I'm in a fair way to get enough of it. The girls are ever so good to me, and Alice confided to May that she liked me very much. May and she are great cronies, and I make fine duenna for I let them do as they like in everything. Alice sends a fine pen and ink sketch of me as I now appear: for the minute, my legs behave, I pick up and we train like mad. Alice is very funny and has just grabbed May, and cut off a bit of her hair. A. is the strongest and she whacks May round like a doll, "for exercise therapy" she says. Dr. Kane is to lend me a boat and then they can let of[f] their steam in that way.

Sat. May 14th 11 A.M.

I have nothing to say, so must scribble off a few odds and ends and despatch the letter. I shall pay the postage so that there can be no mistake. Let me hear if you have to pay it over again, and if you have got four or five from us.

Dr Kane and his neice are coming to breakfast in an hour, and Coste is flying round getting up all sorts of funny messes. May is primping and A. is putting on her silk dress. The handsome old Dr. is to be fascinated by some of us; it don't matter much which, and then we can travel in style with an M.D. in our train.

We had the first rain for a month yesterday and now every thing looks lovely.

Lu

MS: Unlocated; manuscript copy by Bronson at Houghton Library, Harvard University. Printed: Cheney, p. 223 (partial).

1. A. Prescott Baker married Ellen T. Smith on 9 May, and they were honeymooning in Europe (*Boston Daily Evening Transcript*, 10 May 1870, p. 1; see May's letters of 30 May and 30 August 1870 to her family, manuscript copies by Bronson at Houghton Library, Harvard University).

2. Dr. William Kane, an "army surgeon in India, and Dr in England for forty years" (see 30 May 1870), was substituting for his brother John Kane. Dr. John Kane was a widower with two girls, one of whom was named Amy (LMA to Anna Alcott Pratt, 4–9 June 1870, manuscript copy by Bronson at Houghton Library, Harvard University). LMA discusses in great detail how her "dear old Dr. K." was replaced in a letter to her family of 1 June 1870 (manuscript copy by Bronson at Houghton Library, Harvard University). It appears she was quite fond of William, but not of John.

3. The picturesque old Chateau du Guildo was a small seaport and bathing resort near St.-Jacut-de-la-Mer.

4. In response to hearing "such good news" about *An Old-Fashioned Girl*, LMA wrote her family: "Stow away the $3000 when it comes and live on it as cosily as you can. Don't scrimp, Marmee; have clothes and good food and be as jolly as possible. Then I shall not feel as if I was the only one who was spending money" (29 April 1870, manuscript copy by Bronson at Houghton Library, Harvard University).

5. But by the next week, LMA was again looking for material for her literary works: "Sunday was a great day here, for the children were confirmed. It was a pretty sight to see the long procession of little girls in white gowns and viels, winding through the flowery garden and the antique Square into the old Church, with their happy mothers following, and the boys in their church robes singing as they went. The old priest was too ill to perform the service, but the young one who did, announced afterward that if the children would pass the house, the old man would bless them from his bed. So all marched away down the narrow street with crosses and candles; and it was very touching to see the feeble old man stretch out his hands

Drawing of Louisa, probably, as a child, found in the
Alcott Papers, Houghton Library, Harvard University

Dove Cottage in Concord, where the Alcotts moved in 1840

Main building at Fruitlands

Hillside (Hawthorne's Wayside) in Concord, where the Alcotts moved in 1845

The Olive Leaf.

Samuel Pickwick   Friday Evening July 19 1849   No 1

Poets Corner.

To Pat Paw

By Augustus Snodgrass

Oh my kitty Oh my darling
Purring softly on my knee
While your sleepy little eyes dear
Look so fondly up on me

I will shrine you in my heart
Where no dogs can ever reach you
Oh my precious little guiwart

No other kiss can boast such being
Such a form of matchless grace
Such lustrous eyes so full of feeling
Such an intellectual face

The stately perch the playful spring
The graceful waving tail
Afford a store of pleasure
That can never never fail

The snowy breast beneath which
As true a little heart
Never beat in pussy's breast
My excellent little guiwart

May the biggest fattest mouse
Be your never failing potion
Softest crumbs in heaps around you
And of dops a boundless ocean

The sweetest fairest best and dearest
Earthly words cannot express
The perfect love and adoration
Of the friends gone born to bless

Soft and warm as thy own bosom
Shall thy little pillow be
Bright and happy as thy own face
Shall thy life dear pussy be

Botany

From a young correspondant

Botany is a beautiful study
The parts of the flower are
The calix or cup
Corolla or blossom
Stamens the parts filament
and anther
Pistal germ style stigma
parts of the flower
Pericarp around the seed
I analysed a lily the other
day and found it easier
than I thought
In the city it is not
so pleasant to study
Botany as there are not
any flowers to analyse
or look at
If we go into the county
again soon I shall study
it then   yours truly

M L M

"The Olive Leaf," the family newspaper (1849)

Elizabeth Sewall Alcott

*Early daguerreotype of
Louisa May Alcott*

Abigail May Alcott   *Early daguerreotype of Anna Alcott Pratt*

PARLOR
Entertainment.

LAST TIME OF THE SEASON ! !
Tuesday Evening April 22, '56.

When will be presented the following attractive entertainment for the amusement of our friends,

THE JACOBITE!

Supported by all the talent of Syracuse.

THE WIDOW'S VICTIM !

Or Stage Struck Barber.

Supported by the Comic power of all creation.

Doors open at 7 P. M. Admission to the front seats Nothing !! to the back seats 5 per cent. off ! ! ! Children under ten years of age, half price.

The Entertainment will commence with the very high Comedy of

THE JACOBITE.

In two Acts.

Sir Richard Wroughton	Doct. Pense.
Major Murray	Mr. W. B. Cogswell.
John Duck	Mr. Geo. Barnes.
Lady Somerford	Mrs. Wilkinson.
Widow Pottle	Miss Wheaton.
PATTY POTTLE	MISS ALLCOTT.

Soldiers, Corporal, Servants, &c.

(A VACUUM FOR ABOUT TEN MINUTES HEREABOUTS.)

To Conclude with

The Widow's Victim.

In one Act.

Mr. Twitter	Mr. C. Davis.
Jeremiah Clipp	Mr. Randall.
Tinsel John	" "
Distinguished Foreigner	" "
Byron, Tremaine, Pelham, Podge	Mr. J. E. May.
Mrs. Twitter	Miss Colvin.
Mrs. Rattleton	Mrs. Gott.
JANE	MISS ALLCOTT.

A tremendous Hydraulic force has been engaged to preserve order Curtain will slide at 7½ P. M. and will slide back when the thing is over.

Manager, - - - - - Abbe ! !

Playbill for The Jacobite and The Widow's Victim (1856)

Amateur Dramatic Company.

SECOND SEASON---SECOND PERFORMANCE.

TUESDAY EVENING, SEPT. 11, 1855.

Stage Manager,—Miss Louisa Hayward.
Prompter,—Miss Abbie M. Alcott.
New Scenery, by Alfred C. Howland.

The Company take great pleasure in producing, this Evening, the much admired play, in Two Acts, by J. R. Planche, entitled "The Jacobite," to be followed by the celebrated Farce, "The Two Bonny-Castles," by John Madison Morton.

THE JACOBITE.

Sir Richard Wroughton, ... Mr. Alfred Hasmer
Major Munny, ... Mr. Henry E. Howland.
John Duck, ... Mr. Waldo F. Hayward.
Corporal, ... Mr. Thomas B. Kittredge.
Servant, ... Master Samuel G. Kittredge.
Lady Somerford, ... Miss Louisa Hayward.
Widow Pottle, ... Miss Louisa M. Alcott.
Patty Pottle, ... Miss Annie B. Alcott.

THE TWO BONNYCASTLES.

Mr. Smuggins, ... Mr. Waldo F. Hayward.
Mr. John James Johnson, ... Mr. Henry E. Howland.
Mr. Bonnycastle, alias Jeremiah Jorund, ... Dr. Geo. A. Blake.
Mrs. Bonnycastle, ... Miss Louisa M. Alcott.
Helen, (Niece of Mr. Smuggins,) . . . . Miss Annie B. Alcott.
Patty, ... Miss Sarah Kittredge.

DOORS OPEN AT 7 . . . . CURTAIN RISES AT 8.

The Company return their heartfelt thanks to the public for their liberal patronage, and hope, by increased exertions, to merit a continuance of their favor.

Playbill for The Jacobite *and* The Two Bonnycastles *(1856)*

Walpole Sept 21st

Dear Miss Seymour

Mother forgot to send my
message in her letter so I make bold to do
it myself knowing you will excuse me
for trespassing on your time & troubling
you with my concerns.

Will you be so kind as to ask Mr Norris
of the "Olive Branch", or Mrs Jennison of
the "Ladies Enterprise", if they would take
some stories from me. I am writing
for the "Gazette" & "Sunday News" but
neither of them pay very well, & as
money is the principle object of my life

Letter to Miss Seymour of 21 September [1856]

Caroline Hildreth's portrait
of Bronson Alcott (1857)

Lu

her hair exactly
but nothing else

Pen Sketch of Louisa drawn by Abby.

May Alcott's drawing of Louisa (1857)

Alfred Whitman

Louisa May Alcott

Boston July 13th—

My Dear Miss Russel.

Had your proposal come
to me a year ago I should very
gladly have availed myself of
it if we had suited each other.
But now my time is fully occupied
with my pen & I find story writing
not only pleasanter than teaching
but far more profitable, so I
am glad to change the work which
I have done for fifteen years
for more congenial employment.

Hoping that you may succeed in
your search I am

very truly yours

L. M. Alcott.

Letter to Miss Russel of 13 July [1863?]

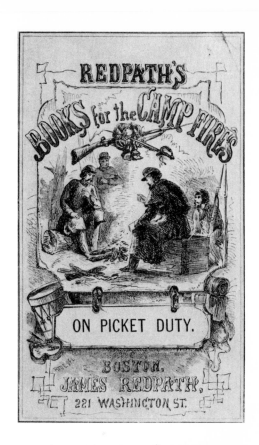

Cover of On Picket Duty,
and Other Tales *(1864)*

Cover of "A. M. Barnard's" V. V.: or,
Plots and Counterplots *(1865)*

Orchard House in the mid-1860s, with the Alcott family standing before it

Silhouette of Louisa May Alcott (1865)

Central Concord in the mid-1860s

Thomas Niles   *May Alcott Nieriker*

above them as the little white brides passed by with bended heads, while the fresh boyish voices chanted the responses. This old priest is a very interesting man, for he is [a] regular Saint, helping every one, keeping his house as a refuge for poor and old priests, settling quarrels among the people, and watching over the young people as if they were his own. I shall put him in a story" (to Anna Alcott Pratt, 25 May 1870, manuscript copy by Bronson at Houghton Library, Harvard University).

To the Alcott Family

Dinan May 30th 1870

Dear Folks,

May has made up such a big letter that I will only add a line to give you the last news of the health of her Highness Princess Louisa. She is such a public character now-a-days that even her bones are not her own, and her wails of woe, cannot be kept from long ears of the world — Old Donkey as it is! Dr. Kane who was army surgeon in India, and Dr in England for forty years, says, my leg trouble and many of my other woes, come from the calomel they gave me in Washington. He has been through the same thing with an Indian-Jungle-fever, and has never got the calomel out of him. The bunches on my leg are owing to that, for the mercury lies round in a body and don't do much harm till a weak spot appears when it goes there and makes trouble. I dont know anything about it, only [my] leg is the curse of my life. But I think Dr. K's Iodine of Potash will cure it in the end as it did his arms, after taking it for three months. It is simple, pleasant, and seems to do something to the bones that gives them ease; so I shall sip away and give it a good trial.

We are now revelling in big strawberries, green peas, early potatos, and other nice things, on which we shall grow fat as pigs.

We are beginning to think of a trip into Normandy where the Howes are. Direct to Munroe and Co. and no one else, then we shall get them without delay.

Love to all. XX By, by.

Your loving Lu.

P. S.

I sent a letter to Nan last week.

MS: Unlocated; manuscript copy by Bronson at Houghton Library, Harvard University. Printed: Cheney, pp. 226–227, who adds two final paragraphs not in Bronson's transcription from a later letter.

To Abigail May Alcott

Blois[1] June 24th[-2 July] 1870

Dear Marmee,

On this Lizzie's and Donny's[2] birth day, Ill begin a letter to you. The last letter from home was from Pa, and we got it a week ago at Tours. I have a "feelin" that one from you and Nan is somewhere on the way and will soon appear. We found at the Post Restante here two "Moods"[3] and a paper for me. One book from Loring and one from Niles.[4] I think the pictures horrid and sent them floating down the Loire as soon as possible, and put one book at the bottom of my trunk and left the other where no one will find it. I could'nt read the story and try to forget that I ever wrote it. Much obliged to Niles for it. I don't get any letter from him about Sampson Low &c.[5] Why dont he answer the letter I wrote ages ago, and tell me about figuring the agreement? If he has written, the letter is lost, and I must S. and L. soon or they will think I'm a Hottentot.[6] Ask Niles about it sometime when Pa is in town.

Blois is a noisy, dusty, soldierly city with nothing to admire but the river (nearly dry now with this four months drought,) and the old castle where Francis I, Louis XII, Catharine de Medicis, and other great folks lived. It has been very splendidly restored by the Government, and the ceilings are made with beams blazoned with coats of arms, the walls hung with cameos painted with the same designs as the stamped leather in old times; and the floors inlaid with colored tiles. Brown and gold, scarlet blue and silver, quaint dragons and flowers, porcupines and salamanders, crowns and letters, glittered every where. We saw the guardroom and the very chimney where the Duc de Guise was leaning when the King, Henry III, sent for him; the little door where the king's gentlemen fell upon and stabbed him with forty wounds. The cabinet where the King and his mother plotted the deed, the Chapel where the monks prayed for its success and the great hall where the body lay covered with a cloak till the King came and looked at it and kicked his dead enemy, saying, "I did not think he was so large." We also saw the cell where the brother of the Duc was murdered the next day, and the attic entire where their bodies were burnt, after which the ashes were thrown into the Loire by order of the King. The window out of which Marie de Medicis lowered herself when her son Louis XIII. imprisoned her there. The recess where Catharine de Medicis died, and many other interesting places. What a set of rascals these old Kings and Queens were!

The Salle des Etats was very georgeous, and here in a week or so are to be tried the men who lately fired at the Emperor. It will be a grand, a fine sight when the great arched hall is full. I got a picture of the castle, and one of a fire place for Pa. It is a mass of gold and color with the porcupine of Louis XII. and the ermine of his wife Anne of Brittany, their arms, in medallion over it.

At 5 P.M. we go onto Orleans for a day where I shall get some relics of Joan of Arc, for Nan. We shall pass Sunday at Bourges where the great church is, and then either to Geneva or the Jura, for a few weeks of rest.

Private

Travelling gets more expensive as we come onto the great routes, for we have to stop at good hotels being women, and sometimes we must go first class when the trains are express. I hate to spend the money, but I'm getting better so fast and enjoying so much that I shall go on till my year is out, and then if the expense is very great, come home and go to work. I have May's washing and sundry little expenses for her which did'nt expect, but her passage and dress took about all her money and she must be taken care of. I hope July will put a nice little plum "in crib" for us all. Let me know how it is, and what Lorings $12. was for.

Geneva June 29th 1870.

It seems almost like getting home again to be here where I never thought to come again when I went away five years ago with my Weld incumbrances. We are at the Metripole Hotel[7] right on the Lake with a glimpse of Mount Blanc from our windows. It is rather fine after the grimy little Inns of Brittany, and we enjoy a sip of luxury and put on our best gowns with feminine satisfaction after living in old travelling suits for a fortnight.

As we went into dinner yesterday, a voice called out as I passed, "Why Miss Alcott how do you do?" and a handsomely dressed lady at table put out her hand smiling and beaming. It was Mrs Bates whom I saw at Mrs Whipples'[8] party last spring, the sister of the Mr. Howe who flirted and flattered on the same occasion. It was pleasant to see a face I'd ever seen before, and as Alice knew her, and she is here with her brother, husband and three boys, it wont be bad to have them to go round with &c.

As it was rather a long hull from Lyons here we are to rest and write letters today, and tomorrow take the early boat to Oilleneuve[?] where Alice's cousins, the Warrens[9] are, and then stay some weeks if we can find a good Pension.

I began my letter at Blois where we spent a day or two. At Orleans we only passed a night, but we had time to see the famous statue of the Maid put up in gratitude by the people of the city she saved. It is a fine statue of Joan in her armor on horseback with her sword drawn. Round the base of the statue are bronze bas-reliefs of her life from the girl with her sheep to the martyr at the stake. They were very fine but dont show much in the photograph which I got for Nan, remembering the time when she translated Schillers' play for me.[10]

At Bourges we saw the great Cathedral, but did'nt like it as well as that in Tours. We only spent a night here, and Alice bought an antique ring of the time of Francis I.: an emerald set in diamonds. It cost $9.00, and is very quaint and handsome.[11]

Moulins we reached Sunday noon, and at 3 oclock went to vespers in the old church where we saw a good deal of mumbo jumbo by red, purple and yellow priests, and heard a boy with a lovely voice sing up [in] the hidden choir like a little angel among the clouds. Alice had a fancy to stay a week if we could find rooms out of the town in some farm house, for the hand-some white cattle have captivated her, and we were rather tired. So the old lady at the Hotel said she had a little summer house out in the fields and we should go and see it with her in basket chay. After dinner we all piled in and went along a dusty road to a little dirty garden house with two rooms and a few cabbages and rose bushes round it. She said we could sleep and eat at the Hotel and come down here for the day. That did'nt suit at all,[12] so we declined and on Monday morning we set out for Lyons. It was a very interesting trip under, over and through the mountains with two engines and much tunneling and up and down grading. May was greatly excited at the queer things we did and never knew that cars could [blank space] such sharp corners. We wound about so that we could see the engines whisking out of sight round one corner while we were turning another, and the long train looked like a snake winding through the hills. The tunnels were so long that lamps were lighted, and so cold we put on our jacks while passing in the darkness. The scenery was very fine, and after we left Lyons, where we merely slept, the Alps began to appear, and May and I stared in blissful silence, for we had two fat old men opposite, and a little priest, so young that we called him the Rev. boy. He slept and said his prayers most of the time, stealing sly looks at May's hair, Alice's pretty hands, and my buckled shoes which were like his own and seemed to strike him as a liberty on my part. The old boys were very jolly, especially the the one with three chins, who smiled paternally upon us and tried to talk. But we were very English and mum, and he thought we didn't understand French and confided to his friend that he didn't see "how the English could travel and know not the French tongue." They sung, gabbled, slept and slapped one another at in-tervals, and were very amusing till they left, and another very handsome Booth-like priest took their places.

Hurrah! A knock just came to our door, and there was Sophy Bond! We howled and flew at her, and she told us Aunty and Mr. B. were below,[13] so down we rushed and have had a good pow-wow. All very "jolly and kind and *so* glad to see us." They are going to stay here some time in a Pension, so we shall see more of them. They saw our names in the book this A.M. and Sophy came up at once to find us. They arrived last eve after we did so did'nt meet at dinner. Auntie is nicely, Sophy very handsome, and Mr B as jolly as ever. A Miss Wells is travelling with them,[14] and they were all in high feather and seemed to think it great larks to meet us here.

Evening.

We have had a busy pleasant day, for after a social chat, May and Sophy went out shopping, and Alice and I went with Mr Bond to the bankers. Then we took a drive. The Bonds are going to stay in a Pension here for a few weeks and we went to see if we could get rooms with them. We could, but not till Saturday, so as Alice's cousins were at the end of the Lake we thought we would only make one more. The Bonds went to their Pension in the P.M. and we called on them in eve and they showed us some lovely pictures. Mr. B. and and Sophy walked home with us, and we sat in the big parlor with some ladies whom they knew talking till 11, when we packed up and went to bed. Next morning at 8 we went to the boat, where Mr. Bond came to see us off, and after a fine sail of three or four hours came to Vevey[15] and drove to Pension Du Rivage, near my old Pension Victoria. A neat pleasant place where we pay 6 francs a day, live well, and have very nice rooms. Russian and English people with a Spanish Bishop are all who are here now. I was so tired that I have done nothing but rest since I came.

Vevey July 2nd

Two days at a great Hotel, used me up as much as two weeks of travel. Alice and I both got cold by the way, and have laid round till today, when A. has gone to see her cousins at Bex and I begin to feel better. Things look very natural here, but more lovely than before, and the girls like it, so we may stay sometime. Aunt and Sophia may join us if Mr. B. goes to Austria. They wanted May to go to Chamoanni [Chamonix?] with them but as it costs about $20, she did'nt feel as if she ought. Mr B. might have invited her, but rich men always feel *so* poor, he did'nt. We telegraphed at once to Paris for our letters but none have come, and we are much disappointed, for there must be a pile somewhere.

I have kept this hoping to acknowledge yours in it, but shall send it off now and wait no longer, or you will think we are lost and gone.

I have got a note from Niles and have signed the agreement.[16] Aunty read me a letter from Lizzy Wells in which she says Mr. Wells is very well and old Ben as usual, so they are not dying as you wrote us.

This is a very dull letter, but I dont feel like writing now-a-days and have very little to tell.

5 P.M. May has just brought in some letters but none from you. One from Tilton asking me to write for "The Revolution,"[17] one from Low saying that £20 had been sent to Munroe,[18] and one from Munroe saying he had recieved the money for me, so that is all right. I am much disappointed but hope to get my home budget tomorrow.

Give my love to everyone who wants it, and don't read my letters to everybody for I hate to write if Tom, Dick and Harry are to see 'em.

By, By. It is "morning on the mountains" just now and it is very sweet for July 2nd.

Kiss my lovers.

Your Lu.

MS: Unlocated; manuscript copy by Bronson at Houghton Library, Harvard University. Printed: Cheney, pp. 235–239 (partial).

    1. Blois, France, on the Loire River on the route from Dinan to Bex, Switzerland.

    2. John or Donny Sewall Pratt and Elizabeth Sewall Alcott shared the birth date of 24 June, she in 1835 and he in 1855.

    3. LMA disliked Loring's capitalizing on her new fame by reissuing *Moods* without her consent, especially since she had revised it under protest to ensure publication: "I see by a Transcript that Niles sent, that Loring is selling "Moods" again. I told him not to do it, and he said he would'nt, for there was no call for it. I won't have it; for it is not *my Book.* So I wish Papa would would see if it can't be stopped. Niles will know if I hav'nt the right to do it. I have the copy right and don't wish the book sold as it is" (to her family, 29 April 180, manuscript copy by Bronson, Houghton Library, Harvard University). And on 1 June, she wrote her family: "I am so mad at Lorings doings and letter that I must begin a new budget to you, by way of frothing my wrath. The dreadful man says that he has a *right to print as many editions as [he] likes for fourteen years!* What rights has an author then I beg to know? and where does 'the *courtesy*' of a publisher come in? He has sent me a book, and if you hear I'm dead, you may know that a sight of the *picters* slew me, for I expect to have fits when I behold Sylvia with a top-knot, Moore with mutton chop whiskers, and Adam in the inevitable checkered trowsers which all modern heroes wear. If the law gives over an author and her work to such slaverery, as L. says, I shall write no more books but take in washing, and say adieu to glory" (manuscript copy by Bronson, Houghton Library, Harvard University).

    4. Both Loring and Niles had sent LMA copies of *Moods.* On 8 June 1870, Niles wrote LMA: "I mailed you last week a copy of Loring's Moods. He tells me he has printed 4000 & I imagine he may have sold 1000 in paper & 1500 in cloth. I don't think the sale will be large & all of these by the excitement over the success of LW & OFG. See if I'm not right." Niles, however, wrote back on 8 November that the sales of *Moods* were larger than he had predicted because people thought it to be a new book (both, Houghton Library, Harvard University).

    5. Concerning Sampson Low, LMA wrote, "The only event of interest is the arrival of English Edition of O. F. G. It is very handsome, scarlet and gold, with gilt edges and type

that would delight father. Initial letters to the chapters and all very elegant. I suppose Niles will have one which you can see. Sampson and Low write me very polite notes and sent me a printed agreement to sign, giving them the 'sole right to print during the legal term of copy right.' " She added, "If that means fourteen years as as Loring says, I prefer not to do it, but should wait to hear from Niles about it before I sign" (to Anna Alcott Pratt, 4–9 June 1870, manuscript copy by Bronson, Houghton Library, Harvard University).

    6. During LMA's time, "Hottentot" was used to describe a person of inferior intellect or culture.

    7. The Metropole Hotel in Geneva is located on the left bank with a view of Lake Geneva (known in French as Lac Léman).

    8. Charlotte Whipple, wife of Edwin Percy Whipple.

    9. Alice Bartlett's cousins, the Warrens, were nieces of Judge Warren of Boston. LMA comments on the two girls in a letter to Anna Alcott Pratt of 24–27 July 1870: "The Warrens dont particularly interest us. Lena is a stubby little girl of 24, very blunt, smart, common-sensical and rough. Her one soft spot is her dog, a scrabbly Skye, whom she frets and fusses over more than she does her sister. She is full of fight as a game chicken, but kind and funny. Emma is 30 years old, is pretty and mild, but affected, and not at all interesting. She sits or lies in a wheeled-chair all the time. Alice thinks she is lovely and is very fond of her, which is a good thing as it gives A. something to do" (manuscript copy by Bronson, Houghton Library, Harvard University).

    10. Friedrich Schiller's play *The Maid of Orleans* was first translated into English in 1835.

    11. LMA and Alice later "made a bargain" with this ring: "she gave me her lovely Francis Ist ring — antique emerald and diamond, in a quaint setting, also a pretty gold chain for watch or locket, and I was to give her a crystal watch, now the rage. It was a fine bargain for me, for the chain was worth $25 or 30 in America and the ring would bring sums among a certain antiquity-loving set. The watch is a round crystal ball hung by a chain from a hook at the belt. I don't admire them but A. does, and was going to sell the ring and chain to get one. So I exchanged and as her watch only cost $28, it was a good speculation. I got a plain new [o]rnamented watch for $30, and with my chain am all fixed. We had great fun over the bargain, and the Bigelows offered sums for my ring, but as a piece of "portable property" I prefer to keep it, and speculate on it in America, where I can do better. My watch is by a good maker and he gave me a sort of pledge to keep it in order through his agents in Rome, London, Paris, Madrid, or New York, whenever I applied to them to regulate it" (to her family, 19 September 1870, manuscript copy by Bronson, Houghton Library, Harvard University).

    12. Earlier, LMA had had different sorts of troubles with a rural visit: "We went to a ruin one day, and were about to explore the castle, when a sow with her family of twelve charged through the gateway at us so fiercely that we fled in dismay, for pigs are not nice when they attack, as we dont know where to bone 'em, and I saw a woman one day whose nose had been bitten off by an angry pig. I flew over a hedge; May tried to follow but stuck and lay with her long legs up and her head in a ditch howling for me to save her, as the sow was charging in the rear, and a dog, two cows, and a boy looking on. I pulled her over head first, and we tumbled into the tower, like a routed garrison. It was'nt a nice ruin, but we were bound to see it, having suffered so much. And we did see it in spite of the pigs, who waylaid us on all sides; and squealed in triumph when we left, dirty, torn and tired. The ugly things wander at their own sweet will, and are tall, round-backed, thin wretches who run like race horses and are no respecters of persons" (to Anna Alcott Pratt, 25 May 1870, manuscript copy by Bronson, Houghton Library, Harvard University).

    13. LMA's aunt and uncle Louisa Caroline Greenwood Bond and George Bond and their daughter Sophy.

    14. Clara Wells (see May Alcott to her family, 29 June 1870, manuscript copy by Bronson, Houghton Library, Harvard University).

    15. Vevey, Switzerland, situated on the left bank of the Veveyse River. It was in Vevey that LMA had met Ladislas Wisniewski in 1865.

16. About LMA's contract with Sampson Low, Niles wrote on 8 June 1870: "The substance of Low's agreement is that they agree to pay you one half the profits of every edit. of O. F. G. which they print, *after they are sold*, said profits being the amount of sales calculated at ⅓ off from retail price, 13 or 12, less cost of printing etc. I should sign it by all means. You are at their mercy but you can't lose anything by signing it. If the book proves a success in England, the house is respectable & you would probably receive the exact amount of profits as indicated in the agreement." In a letter to Sampson Low and Marston of 24 June 1870, LMA writes that she has just heard from Niles and is signing and forwarding the agreement (both, Houghton Library, Harvard University).

17. Theodore Tilton supported the *Revolution*, a feminist weekly edited by Elizabeth Cady Stanton and others. On 8 July 1870, LMA would write to her family: "Did I tell you that Tilton sent me a gushing letter asking me to write for 'The Revolution?' I shall not: for it is not our party unless the Boston and New York squabblers have joined forces. Have they? If I wrote for any Woman's thing it would be for Livermore's paper [*Woman's Journal*]. I think I'd rather keep to my own work and lecture the public in a story, than hold forth . . . in the papers. Old Tilton never answered my last letter, so he can wait for an answer to his signed 'Yours, with all brotherly love' " (manuscript copy by Bronson, Houghton Library, Harvard University).

18. On 27 June 1870, Sampson Low wrote LMA to inform her that their banker was forwarding twenty pounds to Munroe (Houghton Library, Harvard University).

To Thomas Niles

Bex[1] August 7 1870.

Dear Mr. Niles,

I keep receiving requests from editors to write for their papers or magazines. I am duly grateful, but having come abroad for rest, I am not inclined to try the treadmill till my year's vacation is over. So, to appease these worthy gentlemen and excuse my seeming idleness I send you a trifle in rhyme[2] which you can (if you think it worth the trouble) set going as a general answer to everybody, for I cant pay postage in replies to each separately, "its werry costly."

Mr Ford said he would pay me $10, 15, 20, for any little things I would send him, so perhaps you will let him have it first.

The war makes the bankers take double toll on our money, so we feel very poor[3] and as if we ought to be earning not spending, only we are *so* lazy we can't bear to think of it in earnest. Street and Smith of the "N.Y. Weekly" were the last applicants,[4] asking for a serial, and in a brief business way, and ending with; "Name your own price". But I did not like the list of contributors Ned Buntline, Lu Billings, Spaulding, Philander Doesticks, and other great lights,[5] so I could not think of it, and prefer the "heavy moral."

We shall probably go to London next month, if the war forbids Italy for

144

the winter, and if we cant get one dollar without paying five for it, we shall come home disgusted.

If a chance ever comes to get hold of "Morning Glories"[6] please do it for me. Perhaps if I can do nothing else this year, I could have a book of short stories old and new for Christmas. Ford and Fuller have some good ones, and I have the right to use them. We could call them, "Jo March's Necessity Stories." Would, would it go with new ones added and good illustrations?

I am rising from my ashes in a most phoenix-like manner.

L. M. A.

MS: Unlocated; manuscript copy by Bronson at Houghton Library, Harvard University. Printed: Cheney, pp. 243–244 (partial).

    1. Bex, Switzerland, located on the Avançon River and a popular resort area in the spring and autumn.

    2. The poem she refers to is "The Lay of a Golden Goose," printed in Cheney, pp. 204–207. LMA's answer to the incessant queries about her next work ended with these stanzas:

> Soon up among the grand old Alps
>   She found two blessed things,
> The health she had so nearly lost,
>   And rest for weary limbs.
>
> But still across the briny deep
>   Couched in most friendly words,
> Came prayers for letters, tales, or verse,
>   From literary birds.
>
> Whereat the renovated fowl
>   With grateful thanks profuse,
> Took from her wing a quill and wrote
>   This lay of a Golden Goose.

    3. Despite LMA's complaints about money, Niles's July account had been for $6,212. This was "a neat little sum," LMA told her family, for " 'the Alcotts, who can't make money!' " (incorrectly dated 30 May 1870, Cheney, p. 227). She continued on financial matters in another letter to her family on 18–20 July 1870: "About S. E. S. and my money, I have only to say that I want to know that $10,000 is invested, and the rest, if there is any over, so fixed that I can get it as I need it. For now that May's money is used up, I have many small expenses for her, as Alice only pays her travelling expenses. I have still $600. on my letter of credit which I have not touched; also $200 on my bills of exchange, for I have used only one. The war may affect money, and I guess we can do very well and I want things easy for everyone. With $10,000 well invested, and more coming in all the time, I think we may venture to enjoy ourselves after the hard times we have all had. The cream of the joke is that we made our own money ourselves and no one gave us a blessed penny" (manuscript copy by Bronson, Houghton Library, Harvard University).

    4. Street and Smith were publishers of the *New York Weekly*, a pulp paper that ran gripping serials.

    5. The dime novelist Ned Buntline (pseudonym of Edward Z. C. Judson); the humorists Josh Billings (pseudonym of Henry Wheeler Shaw) and Philander Doesticks (pseudonym of Mortimer Thompson); the journalist James Reed Spaulding.

    6. *Morning-Glories, and Other Stories* had been published by Horace B. Fuller.

To Abigail May Alcott

Vevey Aug 21st 1870

Dear Marmee,

Your letters of July 26th came just after our last was sent. The Bonds were here, and by them I sent my watch for Pa, a little Madonna Dolorosa for you, and a pair of gloves for Nan. I wanted to send the plaid purple silk, as I dont wear it, and it is a pity Nan should not have it, but Sophy had but little room; so the box is all.

I had such a droll dream last night, I must tell you. I thought I was returning to Concord after my trip, and was alone. As I walked from the Station, I missed Mr. Moore's house,[1] and turning the corner, found the scene so changed that I did'nt know where I was. Our house was gone, and in its place stood a great grey stone castle with towers and arches and lawns and bridges very fine and antique. Somehow I got into it without meeting any one of you, and wandered about trying to find my family. At last I came across Mr. Moore papering a room, and asked him where his house was? He did n't know me and said, "Oh! I sold it to Mr Alcott for his school, and we live in Acton now." "Where did Mr. Alcott get the means to build this great concern", I asked. "Well, he *gave* his own land and took the great fortune his daughter left him, the one that died some ten years ago." "So I am dead, am I?" says I to myself, feeling so queerly. "Government helped build this place, and Mr. A. has a fine College here," said Mr Moore papering away again. I went on wondering at the news and looked into a glass to see how I looked dead. I found myself a fat old lady with grey hair and specs, very like E[lizabeth]. P[almer]. P[eabody]. I laughed, and coming to a Gothic window, looked out and saw hundreds of young men and boys in a queer flowing dress roaming about the parks and lawns, and among them was Pa, looking as he looked thirty years ago, with brown hair and a big white neckcloth as in the old times. He looked so plump and placid and young and happy, I was charmed to see him, and nodded, but he did n't know me, and I was so grieved and troubled at being a Rip Van Winkle, I cried, and said I had better go away and not disturb anyone, and in the midst of my woe, I woke up. It was all so clear and funny I can't help thinking that it may be a foreshadowing of something real. I used to dream of being famous, and it has partly become true. So why not Pa's College blossom, and he yet young and happy with his disciples? I only hope he won't quite forget me when I come back, fat and grey and old. Perhaps his dream is to come in another world where every thing is fresh and calm, and the reason why he did'nt recognize me was because I was still in this work-a-day world, and so felt old and strange in his lovely castle in the air. Well, he is welcome to my fortune, but the daughter who did die ten years ago, is more likely to be the one who helped him build his School of Concord up aloft.

I can see how the dream came, for I had been looking at Silling's boys[2] in their fine garden, and wishing I could go in, and know the dear little lads larking about there. Then in the forenoon, I had got a top knot at the barbers and talked about my grey hairs, and looking in the glass thought how fat and old I was getting, and had shown the Bond's, Pa's picture, which they thought saintly, &c. I believe in dreams, though I am free to confess that "cowcumbers" for tea may have been the basis of this *"ally-gorry-cal wision."*

May has two devoted croquet followers, the young Frenchman and the little twenty years old Spaniard with the dark blue eyes and black lashes. His name is Silvio Mirandda and his Pa is a Count. Both were in the army and are refugees not daring to go home yet. Vevey is full of Spaniards who are gathered round the Ex-Queen Isabella and Don Carlos,[3] all plotting and planning some mad revolution. Mysterious little brown men come and take the Count out from his meals to jabber darkly in corners, and then vanish as mysteriously as they came. Don Carlos, a plain brown man of twenty four, goes driving round with his little wife and baby.[4] At the christening of said baby all the dingy Spaniards in Vevey burst forth in grand rigs with orders and stars, and our old ladys nineteen generals were gorgeous to behold, she says. One funny weak little man who sits opposite me at table, and spills his soup, puts his knife in his mouth and talks fearful French, turns out to be a great Spanish General, and on gala days is stuck as full of orders as cushion of pins: blue ribbon round his neck with stars, red ribbons on the left breast, yellow ditto on the right, and a green one with a great gold key hanging down his back. His clothes are very shabby, and his hands very dirty, but the orders cover the shabbyness, several rings adorn the unwashed hands, and the little hero is as perky and mild as a baa-lamb when he is not plotting privy conspiracy and rebellion, like bald-headed demon.

There are a good many strangers in town now. The Weld party have been at the Grand Hotel, and we saw many American names in the list of strangers. The Bigelows, sister and brother,[5] come to morrow to visit Alice and will stay a little while. So a week more will slip by pleasantly, and then we can decide what to do. Mr Bond thought we could go to Italy with perfect safety if the money question is fixed. We have had to get new passports from Berne and they are viséd for Italy, so we can be at Milan in a day or so, if we like. I dont want to be cheated out of my Italian winter, and the war can't last long if Prussia goes on beating the French in every battle, and the French continue to mow down the Prussians like grass before they retreat. It will be like the Kilkenny cats, and old Nap will retire to private life a last piece of unnecessary wickedness. I don't envy him. His people hate and distrust him and things look badly for the Naps.

As we know the Consul at Spazia, that is, we have letters to him as well as to many folks in Rome, &c, I guess we shall go, for the danger of Europe getting into the fight is over now, and we can sail to England or home any time from Italy.

Don't send me any more letters from *so cracked* girls. I can't answer them, and have to pay Munroe for every one he forwards. Just put them away and dont reply to them; it is too expensive, and the rampant infants must wait.

I put in a bit of a note to Tommy on the same subject, for I dont want any *"hifalutin"* notes to come disappointing me when I look for letters from family.[6]

I am tip top now and keep so in spite of rain or shine, and a warm winter will finish me off I trust, and let me come home in the spring to work *"in moderation"*, for doing nothing is *awful* when I have nt "my bones" to tend.

Use thicker envelopes for yours are worn out, and have to be tied up before we got them.

Love to every one. I'll write to the poor Mansfields.

Kiss *my lovies* for me.

Ever your
Lu.

MS: Unlocated; manuscript copy by Bronson at Houghton Library, Harvard University. Printed: Cheney, pp. 245–247, where it is listed as being written to Anna Alcott Pratt.

1. John Moore had sold Orchard House to the Alcotts in September 1857.

2. Bellerive School in Vevey was run by Edouard Sillig; it was comparable to Sanborn's Concord school. In a letter to Niles of 23 August 1870, LMA said, "The boys at Sillings school here are a perpetual source of delight to me. . . . The young ladies who want to find live Lauries can be supplied here for Silling has a large assortment always on hand" (manuscript copy by Bronson, Houghton Library, Harvard University).

3. Queen Isabella II of Spain abdicated in favor of her son, Alfonso XII, in 1870.

4. Don Carlos, a Bourbon prince, was a claimant to the Spanish throne as Don Carlos VII. He and his wife, Princess Marguerite, had a son, Don Jaime, born in 1870.

5. On 11–13 August 1870, LMA wrote her mother: "Alice's friends Annie and Addie Bigelow and their brother Joe, are coming here soon." On the twenty-ninth, she wrote her family: "The Bigelow girls are here and we like them much, pretty, gay, kind and accomplished" (manuscript copies by Bronson, Houghton Library, Harvard University).

6. Also distressing to LMA was the receipt, from Niles, of "a notice in the gossipy old Republican telling about my 'good old English Dr. and my legs, and my grief for Dickens (dont care a pin) and all my plans and ails &c.' I suppose [Ellery] Channing or Bun [Sanborn] wrote it, and I should like to knock their heads off for meddling with what dont concern them old tattle tails! — Another notice said I wrote diaries at 6, plays at 10, went out to service at 13, and was governess and dragged a baby round the Common. I recognize Pa's nice derangement of dates here, and fancy it was written by some of his admirers. I suppose I ought to like it,

but I dont. (Oh aint Lu cross?)" (to her family, 8 July 1870, manuscript copy by Bronson, Houghton Library, Harvard University). Sanborn's "From Boston" column in the 15 June 1870 *Springfield Republican* calls LMA one of the "sincerest mourners" of Dickens, who had died on 9 June (p. 2).

To the Alcott Family

Vevey September 10th 1870.

Dear People,

As all Europe seems to be going to destruction, I hasten to drop a line before the grand smash arrives. We mean to skip over the Alps next week if weather and war permit, for we are bound to see Milan and the lakes, even if we have to turn and come back without a glimpse of Rome. The Pope is beginning to perk up, and Italy and England and Russia seem ready to join in the war now that France is down. Think of Paris being bombarded and smashed up like Strasbourg. We never shall see the grand old Cathedral at Strasbourg now, it is so spoilt.

Vevey is crammed with refugees from Paris and Strasbourg. Ten families applied here yesterday. It is awful to think of the misery that wretch Nap has made, and I don't wonder his people curse him after he got them into such a war, and then slipt out like a coward. Hope his ills will increase, and every inch of him will suffer for such a shameful act. I wish you could hear the French talk about him; they stamp and rave and scold, like theatrical children as they are. I like them less and less, the more I see of them. They are so unstable and absurd. Now they howl, "Vive la Republique," and within months they ask one of the Bourbons to come back and reign over them. A bad lot.

Our house is brim full and we have funny times. The sick Russian lady and her old ma[1] make a great fuss if a breath of air comes in at meal times, and expect twenty people to sit shut tight in a smallish room for an hour on a hot day. We protested, and Madame put them in the parlor where they glower as we pass and lock the door when they can. The German Professor is learning English and is a quiet pleasant man.[2] The Polish General, a little crooked, is very droll and bursts out in the middle of the general chat with stories about transparent apples and golden horses. Mrs Munroe and Julia, her daughter, (with a Russian lover whom Julia is to marry next month) are from Syracuse N.Y. and know Uncle Sam.[3] They are rather ordinary, and we dont say much to them. They asked the first thing for my works, "for

149

the Russian bear to read." Benda, the crack book and picture man here asked May, "if she was the Miss Alcott who wrote the popular books," for he said he had many calls for them, and wished to know where they could be found. We told him at London and felt puffed up.

The other eve, as we sat in our wrappers, the maid came up with H. J. Pratts card.[4] We asked him up and he appeared as brown and jolly and handsome as ever. He had been to Bex for us and hunted all day along the Lake to find us. At Montraux he met Charley Howe[5] who told him the Alcotts' were here and on he came. He has been here some days and will remain till we go to Italy, when he will go on to Paris, if Paris isnt blown up. We have had lively times since he came, for he has travelled far and wide, and can tell his adventures well. He went to Tunis and Carthage and dug up marbles among the ruins for classic sleeve buttons, &c. He dances wild dances for us, sings songs in many languages. We had a moonlight ball in the road the other night coming from the Warrens — fine affair. He is much improved and quite appals us by talking Arabic, French, German, Italian, and Armenian in one grand burst.

May and I delve away at French, but it makes my head ache and I don't learn enough to pay for the trouble. I never could *study*, you know, and suffer such agony when I try, that it is piteous to behold. The little brains I have left, I want to keep for future works, and not exhaust them on grammar — vile invention of Satan! May gets on slowly and dont have fits over it, so she had better go on, the lessons only cost two francs.

I don't know as you will ever get this letter or the others lately sent, for Paris is in such a mess no letters go in or come out, and all ours *from* you go Munroe's care, so when we see them, no one knows. Alice has written to have her letters sent to the care of "Baring Brothers, London." I think we had better do the same. So direct your next letters *there*, and I will send Baring our address in Italy, if we go.

MS: Unlocated; manuscript copy by Bronson at Houghton Library, Harvard University. Printed: Cheney, pp. 250–251 (partial).

1. On 2 September 1870, LMA wrote her family about "two Russian ladies" staying there, one "dying of consumption" (manuscript copy by Bronson, Houghton Library, Harvard University).

2. On 2 September 1870, LMA mentioned to her family that a "young German, Eugene Knorsing, very elegant and pleasant, but shy is here" (manuscript copy by Bronson, Houghton Library, Harvard University).

3. LMA's uncle Samuel Joseph May of Syracuse.

4. Herbert J. Pratt (see May Alcott to her family, 29? April 1870, copy by Bronson, Houghton Library, Harvard University).

5. See 14 April 1870.

To the Alcott Family

Private

Dear People,

Pa's letter containing Marmee's picture and Mr Sewall's Accounts has just come.[1] The picture is very soft and pleasant though not quite clear and strong enough, but it will be a great comfort to us, for the old one is so faded you can hardly see it. Alice and Lena[2] who were with us at the P. Office admired it very much, and Lena said at at once, "What a dear, lovely, motherly face, I must know her when we go home." She lost her own mother when a child and does not like her step-mother, so I told her she should come and love my Marmee.

The Account looks all right, but I don't seem to know much about it, and am willing to take it on trust. I am only sorry that Mrs S — [3] had any of my money, for I never wanted to accept the favor, and don't think she had any right to be paid. However we are out of the mess now, and I hope can keep so.

I have only to say, as before, about the *money*, I should like the sums that Roberts pays me safely invested somewhere and we live on the interest so far as we can. When I get home and at work again I can supply all the extra needs by short tales &c, so till then I suppose we must draw and spend, and trust to luck to make the sums hold out. I see that my trip is to cost a good deal more than I expected, for being in a party, I have to pay my share in some things that I dont care for, though Alice is perfectly fair and generous, and kind. May has no money for her private wants, and these I shall of course supply — Drs. bills, French Lessons, and amusements included. So that I shall spend a thousand or two before I get back. If I get well and May has a good time it will be worth the money and I shan't complain.

I dont see why S. E. S. dont invest some of the money in *Government Bonds*, they cant fail like railroads, and every one says they are an excellent investment. If I have a good sum in January from Niles, I wish S. E. S. would buy me some bonds. John will draw the dividends for Ma while Papa is gone. I wish her to have all she wants, to pay Nan a good board — $6 or 8 a week, and have without stint every comfort or luxury she expresses the least wish for. Now our John must see to it that she is well cared for in every way, and let her feel that the income of my money is all her own to use and enjoy to her heart's content. Another thousand by and by will be all May and I shall want, for I have'nt spent my first money yet, and *that* can be put aside in a lump when the January return comes in — the second $1000 I mean. Niles sent me a long letter about Low &c.[4] I suppose he has told you the story, so I won't repeat. I hope Low will "play fair," and Tom keep his temper, and not spend too much in puffing the books, which seem to be doing well enough to be let alone now. I don't think the printing of the "Lay of the Golden Goose" would do us any harm, but I don't care any thing about it either way, so you can let it pass.[5] I am glad the books continue to go well since I am doing nothing now. I am afraid I shall not write till I get home, for all I do is to scribble odds and ends as notes, and dawdle round without an idea in my head. Alice says no one does anything in Italy; so after another six months of idleness, I may get back and go to work. In the spring one of us will come home to run the machine. I fancy it may be May, if I can make up my mind to stay, for Alice cant remain without duenna, and I can be one and also *pay my own way.* A year of pleasure at A's expense is all May should expect or accept *I* think, and she is ready to fall to again, being grateful for sips of fun. I dont want to stay, but if I'm not tip top by spring, I should feel as if I ought, for fifteen years' mischief cant be mended in twelve months, at least not thoroughly, I am afraid. However, I shall leave that point for time to settle.

I think Plato had better not try San Francisco.[6] He would be as much out of place as a saint in a bar-room; besides, he is too old to slamming[?] across the continent in a week. Dont!

Please give the note to Niles and tell him to send our next letters to Baring Brothers, London.

I hope that Nan and Ma are getting off a fat letter to us.

Good bye to all

May sends love, but is rather "absorbed" just now.

Your Lu.

MS: Unlocated; manuscript copy by Bronson at Houghton Library, Harvard University.

1. Bronson's letter of [August] 1870 enclosed Sewall's account, showing that LMA's income from 3 May 1869 to 27 July 1870 was $10,485, and listed the more than $9,000 in stocks that she owned (*Letters,* pp. 520–521).

2. Lena Warren.

3. Bronson paid $300 to Mary Preston Stearns in August 1870 (*Letters,* p. 520).

4. This letter is part of the correspondence about Low's contract for *An Old-Fashioned Girl.*

5. "The Lay of a Golden Goose" was first published in the 8 May 1886 *Woman's Journal.*

6. Bronson wrote LMA in [August] 1870: "My prospects are fair as to my Western tour. I ought not to return home without my $2000 at least, since I go advertised . . . and I may get as far as San Francisco" (*Letters,* p. 521).

To Anna Alcott Pratt

[December? 1870?]

Dear Nannie: You need not be told what he was to me, or how I mourn for him, for no born brother was ever dearer, & each year I loved & respected & admired him more & more. His quiet integrity, his patient spirit, so cheerful & so persistent, his manly love of independence & his brave efforts to earn it for those he loved. How beautiful simple & upright his life looks now. Good son, brother, husband, father & friend. I think that record is a noble one for any man & his 37 quiet years are very precious to those who knew him. He did more to make us trust & respect men than any one I know & with him I lose the one young man whom I sincerely honored in my heart. Good bye my dear, honest, tender, noble John! your place never will be filled your love never lost, your life never forgotten. The world is better for your simple virtues, & those who loved your riches for the faithful heart you showed them.[1]

MS: Unlocated; manuscript copy (partial) at the Henry W. and Albert A. Berg Collection, New York Public Library, Astor, Lenox, and Tilden Foundations. The letter is written from Rome; for more on LMA's stay there, see Alice B. Bartlett, "Our Apartment. A Practical Guide to Those Intending to Spend a Winter in Rome," *Old and New* 3 (April, June 1871): 399–407, 663–671.

1. John Bridge Pratt died on 27 November 1870. LMA commented further on his death in a letter to a friend: "I cannot wish you both any better wish than many years of such love & happiness as the ten which have blessed Annie & John. The memory of them is her best comfort in the present, & the certainty of knowing a still happier & more united life here after is her sustaining hope in the future. She bears her loss so beautifully that I know the burden will not be too heavy or life lose all its satisfactions" (to Mrs. Edward Henry Barton, 9 January [1871], Berg Collection, New York Public Library).

To an Unknown Recipient

RECENT EXCITING SCENES IN ROME.

Rome, December 29, 1870.

My Dear Mr.[1] ——————— : As we are having very exciting times just now, I will send you a little account of the two last "sensations," though I dare say the news will be rather old by the time you receive it.

Yesterday morning at breakfast our maid, Lavinia, came flying in from market with the news that the Tiber had overflowed its banks and inundated the lower part of the city; that people just outside the walls were drowned; others in the Ghetto were washed out of their houses, the Corso was under water, and the world generally coming to an end. We instantly went out to see how things stood, or rather floated, and found that Lavinia's story was true. The heavy rains and warm winds had swelled the river and melted the snow on the mountains, till the Tiber rose higher than at any time since 1805, and had done much damage in a few hours.

When we reached the Piazza di Spagna it seemed as if we were in Venice; for all the long streets leading up to it from the lower part of the city were under water, and rafts and boats were already floating about. The Piazza del Popolo was a lake, with the four stone lions just above the surface, still faithfully spouting water, though it was a drug in the market. Garrett's great stables were flooded, and his horses and carriages were standing disconsolately on the banks about the Piazza. In at the open gates rolled a muddy stream bearing haystacks and brushwood from the country along the Corso. People stood on their balconies, wondering what they should do, many breakfastless; for meals are sent in, and how were the trattoria boys to reach them with the coffee-pots across such canals of water? Carriages splashed about in the shallower parts with agitated loads of people hurrying to safer quarters; many were coming down ladders into boats, and flocks stood waiting their turn with little bundles of valuables in their hands.

THE SOLDIERS AND PRIESTS.

The soldiers were out in full force, working gallantly to save life and property; making rafts, carrying people on their backs, and later, going through the inundated streets with boatloads of food for the hungry, shut up in their ill-provided houses. It has since been said that usually at such times the priests have done this work; but now, they stand looking on and smile maliciously, saying it is a judgment on the people for their treatment of the Pope.[2] The people are troubled because the priests refuse to pray for them; but otherwise they snap their fingers at the sullen old gentleman in the Vatican, and the brisk, brave troops work for the city quite as well (we heretics think better) than the snuffy priests. Some of the saintly young Jesuits amused themselves by throwing stones at the soldiers while they were working during the flood; for which cowardly trick the aforesaid heretics feel a strong desire to box the long-coated boys' ears and cast their shovel-hats in the mud. By the way, I heard that one whole college of lads left in a body and went to the free school the King has opened, demanding to be taken in and taught something, being disgusted with their Jesuitical masters; a sure sign that young Italy is waking up. Three cheers for the boys!

The Flood

To return to the flood. In the Ghetto, the disaster was really terrible, for the flood came so suddenly that the whole quarter was under water in an hour. At five no one dreamed of such a danger; at seven all the lower part of the city was covered, up to the first story in many places. A friend who promptly went to the rescue of the Jews, told us that the scene was pitiful; for the poor souls live in cellars, packed like sardines in a box, and being washed out all of a sudden were utterly destitute. In one street he saw a man and woman pushing a mattress before them as they waded nearly to their waists in water, and on the mattress were their little children — all they could save. Later in the day, as the boats of provisions came along, women and children swarmed at the windows, crying "Bread! bread!" and their wants could not be supplied, in spite of the generosity and care of the city authorities. One old woman who had lost everything but her life besought the rescuers to bring her a little snuff for the love of heaven; which was very characteristic of the Italian race. One poor man, in trying to save his wife and children in a cart, upset them, and the little ones were drowned at their own door. Tragedy and comedy, side by side.

Outside the city houses were carried away, and people saved with difficulty, so sudden and rapid was the overflow. A bridge near the Ghetto was destroyed, and a boatful of soldiers upset in the current and several men drowned. In the Corso several shops were spoilt, and many people were ruined by the mishap. Friends of ours from Boston were cut off from supplies for two days, and lived on bread and water till help came. A pleasant little experience for the Christmas holidays.

We fared better, for our piazza is on the hill and our Lavinia, forseeing a famine, laid in stores; among them live fowls, who roost in the kitchen with the cats and L.'s relatives, who infest that region in swarms. If the heavy rains continue we may come to want; for the woodyards are under water, the railroads down in all directions, and the peasants from outside cannot get in to bring supplies, unless the donkeys swim. So far we enjoy the excitement; for the sleepy old city is all astir, and we drive about seeing unexpected sights in every direction. Being a Goth and a Vandal, I enjoy it more than chilly galleries or mouldy pictures. It thrills *me* more to see one live man work like a Trojan to save suffering women and babies, than to sit hours before a Dying Gladiator who has been gasping for centuries in immortal marble. It's sad, but I can't help it.

Darkness.

Last night the gas went out in many parts of the city, and people were ordered to put lamps at their windows — for thieves abound. We prepared our arms, consisting of one pistol, two daggers, and a heavy umbrella, and slept peacefully, although it was possible that we might wake to find ourselves floating gently out at the Porta Pia. My last idea was a naughty hope that the Pope might get his pontifical petticoats very wet, be a little drowned, and terribly scared by the flood; for he deserves it.

NOVEL SCENES.

Today the water is abating, and we are becoming accustomed to the sight of boats in the market-place, gentlemen paying visits on the backs of stout soldiers, and family dinners being hoisted in at two-story windows. All the world is up on the Pincio looking at the flood; and a sad sight it is. Outside the Popolo Gate a wide sea stretches down the valley, with roofs and trees sticking up dismally from the muddy water. A raging river foams between us and the Vatican, and the Corso is a grand canal where unhappy shopkeepers float lamenting. The Pantheon is under water over the railing, the Post Office has ceased to work, the people have become amphibious, and Rome is what Grandmother Rigglesty would call "a wash."

THE POOR.

The city officers are working splendidly, having fed and housed the poor; but there will be much misery, and beggars already begin to come to us with long tales of their woes. Lavinia's five grandmothers, six aunts and two dozen small nephews and nieces will settle for the winter in our tiny kitchen probably, although none of them have suffered by the flood; and we shall not have the heart to object, they look so comfortable and be so easy about it. Lavinia herself is as good as a whole opera troupe, she is so dramatic and demonstrative. Ristori[3] is feeble beside L. when she shakes her fist at the Pope and cheers for the King, with a ladle in one hand, and her Italian eyes flashing as she prances with excitement, regardless of our *polenta* burning in the frying-pan.

January 1, 1871.

THE CLIMATE AND THE KING.

A happy new year to you and a pleasanter day than we have here in balmy Italy; which, by the way, is the greatest humbug in the way of climate that I ever saw. Rain, wind, hail, snow and general disorder among the elements. Boston is a paradise compared to Rome just now. Never mind; we had a new sensation yesterday, for the King came in the first train from Florence to see what he could do for his poor Romans. He arrived at 4 A. M., and though unexpected, except by a few officials, the news flew through the city, and a crowd turned out with torches to escort him to the Quirinal. Lavinia burst in like a tornado to tell us the joyful news; for the people have begun to think that he never would come, and they are especially touched by this prompt visit in the midst of their trouble. He is to come on the 10th of January and make a grand entry; but the kind soul could not wait, so came as soon as the road was passable, and brought 300,000 francs for the sufferers with his own royal hands.

VICTOR EMMANUEL.

Of course we rushed up to the Quirinal at once, though it rained hard. Before the palace stood a crowd waiting eagerly for the first sight of the King, and cheering heartily every one who went in or out.

There was a great flurry among the officials, and splendid creatures in new uniforms flew about in all directions. Grand carriages arrived, bringing the high and mighty to welcome the King. General Marmora, looking like a seedy French rowdy, went in and out, full of business. Dorias and Collonas gladdened our plebeian eyes, and we cheered everything, from the Commander-in-Chief to somebody's breakfast, borne, through the crowd by a stately "Jeames" in a splendid livery. We stood one mortal hour in a pelting rain, and then retired; feeling that the sacrifice of our best bonnet was all that could reasonably be expected of a free-born American. We consoled ourselves by putting out Lavinia's fine Italian banner, supported by our two little ones proudly bearing the stars and stripes, and much perplexing the boys and donkeys who disport themselves in the Piazza Barberini.

Feeling that neuralgia would claim me for its own if I went out, I sat over the fire and read Roba di Roma; [4] while M. and A. took a carriage and chased the King all over the city, till they caught him at the Capitol. They had a fine view of him as he came down the steps of the Capitol, through a mass of people cheering frantically and whitening the streets with waving handkerchiefs.

ENTHUSIASTIC RECEPTION.

My enthusiastic damsels mounted up with the driver and cheered with all their hearts, as well they might, for it certainly was a sight to see. They had another view of the King on the balcony of the Quirinal; for the people clamored so for another sight of "Il Re" that the Pope's best velvet hangings were hastily spread on the balcony and Victor Emmanuel came out and bowed to his people, "who stood on their heads with rapture," as one young lady expressed it. He was in citizen's dress; and looked like a stout, brown, soldiery man, M. said. He hates ceremony and splendor, and would not have the fine appartments offered him, but chose a plain room and said:

"Keep the finery for my sons, if you like; I prefer this." He asked the city fathers to give the money they intended to spend on welcoming him, to the poor. But they insist on giving him a Roman welcome when he comes on the 10th. He only passed one day here, and went back to Florence last night at five. All Rome was at the station to see him off. Ladies with carriages full of flowers were tearing by at dusk, and there was a great demonstration; for this kingly sympathy has won all hearts.

We are preparing to decorate our balcony for the 10th, and have our six windows full of cheering Yankees; for our rooms are directly on the street he will pass by, and our balcony on the Piazza, where two great arches are now being set up. The prudent A. suggests that we let these windows and make our fortunes, but we decline and intend to hurrah our best for the "honest man," as they call Victor Emmanuel — and that is high praise for a king ***

LITERARY WORK.

I hope the New Year opens well and prosperously with you. I was just getting well into my work on "L.M.," when sad news of dear "John Brooke's" death came to darken our Christmas and unsettle my mind. But I now have a motive for work stronger than before; and if the book can be written, it shall be, for the good of the two dear little men now left to my care, for long ago I promised to try and fill John's place if they were left fatherless.

We all send best wishes, and I am as ever

Yours truly,   L.M.A.

MS: Unlocated. Printed: "Recent Exciting Scenes in Rome," *Boston Daily Evening Transcript*, 3 February 1871, p. 1. In the same issue is the following (p. 2): "The Letter from Rome on our first page will be read with pleasure; not only for its lively and graphic descriptions of recent events in that city, but also for the assurance it gives of the improved health of an author whom tens of thousands have learned to value as a friend. Without the help of the initials appended to it, readers will at once see from whose pen it comes and rejoice at the intimation, in the last paragraph, that the 'Little Women' are to be matched ere long with the 'Little Men;' even whilst they sympathize with the sorrow implied in the added motive for the care to be taken of the fatherless boys."

Earlier, reports had been circulating in the Boston papers about LMA's supposed ill health and even death. Niles tracked the rumors back to a letter from Mrs. Howe to her brother, in which she said LMA had died of diphtheria. Beginning his letter of 20 January 1871 to LMA with "Are you dead?" Niles went on: "I have had a continual stream of excited individuals men, women, boys & girls rushing in, with tears in their eyes, to ascertain the facts" (Houghton Library, Harvard University).

1. This letter may have been written to Daniel Noyes Haskell, editor of the *Transcript*.

2. Victor Emmanuel had upset Pope Pius IX by taking possession of church revenues, allowing the opening of the first Protestant church in Rome, and upholding secular law over ecclesiastical. In return, the Pope refused to receive the king's official congratulations on his Papal Jubilee on 16 June 1871.

3. LMA had heard Adelaide Ristori sing at the opera in Nice in April.
4. William Wetmore Story's *Roba di Roma* (1862).

To Elizabeth Wells

Rome   Jan. 9th [1871]

Dear Lizzie.[1]

Annie in her letters speaks of your being with her during that sad week & of your helping to make dear John ready for his last sleep. Also that Marmee is to make you a little visit. All these kind & tender things come right home to my heart though so far away, & I *must* thank you in this poor way.

Annie bears her loss so beautifully that it makes it possible to stay away now in order that I may be more useful by & by. But *you* know how hard it is for me to be even in Rome when my heart is at home & every day a burden till I can come.

John leaves so sweet & precious a memory of his simple upright life & lovely character that Annie has much to sustain & comfort her. Real goodness is so rare & bea[u]tiful, & he possessed it so truly that the dear boys inherit a better fortune in their father's virtues & honest name than millions of money or much fame. The ten perfectly happy & united years Annie has spent with John are a treasure which nothing can take away, for such a love must be immortal & will not be divided even by death.

Dear Lizzie, I hope I need not say to you what your own loving heart will prompt you to do, *fill my place a little till I come,* for of all our many relatives you are the nearest & dearest to us. Your daughterly care & love for Mother in her dark hour is never forgotten by me, or your regard for John who loved you much. Both mother & Annie find great comfort in your thoughtful kindness, & *I* hold it as one of the debts which I shall hope to pay in the years to come if your daughters are sick or absent when you need them. My heart is very anxious about mother & I ache to go to her, but winter, distance, health, & my duty to Alice hold me till April. I think God will keep my Marmee for me because I couldn't bear to miss my Good bye & the keeping of my promise to close her dear eyes. Annie says she is not well & so I dread another loss before I have learned to bear the last. God bless you dear L.

Ever yrs
L. M. A.

ALS: Houghton Library, Harvard University.

1. Elizabeth Sewall Willis Wells, daughter of Mrs. Alcott's sister Elizabeth Sewall May and a friend of LMA's since the latter's Boston days with Lizzie's brother Hamilton.

To James T. Fields

Dear Mr Fields

Once upon a time you lent me forty dollars,[1] kindly saying that I might return them when I had made "a pot of gold".

As the miracle has been unexpectedly wrought I wish to fulfil my part of the bargain, & herewith repay my debt with many thanks.[2]

> Very truly yours
> L. M. ALCOTT

Concord July 3rd / 71

ALS: Allyn Kellogg Ford Collection of Historical Manuscripts, Minnesota Historical Society.

1. Fields had lent LMA forty dollars "to fit up" her kindergarten in January 1862 (journal entry, Cheney, p. 130).

2. Later, LMA wrote to Louise Chandler Moulton about this incident that "Fields wanted the school for a little nephew & lent me forty dollars to get books, chairs &c, telling me to give up trying to write & stick to my teaching," and that when *Little Women* came out, "I returned the money & said I found writing paid so much better than teaching that I thought I'd stick to my pen. He laughed & owned that he made a mistake" ([1883?], Houghton Library, Harvard University).

To John Seely Hart

Concord Sept. 13th [1871]

Mr. Hart[1]
Dear Sir.

I send you an account of myself & books done by my friend Sanborn which is better than any thing I could do myself on so uninteresting a subject.[2]

To this I can only add the following facts.

I was born on Nov. 29 1832 in Germantown Penn. Was educated at home in my father's somewhat peculiar manner.

Was a teacher for ten years.

Began to write for the papers at sixteen & kept it up with varying success for fifteen years. At twenty five supported myself by needle & pen. At thirty five supported the family by pen alone.

The best proof I can give of the success of my stories is the following account lately sent me by my publishers —

87th 1000 of Little Women —   now selling fast,

47th 1000 of Old Fashioned Girl —   "   "   "

48th 1000 of Little Men — which came out in June last.[3]

Roberts Bros. of Boston can supply you with the notices & the names of the papers & periodicals in which they appeared if you wish to quote from them.

Hoping these facts are what you desire, & thanking you for the honor done me I remain

Yours respectfully — L. M. ALCOTT

Over a hundred letters from boys & girls, & many from teachers & parents assure me that my little books are read & valued in a way I never dreamed of seeing them. This success is more agreeable to me than money or reputation.

ALS: Cornell University Library.

1. John Seely Hart, a professor of rhetoric at Princeton University, was preparing *A Manual of American Literature*, in which a sketch of LMA would appear, using the facts from this letter and many of its phrases ([Philadelphia: Eldredge and Brother, 1873], pp. 499–500).

2. "The Author of Little Women," *Hearth and Home* 2 (16 July 1870): 1. Accompanying this letter is Sanborn's unsigned article, which includes a picture of LMA, at the top of which she has written "Not a good likeness — Too dark, & the nose all wrong." She had also crossed out a description of *Moods* in the article as "embodying but incompletely her idea of love and marriage and failing, for that reason, perhaps, to take the position in literature which the author's talent justified."

3. By September 1871, Roberts Brothers had printed 41,000 copies of the first volume of *Little Women*, 39,000 copies of the second volume, 45,000 copies of *An Old-Fashioned Girl*, and 43,000 copies of *Little Men*.

To Mary Peabody Mann

81 Pinckney St.
[ca. 17 October 1871]

Dear Mrs Mann.[1]

Mr Niles sends me your note to Mr Wilson.[2] I think Mr Ns. civil note to your sister deserved a different sort of reply.

I have nothing to do with the matter but to give father the help of my very undeserved reputation by adding a preface which links a popular book to a long forgotten one.

As the copy right is out the Record belongs by law to the world, & as Miss P. *gave* the book to fath[er] some time ago he fel[t th]at he had a right to reprint. But as his ideas of justice & courtesy are strong he never thought of doing any thing till he had spoken to her. That was done after he had offered Niles the book to read, & while father was away Niles put the book to press without saying any thing about it, believing it to be father's, as we all did.

As father wished Miss P. to have the profits, which might be something considerable owing to the interest in Little Men, he thought she would be satisfied & pleased. It was not only just but generous in him & I was sorry that his plan should be spoilt, for he has waited thirty years to have his school known, & now the world seems ready to value his efforts & acknowledge thier worth.

Miss P.s. prefaces &c. confuse the readers mind, add nothing to the book, & seem to give an impression that the Recorder did not approve of what she recorded. She says she wishes to explain her own views, & retract certain observations of her own in the book. I think if she took out the observations & let the book stand simply as a Record of the school without implicating her in the least, it would be the best plan.

Mr N. says he will not print without my preface as that ensures the sale. *I* dont care in the least except for father's sake, & we should wait another thirty years without doubt only as Niles has the plates it seems unfair that the loss should be his through our mistaken belief in Miss P's gift of the book to father.

As it stands I advise Mr Niles to let the [matter?] rest for I dont want to have any trouble.

Yours respectfully L. M. ALCOTT.

ALS: Massachusetts Historical Society. The manuscript is torn; missing words or letters are supplied in brackets. Niles had given the letter Elizabeth Palmer Peabody had written to LMA on 17 October (Bronson's "Diary for 1871," pp. 664–665, Houghton Library, Harvard University).

1. Mary Peabody Mann, Elizabeth Palmer Peabody's sister, was writing about Roberts Brothers' plan to do a new edition of *Record of a School*, Peabody's account of Bronson's Temple School, first published in 1835. Plans for the book, to be called *Record of Mr. Alcott's School* in order to capitalize on the success of LMA's works (and particularly the Plumfield School she describes in *Little Men*), began in 1871. The book was actually printed and reviewed by September before Niles and the Alcotts decided to hold off publication until Peabody had finished making some additions. However, Peabody's departure for England in September for a trip that lasted until May 1872, her delays in writing a new preface in which she insisted on promoting

the German educator Friedrich Froebel over Bronson, and her plans for a lengthy appendix (never completed) all put off publication until 1874. LMA's preface did appear in the book. For more information, see Bronson's "Diary for 1871," pp. 340–665 passim (Houghton Library, Harvard University), and his *Letters*, pp. 535, 538; 29 July, 22 August, and 30 August 1871, *Letters of Elizabeth Palmer Peabody*, ed. Bruce A. Ronda (Middletown, Conn.: Wesleyan University Press, 1984), pp. 365–369; and Joel Myerson, " 'Our Children Are Our Best Works': Bronson and Louisa May Alcott," *Critical Essays on Louisa May Alcott*, ed. Madeleine B. Stern (Boston: G. K. Hall, 1984), pp. 261–264.

    2. John Wilson and Sons, a Boston printer.

To Louisa Wells(?)

[1871?]

    I send you a Parody on "The Graves Of a Household," suggested by my late afflictions with my teeth.

"They grew in beauty side by side,
    They filled one mouth with glee;
Thier graves are severed far & wide
    By mount & stream & sea.
The same fond toothbrush went at night
    O'er each fair pearly row,
It had each perfect one in sight;
    Where are those *toothies* now?
One sleeps in the forests of the West,
    For in old Concord's shade,
It was the first that openly confest
    The ruin *Calomel* had made.
The sea, the blue lone sea has one —
    It lies where pearls lie deep.
Nuts aboard ship that deed hath done,
    I think of it & weep!
One snapped at Milan; to me, bereaved,
    No splendors can atone,
We asked for bread & we recieved
    At *St Marc's* hands a stone.
One crumbled like the Roman towers
    That tottering round us stand,

*name of our Hotel.

It perished mid Italia's bowers
    The last of that bright band.
And parted thus they rest who stood
    Together in one gum,
Whose chomping mingled as they chewed
    Life's sweet or sour plum.
Farewell my teeth! of thee bereft
    I know no peace nor mirth;
Alas for me, if there were left
    No dentists upon earth!

———

I think this plaintive gem may make you laugh & that will do you good. My mouth is now fair to see, for the ruins are gone & a choice collection of china-ware gleams before the eye. They tumble out now & then, but I am learning to rattle them in with an unmoved face, & in time wont know which are my own & which my "store teeth". I only want a wig to be quite beautiful. Gray hair is the fashion however so I shall wait a while.

AL: Special Collections, Jean and Alexander Heard Library, Vanderbilt University (partial?). This letter was at one time in the possession of Louisa Wells (Elizabeth Sewall Willis Wells's daughter), to whom it may have been sent. LMA had visited Milan in October 1870 and probably wrote this letter the following year, after her return from Europe.

To Amos Bronson Alcott

[6 March 1872]

Dear Papa.

I had a chat with Niles yesterday & asked him about the cost of getting out a book ourselves. I told him that your "Concord Days"[1] would be a very pleasant work & I wanted it printed, so if he didn't feel like doing it himself I should.

He said he did want to do it, & would take it as soon as it was done. A volume a little larger than Tablets would go well. He was very fond of reading Tablets & admired it much, & would like a companion volume.

I told him I thought the sketches of men & books would make it popular & he agreed.

So peg away, Daddy, simmer it well down & let Niles have it in April, then it can come out late in May & be in time for the summer sales.

Niles says it will more than pay for itself he has no doubt.

I shall come up again after the Ball fuss is over & have a quiet day with you. Get the Ms. into shape & then we can confer & judge about the plums to leave in & the plums to take out.

your fellow scribbler L.

ALS: Houghton Library, Harvard University.

1. Bronson's *Concord Days* was published by Roberts Brothers in late September 1872.

To Abigail May Alcott

Boston, [15 April] 1872.

Dear Marmee, — Had a very transcendental day yesterday, and at night my head was "swelling wisibly" with the ideas cast into it.

The club[1] was a funny mixture of rabbis and weedy old ladies, the "oversoul" and oysters. Papa and B.[2] flew clean out of sight like a pair of Platonic balloons, and we tried to follow, but could n't.

In the P.M. went to R. W. E.'s reading.[3] All the literary birds were out in full feather. This " 'umble" worm was treated with distinguished conde-scension. Dr. B. gave me his noble hand to press, and murmured compliments with the air of a bishop bestowing a benediction. Dear B. beamed upon me from the depths of his funny little cloak and said, "We are getting on well, ain't we?" W.[4] bowed his Jewish head, and rolled his fine eye at me. Several dreadful women purred about me, and I fled.

M. said what I liked, — that he'd sent my works to his mother, and the good old lady told him to tell me that she could n't do a stroke of work, but just sat and read 'em right through; she wished she was young so as to have a long life in which to keep on enjoying such books. The peacock liked that.

I have paid all my own expenses out of the money earned by my little tales; so I have not touched the family income.

Did n't mean to write; but it has been an expensive winter, and my five hundred has made me all right. The $500 I lent K. makes a difference in the income; but I could not refuse her, she was so kind in the old hard times.

At the reading a man in front of me sat listening and knitting his brows for a time, but had to give it up and go to sleep. After it was over some one said to him, "Well, what do you think of it?" "It's all very fine I have no doubt; but I'm blessed if I can understand a word of it," was the reply. . . .

The believers glow when the oracle is stuck, rustle and beam when he is audible, and nod and smile as if they understood perfectly when he murmurs under the desk! We are a foolish set!

MS: Unlocated. Printed: Cheney, pp. 268–269.
    1. For the Radical Club, see 22 January [1869].
    2. Cyrus A. Bartol, a minister at whose house the Radical Club often met.
    3. Emerson was giving a series of lectures in Boston in April and May 1872. The only days on which the Radical Club met and Emerson lectured seem to have been 15 April and 20 May; however, Bronson lectured at a second (evening) meeting of the Radical Club on 20 May, and it seems unlikely that LMA would have left out an account of that meeting. At the Radical Club, the Reverend Jesse Hutton Temple spoke on assumption as the basis of thought, while Emerson's address was called "Books" (Bronson's "Diary for 1872," pp. 248–252, Houghton Library, Harvard University).
    4. Possibly John Weiss, a minister and Theodore Parker's biographer, who often attended Radical Club meetings.

To Mr. Farmer

Mr Farmer
    I find that Mr Sewall got ten shares in the Boston & Albany R.R. last Jan. Also twenty shares in the Philadelphia Wilmington & Baltimore R.R. in Feb.
    In Jan 1872 I received from Roberts Bros. $4403.70 for books sold. We lost some by the fire in Chicago. I made by stories $500 last winter — & lent $500.
    The July account is not yet in, so that [is] all I know about my income.[1]

Respectfully
L. M. ALCOTT.

Concord June 17th 1872.

ALS: Louisa May Alcott Collection, Barrett Library, University of Virginia Library.
    1. LMA's journal entry for January 1872 shows that of the $4,400 paid her by Roberts Brothers, she gave $3,000 to Samuel E. Sewall to invest (Cheney, p. 261).

To Louisa Wells

Sat. a.m.
[27? July 1872]

Dear Lu.
    Your two notes were not as cheery as I could have wished, but I see that you are the right girl in the right place, & that's well.
    We had a topsy turvy day at the fire.[1] I saved some valuable papers for my Ralph, & most of their furniture, books & pictures were safe. The upper

story is all gone & the lawn strewed with wrecks of beds, books & clothes. They all take it very coolly & in a truly Emersonian way. Ellen says, she only regrets not selling the old papers and rags up garret. Mrs E. floats about trying to find her clothes, & Mr E. beams affably upon the world, & remarks with his head cocked up like a sparrow — "I now see my library under a new aspect."

He looked pathetically funny that morning wandering about in his night gown, pants, old coat & no hose. His dear bald head lightly covered with his best hat, & an old pair of rubbers wobbling on his Platonic feet.

Our entry is full of half burnt papers & books, & the neighbors are collecting the clothes of the family nicely mixed up with pots & pans, works of art, & cinders. Sad but funny. The house was insured & will be built right up at once. "Our turn next," Ma darkly predicts.

May goes off to the lonely & dissolute Island[2] a Wed, & Nan & boys soon go to Plymouth. Ellen (the incapable Jade) is to depart also[3] & leave me to housekeeping & dispair. The prayers of the congregation is requested that this affliction may be sanctified to me.

Herbert's tale is too big & foolish to waste postage on so I'll keep it for the September gale when "you & me" laugh over it.

Love to all. No news except that Gusty May & M. Edes loom dimly in the distance. Selah.

Yrs ever L. M. A.

ALS: Special Collections, Jean and Alexander Heard Library, Vanderbilt University. Printed: Madeleine B. Stern, "The Alcotts and the Emerson Fire," *American Transcendental Quarterly* no. 36 (Fall 1977), pt. 1, 7–9, which also prints Anna's description of the fire. At the top of the first page is a note by Louisa Wells: "I had spent the night with the Alcotts & left in the morning just as the alarm sounded for the fire in Mr Emerson's house. 1872."

    1. For the *Boston Daily Advertiser's* account of the fire at Emerson's house on 24 July, see *The Letters of Ralph Waldo Emerson*, ed. Ralph L. Rusk, 6 vols. (New York: Columbia University Press, 1939), 6:214. Ellen Emerson's account of the fire and its aftermath is in her *The Letters of Ellen Tucker Emerson*, ed. Edith E. W. Gregg, 2 vols. (Kent, Ohio: Kent State University Press, 1982), 1:676–682.

    2. May went to Clarks Island "for rest" (journal entry, August 1872, Cheney, p. 266).

    3. Probably Ellen Emerson, who took her father to Northampton, Massachusetts, in August to recover from the effects of the fire.

To Miss Holmes

Dear Miss Holmes
    "Tom" is no more Edward Emerson than "Laurie" is Julian Hawthorne.[1] None of the characters in my books are drawn from life but the Marches.

Never believe anything "they" say, or anything you see in the papers. Its never true.

I am glad my little books amused you. Being written on a sick bed may account for the interest invalids take in them.

With thanks for the expressions of regard you send me

I am yours truly
L. M. ALCOTT

Concord Aug. 16th [ca. 1872]

ALS: Fruitlands Museums, Harvard, Massachusetts.
   1. Characters in LMA's *An Old-Fashioned Girl* and *Little Women*, respectively.

To the Lukens Sisters

Concord Aug 23rd [1872]

My Dear Little Women —

I will certainly answer your pleasant letter & very glady subscribe to your paper, although it has not yet arrived.[1]

My two little men at once demanded it & were much impressed by the idea of girls having a printing press & getting out a "truly paper."

I admire your [pluck] & perseverence [and h]eartily believe in [w]omens' right to any branch of labor for which they prove thier fitness.

Work is such a beautiful & helpful thing & independence so delightful that I wonder there are any lazy people in the world.

I hope you preach that doctrine in your paper, not in the rampant Womans Rights fashion but by showing how much women can do even in attending skilfully & cheerfully to the little things that have such an [in]fluence on home-life & through [i]t upon the world outside.

I should like to see that [prin]ting office of yours & the [manuscript torn] five sisters getting out [manuscript torn] thier paper. Wont you tell [manuscript torn] about it? for I find it more interesting than the famous Riverside Printing House & so do Demi & Daisy who went to see it the other day.

Do you let any one write for [your paper] but yourselves? Which of you [is edi]tor? & dont you have great [fun] over it?

[P]lease present my respects [to the] wise father of the five [h]appy girls,

& with the best wishes for the success of the paper believe me very sincerely your friend & fellow worker

L. M. ALCOTT
Concord Mass.

ALS: Boston Public Library. Printed: Bok, 1, where it is incorrectly dated 3 August 1872. The manuscript is torn; missing words are supplied from the printed text. Information on the Lukenses comes from this article.

1. Carrie, Maggie, Nellie, Emma, and Helen Lukens, the oldest of whom was barely seventeen, had convinced their father to print their own journal, *Little Things*, after the example of the March sisters in *Little Women*. Started in March 1871 as a handwritten newspaper, it was typeset by the third monthly issue. In August 1873, the title was changed to *Young Folks' Journal* and the format enlarged. By May of the next year, there were more than a thousand subscribers, and the girls gave it up, selling their subscription list to another publisher (Belle Moses, " 'Little Things,' " *St. Nicholas* 48 [December 1920]: 110–118).

To Anna Alcott Pratt

Boston Fire.[1]

[10? November 1872]

Dear Nan.

I dont know as there is any P.O. left to send this to you through, but at last accounts it was still standing, though injured by the great fire which has burnt from Bedford to State St.

An awful time since Sat night! I wish you had been here to see. The alarm was given about seven, but no one minded it till between 8 & 9 when the light & the alarms increased. I was going to bed, tired with a hard day's writing on "Work," but the excitement kept me up till some of the young men came rushing in to say that Summer St. was burning & the city in a panic. So I bundled up & went out to see the fire like a true descendent of Fire Warden May. I stood in Winter St. looking down into a soaring blaze for everything from Kingston to Summer was burning. Trinity Church was beginning to smoke, & all the great granite blocks of stones were melting like ice in the awful heat.

The Common was a scene of distraction, for the poor shop keepers carried thier goods there & stacked them up in great heaps with men to stand guard.

Our waiter told us that in Summer St. he walked knee deep in silks, laces & elegant shawls thrown out from the great stores. One merchant told his clerks to save what they liked as all must go, & they carried off heaps of costly laces, jewelry & rich things.

The horses are all sick, & that added to the dismay, so every sort of cart was in use, & I saw venerable Beacon St. gentlemen riding in coal carts full of books, others wheeling trucks & barrows, & many lugging thier treasures in thier arms to places of safety. Shop girls ran about with thier little bundles, & boys were hired at high prices to become beasts of burden for awhile.

The fire went along behind Washington St. leaping from one tall roof to another but did not break through till it reached Franklin St. Then great fear was felt that it would sweep up Bromfield to the West End. Water had no effect, & they began to blow up buildings to stop the flames.

Hovey's store was saved by thier own energy, but poor Holbrook's went, & his fine laces flew away in sparks as his plate glass windows melted & ran down in drops. Trinity was burnt, & H. W. was with Philips Brooks inside & they walked calmly out carrying the Bibles & other valuable articles. [2]

The fire was so great that it created a whirlwind & an awful roar. I saw blazing boards, great pieces of cloth, & rolls of paper flying in all directions falling on roofs & spreading the fire. The granite blocks in Franklin St. went down like card houses, & heavy cornices peeled off as if of paper. Fire men could not go up thier ladders the heat was so intense & many were killed by falling walls.

In one of the streets near the P.O. we stood looking up another street which was black with a crowd watching the fire creep, or rather leap, down Federal St, when a load of powder went by to blow up a block, & orders were passed to clear the place. At the word "Powder," the crowd turned like one man & the black mass grew white in a moment with startled faces as people came rushing back. W. C. & I ran off to the steps of the Granery Cemetary & there watched the flames rising & falling behind the low, old stores in Washington St. that saved this part of the city, for men could mount them & pour water into the blaze below.

The red glare, the strange roar, the flying people, all made night terrible, & I kept thinking of the Last Days of Pompeii. I enjoyed it immensely till two o clock, & then we went home to get warm. My room was the only one with a fire in it, & my little tea kettle simmering atop. So I made some hot drink, got out my cake box, & comforted the poor, wet, tired boys who came bringing thier employers' books home for safe keeping, many of the clerks having the keys & the gentlemen being out of town.

As we sat munching & telling our adventures B. [3] came flying in to say that the fire was coming our way & we must each pack a few valuables & be ready to run. No horse could be got, but the boys had a wagon & into it we ladies

170

& our bundles were to get & the good fellows would drag us over Cambridge bridge. I used to dream of being drawn by an admiring crowd as a great actress, but this was better fun. So I packed my Mss, my one good gown, a pair of new boots, & few books into my army blanket & was soon ready. My room looked like Chaos, for I told the lads to leave thier loads there as thier rooms were small & high up. So ledgers reposed upon my bed, tin boxes hid behind the door, manly garments adorned my chairs, & boots clustered round my stove.

We waited, but the fire spared us, & after a while we went out again to see if Parkers & the Tremont House still stood. They did, but State St. was in danger & the energies of the city were bent on saving that precious spot. Engines from Worcester came on express, & even from N.Y. as our men were exhausted by two nights & a day of work.

All day Sunday the fire burned & last night the sky still glowed red with the tons of coal smoldering on the wharves & small fires breaking out all over the burnt district. Soldiers guarded the streets, for tottering walls were dangerous, & thieves so thick the police had no place to hold them when caught.

The fire went back to Fort Hill, & that part is a ruin. The loss in money beats Chicago, but the loss of life is much less, thank God. Mr B's. store burnt to the ground. H. W. saw the sign shrivel like a leaf. The little old houses still stand when the tall blocks with thier flimsy Mansard roofs have vanished.

"He that is low need fear no fall."[4]

I was up all Sat. night larking about with the boys & Mrs F. & had a fine time. To day I am worn out & stay at home to tend the cats one of the boys saved. His master told him to take a basket of wine, as the office was afire, but when he ran back for it old Puss implored him to save her family, trembling in another hamper. "She looked so pitiful & begged so hard I couldn't leave her, for she wouldn't come without the kits," said the good fellow. So he left the wine & saved the poor mother & her babies. He had an extra big slice of cake for that, & the interesting family repose on my hearth in peace today.

The poor spotted dog I saw howling over the ruins of a house I shall put in a story he was so pathetic & so very ugly.[5]

The Museum is safe! So rejoice, for when that goes Boston loses its great charm for us.

I thought Roberts Bros. was gone & the Old South. But R. B. escaped with melted window panes, & the old church is still there with another event to meditate over.

171

AL: Houghton Library, Harvard University.

1. This fire, which started on 9 November, spread over sixty acres in the business center of Boston, destroying some three thousand stores, warehouses, and businesses, with a total loss of nearly eighty million dollars.

2. The dry goods merchants C. F. Hovey and Company at 33 Summer Street and C. C. Holbrook and Company at 12 Summer Street; possibly Hamilton Willis; Phillips Brooks was pastor of Trinity Church.

3. Possibly George William Bond, whose store was lost in the fire.

4. From *Pilgrim's Progress*, misquoting "low" for "down."

5. In a later hand, LMA had written "Huckleberry" here. The story of that title appeared in the 16 January 1873 *Youth's Companion*.

To William Henry Venable

Boston Nov. 21st [1872]

Mr Venable[1]

Dear Sir.

I am quite willing that you should use the scenes in Little Women in any way you like.[2]

Some of them have already been dramatized & acted here, & went very well.

I esteem it an honor that my little stories are considered worthy to be used for the instruction as well as the amusement of young people, & have often wondered why some one did not get up simple, innocent plays for the use of the little actors & actresses who so early begin to play thier parts in the drama of life.

With best wishes for the success of your work.

I am respectfully yours

L. M. ALCOTT.

ALS: Whelpley Collection in the Cincinnati Historical Society.

1. William Henry Venable taught at the Chickering Institute in Cincinnati.

2. Venable's *The School Stage: A Collection of Juvenile Acting Plays* (1873) included two short plays dramatized from *Little Women*.

To Amos Bronson Alcott

Spinster's Retreat

Nov. 29th 1872.

———

Dear Papa.

I mailed you one of the new books yesterday.[1] It is not good but a partial parent will accept it as a birthday gift from his 40 year old "girl."

They gave me a lovely celebration at home, quite perfect if the dear "father bird" had been there to make the nest full & the assembled brood happy.

The boys met me at the gate with lanterns & flags & bore me into the house illuminated hung with garla[nds &] bright with loving faces in honor of the occasion.

Your study was all flowers & light, & a roaring fire shone over the two tables ready for the double birthday, though you were so far away.[2]

Marmee sat in the big red chair waiting with open arms to embrace the wanderer, & the boys danced about waving flags, while Nan & May beamed over me as I examined the pretty treasures the dear souls had made for me.

We had a happy eve talking over past present & future, & coming to the conclusion that Alcotts were prospering after years of patient work & waiting. You the champion [manuscript torn] of the West, love[d,] welcomed, honored & *paid*. Mother at rest in a cosy hom[e] with no money troubles to vex her dear soul now. Nan happy with her fine boys, & May busy at the work she loves, studying & teaching art, & helping several poor girls to the help she needed so long & loves so much to give now that she can.

You will be glad to hear what a bit of luck I've had. Mr C. (one of the editors of the Christian Union,) came to me lately with letters from H. W. Beecher & J. M. Ford both begging for a story for the paper.[3] They have been at me for two years, even in Rome & London they sent men to ask for it. I refused the $2000 they offer[ed, so] now they offer $3000[4] for a [t]ale no longer than Little Me[n] to run six months & be mine to use in book form afterward. T. N. said it was a splendid offer, as Jean Ingelow for her long story did not get half so much.[5] I agreed to rewrite "Work", & Mr C. telegraphed to B. & F. at once in great glee. It is to begin in the Xmas number & a check for $1000 is to come on Monday with the contract. T. N. was rather taken aback & felt that others were bidding high for his golden goose.[6] But he was very kind about it, & will sell it to people in Canada & London so we shall put money [in] our purse. I was needing something to [m]ake me forget my bones. Th[e] fine offer gave me a motive & I fe[ll] to at once. Work is always [my s]alvation & I will celebrate it.

Good bye ever yr L.

ALS: Louisa May Alcott Collection, Barrett Library, University of Virginia Library. The manuscript is torn; missing words or letters are supplied in brackets. At a later date, LMA wrote "Papa 73 — L. 40" at the top of the first page.

1. *Shawl-Straps*, volume two of *Aunt Jo's Scrap-Bag*, was published by Roberts Brothers in late November 1872.

2. Bronson had left on 8 November on another of his midwestern lecture tours.

3. Possibly Henry E. Childs, former editor; Henry Ward Beecher, editor; and J. B. Ford, publisher, all of the *Christian Union*. "Work; or Christie's Experiment" appeared in the paper between 18 December 1872 and 18 June 1873.

4. LMA's "Notes and Memoranda" shows that she did receive three thousand dollars from the *Christian Union* for her story (Houghton Library, Harvard University).

5. Ingelow's novel *Off the Skelligs*, serialized in *Littell's Living Age*.

6. Niles was very upset at the prior serialization of LMA's novel, calling the editors of the *Christian Union* "thieves" (see his letters to LMA in November and December 1872 at Houghton Library, Harvard University).

To Amos Bronson Alcott

Concord Dec. 8th [1872]

Dear Papa.

Being storm bound over Sunday I take advantage of the leisure day to write letters.

I have been having lively times among the publishers, for Beecher, Hale & Niles have been outbidding each other for a story.[1] Telegrams have been flying to & fro, fierce letters were interchanged, & names were called by the irate gentlemen, while the bids varied from $2,500 to $3000.

I nearly lost my wits among all this bribing & corruption & after asking other people['s] advice ended by following my own as usual.

Four chapters are done, the first will appear in the Christmas Number of the Christian Union. It is called "Wor[k"] & has some of your girls experiences in it.

I think it dull so it will probably go well. Ford & Co sent me $1000 on account & I shall invest it at once. The rest is to be paid month[l]y in installments of $250 a month. So for six months to come I have something to do, & shal[l] be the better for work, as will the story.

The boys seem well & are all at home again. Fred is to take music lessons & skate. Little [D]onny[2] cuddles Mamma & makes [s]unshine for the family.

Ma has her ups & downs but seems well. Nan purrs [a]long as usual, & May combines art & housekeeping with her usual success.

I send you two photographs of an old lady you may have met. They are rather punchy & funny, but are better than the others. The sitting one pleases Mamma & sisters best. It looks to me [r]ather sentimental, but Nan says "That's Lu as she looks [w]hen reading [manuscript torn] she knows.

What fine times you are having, & how kind they are to you out there. I see I shall have to go & thank them some time. The cane was a very pretty attention to the old gentleman who seems very festive in his 73rd year. I am 40 *not* 41, sir. It is a wise man that knows the age of his own child.

Dont get small pox at St Louis, & if you are sick let us know at once.

"Shawl Straps" goes well & good notices appear. *Bun*[3] likes it so I can die content.

Regards to all the good people & much love from your [signature cut out]

AL: Louisa May Alcott Collection, Barrett Library, University of Virginia Library. The manuscript is torn; missing words or letters are supplied in brackets.

1. Henry Ward Beecher; possibly Edward Everett Hale, editor of *Old and New*, which Roberts Brothers published; and Thomas Niles. For more on this bidding war for *Work*, see 29 November 1872.

2. John Sewall Pratt, born on 24 June 1865.

3. Frank B. Sanborn.

To Mr. Wiley

Concord May 13th [1873]

Dear Mr. Wiley,

As father is deep in garden ploughing & orchard pruning he desires me to answer for him.

The original "Plumfield" was quenched forty years ago in Boston, & has never sprung up again except on paper.

The only school we can think of is Mr Allen's at West Newton.[1]

Several people whom we know have sent boys there & seemed to like it. The Allen tribe are excellent men & many of them teachers.

I have a vague idea that Sam Greele[2] sent one of his boys there, or talked of it. Uncle Sam J. May sent his youngest son[3] I know, & liked the Allen's very much.

Any Western boy will *howl* at first at Eastern ways, but I have a firm belief in the calming & polishing effects of Eastern manners & morals.

I hope the little man will find a good place our way & be "an honor to his country & a terror to the foe", as my Demi[4] says.

With kind regards from all

I am yours truly

L. M. ALCOTT.

P. S.

When father gets his Socratic Seminary started here we shall be at no loss where to direct anxious parents. I know he will have it in time because he has waited so patiently forty years. And when it *is* underway the whole West is cordially invited to come & discuss chaos, cosmos & the Oversoul.

ALS: Fruitlands Museums, Harvard, Massachusetts.

1. Nathaniel Topliff Allen ran a progressive school at West Newton, Massachusetts, based in part on the educational ideas of his aunt and uncle, Lucy Clark Ware Allen and Joseph Henry Allen (for a description of the Allens' school, see *Memorial of Joseph and Lucy Clark Allen* [Boston: George H. Ellis, 1891], pp. 87–119, and Judith Strong Albert, "The Allen School: An Alternative Nineteenth-Century Education," *Harvard Educational Review* 51 [November 1981]: 565–576).

2. Samuel Greele, deacon of the Federal Street Church for almost fifty years, married Louisa May, Mrs. Alcott's sister, in 1823.

3. George Emerson May (b. 1844), youngest son of Mrs. Alcott's brother Samuel Joseph May.

4. Fred Pratt.

To the Lukens Sisters

Concord Sept. 4th [1873]

Dear Sisters,

You ask about little stories. Well, D. Ford of the Companion pays $50 apiece for them.[1] Much more than they are worth of course, but he says he pays for the name, & seems satisfied with his bargain. I write for nothing else except a tale for the Independent now & then, which brings $100. This winter I shall write for Scribner at thier request, as I have no book on the stacks.[2]

For you I will, if I have time, write a tale or sketch now & then for love not money, & if the name is of any use you are very welcome to it.

I remember the dear little Pickwick Portfolio of twenty years ago,[3] & the spirit of an editor stirs within me prompting me to lend a hand to a sister editor.

I like to help women help themselves, as that is, in my opinion, the best way to settle the Woman question. Whatever we can do & do well we have a right to, & I dont think any one will deny us.

So best wishes for the success of Little Things & its brave young proprietors.

yrs truly L. M. ALCOTT.

P.S.

I did not like the suicide in "Work," but as much of that chapter was true I let it stand as a warning to several people who need it to my knowledge, & to many whom I do not know.[4] I have already had letters from strangers thanking me for it, so I am not sorry it went in. One must have both the dark & the light side to paint life truly.

I'll write from imagination not cuts. I send you the last style of photo I have. Not very good but you can't make a Venus out of a tired old lady. Let me see yours by all means.

ALS: Boston Public Library. Printed: Bok, 1.
    1. Daniel Ford, editor of the *Youth's Companion*.
    2. "Roses and Forget-Me-Nots" appeared in the March 1874 *St. Nicholas*, published by Scribner.
    3. The "Pickwick Portfolio" was LMA's childhood newspaper as named and described in *Little Women*. Manuscript copies of "The Pickwick" are at Houghton Library, Harvard University, and the Louisa May Alcott Collection, Barrett Library, University of Virginia Library.
    4. For LMA's own plans to have "jumped into the river" when her "courage most gave out," see [October 1858].

To the Lukens Sisters

Concord Sept. 20th [1873]

Dear Sisters.

I waited till the five were all here before I sent my thanks for them.[1]

They make a very pretty little "landscape", as Jo used to say, all in a group on my table, & I am glad to show such a posy of bright, enterprising girls. Long may they wave!

My Marmee, though very feeble now, was much pleased at your message & said in her motherly way, as she looked at the five faces, "Little dears, I wish I could see em all, & do something for em."

Perhaps some of these summers we may see a band of pilgrims coming up to our door, & then the three old March girls & the five young Lukens ditto will sit in a bunch & spin yarns. Play we do?

Of one thing let me an old scribbler warn you. Dont write with *steel pens* or you will get what is called "writers cramp," & lose the use of your thumb

177

as I have. I have to wobble round with two fingers while my absurd thumb is folded under & no good for pen work, though all right for other things.

Look at my wild scribbles & use cork pen-holders or gold pens, & dont write fourteen hours at a stretch as I used to do.

I'm glad there is ironing & preserving to rest the busy brains with good wholesome work, I believe in it so heartily that I sweep my eight rooms twice a week, iron & scrub round for healths sake, as I have found it better medicine than any Dr ever gave me.

Keep the bodies strong & healthy & the nerves wont get out of order or the spirits turn blue. Old ladies *will* advise.

With many thanks & best love I am yours truly

L. M. A.

You may like to know that my Polish boy Laddie (or Laurie) has turned up in N.Y. alive & well with a wife & "little two daughters" as he says in his funny English.[2] He is coming to see me & I expect to find my romantic boy a stout Papa, the glory all gone. Is n't it sad?

As I cant give or lend you the dear old original I send you a picture of Marmee, taken some ten or fifteen years ago. She is much changed now, wears caps & is old & broken sadly.

ALS: Boston Public Library. Printed: Bok, 1.
    1. These pictures of the five Lukens girls are reproduced in Belle Moses, " 'Little Things,' " *St. Nicholas* 48 (December 1920): 110.
    2. When she learned that Ladislas Wisniewski and his wife and two daughters had arrived in New York, LMA instructed Roberts Brothers to pay him four hundred dollars, probably in recognition of his being part model for Laurie (see *LMA*, p. 233, and the canceled Roberts Brothers check for four hundred dollars, dated 9 October 1873, at Houghton Library, Harvard University).

To Lucy Stone

Concord, Mass., Oct. 1, 1873.

Dear Mrs. Stone:[1] — I am so busy just now proving "Woman's Right to Labor" that I have no time to help prove "Woman's Right to Vote." When I read your note aloud to the family, asking "What shall I say to Mrs Stone?"[2] my honored father instantly replied: "Tell her you are ready to follow your leader, sure that you could not have a better one." My brave old mother, with the ardor of many unquenchable Mays shining in her face, cried out: "Tell her I am seventy-three, but I mean to go to the polls before I die, even if my three daughters have to carry me." And two little men already mustered in added the cheering words: "Go ahead, Aunt Weedy,[3] we will let you vote as much as you like." Such being the temper of the small convention of which I am now President, I can not hesitate to say that though I may not be with you in the body I shall be in spirit, and I am, as ever, hopefully and heartily yours,

LOUISA MAY ALCOTT.

MS: Unlocated. Printed: "Suffrage Extension," *New York Daily Tribune*, 15 October 1873, p. 2; *History of Woman Suffrage*, ed. Elizabeth Cady Stanton et al., 6 vols. (New York and Rochester: Fowler & Wells — S. B. Anthony, 1881–1922), 2:831–832; *LAFL*, pp. 437–438. This letter was read by Thomas Wentworth Higginson at the second session of the Woman's Suffrage Convention in Brooklyn's Plymouth Church.

    1. Lucy Stone, woman's rights activist and editor of the *Woman's Journal*.

    2. The text in the *History of Woman Suffrage* has "a voice from the transcendental mist which usually surrounds" here; Higginson probably omitted it when he read the letter.

    3. Aunt Wee, LMA's persona in the stories collected in *Morning-Glories*. She was often called Weedy by her family, and she was Aunt Weedy to her nephews (and later to May's daughter, Lulu).

To Edward Marston

Concord Oct. 5th [1873]

Mr Marston.[1]

Dear Sir.

    I am sorry you think my letter cruel for it was not intended to be unjust, but merely an expression of dissatisfaction at the state of things in the accounts. I said that some of these charges might only be the usual way of doing business in England, but it seemed unfair to us & we found it hard to understand. $600 for 16,247 books is not a very profitable speculation. One of the points is this — you deduct about 8 per cent from the actual number of books sold — for every 100 copies sold I am allowed 92 copies. This my friend says may be "custom", but you also deduct 10 per cent from the amount of sales when put into pounds, & this is probably "custom" also, but we cannot see the justice of it.[2]

    Then on neither Scrap Bag was I allowed 10 per cent though I had expressly desired to have no more half profits after Little Men. "Shawl Straps" I find has been corrected, but Aunt Jo or My Boys has not been as yet.

    It is not a great matter but it makes confusion, & as the half profit plan does not suit us at all we prefer to have all future books on the other plan if you please.

    The accounts last sent are only up to Jan. 1873, & six months or more still remain to be accounted for. All publishers here settle twice a year Jan. & July — & this is a great satisfaction & convenience to authors whose books sell well & who live on the income of said sales.

I do not wish to be unjust or uncivil, but when I am constantly hearing from friends abroad that my books are found every where, especially every railway book-stall in England, & I am frequently recieving letters from English people about them I cannot help feeling that if they sell so well they should be more profitable to me. I do not expect returns like those I get here, & until many persons on both sides of the water had assured me that my books *were* popular in England I was content with small returns.

As to other houses stealing American books &c, I have given up expecting any thing like honesty on that point, for I cannot discover any laws to protect authors, & till there are some I suppose we must do the best we can.

Routledge had my first book "Moods," & seems inclined to do things in our American style, but I shall do nothing uncourteous or unfair toward you without due notice, of this please rest assured.

A third "Scrap Bag" is to come out at Christmas,[3] & if you care to have it on the same terms as the others I will ask Mr Niles to forward you the sheets as soon as possible.

With regards to Mr Low I am yours respectfully

L. M. ALCOTT

ALS: Houghton Library, Harvard University.
    1. Edward Marston, a partner in the English publishing firm of Sampson Low, Marston.
    2. A friend of LMA's had told her that she should be getting more profits than she had been receiving from her English publishers, because the same number of works sold in America would have returned more money. Marston explained to LMA that a comparison based solely on the number of copies sold was wrong and went on to spell out the advantages of the half-profits system over that which would give her a straight 10 percent royalty. For more information, see Sampson Low to LMA, 13 September 1873, and Marston to LMA, 20 September 1873 (both at Houghton Library, Harvard University).
    3. *Aunt Jo's Scrap-Bag: Cupid and Chow-Chow* was published by both Roberts Brothers and Sampson Low in December.

To James R. Osgood

Boston Jan. 28th [1874?]

Mr Osgood[1]
Dear Sir.

Mr Niles tells me that my long lost Ms. has been found.[2] As the tales have most of them been published singly the book is no longer of much value I fancy & I should be glad to put it in the fire.

The facts of the case are these. Eight or nine years ago H. Ticknor accepted the Ms. & was to bring it out as a Christmas book I think. But it did not appear & on my return from Europe I was told that the Ms. was lost. So I rewrote it & waited a year or two longer, when, in the great move from School to Tremont St the doomed Ms. again vanished illustrations & all. I paid E. B. Greene for the pictures $30, & in the course of time the blocks were found & sent to me. I did not try the book again but at intervals sent several of the tales to various magazines & papers, for I considered them mine as Mr Fields gave me $150 for my loss of time & trouble & the matter was considered ended with him.

Even in my day of small things I fancy $150 would not be considered sufficient remuneration for a book, & not an unduly large compensation for the labor, loss & disappointment of the affair.

I should like to reclaim the Ms. which does not seem to have been of much value to any one but its author. Will you kindly let me know the rights of the case.

Respectfully yours,
L. M. ALCOTT.

26 East Brookline St.

ALS: Boston Public Library. Printed: Madeleine B. Stern, *Louisa's Wonder Book — An Unknown Alcott Juvenile* (Mount Pleasant: Central Michigan University, 1975), pp. 12–13.
  1. James Ripley Osgood, whose firm, James R. Osgood and Company, had succeeded to the business of Ticknor and Fields.
  2. For more information, see Stern, *Louisa's Wonder Book*, pp. 11–13.

To Florence Hilton

Boston, March 13 [1874].

Dear Miss President: [1]

Thanks for the notes and papers telling about your pleasant society and its doings.

I am glad if any thing from my little stories is found worthy of representation, and if you had half as much fun over that immortal play as we did, it has a right to be approved.

The original libretto still exists, written in an old account book, with stage directions, which would convulse any manager, and a list of properties and costumes seldom surpassed. [2]

Did you have russet boots? I would have lent you the genuine articles, for they still adorn my wardrobe, and occasionally my feet.

Did the bed actually shut up? If not, you missed one of the finest stage effects ever seen. When the play was acted here by some Sunday-school children, that crash brought down the house, and I felt myself covered with glory, as the author of this superb idea.

My acting days are over, but I still prance now and then with my boys, for in spite of age, much work, and the proprieties, an occasional fit of the old jollity comes over me, and I find I have not forgotten how to romp as in my Joian days.

You may care to know that the Marches are all well, Mr. M. preaching to churches, schools, and divinity students as a peripatetic philosopher should. Marmee sits in her easy arm-chair and makes sunshine for the family. Meg still broods over her babies, doing double duty now that her John is gone. Daisy and Demi are trying school for the first time, and it is unnecessary to say that they are the most remarkable children in America.

Amy, after a year of study in England, is on her way home with such a load of great works that she says "in case of wreck I shall build a raft of my pictures and paddle gaily to shore." Jo is writing, nursing, croaking, and laughing in the old way. Laurie ("my polish boy") is married to a country woman and has "dear little two daughters," as he says.

Hoping this report will prove satisfactory, I am with best wishes to all, Yours truly, L. M. ALCOTT.

MS: Unlocated. Printed: "Little Women," *Chicago Tribune*, 22 March 1874, p. 13.

    1. According to the introduction, this letter was written to the president of the Philocalian Society of Chicago, who had played the part of Jo in *Scenes from Little Women* at the group's last entertainment at Standard Hall. The 1 March 1874 *Tribune* reported that the performance included *Playing Pilgrims*, *Jo's Christmas Play*, and *The Witch's Curse*, "a operatic tragedy in five acts," with Florence Hilton playing Jo ("The Philocalian Society," p. 13).

    2. See Anna Alcott Pratt's edition of *Comic Tragedies Written by "Jo" and "Meg" and Acted by the "Little Women"* (Boston: Roberts Brothers, 1893).

To Edwin Munroe Bacon

Concord   July 14th [1874]

Mr. Bacon [1]
Dear Sir,

In reply to your letter I have to say that I can supply a serial in the style, & about the same length as Little Women.

But for it I want as much as I got for Work, $2500. I was offered $3000 & accepted the offer but only got $2500 because I would not allow Mr Ford to print the book also.[2]

That right I should wish to reserve with the next story.

The St. Nicholas wanted a serial & would have paid well for it last year, but I had no time then.

I find that I must make hay while my sun shines, & so wish to earn all I can before Fortune's wheel takes a turn & carries me down again.

If this arrangement suits you will you let me know when you would want to begin the tale. One month of steady work is all I need, but time is not always to be had, & I have other work to do.

I should like to lend a hand toward helping or improving The Globe in any sense of the word, & in this story plan to have my young folks interested in several reforms, hoping thereby to inspire real boys & girls with good aims.

Yours truly
L. M. ALCOTT.

ALS: Fruitlands Museums, Harvard, Massachusetts.
    1. Edwin Munroe Bacon, editor of the *Boston Globe*.
    2. Apparently, LMA received only two thousand dollars from *St. Nicholas* (see 31 July, Bronson's "Diary for 1874," p. 842, Houghton Library, Harvard University).

To Edwin Munroe Bacon

Conway Centre
Aug. 13th [1874]

My dear Mr Bacon,

I am sorry that my last letter was not definite enough. I thought the matter was *settled* when I declined the offer & heard no further from you.

It is now too late to reconsider the affair as the story is disposed of to St Nicholas & the bargain concluded.[1]

I felt that I owed the Magazine a story as they asked for one some time ago & made a good offer. I waited some days before closing with their last offer thinking you might reconsider yours, & hearing no more from you I agreed to give them a shorter tale at the same price, securing illustrations for the book at half cost.

From various sources I hear that it is likely to be a bad year for books, so

I fancy literary enterprises of all sorts will not flourish as we could hope. I shall not venture any book I think but make what I can from short stories.

The Springfield Republican *is* a great gossip, & as one of the editors lives in Concord[2] it is vain to try & keep anything private. It does not know *everything* however or it would have said that Miss Alcott had declined to write a serial for more than one Boston paper, if that is any comfort.

If I were at North Conway I should do myself the pleasure of calling on *Miss Bacon.*[3] But we are eight miles away & I am busily at work.

Yours truly
L. M. ALCOTT.

ALS: Fruitlands Museums, Harvard, Massachusetts.

    1. Possibly a reference to "The Autobiography of an Omnibus," which appeared in the October 1874 *St. Nicholas,* although this might be another reference to *Eight Cousins,* which also appeared there.

    2. Frank Sanborn was an editor of the *Springfield Republican* and contributed a regular column of literary gossip.

    3. LMA was spending the summer in Conway, New Hampshire.

To Abigail Williams May

Boston Sept. 25th [1874]
15 Joy St.

Dear Abby[1]

I address you on the subject of boots & beer or legs & lager if you prefer it, or gas & gaiters. I have been told that you, in memory of my honored grand pa I suppose, wear the latter articles upon your aristocratic legs. I would fain do likewise as one [of] my highly connected limbs is afflicted with — let us say gout as rheumatism is a vulgar malady — so much so — referring now to the leg not the gout, that I cannot wear a boot with any comfort. Therefore the question arises, Where does A. W. M. get her noble gaiters? I have asked here & there at stores & the men look as scandalized as if I had demanded the ballot. I mean to have both ballot & gaiters however, & beginning with the smaller desire of my soul ask you, man to man, "Who makes em for you?"

Likewise having been ordered to drink lager that the intense brilliancy & activity of my brain may be somewhat quenched & a pleasing doziness produced so I can sleep & rest my colossal mind, therefore, dearly beloved, I ask you, Where does your venerable parent procure *her* lager? I know this was a deep & awful family-secret till Leicester burglars revealed it to an astonished world. But I will keep it & no one can think ill of aged ladies who need a drop of comfort as we do.

As you are *not* a busy woman I dont expect a speedy reply — Any time before frost sets in will do. *Then* my legs are nipped & perish like other morning glories.

Yrs truly L. M. A.

As I have no idea in what part of the world you are I cast my note upon the tender mercies of the P. O. trusting that you may get it in the fulness of time. Love to Aunt. L.

ALS: Schlesinger Library, Radcliffe College.
    1. Abigail Williams May, youngest daughter of Samuel May and Mary Goddard May, was Mrs. Alcott's first cousin and active in the New England Women's Club.

To the Lukens Sisters

Boston Oct. 2ond [1874]

Dear Girls.

I *am* writing a story, but it is *not* about you for I did not know enough to do it. I shall like any thing you may choose to send me about your paper & yourselves as I may like to use it some time however.

I shall not go West this Fall as I am not well enough to travel. My Father has already started but I am in my winter den, 17 Beacon St.[1] Boston spinning away at "The Aunt Hill"[2] or "Rose & the Rest", haven't decided which the name shall be. I'm afraid it will be a dull story for my head is not in it a bit & my bones ache like fun most of the time.

However as I wrote Little Women with one arm in a sling, my head tied up & one foot in misery perhaps pain has a good effect upon my works.

I sympathize with the disappointment of your friends on seeing my picture[3] for I remember I was so upset when I saw Frederika Bremer,[4] whose books I loved, that my sister, Nan & I went into the closet & cried though we were great girls of 16 & 18.

Why people will think Jo small when she is described as tall I dont see; & why insist that she must be young when she is said to be 30 at the end of the book?

After seeing the photograph it is hardly necessary to say that Jo & L. M. A. are *not* one, & that the latter is a tired out old lady of 42 with nothing left of her youth but a yard or more of chestnut hair that *wont* turn grey though it is time it did.

Yes, I got your letter about the paper, & though I was sorry to lose the little sheet I think you were wise to give it up.

As you are in the business I'll tell you that I'm going, D. V., to write Youth's Companion a serial of six chapters this winter.[5] A temperance tale, so if you have any facts to contribute pray do so.

With love to all the sisters I am as ever your friend L. M. A.

If you ever come to Boston dont forget to call on me.

ALS: Boston Public Library. Printed: Bok, 1, where it is incorrectly dated 1873. In early October 1873, LMA was still in Concord.

1. The Bellevue Hotel, 17 Beacon Street, where LMA often stayed while in Boston.

2. *Eight Cousins* was serialized in England in *Good Things: A Picturesque Magazine for Youth of All Ages* between 5 December 1874 and 27 November 1875 and in *St. Nicholas* between January and October 1875 before being published as *Eight Cousins; or, the Aunt-Hill* by Roberts Brothers in late September 1875.

3. A photograph, identified as the one to which LMA is referring, is reproduced in Bok's article.

4. Fredrika Bremer, Swedish travel writer most noted for her *Homes of the New World* (1852), which included a description of her visit to the Emerson house in Concord, at which time the eighteen-year-old LMA met her. As Mrs. Alcott described this "red-letter day" in her diary, her children "have long read and loved [Bremer] in her works, but little dreamed they should ever meet face to face" (20 February 1850, Houghton Library, Harvard University).

5. *Silver Pitchers* was serialized in the *Youth's Companion* between 6 May and 10 June 1875.

To Scribner & Co.

Boston Oct. 30th [1874]

Scribner & Co.

Gentlemen.

I was not aware that Mr Niles had written to you until he showed me your replies.[1]

If the copyright matter annoys publishers it certainly bewilders authors & leaves them in very defenceless positions at times, for there seems to be no law to guide or protect them.

Had I the money I should think it well spent in testing the question; as it is I can only try to do the honest thing as far as I can discover it.

It is certainly for my own interest to keep faith with American publishers as I find them far more generous, active & obliging than English ones. If it were not for protecting the interests of Roberts Bros. I should prefer to lose the little John Bull pays me than to be worried by delay, small returns & the very peculiar way in which business is done there.

I think if I instruct Low to print the first chapter in pamphlet form & have it out by Dec 15th that it will be all right. Also tell him that it must *not* appear in English magazine or book-form in this country. Does not that protect us all & make things safe on both sides the water?

In order to do this copy should be sent at once to Low. The first chapter or two will be enough, & they are such slow coaches there is little fear of thier getting ahead of any one in wide awake America.

Please let us have some proof as soon as possible. With best wishes for peace & profit all round I am

yrs respectfully
L. M. ALCOTT

ALS: Manuscript Division, Library of Congress.

    1. This letter refers to the protracted negotiations for *Eight Cousins,* see also 2 December [1874].

To Mary Mapes Dodge

Boston   Dec 2d [1874]

Dear Mrs Dodge.

I infer from Scribner's last voluminous epistle that you are troubled about thier & my allusion to your tears.

Of course I understood what they meant, but as the whole affair has seemed like a tempest in a tea cup to me I did not want any more time wasted over it.

The excellent gentlemen have evidently "got a bee in thier bonnet" on this point, & I cannot find out just what it is in spite of the many explanations so kindly given me.

To me the matter appears thus. I make an agreement with S. & Co. about Eight Cousins exactly as I have always done with other serials. Reserving all rights to the tale outside of thier magazine. Among these rights is that of selling it as a serial in England which gives me my copy right there & secures the book hereafter. Of course I protect S. & Co. by forbidding the tale to appear in this country in any English magazine, & if it *does* I have the power to stop it.

If I do not secure myself in England S. & Co. as well as myself are at the mercy of any English publisher who chooses to take the story.

S. & Co. agree as a matter of courtesy, & then proceed to put so many obstacles in the way, & make so many stipulations that the English publisher

187

is perplexed, & I shall probably lose the sum he offered me for the tale in order that he might keep control of the serial. I telegraph, write, explain, & try to be as obliging as I can. Change the name of the tale to suit others, put in babies to suit the artist, & endeavor to go on writing with the whole affair in such a coil that my genius refuses to burn & the story is put away till calmer times.

I value peace & good will much more than money & would gladly give away the whole Eight or put them in the fire if it were fair to others. As it is not I still wait & hope.

I am not well, & with little relief from pain day & night worry wears upon me more than [I] like to have it. If it were not for the blessed fact that everything has its comic as well as tragic side I should have lost my wits long ago with three publishers thundering at me all at once. As a sister woman you can understand this, & know that neither tears nor laughter can keep one from losing patience & spirits sometimes.

Yrs truly L. M. ALCOTT.[1]

I should like to see the pictures, if I may, before they are past change if need be. R. Bros. will like to have them if they suit.

ALS: Special Collections, Harold B. Lee Library, Brigham Young University. Printed: *LASC*, pp. 368–369.

1. This letter concerns the serializations of *Eight Cousins* in *Good Things* and *St. Nicholas*, and the book publication by Roberts Brothers. Prior to publication, Roberts Brothers, Sampson Low of London, and Scribner, publishers of *St. Nicholas*, all engaged in a bidding war (see Cheney, pp. 274–275, and *LMA*, p. 239). Complications also attended publication of the sequel, *Rose in Bloom*. According to Raymond L. Kilgour: "There was a legal dispute between Sampson Low and Son and a Swiss firm, H. Mignot, of Lausanne, over the European rights to *Rose in Bloom*. Sampson Low asserted that the book appeared *first* in England and thus had European copyright, whereas Mignot claimed that the American edition appeared first and hence Sampson, Low had no rights" (*Messrs. Roberts Brothers, Publishers* [Ann Arbor: University of Michigan Press, 1952], p. 296n).

To Scribner & Co.

Boston Dec. 10th [1874]

Scribner & Co.
Gentlemen.

I have heard from Low in reply to my telegram & he says he made a mistake in telling me he had sold the story to "*Kind Words*" — he should have said "*Good Things.*"

It is now too late to undo the bargain & Strahan[1] will print one half of the first instalment which appears in the Jan. St Nicholas in the Jan Good Things, & in like manner follow monthly, keeping behind you one half all the time, or he will keep a whole month behind you if you wish it.

Low says, "We cannot imagine that Messrs Scribner can seriously think that the issue in Good Things *after* it has appeared in St Nicholas can affect them, the sale of Good Things in the United States being extremely limited."

Low also says that I made no restrictions in my first offer to him; which is true, nor did I think it necessary. I sold him the story for publication in *England*, & if he prints it there or causes it to be printed there to send to the United States, he does it on his own responsibility.

All I can now do is what I have proposed before (& what Mr Smith says is all that is necessary to make you easy) namely — that *if* you object to Good Things coming here I shall write to Low to that effect, & if it *does* come here I shall prevent its sale as I have a legal right to do.

Low says he will write you, & you may prefer to wait for his letter before deciding the matter.

I think it very unbusiness like in Low not to know exactly *what* magazine he sold the story to; but fortunately it makes no difference as the sale of Good Things can be stopped as well as of Kind Words & neither come over in any large number.

Respectfully
L. M. ALCOTT.

ALS: Louisa May Alcott Collection, Barrett Library, University of Virginia Library.
   1. The English publisher Alexander Strahan.

To Maria S. Porter

[1874]
    I rejoice greatly therat, and hope that the first thing that you[1] and Mrs. Sewall propose in your first meeting will be to reduce the salary of the head master of the High School, and increase the salary of the first woman assistant, whose work is quite as good as his, and even harder; to make the pay equal. I believe in the same pay for the same good work. Don't you? In future let woman do whatever she can do; let men place no more impediments in the way; above all things let's have fair play, — let *simple justice* be

done, say I. Let us hear no more of "woman's sphere" either from our wise (?) legislators beneath the State House dome, or from our clergymen in their pulpits. I am tired, year after year, of hearing such twaddle about sturdy oaks and clinging vines and man's chivalric protection of woman. Let woman find out her own limitations, and if, as is so confidently asserted, nature has defined her sphere, she will be guided accordingly; but in heaven's name give her a chance! Let the professions be open to her; let fifty years of college education be hers, and then we shall see what we shall see. Then, and not until then, shall we be able to say what woman can and what she cannot do, and coming generations will know and be able to define more clearly what is a "woman's sphere" than these benighted men who now try to do it.

MS: Unlocated. Printed: Maria S. Porter, "Recollections of Louisa May Alcott," *New England Magazine* n.s. 6 (March 1892): 13–14; Maria S. Porter, *Recollections of Louisa May Alcott, John Greenleaf Whittier, and Robert Browning* (N.p.: New England Magazine Corp., 1893), pp. 22–23. Porter writes that LMA wrote this letter to her when she "was elected a member of the school committee of Melrose in 1874."

1. Maria S. Porter knew LMA for about twenty years before her death and was in charge of *The Old Curiosity Shop* when LMA presented *Mrs. Jarley's Waxworks* at the Author's Carnival in Boston in 1879. The wife of Charles Porter of Lynn, she was interested in the abolition movement and contributed poems to the Boston papers (*LMA*, p. 275; *Boston Daily Evening Transcript*, 12 March 1904, p. 17).

To Frank R. Stockton

Boston   Jan. 10th, 1875

F. R. Stockton[1]
Dear Sir.

The story was finished with the old year & has been waiting for the last touches which are most effectually given after an author has got out of the composing "vortex."-[2]

I can easily take out two chapters, which will bring the tale to the right length for St. Nicholas, & they can be put back again when the book appears.[3]

These changes can be made without damage to the little tale as a whole, because I have not attempted much in the serial but a few hints at "Dr Alec's" experiment with Rose.

Pictures of boy & girl life & character with as much fun & as little preaching as possible; this is all the short space allowed will permit me to do, & if the young people get an idea or a laugh or two out of it I shall be satisfied.

There were 24 chapters, but I can make 20 by shortening some & removing two that can be spared; as the Christmas one will come in spring & so seem out of place perhaps; & the frolics of Jamie & Pokey do not help on the story in any way.

Each chapter is fifteen Ms. "pages", & the two for each month make about six printed pages, that being the number Mrs Dodge mentioned as suiting St. Nick best.

Shall it be so? I will at once rearrange the chapters, & send a part if more is needed for the artist.

Yrs respectfully

L. M. ALCOTT.

ALS: Houghton Library, Harvard University. Printed: *LASC*, p. 352.

    1. Frank R. Stockton, assistant editor of *St. Nicholas*, later known for his short story "The Lady or the Tiger?" (1882).

    2. LMA finished writing *Eight Cousins* in December 1874 (journal entry, Cheney, p. 275).

    3. Both the *St. Nicholas* and book printings have twenty-four chapters.

To Frederick W. G. May

April 20th [i.e., 13], 1875.

Tuesday A. M.

Dear Cousin Fred: [1]

Not being sure of meeting you in "The Dary's cool retreat," whither I am about to go for a social swear at the Vermont Central, I drop a line vaguely into time and space for the following purpose, to wit, namely, viz.

My honored Ma coolly begs me to ask the lend of the Hancock punch bowl[2] for the grand Row our unhappy town is to be afflicted with on Monday next.[3] As a dutiful darter [i.e., daughter] I obey, although it may be like asking for the nose off your noble countenance or the heart out of your manly bosom.

One Grant[4] is to be handed round like refreshment on that day (and from all I learn he's about all the refreshments we are likely to get — buncome [bunkum] thrown in) and Judge Hoar[5] (who by the way has a lurid carbuncle on his judicial nose) wishes each man to decorate his mansion and get out his relics, and recieve said Grant with bursts of applause. Especially those who dwell in Revolutionary ruins are ordered to scuttle the dust of ages, the ancestral rats, and venerable bugs out of sight, and put their best foot forward.

Our humble abode used to belong to the Hoars and we are to go in for glory no end, so my Ma's dander is up and she is prancing like an old war horse, demanding that I should go to the ball as Madame Hancock,[6] that you should hand over your cherished treasures, and that a stupendous new cap should be evolved from some inspired woman's brain to deck her aged brow and do honor to the race of May. Hooray.

This being thus you see I can but rush madly to and fro trying to do the impossible while privately wish the whole affair in — well we'll say Washington, or the next best place to the warm regions where political rubbish belongs. If you can grasp my meaning in this incoherent explanation, & if you incline to please your spirited old kinswoman, bless you and come on. May will be in on Thursday and if you will bear the bowl to 17 Beacon St. on that day or Friday, she will take it to Concord clasped to her heart and the boys shall mount guard over it till I bring it home on Tuesday with the thanks of a grateful country.

Addoo — yours in —

L. M. ALCOTT.

MS: Unlocated; typescript copy at Houghton Library, Harvard University. Although the typescript copy is dated 20 April, this must have been an error in transcription; the Centennial Celebration of the Concord Fight was held on Monday, 19 April, and the previous Tuesday would have been the thirteenth.

1. Frederick Warren Goddard May, son of Mrs. Alcott's uncle Samuel May and Mary Goddard May.

2. On [21 April], LMA wrote May that her mother "enjoyed showing off the jolly old bowl immensely, & I shall enjoy getting it off my hands still more; for I have . . . stood guard over it as if my salvation depended on its safety" (Houghton Library, Harvard University).

3. LMA's account of this festive event is in the 1 May 1875 *Woman's Journal* (reprinted in *LAFL*, pp. 438–441); see also *Proceedings at the Centennial Celebration of Concord Fight* (Concord: The Town, 1876).

4. President Ulysses S. Grant.

5. Rockwood Hoar, Concord lawyer and judge.

6. Mrs. Alcott's great-aunt Dorothy Quincy married John Hancock and was known in family tradition as Madame Hancock.

To Mrs. Woods

Dear Mrs Woods,

I am very sorry that it so happens I must seem ungracious & say No, to all your proposals, but my duty makes it necessary for me to play dragon for mother's sake, & to do many disagreeable things that quiet may be secured to her.

I dont believe any one knows how we are bored by company, over a hundred a month, most of them strangers. A whole school came without warning last week & Concord people bring all their company to see us. This may *seem* pleasant, but when kept up a whole season is a great affliction. Mother says we have no home now & no chance to see our own friends. This for a feeble old lady is hard, as Father can go away & enjoy himself & so can we younger folk. So I have resolved to defend Marmee's health & home at the point of the bayonet, & be called a cross patch for my pains. It is only fair that I take the scoldings as I have been, quite innocently, the cause of much of this discomfort.

I am sure you will understand this, & see that it is easier for you to say to your friends that the Alcotts are not on exhibition in any way, than for me to shut the door upon them & seem very rude, as I must for Mother is poorly & dreads to see strangers approach though she need not meet them. [1]

Sometime when you are *alone* we shall be glad to see you, but on Friday please pass by & forgive the seeming rudeness of the daughter for the sake of a very dear old Mother whose state of mind & body needs the most watchful care.

Love to the boys,

Yours truly
L. M. ALCOTT.

July 20th [1875]
I wish you'd write an article on the rights of authors, & try to make the public see that the books belong to them but not the peace, time, comfort and lives of the writers. It is a new kind of slavery & these horrid Paul Prys [2] *must* be put down.

ALS: Fruitlands Museums, Harvard, Massachusetts.
    1. LMA wrote in her journal for the summer of 1875, "ninety-two guests in one month to entertain" (Cheney, p. 276).
    2. Paul Pry, the title character in a well-known comedy by John Poole, who, having no business of his own, was always meddling in other people's affairs.

To Mrs. H. Koorders-Boeke

Concord, 7 August 1875
Dear Madame. [1]

It gave me much pleasure to recieve the letters from you and other friends [2] and then to realize that people far away in Holland know me through my little books.

193

If you want to know something about me, even though there is not much to tell, I would like very much to mention a few little things.

I live with my worthy parents out in the country, just above Boston; they are both old; my father is a minister, my mother is frail. Two sisters still live with me, May ("Amy") a skillful artist, and Anna ("Meg")[3] now a widow with two children, "Daisy and Demi"; and I am the second daughter, an old spinster of 42 years. "Beth" the fourth daughter died a few years past, as in the book.

Many things in my story truly happened; and much of *Little Women* is a reflection of the life led by us four sisters. I am "Jo" in the principal characteristics, not the good ones.[4] I have written, have taught, have worked as a housekeeper, have edited a magazine, and have followed the army in war as a nurse. I went to the hospital in Washington and took care of at least forty "colored men"[5] until I became sick myself, and almost lost my life in the affair. Since then I have never again felt completely well, but I have no regret about the experience that cost me so dearly; that is one of the lessons that makes one's life rich and precious, and measures one's powers.

Now I am at home again, taking care of my mother, and doing that which I can which is beneficial to show what is good in the world.[6]

Since then I have been in Europe, and plan to go there yet again. The last time I was in Antwerp, and would have gladly gone on to Haarlem, had I known that I had such good friends there. When I cross the ocean again I shall try to extend my trip as far as there, but unfortunately I speak no language well other than my own.[7]

I shall receive my books in their Dutch dress with pleasure, as I already have them in their French and German attire. My next book comes out in October, and is called Eight Cousins.[8] I wrote it for a children's magazine, but it did not turn out so well as I had certainly wished, because I had to shorten it. There is to be a sequel in which the cousins are adults.

Young girls in America do not get a good education in various respects, even though much is taught to them. They know nothing of health care, or of housekeeping, and are presented into society too early. My story is intended to encourage a better plan of child-rearing, and my heroine shows that such a plan is feasible.

I could not read the addresses of the other ladies who wrote me, and thus cannot answer them. Be so kind as to convey my gratitude and greetings, and I remain Yours

very gratefully
L. M. ALCOTT

Postscript

My address is Concord, Mass. U.S.A. I enclose my picture but it does not look good. I appear sick. Send me yours.

MS: Unlocated. Printed: H. Koorders-Boeke, "Een Onzer" ("One of Us"), *De Gids* 41, 3d series, no. 15 (1877): 424–431. Koorders-Boeke had translated *Work* into Dutch in 1875. We are grateful to Alexandra Krapels for translating this letter from the Dutch. All the notes below are by Koorders-Boeke.

1. "I do not know why, but it is customary in England, and apparently in America also, to give the title of Madame to all women who are not English, just as formerly all foreigners were called Franks."
2. "It is evident that apparently people wrote her without each other's knowing they had done so."
3. ". . . which is Meta in the translation."
4. "It is, naturally, her humility that makes her speak so, for Jo is Jo and no one else."
5. ". . . we should say 'blacks.' "
6. " 'To help on the good work of the world' is stated there, and that is the only phrase of the letter which I had any difficulty translating; (it is one of the characteristic, but rather noble expressions in her books, by which she thinks a lot more than says, and people must read all between the lines)."
7. "It should exceed her expectations that everyone here understands English."
8. "Since translated into Dutch, or rather revised, by Mr. Andriessen, and published by Mr. Leendertz of Amsterdam."

To Mary Mapes Dodge

Walpole N. H.[1]
Sept. 10th [1875]

Dear Mrs Dodge.

Your letter has just reached me, & as no telegraph goes from this little nook among the hills I write at once to answer your question.

I cannot undertake any long job of pen work as I have another book on hand. But an occasional story is at your service, & one or two papers to the girls if no better person can be found. I have put so many bits of advice into 8 Cousins that I haven't much left, but will try one paper at least.

I heard of your illness from Mr Stockton who told me not to write to you, so I have been waiting for news of you. I am glad you are safe & well again, for where *would* St Nick be without you?

I hope to be in New York for a part of the coming winter if I can find a snug corner somewhere. Dr Bellows[2] mentions a place Mrs Cushmans in 16th St. but is rather vague.

Do you happen to know of a private boarding house where a lone &

literary spinster could abide? Dr Millers did not suit me being too much of a mixture.[3] A central, comfortable & moderately cheap place would satisfy. Dont trouble yourself the least bit, but *you* might understand better than Dr B. or Judge Howland[4] what a woman would like.

With regards to the son I am yours truly

L. M. ALCOTT.

I think the "Talks" an excellent idea. Glad 8 Cousins suit in spite of its many trials & faults.

ALS: Wilkinson Collection of Mary Mapes Dodge, Princeton University Library.

1. LMA had left for New Hampshire on 1 September "to pass a few weeks with her sister and the Little men" (2 September 1875, *Letters*, p. 655).

2. The minister Henry Whitney Bellows of New York.

3. Dr. Eli Peck Miller, supervisor of the Bath Hotel and the New Hygienic Institution in New York. Despite LMA's misgivings, she did stay with him.

4. Possibly William Howland, circuit court commissioner for Lynn, Massachusetts.

To Samuel E. Sewall

Sept. 28th [1875]

Dear Mr Sewall.

I should much like to have Mr Smith pay off his *whole mortgage* as I can invest the money at 6 & 7 p.c. very easily, & dont care to take 5.

I was about to consult you about a matter in which I am interested. It is this. Miss Henrietta Joy & her sister's have bought a house on Warren St. Roxbury where they take boarders & the patients of Mrs Dr Lawrence, the married one. They want to have 3 or $4000 to pay the first installment of the price, which must be done on *Friday next.*[1]

I should like to lend them this sum, as my new book will be very profitable,[2] & the house is just the place many of us used up people need to go to for repairs. Mrs L. offers as security either her note which her life insurance will pay, or a second mortgage on the house which costs twelve thousand.

The other sisters are responsible for the rest of the sum.

Will you kindly tell me *by tomorrow* your opinion of the investment from a business point of view. In justice to the boys & Anna I dont want to do anything unwise, but I *do* very much want to help Mrs L. get a good start. The boarders, her practice, (which brought her $1000 last year though she is just beginning,) & the interest & support of Dr Wesselhoeft[3] & other friends seem to assure success, & I hope we can make it go.

Has Lucy[4] returned? I thought I saw her carriage at the Hospital yesterday.

We shall all be here this week & glad to see you.

As ever yrs
L. M. ALCOTT.

ALS: Massachusetts Historical Society.
    1. Henrietta Joy, Mary Joy, and Dr. Rhoda Ashley Joy Lawrence. Dr. Lawrence attended the Female Seminary in Charlestown, took charge of the Western Union Telegraph office in Jamaica Plain, and studied at the Boston University School of Medicine. She established a nursing home at Dunreath Place, Roxbury, where LMA spent her last years. LMA's "Notes and Memoranda" for 1873 shows a three-thousand-dollar mortgage for "L.," presumably Dr. Lawrence (Houghton Library, Harvard University).
    2. *Eight Cousins.*
    3. Dr. Conrad Wesselhoeft, longtime homeopathic physician to the Alcotts, to whom LMA dedicated *Jo's Boys.*
    4. Lucy Ellen Sewall, Samuel E. Sewall's daughter, was a Boston physician.

To Ariadne Blish

Concord Oct. 9th [1875]

Dear Madam.[1]

Five & thirty years ago I heard the name Ariadne Blish & because of its peculiarity have remembered it ever since, although all knowledge of the child who bore it ended then & there.

When writing Eight Cousins I wanted a name & as this occurred to me first I took it never dreaming that an owner would be found for it so near home.

I have lately been told that you are much annoyed by its appearance in print, & as the only atonement now in my power I hasten to assure you that it was done in entire ignorance of your existence, & that I should have changed the name had I known in time.

It is too late now to alter it in Eight Cousins, but if there should be a sequel Ariadne will be rechristened.[2]

Regretting the annoyance I have innocently caused you, I am

Respectfully yours
L. M. ALCOTT.

ALS: Louisa May Alcott Collection, Barrett Library, University of Virginia Library.

1. Ariadne Blish taught in the Cambridge public schools for eleven years and ran a school at her home for eight. In replying to this letter, she mentioned that she had been *"very very* much hurt" by her name being used in *Eight Cousins* because she was "naturally very shy" (14 October 1875, Barrett Library, University of Virginia Library).

2. LMA later changed the name of the character to Annabel Bliss.

To Amos Bronson Alcott

Monday A.M.

[18 October 1875]

On the last day of the Woman's Congress, Lotty (Mrs Wilkinson) and I went in the P.M. and as we were late, we had to sit on the stage.[1] I got behind a canvass tree, with a painted fire place to lean on, and sat as still as a mouse. Many young folks were in the house, and presently the stage boxes opposite began to fill up with girls all gazing upon the lady in black. Mrs. Manniford and others came and asked for autographs, and I gave them, though I found out afterwards that they were asked to speak to me that the girls might be sure I was I. When the meeting was over, the stage filled in a minute (it seemed to me,) with beaming girls all armed with Albums and cards and begging to speak to Miss A. I wrote some and then said, I could'nt keep Mrs W. waiting. "Do put up your veil so we can see how you really look" said one. "Will you kiss me please," said another. "Oh do write some more," said several, and I finally had to run for my life with more girls all along the way, and Ma's clawing me as I went.[2] Lotty thought it was fun, and we went off to do an errand at Mr [Alfred] Wilkinsons bank. I of course looked out of the window, while Lotty and Forman talked. But soon a flock of girls who had followed gathered on the side walk, and were staring in, so I right aboutfaced, and when we came out, Lotty had another laugh, and so home we went. I did not go in the evening, but Jane Hosmer took a lot of autographs to the girls who had said they must have them, and now I trust I'm done.

I have my "Graphic Story" under way,[3] and shall see Niagara and then slip away to New York.

MS: Unlocated; manuscript copy by Bronson at Houghton Library, Harvard University.

1. According to the *New York Daily Tribune*'s report, the "audience was the largest ever assembled" in the hall, and "many were compelled to sit on the floor" ("Woman's Congress," 15 October 1875, p. 6).

2. LMA's journal gives this account of the occasion: "Write loads of autographs, dodge at the theatre, and am kissed to death by gushing damsels. One energetic lady grasped my

hand in the crowd, exclaiming, 'If you ever come to Oshkosh, your feet will not be allowed to touch the ground; you will be borne in the arms of the people! Will you come?' 'Never,' responded Miss A., trying to look affable, and dying to laugh as the good soul worked my arm like a pump-handle, and from the gallery generations of girls were looking on. 'This, this, is fame!'" (October 1875, Cheney, p. 277).

3. The 22 December 1875 *New York Graphic* announced the *Christmas Graphic*, "entirely separate and distinct from the regular issue . . . [of] twenty pages, including a four-page cover, illuminated with elegant designs" (p. 403). LMA's "The Boy's Joke, and Who Got the Best of It" appeared on pp. 4–5, and she received one hundred dollars for the story ("Notes and Memoranda," Houghton Library, Harvard University).

To Caroline H. Dall

41 West 26th Street.

Dear Mrs Dall.[1]

Having explained the matter to Miss Blish herself as soon as I learned that she was alive & troubled by my use of her name, I do not think it necessary to do anything more.

The name cannot be changed in the book now; in the sequel of course it will be, & as I intended no unkindness or disrespect in using the peculiar name of a child whom I saw for a few days thirty five years ago I consider that in explaining the fact & apologizing for the liberty I have amended my carelessness in the only way possible.

No earring episode ever occurred, & I remember nothing about little Ariadne except that she was a very well behaved child who was held up to naughty Louisa as a model girl.[2]

Any farther discussion of the affair seems to me unwise as everything in this busy world is so soon forgotten if let alone.

yrs in haste
L. M. Alcott.

Nov. 10th / 75

Thanks for defending me, but do not trouble yourself about it for I am used to being mis-understood by a certain class of persons & have learned not to mind it if I honestly do what seems right both to those whom I unwittingly offend & those who offend me. One's best defence is one's life & character.

ALS: Massachusetts Historical Society. Printed: *LASC*, p. 353.

1. Caroline Wells Healey Dall, author and reformer, had been involved with the Concord circle ever since she had attended Margaret Fuller's "Conversations" in the early 1840s.

2. In Chapter 15 of *Eight Cousins*, Ariadne impresses her friend Rose with her earrings and then pierces her ears so that she, too, may have some. Dr. Alec sees this as vanity.

To Amos Bronson Alcott

New York, Nov. 26, 1875.

Dear Seventy-Six, — As I have nothing else to send you on our joint birthday, I'll despatch a letter about some of the people I have lately seen in whom you take an interest.

Tuesday we heard Gough on "Blunders," and it was very good, — both witty and wise, earnest and sensible.[1] Wednesday eve to Mr. Frothingham's for his Fraternity Club meeting.[2] Pleasant people. Ellen F.; Abby Sage Richardson, a very lovely woman; young Putnam and wife; Mrs. Stedman; Mattie G. and her spouse, Dr. B., who read a lively story of Mormon life; Mrs. Dodge; O. Johnson and wife, and many more whose names I forget.[3]

After the story the given subject for discussion was brought up, — "Conformity and Nonconformity." Mr. B., a promising young lawyer, led one side, Miss B. the other, and Mr. F. was in the chair. It was very lively; and being called upon, I piped up, and went in for nonconformity when principle was concerned. Got patted on the head for my remarks, and did n't disgrace myself except by getting very red and talking fast.

Ellen F. was very pleasant, and asked much about May. Proudly I told of our girl's achievements, and E. hoped she would come to New York. Mrs. Richardson was presented, and we had some agreeable chat. She is a great friend of O. B. F., and is lecturing here on "Literature."[4] Shall go and hear her, as she is coming to see me.

O. B. F. was as polished and clear and cool and witty as usual; most gracious to the " 'umble" Concord worm; and Mrs. F. asked me to come and see them.

Yesterday took a drive with Sally H[olley]. in Central Park as it was fine, and she had no fun on her Thanksgiving. I dined at Mrs. Botta's, for she kindly came and asked me.[5] Had a delightful time, and felt as if I'd been to Washington; for Professor Byng, a German ex-consul, was there, full of Capitol gossip about Sumner and all the great beings that there do congregate. Mr. Botta you know, — a handsome, long-haired Italian, very cultivated and affable.[6]

Also about Lord H.,[7] whom B. thought "an amiable old woman," glad to say pretty things, and fond of being lionized. Byng knew Rose and Una, and asked about them; also told funny tales of Victor Emmanuel and his Court, and queer adventures in Greece, where he, B., was a consul, or something official. It was a glimpse into a new sort of world; and as the man was very accomplished, elegant, and witty, I enjoyed it much.

We had music later, and saw some fine pictures. Durant knew Miss Thackeray,[8] J. Ingelow, and other English people whom I did, so we had a good dish of gossip with Mrs. Botta, while the others talked three or four languages at once.

It is a delightful house, and I shall go as often as I may, for it is the sort of thing I like much better than B[ellevue]. H[otel]. and champagne.

To-night we go to hear Bradlaugh; to-morrow, a new play; Sunday, Frothingham and Bellows; and Monday, Mrs. Richardson and Shakespeare.[9]

But it is n't all play, I assure you. I'm a thrifty butterfly, and have written three stories. The "G." has paid for the little Christmas tale; the "I." has "Letty's Tramp;" and my "girl paper" for "St. Nick" is about ready.'[10] Several other papers are waiting for tales, so I have a ballast of work to keep me steady in spite of much fun.

Mr. Powell[11] has been twice to see me, and we go to visit the charities of New York next week. I like to see both sides, and generally find the busy people most interesting.

So far I like New York very much, and feel so well I shall stay on till I'm tired of it. People begin to tell me how much better I look than when I came, and I have not an ache to fret over. This, after such a long lesson in bodily ails, is a blessing for which I am duly grateful.

Hope all goes well with you, and that I shall get a line now and then. I'll keep them for you to *bind* up by and by instead of mine. . . .

We can buy a carriage some other time, and a barn likewise, and a few other necessities of life. Rosa[12] has proved such a good speculation we shall dare to let May venture another when the ship comes in. I am glad the dear "rack-a-bones" is a comfort to her mistress, only don't let her break my boy's bones by any antics when she feels her oats.

I suppose you are thinking of Wilson[13] just now, and his quiet slipping away to the heavenly council chambers where the good senators go. Rather like Sumner's end, was n't it? No wife or children, only men and servants. Wilson was such a genial, friendly soul I should have thought he would have felt the loneliness very much. Hope if he left any last wishes his mates will carry them out faithfully. . . .

Now, dear Plato, the Lord bless you, and keep you serene and happy for as many years as He sees fit, and me likewise, to be a comfort as well as a pride to you.

Ever your loving
FORTY-THREE.

MS: Unlocated. Printed: Cheney, pp. 278–281.

1. John B. Gough, a temperance speaker, gave an untitled lecture on 23 November.

2. Octavius Brooks Frothingham, a leader of the Free Religious Association and LMA's distant cousin, was a prime mover in establishing the literary discussion group known as The Fraternity Club, which lasted from about 1869 through 1874.

3. Not previously identified are Ellen Frothingham, Octavius's younger sister, who lived on Commonwealth Avenue in Boston; Abby Sage Richardson, popular lecturer on literary topics; young Putnam and his wife, possibly a son of the publisher George Palmer Putnam; Laura H. Woodworth Stedman, wife of the poet and anthologist Edmund Clarence Stedman; the reformer Matilda Joslyn Gage and her husband Henry H. Gage.

4. Richardson's lecture series was probably titled "English Literature from the Conquest of Britain to the Death of Walter Scott."

5. Anne Charlotte Lynch Botta ran a famous literary salon in New York for many years.

6. Vincenzo Botta, Anne's husband, had emigrated to America from Turin to accept a professorship at the University of the City of New York.

7. Although the context indicates this reference is to Hawthorne, it may be to the British critic and politician Richard Monckton Milnes, Lord Houghton, who was at this time making a very successful visit to New York. Milnes had visited the Alcotts in Concord on 7 October (Bronson's "Diary for 1875," p. 641, Houghton Library, Harvard University).

8. Anna Isabella Thackeray, daughter of William Makepeace Thackeray and also a novelist.

9. Charles Bradlaugh, author of *A Plea for Atheism* (1880), did not lecture because of illness (*New York Daily Tribune*, 27 November 1875, p. 4); Henry Whitney Bellows, minister of the Church of All Souls in New York.

10. "Letty's Tramp" appeared in the 23 December 1875 *Independent*; the "girl paper" could be either "Marjorie's Birthday Gifts" or "Helping Along," which appeared in, respectively, the January and March issues of *St. Nicholas*; for the "Christmas tale," see [18 October 1875].

11. Aaron Powell, former editor of the *National Anti-Slavery Standard* and active in New York charities.

12. May's horse, Rosa.

13. Henry Wilson, former U.S. senator from Massachusetts and vice-president, died on 22 November 1875.

To Frederick and John Pratt

New York, Dec. 4, 1875.

Dear Fred and Donny, — We went to see the newsboys,[1] and I wish you'd been with us, it was so interesting. A nice big house has been built for them, with dining-room and kitchen on the first floor, bath-rooms and school-room next, two big sleeping-places, — third and fourth stories, — and at the top a laundry and gymnasium. We saw all the tables set for breakfast, — a plate and bowl for each, — and in the kitchen great kettles, four times as big as our copper boiler, for tea and coffee, soup, and meat. They have bread and meat and coffee for breakfast, and bread and cheese and tea for supper, and get their own dinners out. School was just over when we got there, and one hundred and eighty boys were in the immense room with desks down the middle, and all around the walls were little cupboards numbered. Each boy on coming in gives his name, pays six cents, gets a key, and puts away his hat, books, and jacket (if he has 'em) in his own cubby for the night. They pay five cents for supper, and schooling, baths, etc., are free. They were a smart-looking set, larking round in shirts and trousers, barefooted, but the faces were clean, and the heads smooth, and clothes pretty decent; yet they support themselves, for not one of them has any parents or home but this. One little chap, only six, was trotting round as busy as a bee, locking up his small shoes and ragged jacket as if they were great treasures. I asked about little Pete, and the man told us his brother, only nine, supported him and took care of him entirely; and would n't let Pete be sent away to any home, because *he* wished to have "his family" with him.

Think of that, Fred! How would it seem to be all alone in a big city, with no mamma to cuddle you; no two grandpa's houses to take you in; not a penny but what you earned, and Donny to take care of? Could you do it? Nine-year-old Patsey does it capitally; buys Pete's clothes, pays for his bed and supper, and puts pennies in the savings-bank. There's a brave little man for you! I wanted to see him; but he is a newsboy, and sells late papers, because, though harder work, it pays better, and the coast is clear for those who do it.

The savings-bank was a great table all full of slits, each one leading to a little place below and numbered outside, so each boy knew his own. Once a month the bank is opened, and the lads take out what they like, or have it invested in a big bank for them to have when they find homes out West, as many do, and make good farmers. One boy was putting in some pennies as we looked, and I asked how much he had saved this month. "Fourteen dollars, ma'am," says the thirteen-year-older, proudly slipping in the last cent. A prize of $3 is offered to the lad who saves the most in a month.

The beds upstairs were in two immense rooms, ever so much larger than our town hall, — one hundred in one, and one hundred and eighty in another, — all narrow beds with a blue quilt, neat pillow, and clean sheet. They are built in long rows, one over another, and the upper boy has to climb up as on board ship. I'd have liked to see one hundred and eighty all in their "by-lows" at once, and I asked the man if they did n't train when all were in. "Lord, ma'am, they're up at five, poor little chaps, and are so tired at night that they drop off right away. Now and then some boy kicks up a little row, but we have a watchman, and he soon settles 'em."

He also told me how that very day a neat, smart young man came in, and said he was one of their boys who went West with a farmer only a little while ago; and now he owned eighty acres of land, had a good house, and was doing well, and had come to New York to find his sister, and to take her away to live with him. Was n't that nice? Lots of boys do as well. Instead of loafing round the streets and getting into mischief, they are taught to be tidy, industrious, and honest, and then sent away into the wholesome country to support themselves.

It was funny to see 'em scrub in the bath-room, — feet and faces, — comb their hair, fold up their old clothes in the dear cubbies, whch make them so happy because they feel that they *own* something.

The man said every boy wanted one, even though he had neither shoes nor jacket to put in it; but would lay away an old rag of a cap or a dirty tippet with an air of satisfaction fine to see. Some lads sat reading, and the man said they loved it so they'd read all night, if allowed. At nine he gave the word, "Bed!" and away went the lads, trooping up to sleep in shirts and trousers, as nightgowns are not provided. How would a boy I know like that, — a boy who likes to have "trommin" on his nighties? Of course, I don't mean dandy Don! Oh, dear no!

After nine [if late coming in] they are fined five cents; after ten, ten cents; and after eleven they can't come in at all. This makes them steady, keeps them out of harm, and gives them time for study. Some go to the theatre, and sleep anywhere; some sleep at the Home, but go out for a better breakfast than they get there, as the swell ones are fond of goodies, and live well in their funny way. Coffee and cakes at Fulton Market is "the tip-top grub," and they often spend all their day's earnings in a play and a supper, and sleep in boxes or cellars after it.

Lots of pussies were round the kitchen; and one black one I called a bootblack, and a gray kit that yowled loud as a newsboy. That made some chaps laugh, and they nodded at me as I went out. Nice boys! but I know some nicer ones. Write and tell me something about my poor Squabby.

By-by, your
WEEDY.

MS: Unlocated. Printed: Cheney, pp. 281–284. The brackets in the next-to-last paragraph are Cheney's.

1. LMA describes her visit to the Newsboys' Lodging House in New York, which was conducted by Mrs. C. O. O'Connor, the matron of the establishment.

To Daniel Sharp Ford

Dec. 5th [1875]

Dear Mr Ford.[1]

Expecting to have much more time I have been obliged to hurry terribly to finish the story,[2] & it is not what I meant it to be after all. I cannot even copy it, & hope your printers can read the Ms. I should like to see the proof if possible, or be sure it was carefully over looked by some one, else there will be a jumble.

Now in return for my obliging scramble please send me a nice little check for $100, so that I can make my Xmas story pay for my Xmas shopping.

The Ms goes by tonight's mail, to Boston, so you will get it by Wed. I hope.

Yrs truly
L. M. A.

ALS: Overbury Collection, Barnard College Library. Printed: *LASC*, p. 354.

1. Daniel Sharp Ford, editor, publisher, and philanthropist, edited the *Youth's Companion* between 1857 and 1899.

2. "A New Way to Spend Christmas" — LMA's account of Randall's Island — was published in the March 1876 *Youth's Companion*.

To Amos Bronson Alcott

Dec. 12th[−13, 1875]
Sunday P.M.

Dear Father.

At the first quiet hour I find after a gay & busy week I will answer your last. I have told about Sorosis lunch [on] Monday,[1] Tuesday rained so I [d]id not go to Brooklyn but staid at home & wrote, also Wed. till the P.M. when Alf & Lotty came & we saw Stewart's picture gallery.[2] Thursday more pictures & Mrs Richardson's lecture on English Essayists. Friday went about with Lotty & L. Greele [&] in the eve heard Conway on Devils.[3] It was very interesting & after it I went [to] say a word to him. He was very jolly & [the] party of us had a lively chat. Mr & Mrs Botta, Frothingham, O. Johnson, A. Powell & others. There was an excellent report of the lecture in the Times which I will try to get for you. Sat. to the theatre with Lotty to see Fechter in "Camille" to which play you took me years ago when M. Heron

205

played it.[4] This was in French & F. did the lover well but has grown fat & I never ca[re] to see him again.

At 6. Edward May came for me & we went to Mrs Warren Goddard's[5] to a c[o]usin dinner, Mrs John Sewall, E. May, Alf, Lotty & myself with the Goddards made up the set. A fine house a fine dinner, seven or eight courses canvas back ducks & green peas, venison & French messes, five kinds of wine & coffee & cigars to top off with. Near[ly] three hours at table & when we were done it was time to go to Miss Booth's[6] & se[e] Conway. Alf & E. May were all devotion [to] the cousin who used to be called [a]n "odd, graham-ish,[7] transcendental, [h]alf educated tom boy." *Now* she is somebody & wears a good gown & goes [a]mong nice people she is "an old trump[?]," "dear Louisa" & "my cousin the genius." A funny world is n't it?

By ten o clock Miss B[o]oth's three parlors were full, everyone gabbing [a]s hard as they could gabble, so I dived [i]n & splashed round as briskly as the [r]est. Fished Conway from a sea of admiring ladies & had a quiet word with him. He was home sick,[8] & rather disgusted at his small audiences but as queer & jolly as ever & I was just getting into some London gossip when Miss B. came up with some newspaper men to see me & Conway was whisked off by a new set of women.

Chadwick & wife[9] came & we talked about the Concord sages in a way that would have done you good to hear. He told me that Joe May had recieved a call to Mr Furnis's church in Phil.[10] I was glad to hear it as Lotty had just been lamenting over Joe's hard fate, for his people had cut off $500 from his salary. I hope he will go & do something.

Joachin Miller was mooning about, lying on sofa's, gazing into ladies eyes & playing poet as well as he knew how.[11] I didn't see him when he called so he reproached me with it, adding "But I forgive you" — & kissed my hand. I should have liked to box his ears for a conceited puppy. No one seems to like him.

I shall hear Conway this eve if I can & see him at Mrs Croly's afterward.[12]
Tomorrow Lizzie Wells comes & I must do the honors to her.

Monday a.m.

I did not hear Conway lecture last eve as I went to tea with Miss Holly at a cousin's. Pleasant people with a flock of pretty children.

After tea I went to Mrs Crolys & had a capital time. Stedman & Stoddard, Beecher-Moulton, a man with a big red head, Miller, Dr Holland Conway, Ida Greeley & her handsome husband Nicholas Smith, Mrs Moulton & Bullard, Mrs Greatorex & daughters.[13] A Mrs Wells who met May when at Conway with the Mannings, Miss Brackett who asked me to come & see her school & go to the theatre with her next week.[14] Carlton the publisher[15] was there, & begged to be presented that he "might make his peace with Miss Alcott." So he took me out to supper at 11 o clock & we had a lively time. He explained the Morning Glory affair & we found that Fuller had lied all round. Mr C. is a handsome man, a large Tom Wheeler,[16] jolly & elegant & we made up the quarrel over coffee & cake, & I am to go & see his fine store under Fifth Avenue Hotel, & hope to get some books. I told him nothing would soothe my feelings so much as a neat check Jan 1st,[17] no matter whether the books had sold or not. He said he would be glad to buy peace & good will at any price.

Stedman is a delicate little man, an invalid, but keen & bright as a sword, & talked charmingly. Mr Croly invited Conway to speak to the whole company as all wanted to hear him. So a lively discussion followed upon American & English politics.

It was so brisk & interesting that we stayed till past 12 & then all bundled away in great haste. I enjoyed it very much, & had some good talk with Anna Brackett who went home alone without fear, in N.Y. at midnight. Says she always does it & is never molested. I have Charley the boy come for me & pay him half a dollar. A better arrangement than paying $4.00 for a carriage.

Mrs Botta invited me to breakfast with Conway Sunday morning but the note did not reach me till too late, & I was very sorry; for I like to visit at the B's & Conway has improved so much it is pleasanter than ever to hear him talk.

Mr Croly told me that Tilton's daughters had left thier mother & gone back to him feeling that *he* was in the right.[18]

No one seems to believe in Beecher, & slowly but steadily the great hypocrite is going down; his own friends finding it impossible to believe in him.

I should love to have have you here, but dont think Conversations would prosper in N.Y. People are too busy to th[ink] & only gossip prospers. Mrs Botta might make such things go, but eve[n] she is full of society cares & things that you dont enjoy. I shall tir[e] of it by & by, but now the delight [of] feeling well rather upsets me & [I] want to enjoy it. yrs ever L.

Mrs F. D. Gage has sent to ask me "to come & see the old lady in her arm chair & let her tell her love & admiration for the young lady & her good work". As they were good to you I shall go. Kiss *our* old lady for me.

ALS: Louisa May Alcott Collection, Barrett Library, University of Virginia Library. The manuscript is torn; missing words or letters are supplied in brackets.

1. The Sorosis Club, founded by Jane Croly (see note 12) in 1868 for the promotion of women's interests in art, science, and literature. The following report from the *New York Graphic* may refer to this meeting: "Mrs. [sic] Louisa M. Alcott may be credited with inventing a new substitute for a speech. She visited the Sorosis the other day and was formally presented to the club by the President as the 'most successful woman author in America,' and being on

her feet, told a little story. She said at Vassar College the girls, as usual, asked for a speech, and when she also, as usual, told them she never had and never intended to make one, they requested that she would place herself in a prominent position and turn around slowly. This she consented to do, and if revolving would satisfy or gratify Sorosis she was willing to 're-volve' " ("Personalities," 18 December 1875, p. 374).

2. Alfred and Charlotte Wilkinson; Edward J. Stewart's photographic studio.

3. Probably Louisa May Greele, daughter of Mrs. Alcott's sister of the same name and LMA's cousin. Conway's lectures were "Demonology with Pictures of Satan" on 10 December, "St. George and the Dragon" on 11 December, and "Oriental Religions" on 12 December; the first was reported as "Demonology. An Instructive and Entertaining Lecture by Moncure D. Conway" in the 11 December 1875 *New York Times*.

4. LMA may have seen Matilda Heron play in Alexandre Dumas's *Camille* in either May 1857 or January 1858 at the Boston Theatre; Charles Fechter performed in *Camille* in French on 9 December.

5. Mrs. J. Warren Goddard, whose husband had been a trustee of Bellows's church.

6. Mary L. Booth, editor of *Harper's Bazaar*.

7. One who followed the dietary reforms of Sylvester Graham.

8. Conway had been preaching at South Place Chapel in London since 1863.

9. John White Chadwick, author and minister at the Second Unitarian Church of Brooklyn, and his wife, Annie.

10. Joseph May, son of Samuel Joseph and Lucretia Flagge Coffin May; William Henry Furness, longtime Unitarian minister in Philadelphia.

11. Cincinnatus Hiner Miller, who wrote as Joachin Miller, a western poet noted as much for his flamboyant behavior as for his verses.

12. Jane Cunningham Croly, editor of *Demorest's Magazine*.

13. Not previously identified are: Richard Henry Stoddard, popular author and lecturer; Francis Moulton, a New York merchant involved in Henry Ward Beecher's trial (see note 18); Dr. Josiah Gilbert Holland, editor of *Scribner's Monthly Magazine*; Ida Greeley, daughter of the late newspaper editor Horace Greeley, and her husband, Nicholas Smith; Louise Chandler Moulton, a popular poet; possibly Mrs. Laura C. Bullard, who often attended Mrs. Botta's gatherings and was mentioned in the Beecher-Tilton trial; the artist Eliza Pratt Greatorex and her daughters, Kathleen Honora and Elizabeth Eleanor.

14. Anna C. Brackett, educator and author of *The Education of American Girls* (1874), to whom Bronson had written on 13 November 1876 that "Louisa speaks with pleasure of her visit a year since, and of yourself" (*Letters*, p. 676).

15. George W. Carleton had published an abridged edition of LMA's *Morning-Glories* in 1867 without her consent.

16. Thomas Wheeler, husband of LMA's Concord friend Elizabeth Cheney Wheeler.

17. LMA's account books and "Notes and Memoranda" show that Carleton paid her as follows: $100 in 1874, $32 in 1875, $16 in 1876, $20 in 1877, and $10 in 1879 (Houghton Library, Harvard University).

18. In 1872, Henry Ward Beecher of Brooklyn, one of America's most popular preach-ers, was accused of having seduced Theodore Tilton's wife, Elizabeth. His trial in 1875 proved inconclusive, since it resulted in a hung jury, and he never regained his former popularity, especially when Mrs. Tilton admitted to their adultery.

To Amos Bronson Alcott

Monday Dec. 20th [1875]

Dear Father.

It would amuse you to see what a sudden dive I have made from New York fashionable life into St Louis philosophy, & how refreshing I find the change.

Conway's lectures gave me a start, & just as I was wanting the 2ond part of Faust to read, Mr Ames[1] came along with the book & Brockmeyer's letters on the very subject.[2]

So I said "Not at home," to every one & for a week have lived with Goethe's hero. What a wonderful book it is? I admire the grand old gentleman more than ever, & forgive him his fifteen sweethearts, for I've no doubt they helped him do his work, unconsciously. He seems to have believed in the worth of experiences & gone to find them; so I feel set up as that has always been my idea & practice too.

Mr Ames is a very agreeable man, full of Harris[3] & Hegel but does not neglect two sisters whom [he] is educating, & seems busy about [g]ood things. We talk over Concord & its sages at meal times & he enjoys my impious remarks about the sacred sand bank. He makes a pilgrimmage thither once a year, & on one of these trips saw you & had a capital time, for you showed him all over the house & told him much news.

Miss Brackett has been pleased to be very cordial to this lowly worm of an L. M. A. Invites me to visit her school, go to the theatre & discuss education copiously.

So you see I have not been swamped in a sea of frivolity but come ashore on Speculativ[e] Philosophy which seems pretty solid, & inspires me with a sudde[n] desire to read up a bit in that line. I pored over a big book [of] the S. P. Magazine last eve & ca[me] upon certain papers by one A. B. A. which interested me curiously.[4] In one place when Harris says of this person that "he has treated the problem of the *lapse* & *return* far more satisfactorily than Plotinus," I felt proud, for I have the honor to be A. B. A's

affectionate & admiring
daughter — L.

ALS: Houghton Library, Harvard University. The manuscript is torn; missing words or letters are supplied in brackets.

1. Probably the C. H. Ames who contributed "Does Correlation of Forces Imply Personality" to the October 1877 *Journal of Speculative Philosophy* and who attended the first (1879) session of the Concord School of Philosophy (manuscript records, Concord Free Public Library).

2. Henry C. Brockmeyer, a founder of the St. Louis Hegelian movement, published "Letters on Faust" in the 1867 and 1868 volumes of the *Journal of Speculative Philosophy*. LMA was interested in *Faust* at this time because she was preparing to work on *A Modern Mephistopheles*.

3. William Torrey Harris, also a founder of the St. Louis Hegelian movement, later helped to organize the Concord School of Philosophy and co-authored with Frank Sanborn *A. Bronson Alcott: His Life and Philosophy* (1893).

4. LMA's father contributed a number of pieces to Harris's *Journal of Speculative Philosophy*. LMA's reference may be to his "Philosophemes" in the January, April, and July 1875 issues.

To the Alcott Family

Saturday Evening, Dec. 25, 1875.

Dear Family, — . . . I had only time for a word this A.M., as the fourth letter was from Mrs. P. to say they could not go; so I trotted off in the fog at ten to the boat, and there found Mr. and Mrs. G. and piles of goodies for the poor children.[1] She is a dear little old lady in a close, Quakerish bonnet and plain suit, but wide-awake and full of energy. It was grand to see her tackle the big mayor and a still bigger commissioner, and tell them what *ought* to be done for the poor things on the Island, as they are to be routed; for the city wants the land for some dodge or other. Both men fled soon, for the brave little woman was down on 'em in a way that would have made Marmee cry "Ankore!" and clap her dress-gloves to rags.

When the rotundities had retired, she fell upon a demure priest, and read him a sermon; and then won the heart of a boyish reporter so entirely that he stuck to us all day, and helped serve out dolls and candy like a man and a brother. Long life to him![2]

Mr. G. and I discussed pauperism and crime like two old wiseacres; and it was sweet to hear the gray-headed couple say "thee" and "thou," "Abby" and "James," to one another, he following with the bundles wherever the little poke-bonnet led the way. I've had a pretty good variety of Christmases in my day, but never one like this before. First we drove in an old ramshackle hack to the chapel, whither a boy had raced before us, crying joyfully to all he met, "She's come! Miss G. — she's come!" And all faces beamed, as well they might, since for thirty years she has gone to make set after set of little forlornities happy on this day.

The chapel was full. On one side, in front, girls in blue gowns and white pinafores; on the other, small chaps in pinafores likewise; and behind them, bigger boys in gray suits with cropped heads, and larger girls with ribbons in their hair and pink calico gowns. They sang alternately; the girls gave "Juanita" very well, the little chaps a pretty song about poor children asking a "little white angel" to leave the gates of heaven ajar, so they could peep in, if no more. Quite pathetic, coming from poor babies who had no home but this.

The big boys spoke pieces, and I was amused when one bright lad in gray, with a red band on his arm, spoke the lines I gave G., — "Merry Christmas." No one knew me, so I had the joke to myself; and I found afterward that I was taken for the mayoress, who was expected. Then we drove to the hospital, and there the heart-ache began, for me at least, so sad it was to see these poor babies, born of want and sin, suffering every sort of deformity, disease, and pain. Cripples half blind, scarred with scrofula, burns, and abuse, — it was simply awful and indescribable!

As we went in, I with a great box of dolls and the young reporter with a bigger box of candy, a general cry of delight greeted us. Some children tried to run, half-blind ones stretched out their groping hands, little ones crawled, and big ones grinned, while several poor babies sat up in their bed, beckoning us to "come quick."

One poor mite, so eaten up with sores that its whole face was painted with some white salve, — its head covered with an oilskin cap; one eye gone, and the other half filmed over; hands bandaged, and ears bleeding, — could only moan and move its feet till I put a gay red dolly in one hand and a pink candy in the other; then the dim eye brightened, the hoarse voice said feebly, "Tanky, lady!" and I left it contentedly sucking the sweetie, and *trying* to *see* its dear new toy. It can't see another Christmas, and I like to think I helped make this one happy, even for a minute.

It was pleasant to watch the young reporter trot round with the candy-box, and come up to me all interest to say, "One girl has n't got a doll, ma'am, and looks *so* disappointed."

After the hospital, we went to the idiot house; and there I had a chance to see faces and figures that will haunt me a long time. A hundred or so of half-grown boys and girls ranged down a long hall, a table of toys in the middle, and an empty one for Mrs. G.'s gifts. A cheer broke out as the little lady hurried in waving her handkerchief and a handful of gay bead necklaces, and "Oh! Ohs!" followed the appearance of the doll-lady and the candy man.

A pile of gay pictures was a new idea, and Mrs. G. told me to hold up some bright ones and see if the poor innocents would understand and enjoy them. I held up one of two kittens lapping spilt milk, and the girls began to mew and say "Cat! ah, pretty." Then a fine horse, and the boys bounced on their benches with pleasure; while a ship in full sail produced a cheer of rapture from them all.

Some were given out to the good ones, and the rest are to be pinned round the room; so the pictures were a great success. All wanted dolls, even boys of nineteen; for all were children in mind. But the girls had them, and young women of eighteen cuddled their babies and were happy. The boys chose from the toy-table, and it was pathetic to see great fellows pick out a squeaking dog without even the wit to pinch it when it was theirs. One dwarf of thirty-five chose a little Noah's ark, and brooded over it in silent bliss.

Some with beards sucked their candy, and stared at a toy cow or box of blocks as if their cup was full. One French girl sang the Marseillaise in a feeble voice, and was so overcome by her new doll that she had an epileptic fit on the spot, which made two others go off likewise; and a slight pause took place while they were kindly removed to sleep it off.

A little tot of four, who had n't sense to put candy in its mouth, was so fond of music that when the girls sang the vacant face woke up, and a pair of lovely soft hazel eyes stopped staring dully at nothing, and went wandering to and fro with light in them, as if to find the only sound that can reach its poor mind.

I guess I gave away two hundred dolls, and a soap-box of candy was empty when we left. But rows of sticky faces beamed at us, and an array of gay toys wildly waved after us, as if we were angels who had showered goodies on the poor souls.

Pauper women are nurses; and Mrs. G. says the babies die like sheep, many being deserted so young nothing can be hoped or done for them. One of the teachers in the idiot home was a Miss C., who remembered Nan at Dr. Wilbur's. Very lady-like, and all devotion to me. But such a life! Oh, me! Who *can* lead it, and not go mad?

At four, we left and came home, Mrs. G. giving a box of toys and sweeties on board the boat for the children of the men who run it. So leaving a stream of blessings and pleasures behind her, the dear old lady drove away, simply saying, "There now, I shall feel better for the next year!" Well she may; bless her!

She made a speech to the chapel children after the Commissioner had prosed in the usual way, and she told 'em that *she* should come as long as she could, and when she was gone her children would still keep it up in memory of her; so for thirty years more she hoped this, their one holiday, would be made happy for them. I could have hugged her on the spot, the motherly old dear!

Next Wednesday we go to the Tombs, and some day I am to visit the hospital with her, for I like this better than parties, etc.

I got home at five, and then remembered that I'd had no lunch; so I took an apple till six, when I discovered that all had dined at one so the helpers could go early this evening. Thus my Christmas day was without dinner or presents, for the first time since I can remember. Yet it has been a very memorable day, and I feel as if I'd had a splendid feast seeing the poor babies wallow in turkey soup, and that every gift I put into their hands had come back to me in the dumb delight of their unchild-like faces trying to smile.

MS: Unlocated. Printed: Cheney, pp. 284–288.

    1. Mrs. Anna Rice Powell, wife of the reformer Aaron Powell; James Gibbons and his wife, Abby Hopper Gibbons, who ministered to the waifs on Randall's Island. For an account of LMA's visit to Randall's Island, see her letter to Mrs. Powell, 25 December 1875, in Aaron M. Powell, *Personal Reminiscences of the Anti-Slavery and Other Reforms* (New York: Caulon Press, 1899), pp. 240–241, and *LMA*, pp. 254–256.

    2. The "boyish reporter" may have been the author of the brief but favorable description of this visit in "Charity's Open Hand," *New York Daily Tribune*, 27 December 1875, p. 5.

To Abigail May Alcott

New York.
Jan. 1st [−2] 1876.

My Blessed Marmee.

Your letter has just come & so I've had my present. Before I go to recieve calls at Mrs Croly's I'll begin a note to you as I have nothing else to send.

At midnight just as I was going to sleep all the bells began to chime, cannon fired, ditto pistols & crackers, horns blew, people sung, organs played & a general row ushered in the N[ew]. Y[ear]. in a truly American style. It was very provoking but as its the fashion all submit & the young folks enjoy it. The house was astir all night & sleep a lost art.

This morning the sun shines after three mild days of fog so like London that I've felt as if I there, especially when I see one of the few Hansom cabs whisking by with a swell inside "going to the Club, dont you know".

I have been nursing my cold & putting new braids on my skirts this week. Also called on Mrs Henry & Mrs John Sewall who called on me. Mrs Henry is a plain, oldish lady but kindly & said, "We did so want to know you that we ventured to call, for Mary S. thinks every thing of you & we are proud to be relations." I am to tea with them Sunday eve so Mr S. can see me. A pleasant house not in a fashionable street.

Mrs John is a sister of Mrs Sedgwick, a pretty woman & a widow now boarding near by. Has a little daughter & was very sweet & Gannetty. I wanted to know them because Sewalls wear well & I like the breed better than the May ditto.

Dear Mrs Gibbons wrote me a kind note saying she was not well enough for the Tombs last Wed. but next Wed we'd go, & ended off "with pleasant memories of the day we spent together cordially thy friend Abby Gibbons." She's an old saint, & still goes every week to the "Hopper Home" for women just out of jail founded by her good father.[1]

Now I must go & dress for the day's business, but this eve I'll finish. Miss Booth's reception tonight, tea at H. Sewall's tomorrow eve, Julius Caesar at Booth's theatre on Monday eve with Mr Heath,[2] Brooklyn Woman's Club reception Tuesday, Tombs Wed & so it goes from grave to gay from lively to severe. "Pope"[3] Sunday a.m.

I still live after twelve hours of New Years calling. I went at 11 to Mrs Croly's in my black & gold suit, & found Mrs C. her pretty daughter & Mrs Lamb[4] a friend all ready & hard at it ever since 9 entertaining gentlemen. As I went up the streets were full of swells dashing in & out of carriages all in thier best, buff kids, nosegays, white ties, & all with long lists & packs of cards in thier hands.

From 11 a.m. till 11 p.m. at Mrs C's a steady stream came & went, few taking any lunch though a nice one was set out & two pretty girls in light silks were ready to wait. Conway, Dr Holland, Mr Cleveland, Stoddard, Whitelaw Reid, Carleton, A. J. Davis & a man from the west who knows Pa, Fuller Walker, Barney Williams & Florence, the actors, very gentlemanly men, Clara Morris's husband who told me about Mrs Barrow who lives here in elegant retirement.[5] No end of newspaper men, Count Bodisco[6] the Russian minister's two sons, many officers & superior beings whose names I dont know. We were so busy we couldn't get our dinner till 8 & at 11 1/2 Mrs Lamb took me home tired out.

Conway was very jolly & I'm going to hear him preach at O. F's today, Mrs O. F. called last week.

Stoddard who was very chatty & an invalid, so let to do as he likes, came & sat on a cosy sofa by me & we had a good gossipy talk about literary N.Y. He said J. Miller is a humbug & will "get kicked some day he is so rude". That Lord Houghton was a *hard drinker*, & often quite gay at the Century Club. That Mrs Bullard's husband is a confirmed drunkard but an amiable man & a gentleman in spite of his weakness. Mrs B. merely keeps his house for looks sake & he adores but leaves her to her own set & bibes in private. This is the tie between Laura B. & L. C. Moulton, only Roman-faced Laura doesn't wail about it & pug-nosed Louise does in "werse" & prose, but is fat & coquettish in spite of woe.[7]

214

Miller's wife & children are supported by charity & he is loping round with big diamond rings & living at hotels, & putting on the airs of a first class genius.[8] Mr Stoddard blew up Gill & told me what horrid *mean* things he did. Has G. ever paid Pa for his article or sent him a book?[9] Let me know.[10] Mr Swinton & I had a good talk also, he is brother of William Swinton whom Pa knows & Mr Calvert of Newport.[11] We talked Emerson & genius, & he sat an hour in my corner & only got up to make room for Dr Holland who congratulated me on being a New yorker. It seems to please folks that I like N.Y. & am not a prim, prejudiced Bostonian. I tell em I dont belong anywhere & shall stay as long as I like N.Y.

Mr Elderkin, Eli Perkins, Prof. Bird &c all trotted up & said a word.[12] Jimmy Alliger & two young sprigs called on me, & May Croly was charmed with the little beaux. I've got some pretty bon-bons for the boys made like lilies, honey suckles & roses of delicate tinted paper with the motto & sweetie inside. Also a Swiss town to be made out of the stamped bits. It came too late for the parcel & I'll bring or send them some day. Mrs Dodge gave it to em. Wish F. would write & thank her prettily.

On the whole the N. year's day was a jolly one, & I was glad to see no drinking among the men. Mrs C. had wine but all took coffee or lemonade & she didn't press the wine, merely had it for manners. Mr C. would have no brandy or heavy drinks, & came home from his round of calls as calm & sober as a judge. It got to be very bad at one time & many ladies refused to recieve on that account, others had no wine & so the men behaved properly at once. Even in the eve when they had been on the go all day some making over a 100 calls I saw none tipsey, not even a "multiplying eye" & I watched on purpose. Give the devil his due. About 200 called on Mrs C. & I liked her ways very much, simple & kind, with her children round her, & she more intent on good conversation with the best men than on eating, flirting or nonsense of any kind.

Sunday p.m.

Such a sermon from Conway![13] I wish you had heard it, so like Parker & yet with the new twang of English science & religion. He showed some of the great superstitions of the past & then suddenly brought up the New Testament as one of the superstitions of the present. Showing how false much of it was & how priests even to day refuse to translate the story of Christ *truly*, but put in whatever will support *their* ideas. Today in Westminster Abbey a set of men are revising the book & exclude some of the most learned scholars & thinkers because they will tell the honest truth & upset the old theories of the Trinity, Incarnation &c which have no foundation in fact as some of them were ideas & beliefs that didn't exist till after Christ's time, & are not spoken of at all in the letters of Paul which are ackno[w]ledged to be the truest accounts.

I met Mrs Groat, Mrs Bullard & Mrs Wallace [14] "the three handsome women with brains," as they are called & they were charmed & full of fun at the idea of the effect of such a sermon in some of the great N.Y. churches, the steeples of which would fall on Conway's sinful head for saying the miracles did not happen, & Christ was not God though made so by the addition of two letters in several places put in by priests.

Conway has a lecture this eve on Science & Religion [15] & if I can get away from the Sewall's I shall go. I saw them at church & Mr S. has the Sewall nose & mild stare.

Miss Wallace asked if Pa was coming to N.Y. to talk this winter, & I said he would if people made it worth his while. But I think N.Y. is too busy a place & with too few really *earnest* people to make it pay, unless he had some other reason for coming. I should be proud to show my handsome old Papa for I haven't seen such a splendid man anywhere. Mr Swinton admires him immensely & begged I'd write the Life; said "Alcott & Emerson were *the* geniuses of the age & he wasn't sure that Alcott's wisdom was not greater than Emerson's as it came less from books & observation & more by natural gifts & processes."

I'll slyly spur about & see if anything can be done, as by & by in Lent when gayieties end folks may be glad to take breath & hear "Plato sweet lipped." No Genesis or Lapse, Papa, but Concord Authors or Western Evenings, or Books, or Social Life, that sort would go & perhaps with me to lend a hand we might turn a penny if some one would give the parlor. I'd have it myself free gratis & in style if I had rooms & invite the cream of N.Y. pan[?]. Botta's & that rather exclusive set which gives a relish & tells, jes see. [16]

I hope you will be spared to get through this screed, but I thought you'd like to know how the New year went out & came in with me.

I wish Papa would tell me how many of Goethe's books we *own*. As Mr Heath (who is a book man) can get me a complete set of Bohn for $1.25 a vol. I want the *whole* of Faust Meister, & Affinities. We have the plays & a part of Faust & W. M. Take a look & let me know if they are *ours* or R. W. E's.

Happy New Year & bless you all ever your loving black sheep Lu.

What do you mean about May's diamond ring? Has she really got one?

"Trift" is a good thing to have round.

216

ALS: Houghton Library, Harvard University.

1. The Isaac T. Hopper home, named after the Quaker reformer and father of Abby Gibbons.

2. Daniel Collamore Heath, a New York publisher. The *New York Times* reported on the "dazzling splendor" of the great Shakespearean actor Edwin Booth's *Julius Caesar* on 2 January 1876 ("Booth's Theatre," p. 6).

3. Alexander Pope, *An Essay on Man*, Epistle IV, line 380.

4. Possibly Martha Lamb, author of *History of New York* (1877–1880).

5. Not previously identified are: Whitelaw Reid, editor of the *New York Tribune;* Andrew Jackson Davis, a spiritualist; the actors Barney Williams, W. J. Florence, Clara Morris, and her husband; the British actress Julia Bennett Barrow.

6. Count Waldmar de Bodisco, Russian consul-general in New York.

7. The section from "humbug & will" to "spite of woe" is crossed out with a large X in a later hand.

8. After Miller and his wife Theresa Dyer Miller were divorced in 1869, she went on the lecture circuit to tell her tale (probably exaggerated) that he had disowned her and their two children, forcing her to live in penury above a Chinese laundry in Portland, Oregon.

9. William F. Gill published Bronson's "Books" in his *Laurel Leaves* (1876).

10. The section from "Miller's wife" to "Let me know" is crossed out with a large X in a later hand.

11. John Swinton, editor of the *New York Times* and *New York Sun*, and his brother William Swinton, author of numerous textbooks in various fields; George Henry Calvert, prolific dramatist, poet, and travel writer.

12. John Elderkin, a journalist who became editor of the *New York Ledger* in 1877; the humorist Eli Perkins (pseudonym of Melville de Lancey Landon).

13. Conway lectured on the New Testament on the morning of 2 January.

14. Possibly Mrs. Zerilda Wallace, a temperance and suffrage leader.

15. Conway's lecture on the evening of 2 January was entitled "Science and Religion in England."

16. This sentence is crossed out in a later hand.

To Lucy Stone

Dear Mrs. Stone: — One should be especially inspired this Centennial year before venturing to speak or write. I am not so blest, and find myself so busy trying to get ready for the good time that is surely coming, I can only in a very humble way, help on the cause all women should have at heart.

As reports are in order, I should like to say a word for the girls, on whom in a great measure, depends the success of the next generation.

My lines fell in pleasant places last year, and I looked well about me as I went among the young people, who unconsciously gave me some very cheering facts in return for very poor fictions.

I was both surprised and delighted with the nerve and courage, the high aims and patient persistence which appeared, not only among the laborious young women whose teacher is necessity, but among tenderly nurtured girls who cherished the noblest ambitions and had learned to earn the happiness no wealth could buy them.

Having great faith in young America, it gave me infinite satisfaction to find such eager interest in all good things, and to see how irresistably the spirit of our new revolution, stirring in the hearts of sisters and daughters, was converting the fathers and brothers who loved them. One shrewd, business man said, when talking of Woman Suffrage, "How *can* I help believing in it, when I've got a wife and six girls who are *bound* to have it?"

And many a grateful brother declared he could not be mean enough to shut any door in the face of the sister who had made him what he was.

So I close this hasty note by proposing three cheers for the girls of 1876 — and the hope that they will prove themselves worthy descendants of the mothers of this Revolution, remembering that

> "Earth's fanatics make
> Too often Heaven's saints."[1]

L. M. ALCOTT.

Concord, June 29 [1876].

MS: Unlocated. Printed: *Woman's Journal* 7 (15 July 1876): 225; *LAFL,* p. 442.
    1. Elizabeth Barrett Browning, *Aurora Leigh,* Book II, line 449. LMA changes "frequently" to "often."

To Sallie Holley

Concord Nov. 26th [1876]

Dear Miss Holly.[1]

I have been trying to get a moment to drop you a line & tell why I did not continue the Independent.

I have lost quite a sum by the swindling railroads,[2] & as May is in Paris hard at work as an artist I have to help her till she can sell her pictures & pay her own way. This makes economy more than ever necessary, as my dear old people need many small comforts & my boys a lift with thier education. So cant do all I would.

I am at home keeping house, & mother & I are trying to get our Xmas barrel ready. Books & papers I have, & E. Emerson has sent a few clothes, so I hope to have a small offering to send for your good work.

I never forget what you told us of it, & was much disappointed that my visit had to be given up. But my place is here now till May returns & I must live on remembered pleasures.

I shall send you my years supply of Woman's Journals, Youth's Companion, Harper, Scribner & St Nicholas, so there will be something for old & young.[3]

I hope you are well & prosperous, & with all good wishes I am

Yours truly
L. M. ALCOTT.

ALS: Smith College Library Rare Book Room.
    1. In her reply of 8 December, Holley mentioned that the *Independent* had kept coming anyway (Houghton Library, Harvard University).
    2. Letters from Samuel Sewall to LMA at this time indicate that her many railroad stocks were paying smaller dividends than usual (Houghton Library, Harvard University).
    3. The previous year, LMA had asked to have sent "The Independent for a year to Miss Sallie Holley, Lattsburgh, Northumberland Co. Virginia. . . . She is one of the saints, & after working for Anti slavery many years now buries herself in a lonely place among the Freedmen to teach them. Has been there for seven years & done wonders. Reading for herself & pupils & neighbors, black & white, is very necessary for the winter as *she* has no society but Miss Putnam her partner" (to Mr. Ward, 3 December [1875], from the collection of Morristown National Historic Park, New Jersey).

To Mrs. Graham

Boston Feb. 2ond [1877]

My Dear Mrs Graham.

Marmee is so ill that I have time only to say a few words in return for your kind notice.

I had already seen the notice, & said with real satisfaction, "There, that person has caught my idea & understands what I meant to say or suggest." I long ago gave up feeling "low in my mind" about being cut up by the critics, or much elated by the very undeserved praise of more partial friends, but it *is* pleasant to be understood & have one's purpose recognized in spite of the imperfection of one's performance.

I should have liked to pay a visit to the pleasant party at the Hillside but my vacation time has not come yet & I begin to think it wont come till I am too old to enjoy it.

I seem to have so many young friends all over the country that I cannot hope to accept all the invitations they kindly send me, & can only thank them trusting to meet some day some where.

I am thinking of a new book like Old Fashioned Girl,[1] as my publisher tells me that sells better than any other of my immortal tales. So if Miss Alice has any good experiences, funny adventures or interesting incidents in girl-life I shall be very glad to hear of them, & shall calmly put em in & then take all the credit for "those life-like pictures & touching episodes." That's the way books are made, for there is nothing original in the world & the young folks write thier own stories; we only steal & publish them.

The Marches send thier regards & are all robust except Marmee who is much broken & is now the cherished "old baby" as she calls herself. Amy is painting away in London & coming home to keep house in March. Meg & the lads are with us here in Boston for the winter. Mr M. lectures & takes care of his large parish of young men & women. Jo is nurse, housekeeper, scribbler & Papa to the boys. She desires to be most kindly remembered to the Hillside party & is very truly yours — L. M. A.

ALS: Lilly Library, Indiana University.
    1. Probably *Under the Lilacs*, which was serialized in *St. Nicholas* between December 1877 and October 1878, and published by Roberts Brothers in 1878.

To Abigail Williams May

Concord Feb. 23d [1877]

Dear Abby.

I went home a week sooner than I had intended as I found Mother a little poorly & the Belles of the Kitchen on a strike. I do *so* love to say to em "Go, I can do without you," when they get rampageous.

I have now done this to our "Mistress Mary, *quite* contrairy," & plunge from litteratoer to slaps & cinders at one dive.

Shall come to the surface next week, & run to town for a day on business, if the weather holds. So if you are starving for your lunch bring on the crackers & cheese any day & let me know.

Hold up your right hand & swear that you wont ask me to make or murder a speech, or I wont come; no, not if you have nightengales tongues & calves brains right from the Parker House!

By all mean[s] come up & see your relations as often as you can. Nothing would please mother more than a good crack about *the* family, & good works generally. Concord is not at all "bad to take" when apple-blossoms & dandelions give a relish to the mixture.

Love to all,
yours as ever
L. M. A.

ALS: Schlesinger Library, Radcliffe College.

To George A. Thatcher

Concord Mar. 6th [1877]

Mr Thatcher.[1]
Dear Sir.

I find on consulting various Concord men who know the worth of the Thoreau place that $5000 is considered a high price.

Our lawyer, S. E. Sewall, also thinks it too much, as the taxes upon it seem to show that it is not so valuable a property as we thought it.

Real estate is so low just now that prices are expected to fall also, & we will offer $4500 for the place.[2]

On examining the house we find it needs considerable repairing; as several ceilings must be done over & some painting is necessary as we do not want to buy a shabby house.

I do not know whether Mr Sanborn is expected to do this or the owners before selling it.[3]

Awaiting your reply I am

respectfully yours
L. M. ALCOTT.

P. S.

If you are in Boston & will call at No. 5 Pemberton Sq. Mr Sewall will be glad to see you about the matter.

ALS: Pierpont Morgan Library. Printed: Thomas Blanding [untitled column about Louisa May Alcott], *Concord Saunterer* 13, no. 2 (Summer 1978): 12–13.

1. George A. Thatcher of Bangor, Maine, a cousin of Thoreau's, was handling the estate after Sophia Thoreau's death in 1876.

2. In his reply of 10 March, Thatcher accepted the offer of $4,500 (Houghton Library, Harvard University).

3. Frank Sanborn was leasing the house through June.

To Thomas Niles

[ca. 28? April? 1877]

Dear Mr. Niles, — I had to keep the proof longer than I meant because a funeral came in the way.

The book as last sent is lovely, and much bigger than I expected.[1]

Poor "Marmee," ill in bed, hugged it, and said, "It is perfect! only I do wish your name could be on it." She is very proud of it; and tender-hearted Anna weeps and broods over it, calling Gladys the best and sweetest character I ever did. So much for home opinion; now let's see what the public will say.

May clamors for it; but I don't want to send this till she has had one or two of the others. Have you sent her "Is That All?"[2] If not, please do; then it won't look suspicious to send only "M. M."

I am so glad the job is done, and hope it won't disgrace the series. Is not another to come before this? I hope so; for many people suspect what is up, and I could tell my fibs about No. 6 better if it was *not* mine.

Thanks for the trouble you have taken to keep the secret. Now the fun will begin.

Yours truly, L. M. A.

P.S. — Bean's expressman grins when he hands in the daily parcel. He is a Concord man.

MS: Unlocated. Printed: Cheney, p. 294.
1. *A Modern Mephistopheles* was published anonymously by Roberts Brothers in its No Name Series in late April 1877.
2. *Is That All?* by Harriet Preston was published anonymously as the third volume of the No Name Series in December 1876.

To Mary Mapes Dodge

Concord June 3rd [1877]

Dear Mrs Dodge.

The tale goes slowly owing to interruptions,[1] for summer is a busy time & I get few quiet days. Twelve chapters are done, but are short ones & so will make about six or seven numbers in St Nicholas.

I will leave them divided in this way that you may put in as many as you please each month, for trying to suit the magazine hurts the story in its book form, though this way does no harm to the monthly parts I think.

I will send you the first few chapters during the week for Mrs Foote,[2] & with them the schedule you suggest, so that my infants may not be drawn with whiskers & my big boys & girls in pinafores as in Eight Cousins.

I hope the new baby wont be set aside too soon for my illustrations, but I do feel a natural wish to have one story prettily adorned with good pictures, as hitherto artists have much afflicted me.

I am daily waiting with anxiety for an illumination of some sort as my plot is very vague so far & though I dont approve of "sensations" in childrens books, one must have a certain thread on which to string the small events which make up the true sort of child life.

I intend to go & simmer an afternoon at Van Amburg's great show,[3] that I may get hints for the further embellishment of Ben & his dog. I have also put in a poem by F. B. S's small son,[4] & that bit will give Mrs Foote a good scene with the six-year-old poet reciting his verses under the lilacs.

I shall expect the small tots to be unusually good since the artist has a live model to study from. Please present my congratulations to the happy Mamma & Mr Foote Jr.

yours *warmly*

L. M. A.

ALS: Wilkinson Collection of Mary Mapes Dodge, Princeton University Library. Printed: Cheney, pp. 301–302; *LASC*, pp. 369–370.

1. LMA was writing *Under the Lilacs*, which would begin serialization in *St. Nicholas* in December 1877 and for which she was paid three thousand dollars (24 August, Bronson's "Diary for 1877," p. 606, Houghton Library, Harvard University).

2. Mary Anna Foote provided the illustrations of "Bob and Betty" and "The Blue Beard Group" for the serialization of *Under the Lilacs* in *St. Nicholas*.

3. LMA had visited I. A. Van Amburgh's Mammoth Menagerie and New Great Golden Menagerie in Boston to get some ideas for *Under the Lilacs*.

4. The poem by five-year-old Francis Bachiler Sanborn appeared in *Under the Lilacs*, p. 78.

To Richard Rogers Bowker

Concord Oct. 4th [1877?]

R. R. Bowker.[1]

Dear Sir.

In reply to your questions I can only say that Low[2] honorably pays me for all books of mine which he publishes.

I recognize no other person's right to bring out the books, & recieve nothing from such piratical publications, which have been a great injury to me pecuniarily.

I *should* very much object to being in any way connected with "Happy Days,"[3] as my relations with Merry's Museum were of a very disagreeable nature throughout; & I have had more trouble with American publishers than with English.

Respectfully

L. M. ALCOTT.

ALS: R. R. Bowker Papers, Rare Books and Manuscripts Division, New York Public Library, Astor, Lenox, and Tilden Foundations.

    1. Richard Rogers Bowker, editor of *Publishers Weekly* and *Library Journal.*

    2. LMA's English publisher, Sampson Low.

    3. The only work published with this title between 1868 and 1888 seems to be the anthology *Happy Days for Boys and Girls* (Philadelphia: Porter and Coates, 1877), which reprints four short portions from LMA's works.

To Caroline H. Dall

Concord Oct. 11th [1877]

Dear Mrs Dall.

I am sorry to hear of your troubles & wish I had some helpful suggestion to make.

We all have known just the same predicament & how hard it is for intelligent women to find thier place when home fails or necessity of any sort pushes them out into the world.

Mother is dying slowly of water on the chest so I cannot apply for advice to her, & have nothing to propose. But I do *not* think your housekeeping plan would work or that a place in any family would suit you. Some literary post would be the thing if it could be found, or business affairs, your executive ability is so great.

Have you no friend at Washington who could get some place there which would suit you?

I long ago discovered that Boston was the hardest spot in the world for a Bostonian to get work in, so I pushed off in various directions & among strangers found the help I could not get there.

I sincerely wish I knew of some fitting niche where you could nestle safe from the hard side of life, for it does seem unfair that a woman of your talent should ever need a support.

Mrs [Lizzie] Wells is with her cousin Mr May in Cambridge, Highland St I think. She is a helpful soul & may be able to do more than

Yours truly
L. M. A.

I read with great interest your Centennial Letters,[1] & felt as if I had been there, so minute & graphic were they. Cannot you find something of that kind which will pay? If I can aid you in any way with Mr Niles or any other publisher I shall be glad to do so. As N. employs translators & copyests & proof readers, maybe he could suggest something in that line. Have you tried him? He is the woman's friend & loves to help us.

ALS: Massachusetts Historical Society. At the end of the letter, Dall has written: "Louisa is very unjust in this letter to Boston wh has always helped *her* & hers. If *I* had been writing this letter I shd have begun it — 'Since you once came to *my* help dear Mrs Dall, I would be glad to come to yrs etc — " Dall is referring to the Ariadne Blish episode; see 9 October [1875] and 10 November 1875.

1. Dall had published a series of forty-three "Centennials," reporting on the Philadelphia Centennial Exhibition, in the *New Age* between 8 July 1876 and 5 May 1877.

To May Alcott

Sunday Eve
Nov. 25th [1877]

Dearest May.

Our Marmee is at rest[1] after two months of pain & weariness as hard to bear as pain. A happy end, thank God! with loving faces to look her last upon & tender hands to serve her. Such sweet peace on her face now I wish you could see it. I took off your ring today, & gave her a good bye kiss for you. Yesterday she pointed up at your picture & said smiling "Little May," & nodded & waved her hand though only conscious at moments, then she looked up at us so sweetly & put up her lips to kiss us.

Once she said "A smile is as good as a prayer," & laid her hands together with a lovely look all round as if she blessed us.[2]

I wish I was with you my darling for I know how hard it will be to bear alone this sorrow, but dont think of it much till time makes it easier & never mourn that you didn't come. All is well & your work was a joy to Marmee. We will write often & tell you all that goes on. God bless you dear, yr Lu.

ALS: Houghton Library, Harvard University.
   1. Mrs. Alcott died on 25 November.
   2. A similar description appears in LMA's journal for November (see Cheney, p. 300).

To Lidian Emerson

Nov. 26th [1877]

Dear Mrs Emerson.

Mother left us last night; a peaceful & happy death as befitted so lovely a life.

The funeral is to be on Wed. next at 1 o clock for the convenience of Boston relatives.[1]

If that is not too early an hour for you we should love to see you & yours as the nearest & dearest of all Concord friends.

Affectionately yours
L. M. ALCOTT.[2]

ALS: Houghton Library, Harvard University.
   1. H. W. Foote, minister of King's Chapel (where the Alcotts had been married), read scriptures; Cyrus A. Bartol gave a eulogy; and William Lloyd Garrison presented his recollections of Mrs. Alcott's role in the antislavery conflict (*Concord Freeman*, 6 December 1877, p. 1).
   2. Writing to Elizabeth Wells on 30 November, LMA reported: "Anna & I are resting or trying to, for we still listen for the fluttering breath, the little call for Brama, & often find our feet going toward the empty room where the fire is out & all the windows stand open now" (Houghton Library, Harvard University).

To Mrs. A. D. Moshier

Concord Dec. 16th [1877]

My Dear Old Friend.[1]

I have been trying to find a quiet moment to send you a word about Mother, for I know you would love to hear of her & her last days.

Miss Dean sends me your address & I need wait no longer.

Dear mother has been failing slowly for some years but enjoyed much in her own bright way, for the days of well-earned rest had come & all that love & care could do made them calm & happy.

Three months ago the family trouble, water on the chest following heart disease, came on & she suffered sadly for weeks.

Her fortitude was great & her patience wonderful when each breath was a pain & every hour an increasing burden. Dr Conrad Wesselhoeft & our own good Dr Cook[2] did much to mitigate the suffering & as strength failed ease came, till weakness & weariness were all she had to bear.

Anna was just settled in the pretty new home she had bought for herself & boys,[3] & we were to spend the winter with her. Mother's illness delayed the moving till about a fortnight before her death. Then she so longed to go that we went & she enjoyed the change very much, for her room was full of sunshine, flowers, & the old fashioned furniture she loved.

Here she quietly failed day by day, only keeping [to] her bed two or three days at the last, & at twilight Sunday Nov. 25th fell asleep without a thought of pain. Her last words to father were, "you are laying a very soft pillow for me to rest upon." & in truth his love has always been that to her energetic spirit through this long companionship of nearly fifty years.

At mother's desire the funeral was a very private one, & she lies beside our Lizzie in Sleepy Hollow. It is a great comfort & happiness to us to think of her as freed from the burdens of infirmity & at home with all the dear family who only waited for her to be complete again. She often spoke of them during the last day as she lay smiling & whispering happily to herself of old times & beloved friends gone before; for the past brightened as the present grew dim.

In looking over her journals I find your name very often in the missionary times, & you seemed to be her stand-by when others failed. I know how much she loved you, not only for the loyal friendship of years but for the same benevolent aims & never tiring good will & good work for others which made her own life a labor of love.

I shall try to come to see you if I pass any time in Boston this winter as Concord always gives me neuralgia toward spring.

May is in Europe studying Art & doing finely. Father & I stay with Anna & her nice boys. Come & see us if you ever feel the spirit move this way. We are close to the station now.

With regards to your son I am affectionately yrs L. M. ALCOTT

ALS: Louisa May Alcott Collection, Barrett Library, University of Virginia Library.

1. Mrs. A. D. Moshier of Cambridge.

2. Joseph Cook, a well-known lecturer on theological subjects, was then delivering a series in Boston. Bronson wrote that Cook "has been most faithful, visiting her lately three times daily" (25 November 1877, *Letters*, p. 704).

3. Anna Pratt purchased the Thoreau House at 26 Main Street in Concord from Sophia Thoreau's estate in April or May 1877 for $4,500. Another inhabitant of the house was a ghost: "This house is haunted by the ghost of old Mrs Thoreau, just seen by a Scotch servant girl who never heard of her, & when things mysteriously vanish & sometimes reappear we say the old lady, being of an inquisitive turn, has taken them to examine" (to Horace P. Chandler, 7 September [1884], Parkman Dexter Howe Library, University of Florida).

To Mrs. A. D. Moshier

April 6th [1878]

Dear Mrs Moshier.

The old house *is* to rent if any one wants it. We none of us care for it now Mother is gone & May married abroad. Annie has her new home & I am to be with her free from the cares always so burdensome to me.

Father still rather clings to the place he made & does not want to sell it yet. The house is dismantled & looks a very different place from the one you knew, for summer, pictures, books & "Marmee" made it lovely. Now it is a shabby old spot with all the infirmities of nearly two hundred years on its head. We made no repairs the last year knowing that it was to stand empty all winter, & now do not care to do more than paper & paint, mend the roof & "tinker up" a little for a summer tenant.

If your friends want quiet, sunshine & strawberries they can be had at Apple Slump, but there is little else to offer.

Our parlor carpets are for sale as they are fitted & we do not want them; also a few pieces of furniture if any one cares to buy or use them.

Father is to be away till Wed. but if your friends like to come up later in the week & look at the place he will be glad to show it though not yet in order.

With thanks for your kind thought of us I am

yours truly
L. M. ALCOTT.

P.S. You may like to know that May was married March 22ond in London to Ernest Nierisker[1] a Swiss gentleman, son of a banker living in Baden, young, comely, accomplished & in a good business. They are very happy & now in Brittany on a honey-moon trip. May says — "To combine art & matrimony is almost too much bliss." I hope she will find it so & prove "Avis" in the wrong. They will live abroad & we must go to her when she is fairly settled.

ALS: Louisa May Alcott Collection, Barrett Library, University of Virginia Library.

1. May had become engaged to twenty-two-year-old Ernest Nieriker in February (LMA has spelled his name incorrectly). After their honeymoon, they settled in Paris.

To Thomas Niles

April 19th [1878]

Dear Mr Niles.

Thanks for the tickets. They are a great improvement on the others & my little cousin is much delighted, also very grateful.

Mr Becket brought a letter from my friend Chase of Dall's, so I did not throw him out of the 6th storey window as I should otherwise have felt it my duty as a hunted bear to have done.

It was amusing to see how patiently he listened to my twaddle about every subject under the sun *but* L. M. A. & how skilfully he slipped in a question now & then which I had to answer whether I wanted to or not.

On the whole I think he let me off pretty well, though a few facts were a little mixed & the low spirited cranky old lady appeared as a sunny, large eyed person of an angelic & dramatic turn. Never mind, let the dear, deluded public be happy.

I was very glad Mr B. gave you credit for the immortal Little Women, for you evoked the book from chaos & made my fortune, & deserve much more honor & thanks than you get.

I dont forget ten years of kindness & hope a day will come when I can in some way prove my appreciation of that which is better than money or fame.

Very truly your friend
L. M. A.

ALS: Boston Public Library.

To Ellen Conway

Concord May 1st [1878]

Dear Mrs Conway.

I was very glad to hear from you though it may not seem so as I have neglected to reply till now. But I too have been very ill & still am ordered to keep still for some months. May does not know how ill I was as I thought she would only worry & had already enough to bear in Mother's loss.

I am "turning the corner" & too much nursing last summer was bad for me. But I could not let any one else care for the dear invalid while I could lift a hand for I had always been her nurse & knew her little ways.

She suffered much for three months, but was spared at the last & fell asleep in my arms so peacefully that we could not find anything but gratitude in our hearts when she had gone.

The feeble old woman whom I had tended for some years seems to be laid tenderly away by Lizzie in Sleepy Hollow & I feel as if I had found again my cheerful, energetic, splendid mother; & cannot mourn in the least but rejoice that her brave, benevolent spirit is free from its burdens & able to work in a grander way & wider sphere than it could here.

It is a fit memory for such a lovely, unselfish life to leave.

May *is* very happy, & we get charming letters from her as she spends her honeymoon in Havre sketching & enjoying fine weather, new sights & a great deal of love.

From all she writes & Ernest's own letters we get the impression of a cultivated, talented, honest & ambitious man. He seems anxious to make a happy home for May & see her gift improved to the utmost. They talk of settling in Paris as several good business offers are made E. in banks. May prefers the country, but things are undecided as yet & the pair live in Paradise for a little while. Pity they need ever come out!

We are settled in the Thoreau house with Anna as house-mother. The old place is to let as it is no longer home without "Marmee."

Concord is much changed, for many of the good grey heads are gone & none so excellent have come to fill thier places. Minot Pratt, Dr Bartlett & Miss E. Hoar are some of the recent losses.[1]

I cannot cross the water till autumn, perhaps not then,[2] but May is no longer lonely & Anna would be if I left her, so I fancy my part henceforth is to be the old maiden aunt & sit in the corner & darn stockings & pet the boys. Fred & Jack are fine big fellows, doing honor to thier good father's name & thier very faithful mother's bringing up.

Best regards to Mr Conway & the young people, & with very sincere wishes for the return of your health I am, dear friend, yrs truly L. M. ALCOTT.

Didn't May's sudden wedding rather surprise you? It did us, but was so like her we soon enjoyed the joke as much as she did. The Swiss Papa & Mamma are very nice & May feels rich in the new family.

ALS: Harry Ransom Humanities Research Center, University of Texas at Austin.

1. Minot Pratt, John's father, had died on 29 March; Dr. Josiah Bartlett on 5 January; and Elizabeth Hoar on 7 April.

2. On 23 June [1878], LMA wrote to Maggie Lukens and her sisters: "So sorrow & joy have been mercifully mixed for us, & we draw closer as the circle grows smaller. I hope in the Autumn to pay Madame a visit over the sea, & get rested after the hard winter just ended" (Boston Public Library).

To John Preston True

Concord, October 24 [1878].

J. P. True [1]

Dear Sir, — I never copy or "polish," so I have no old manuscripts to send you; and if I had it would be of little use, for one person's method is no rule for another. Each must work in his own way; and the only drill needed is to keep writing and profit by criticism. Mind grammar, spelling, and punctuation, use short words, and express as briefly as you can your meaning. Young people use too many adjectives to try to "write fine." The strongest, simplest words are best, and no *foreign* ones if it can be helped.

Write, and print if you can; if not, still write, and improve as you go on. Read the best books, and they will improve your style. See and hear good speakers and wise people, and learn of them. Work for twenty years, and then you may some day find that you have a style and place of your own, and can command good pay for the same things no one would take when you were unknown.

I know little of poetry, as I never read modern attempts, but advise any young person to keep to prose, as only once in a century is there a true poet; and verses are so easy to do that it is not much help to write them. I have so many letters like your own that I can say no more, but wish you success, and give you for a motto Michael Angelo's wise words: "Genius is infinite patience."

Your friend, L. M. ALCOTT.

P.S. — The lines you send me are better than many I see; but boys of nineteen cannot know much about hearts, and had better write of things they understand. Sentiment is apt to become sentimentality; and sense is always safer, as well as better drill, for young fancies and feelings.

Read Ralph Waldo Emerson, and see what good prose is, and some of the best poetry we have. I much prefer him to Longfellow.

MS: Unlocated. Printed: J. P. True, "The Advice of Miss Alcott," *St. Nicholas* 15 (May 1888): 545; Cheney, pp. 399–400; *LASC*, p. 358. True, who was born 13 February 1859, was nineteen when this letter was written, establishing the date as 1878.

　　1. John Preston True, author of children's novels and a member of the editorial department of Houghton, Mifflin for forty years. LMA sent him a letter of praise on 7 September 1883, when he published his first book, *Their Club and Ours* (True, "The Advice of Miss Alcott," 545).

To Miss Churchill

Xmas Day [1878?].

My Dear Miss Churchill.

　　I can only say to you as I do to the many young writers who ask for advice — There is no *easy* road to successful authorship; it has to be earned by long & patient labor, many disappointments, uncertainties & trials. Success is often a lucky accident, coming to those who may not deserve it, while others who do have to wait & hope till they have *earned* it. That is the best sort & the most enduring.

　　I worked for twenty years poorly paid, little known, & quite without any ambition but to eke out a living, as I chose to support myself & began to do it at sixteen. This long drill was of use, & when I wrote Hospital Sketches by the beds of my soldier boys in the shape of letters home I had no idea that I was taking the first step toward what is called fame. It nearly cost my life but I discovered the secret of winning the ear & touching the heart of the public by simply telling the comic & pathetic incidents of life.

　　"Little Women" was written when I was ill, & to prove that I could *not* write books for girls. The publisher thought it *flat*, so did I, & neither hoped much for or from it. We found out our mistake, & since then, though I do not enjoy writing "moral tales" for the young, I do it because it pays well.

　　But the success I value most was making my dear mother happy in her last years & taking care of my family. The rest soon grows wearisome & seems very poor beside the comfort of being an earthly Providence to those we love.

　　I hope you will win this joy at least, & think you *will*, for you seem to have got on well so far, & the stories are better than many sent me. I like the short one best. Lively tales of home-life or children go well, & the Youth's Companion is a good paying paper. I do not like Loring as he is neither honest nor polite. I have had dealings with him & know. Try Roberts Brothers 299 Washington St. They are very kind & just & if the book suits will give it a fair chance. With best wishes for a prosperous & happy New Year I am your friend

L. M. A.

ALS: Henry W. and Albert A. Berg Collection, New York Public Library, Astor, Lenox, and Tilden Foundations.

To Miss Churchill

Sat. Dec. 27th [1878?]

Dear Miss Churchill.

Beginners must take what they can get. Papers usually have a fixed price & till one grows well known one must be content with that. So much a column or page. The True Flag used to pay me $25 or $30 for a long story.[1] Frank Leslie at first $25 for short ones; then $100 for anything I would send.[2] Bonner once paid me, without my asking, $100 for one short column.[3] Now I never write a short tale for less than $100. Serials $3000.

The Evening Gazette used to pay me $10 for a story a month when I began twenty five years ago.[4]

My first story gave me $5.00 & I felt very rich. I was 16 & considered my fortune made.

Now I can ask what I like & get it, but have not time or health to do much & refused $400 for some Xmas tales. A name is considered in the price.

The Atlantic used to pay $10, a page. Mr Ford of the Youth's Companion offered $50 for very short tales such as I could do two of in a day & I sometimes send him a couple & use them in "The Scrap Bag" later. A dollar a page used to be called good pay & Leslie gave me that.

Short stories are harder to do than long ones & it is an art to write good ones. Try Ford, but he wont pay more than $10 $15 or 20 I think.

Please do not speak of these prices *in public*, as I find publishers dont like the big ones mentioned. Do something really good & you can command your own prices.

Yrs truly
L. M. A.

ALS: Henry W. and Albert A. Berg Collection, New York Public Library, Astor, Lenox, and Tilden Foundations.

1. LMA published serials, poems, and novels in *The Flag of Our Union* in the mid-1860s.

2. LMA published a number of works in *Frank Leslie's Illustrated Newspaper* in the early 1860s.

3. Robert Bonner had paid LMA one hundred dollars for "Happy Women," which appeared in the 11 April 1868 *New York Ledger*.

4. LMA published a number of stories in the *Saturday Evening Gazette* in the mid-1850s.

To Annie Langley

June 7th [1879]

Dear Miss Langley.

We are planning to send a box to May in July, early, as that is her birthday month. You asked me to let you know when we were sending, so I do; but anything can go by mail if later suits you better.

Madame is very well & so funny about her preparations, knowing nothing of the needfuls, & calmly saying, "Two gowns & a blanket are quite enough to begin with."[1] Anna's maternal heart is rent at this sad ignorance, & we are sewing away on bibs & frocks lest our beloved nephew or niece, or both, should suffer from an unnatural parent's neglect.

Imagine May's dismay at the appearance of twins with only two gowns & a blanket as wardrobe. It would serve her right. *She* would dress them in canvas robes with palettes for hats & feed them on paint, I suppose.

She has been enjoying the Salon & her own picture hung in a good place. When the artistic fever abates I hope she will return to her maternal duties like a Christian woman.

With regards to your mother & aunt I am as ever, affectionately yours

L. M. ALCOTT.

ALS: Langley Family Papers, Heineman Collection, Department of Rare Books and Special Collections, University of Michigan Library.
1. May was expecting her first child in November.

To Mary Mapes Dodge

Aug. 21st [1879]

Dear Mrs Dodge.

I have not been able to do anything on the Serial[1] as a very sick friend & much company have taken all my time. The poor soul is now at rest, the company gone, &, after a week at the seaside to get braced up for work, I intend to begin.

The Revolutionary tale does not seem to possess me.[2] I have casually asked many of my young folks, when they demand a new story, which they would like, one of that sort or the old Eight Cousin style, & they all say the latter.

It would be much the easier to do as I have a beginning & a plan all ready, a village & the affairs of a party of children. We have many little romances going on among the Concord boys & girls & all sorts of queer things which will work into "Jack & Jill" nicely.

Mrs Croly has been anxious for a story & I am trying to do a short one, as I told her you had the refusal of my next serial.[3]

I hope you will not be very much disappointed about the old time tale. It would take study to do it well, & leisure is just what I have not got & never shall have I fear, when writing is to be done.

I will send you a few chapters of "Jack & Jill" when in order if you like, & you can decide if they will suit. I shall try to have it unlike the others if possible. But the dears *will* cling to the Little Women style.

I have had a very busy summer but have been pretty well & able to do my part in entertaining the 400 philosophers.[4] Yours truly L. M. A.

ALS: Wilkinson Collection of Mary Mapes Dodge, Princeton University Library. Printed: Cheney, pp. 302–307; *LASC*, pp. 370–371 (partial).

    1. *Jack and Jill* was serialized in *St. Nicholas* from December 1879 to October 1880 before being published by Roberts Brothers in October 1880.

    2. LMA apparently never finished this "Revolutionary tale."

    3. Possibly this turned out to be "Victoria. A Woman's Statue," which appeared in the March, April, and May 1881 issues of *Demorest's Magazine*, which Croly edited.

    4. The first session of the Concord School of Philosophy lasted from 15 July to 16 August.

To Ednah Dow Cheney

Sept. 4th [1879]

Dear Mrs Cheney,

As Miss B.s address is rather mixed up I send you the sister's letter to read & the direction to study at your leisure. Please keep it for me.

Our meeting last eve. was a small one, & nobody had registered because of "jelly-making, sewing, sickness or company." So I gave them a good scolding & offered to drive the timid sheep (in a van) to the fatal spot where they seem to expect some awful doom.[1]

A public meeting is proposed, but as they make a fuss about the two dollar poll tax I doubt if they get a meeting unless some energetic member gets it up for them. Then they will go & say afterward "How well *our* meeting went off." So slow!

Ellen Emerson has decided not to register. I dont know why but am very sorry for she has much influence in C. & some already back out because she does. Is n't it a pity? Yours disgustedly

L. M. A.

ALS: Sophia Smith Collection, Smith College.
    1. Ever since July 1879, when she became "the first woman to register my name as a voter," LMA had been campaigning in Concord to get women to register to vote. The results were disappointing: LMA called her neighbors "so timid and slow" when she found it so "hard to move people out of the old ruts," and by October only seven of the more than one hundred eligible women had registered (see her journal entries for July–September, Cheney, pp. 321–322, and [ca. 11 October 1879]).

To George Frisbie Hoar

Concord Sept. 5th [1879]

Mr Hoar. [1]
Dear Sir.

The Woman's Suffrage Society of Concord are anxious to have a public meeting here, hoping to interest & decide their hesitating townswomen on the subject of voting for School Committee. [2]

As Chairwoman of our small society I am requested to ask if it would be possible for you to address us at the Town Hall on Saturday evening Sept. 13th?

We hope to have Mr Higginson & Dr Peabody [3] at the same time, & wake sleepy Concord up to its duty on this question.

A line to me will much oblige

yours respectfully
L. M. ALCOTT.

ALS: Massachusetts Historical Society.
    1. George Frisbie Hoar, U.S. senator from Massachusetts.
    2. For more on the school committee vote, see [ca. 11 October 1879] and 30 March 1880.
    3. Thomas Wentworth Higginson and Nathaniel Peabody, homeopathic physician and brother of the Peabody sisters (Elizabeth Palmer Peabody, Mary Peabody Mann, and Sophia Peabody Hawthorne).

To Mary Mapes Dodge

Sept. 17th [1879]

Dear Mrs Dodge.

I am glad the beginning pleases you.[1] I have four more chapters ready & will send two by to day's mail, the others as soon as those are safely in your hands. You can keep them as I have copies. Hope the artist will be inspired & have some good pictures for us.

Checks are always a pleasing sight & I accept them without a murmur.

Are the chapters or installments the right length? From 30 to 35 of mine are about what you put in to three or four of yours with pictures. I like to know my limits & then I can plan to have each month's allowance complete in itself, or end with an interesting episode.

Dont let me *prose*. If I seem to be declining & falling in to it pull me up & I'll try to prance as of old. Years tone down one's spirit & fancy though they only deepen one's love for the little people & strengthen the desire to serve them wisely as well as cheerfully. Fathers & mothers tell me they use my books as helps for themselves, so now & then I like to slip in a page for them, fresh from the experience of some other parent, for education seems to me to be *the* problem in our times.

"Jack & Jill" are right out of our own little circle, & the boys & girls are in a twitter to know what is going in, so it will be a "truly story" in the main.

Such a long note for a busy woman to read! But your cheery word was my best "starter" & I'm more than ever

yours truly L. M. A.

ALS: Wilkinson Collection of Mary Mapes Dodge, Princeton University Library. Printed: Cheney, p. 303; *LASC*, p. 371.
    1. The beginning of *Jack and Jill*.

To the Woman's Journal

[ca. 11 October 1879]

Editors Journal. Some time ago you asked for a report from Concord as to what was being done about preparing to vote for school committee. So little has been done that it is hardly worth recording, yet honor is due to the few brave and sensible women who have done their duty at the cost of time, money and feeling.

Three meetings were held at our house. Half-a-dozen were expected, and twenty-five came to hear what Mrs. Cheney, Mrs. Dr. Talbot and Mrs. Shattuck[1] could tell us of the proper ways and means. Very informal meetings, where we met and talked over the matter, asked questions, compared notes and got ready to go and register.

I had already been to see the Assessor, and as my interview has been very untruly reported by the gossips, it is only fair to the gentlemen in office to clear them of the absurd blunders they are said to have made. At my first call I was kindly received, and having asked my question, "What must I do?" was told that as a woman paying a property tax I need only take my last year's receipted bill and go to the Registrar.

I did so July 23d, and the interview was as simple and brief as possible. I told what I wanted, showed my bill, was asked where I was born, age and profession; requested to read a few words from the Constitution to prove that I could read, to sign my name to the paper to prove that I could write, and that was all.

The Assessor did not make out my new tax bill, nor did I pay it to him, as the Collector is the person to receive it, and none of the reported conversation took place, except that I said I never felt that my tax was just before, and though not wholly so now I should pay it with pleasure.

Both gentlemen have been very courteous and made matters as easy as they could, though as no one seems to know just how things stand there is some confusion, and each new case has to be settled as well as they can.

Letters were written to Mr. Higginson and Hon. George Hoar, asking them to give us a public meeting; but politics absorbed them and they could not be had till after the 15th of September. We still hope to have a meeting, for it is not too late to stir up the class of women who seem slowest to register. I am ashamed to say that out of a hundred women who pay taxes on property in Concord, only seven have as yet registered, while fourteen have paid a poll tax and put their names down in time.

A very poor record for a town which ought to lead if it really possesses all the intelligence claimed for it.

Yours for reforms of all kinds,

L. M. ALCOTT.[2]

MS: Unlocated. Printed: *Woman's Journal* 10 (11 October 1879): 321; *LAFL*, pp. 442–443.

1. Emily Fairbanks Talbot, philanthropist and co-worker with her husband, the homeopathic physician Israel Tisdale Talbot; Harriette Robinson Shattuck, daughter of the journalist William S. Robinson ("Warrington") and the first woman in Massachusetts to express publicly her desire to vote under the new law.

2. This letter was in part a reply to the notice that had appeared in the 23 August *Woman's Journal* as "Miss Alcott Before the Registrar": "An eye witness reports the appearance of

Louisa M. Alcott before the Selectmen of Concord to secure registration for herself. . . . She said to the authority, 'I want to have my name put on the register that I may vote for School Committee.' 'Very well,' said the Selectman. 'Have you brought your receipt for your last year's tax?' 'No,' said Miss Alcott, 'I did not know it was necessary.' 'You will have to bring it.' 'Won't this year's tax receipt do just as well?' 'Oh, yes, but you have not paid it.' " At this, "Miss Alcott runs over with mirth. A little comical look came on her face, as she said, 'I never did hanker to pay my taxes, but now I am in a hurry to pay them.' The Selectman, as much amused as Miss Alcott, got the tax bill made out by the Assessor, and then and there Miss Alcott paid it. When they put her name on the Register, it was found that Miss Alcott had been the first woman to register in the old town of Concord" (reprinted in *LAFL*, pp. 451–452).

To Ann E. Devens

Nov. 15th [1879]

Mrs Devens.

Dear Madam.

I am writing a Serial[1] about a group of girls & boys somewhat like the little circle of which your dear Elly[2] was a well beloved member. Of course I give no names & merely use such characteristics, events & games as will give life to the picture.

My story will not be complete without some memorial of one who was very dear to us all, but death renders sacred everything concerning those we lose, & I do not venture to use any of the pleasant recollections we have of Elly without asking your permission.

The moral of my story is the influence for good or ill that even young people can exert over one another, & Elly's was so beautiful that I cannot bear to lose so fine & true an example.

At the time of his death both my sister & I longed to come & express to you our sympathy in your great loss, but feared to intrude, though we mourned for him sincerely & still cherish the flowers Maud brought us from his grave.

I should dearly love to record in a few tender pages, for other boys & girls to read & remember, this sweet & noble life whose influence is still felt, whose memory is still green in the hearts of many.

Please reply to me as frankly as I have written, & believe me

your friend for Elly's sake

L. M. ALCOTT.

ALS: Louisa May Alcott Collection, Barrett Library, University of Virginia Library. Printed: Carroll A. Wilson, *Thirteen Author Collections of the Nineteenth Century*, eds. Jean C. S. Wilson and David A. Randall, 2 vols. (New York: Scribners, 1950), 1: 12–13.

1. *Jack and Jill.*

2. Ellsworth Devens died at the age of seventeen on 8 August 1879. *Jack and Jill* is dedicated to "the schoolmates of Ellsworth Devens."

To Louisa Caroline Greenwood Bond

Concord, Jan. 1, 1880.

Dear Auntie, — It is hard to add one more sorrow to your already full heart, particularly one of this sort, but I did not want you to hear it from any one but us. Dear May is dead.[1] Gone to begin the new year with Mother, in a world where I hope there is no grief like this. Gone just when she seemed safest and happiest, after nearly two years of such sweet satisfaction and love that she wrote us, "If I die when baby comes, remember I have been so unspeakably happy for a year that I ought to be content . . ."

And it is all over. The good mother and sister have done everything in the most devoted way. We can never repay them. My May gave me her little Lulu, and in the spring I hope to get my sweet legacy. Meantime the dear grandma takes her to a home full of loving friends and she is safe. I will write more when we know, but the cruel sea divides us and we must wait.

Bless you dear Auntie for all your love for May; she never forgot it, nor do we.

Yours ever,
LOUISA.

MS: Unlocated. Printed: Cheney, p. 312.
    1. May Alcott Nieriker died on 29 December, shortly after the birth of Louisa May Nieriker on 8 November. She left the child, nicknamed Lulu, to LMA to raise.

To the Boston Transcript

For The Transcript.

———

[ca. 2 January 1880]

As the facts in the Advertiser notice of the late May Alcott Nieriker were incorrect will you kindly give place to the following true ones.[1]

Both of the pictures which Madame Nieriker sent at different times to the Salon were accepted, & many of those exhibited in London, Manchester & els[e]where were sold at once.

She was considered by those who knew her best both at home & abroad as one of the most industrious & promising of the young artists, & all her teachers, Hunt, Rimmer, Vautin Johnston, Krug & Müller spoke highly of her talent, ardor & perseverance.[2]

Her large collection of copies from Turner's oil & water colors is the finest in the country & will if possible be exhibited at the Art Museum in the spring. Her own sketches which she brought home at various times sold so rapidly that the modest artist was surprised to find her work preferred to the copies which she valued so much. By the sale of these pictures she was enabled to revisit Europe for another year of hard & most successful work in the Paris studios.

She had been a teacher of drawing & water color, & a [manuscript breaks off]

The year before her last trip abroad she opened a free art school in Concord at her own expence, giving time, teaching, casts, clay, books, & best of all the inspiration of her own patient yet ardent love & labor for her art. More than one pupil will remember gratefully her generous aid, & mourn the loss of a true friend.

Her marriage was not unexpected by her immediate family, nor was her death a surprise to them, letters having apprised them of sudden & severe illness some days before the cable brought the sad tidings that the happy little romance of the past two years was ended.

Madame Nieriker was preparing to pass the winter with her husband's family in Baden, but the unusually bitter weather in Paris was unfavorable to her, & after a brief illness she died of cerebro spinal menengitis Dec 30th in the 39th year of her age, leaving a little daughter seven weeks old.

L. M. A.

ALS: Houghton Library, Harvard University (partial). Printed: "The Sudden Death of one of Concord's Most Gifted Daughters," *Concord Freeman*, 8 January 1880, p. 1. The *Boston Evening Transcript* carried a one-paragraph obituary of May on 1 January (p. 4) but not this eulogy by LMA.

1. LMA objected to the *Boston Daily Advertiser*'s claims that the pictures May submitted to the Paris Salon had been rejected, her marriage was "quite unexpected," and her death "sudden" (2 January 1880, p. 1).

2. Artists William Morris Hunt and William Rimmer; Boston artists Henry Vautin and David Claypoole Johnston (one of May's teachers in 1860); Edouard Krug, under whom May studied in Paris; and Charles Louis Müller.

To Louisa Caroline Greenwood Bond

January 4 [1880].

Dear Auntie, — I have little further news to tell, but it seems to comfort me to answer the shower of tender sympathetic letters that each mail brings us. . . .

So we must wait to learn how the end came at last, where the dear dust is to lie, and how soon the desolate little home is to be broken up. It only remains for May's baby to be taken away to fill our cup to overflowing. But perhaps it would be best so, for even in Heaven with Mother, I know May will yearn for the darling so ardently desired, so tenderly welcomed, bought at such a price.

In all the troubles of my life I never had one so hard to bear, for the sudden fall from such high happiness to such a depth of sorrow finds me unprepared to accept or bear it as I ought.

Sometime I shall know why such things are; till then I must try to trust and wait and hope as you do. . . . Sorrow has its lonely side, and sympathy is so sweet it takes half its bitterness away.

Yours ever, L.

MS: Unlocated. Printed: Cheney, p. 313.

To Mary Preston Stearns

Jan. 4th [1880]

Dear Friend.[1]

We all thank you most sincerely for the true and tender words you have written of May.

They were just what we wanted, and no one but yourself could so well say them.

Her ambition was to be known as an artist, and she agreed with me that her life as a woman was not for the world except such glimpses as would show from time to time the inspiration which kept her love for her art, or the obstacles, which delayed its fuller success. Come in sometime and tell us about the club. I know kind things were said and felt by many, and at such a time *we* must try to forget that actions ever belie the words of some.

Gratefully yours

L. M. ALCOTT.

Can you secure a few copies of the paper for us.[2] We shall love to send it to the Nierikers and other friends.

MS: Unlocated; typescript copy at Fruitlands Museums, Harvard, Massachusetts.
    1. Mary Preston Stearns, a friend of LMA's father from Medford, Massachusetts, and wife of Major George Luther Stearns.
    2. Possibly the obituary "May Alcott, Artist," by Frank Sanborn in the 3 January 1880 *Springfield Daily Republican* (p. 4).

To Elizabeth Wells

Jan. 14th [1880]

Dear Lizzie.

    You will be glad to hear that in our last letters from Miss Plummer[1] (who saw May often) she tells us how quietly the dear little child died in her sleep at 9 a. m. Dec. 29th.

    She was buried in the cemetery of Montrouge, a pretty place where she once said when walking with E[rnest]. before baby came,

"If I die lay me here."

Miss P. knew an American clergyman who had met father at the West & was in Paris. So he read the service at the funeral where E's friends & May's neighbors, all of whom loved & mourned her, met to pay her the last respect. A simple, pretty funeral with flowers & sunshine in the little salon, loving people, & then with three carriages & a dozen gentlemen walking behind the hearse in French fashion, she was carried to her grave; all the men they met, rich or poor lifting their hats as the procession passed. In a green corner of the quiet cemetery, where Miss P. says she shall watch over the new mound, lies our bright, happy May just as she wished to lie in the country she loved more than America.

    She had not suffered for the last week but lay asleep most of the time, waking to know them & speak gently, then to drift away again till the morning she died without a sigh or struggle, just folded her hands as she always did when easy & so fell into the last long sleep. I am resigned now for she would never have been well had she lived. Baby has gone to Baden with Grandma, Sophie[2] is in a Paris pension, & poor E. still clings to the home though his mate is gone. He means to stay till spring with a friend as company, & I think he is wise.

I shall not go out but send some one if no N[ieriker]. comes over. Annie cant let me go & we are all left now, so I shall not venture as I could not stay. Baby must be here in May before the hot weather as she will be teething, & Fall is too long to wait for her.

About the house,[3] all is so uncertain we had better not plan. The C[oncord]. house wouldn't suit as we want to be in the *city*, & now the family is to be so mixed it may be better to keep still. At any rate I cant decide till *autumn*, & that wouldn't suit you. Nothing seems *sure* to me now & I dont care much for anything. Nan is pretty well & sends love. yrs Lu.

ALS: Houghton Library, Harvard University.
    1. Copies of Plummer's letters of 21[–29] December and 31 December [1879], describing May's death and funeral in much the same terms as in LMA's letter, are at Houghton Library, Harvard University.
    2. Sophie Nieriker, Ernest's sister, accompanied Lulu to Boston, arriving on 19 September 1880.
    3. LMA was planning to rent Elizabeth Sewall Willis Wells's house in Boston for the next winter.

To Mary Mapes Dodge

Jan. 20th [1880]

Dear Mrs Dodge.
    I have been so bowed down with grief at the loss of my dear sister just when our anxiety was over, that I have not had a thought or care for anything else.
    The story is done,[1] but the last chapters are not copied, & I thought it best to let them lie till I could give my mind to the work.[2]
    I never get a good chance to do a story without interruption of some sort. "Under the Lilacs"[3] was finished by my mother's bedside in her last illness, & this one when my heart was full of care & hope & then grief over poor May.
    I trust the misery did not get into the story, but I'm afraid it is not as gay as I meant most of it to be.
    I forgot to number the pages of the last two chapters, & so cannot number these. I usually keep the sum, but this time sent off the parcel in a hurry.

Can you send me the right number to go on with in Chapter 17? I can send you four more as soon as I hear.

I dont believe I shall come to N.Y. this winter. May left me her little daughter for my own, & if she comes over soon I shall be too busy singing lullabies to one child to write tales for others or go anywhere even to see my kind friends.

A sweeter little romance has just ended in Paris than any I can ever make, & the sad facts of life leave me no heart for cheerful fiction.

Yours truly
L. M. ALCOTT.

ALS: Wilkinson Collection of Mary Mapes Dodge, Princeton University Library.
    1. *Jack and Jill.*
    2. Later, LMA added that "People told me to make the tale 'a little pious,' so I have here & there tried to suit them without being too preachy." This tone did not offend the "Concord children [who] enjoy the numbers as they come out, & my other infants seem satisfied, so I trust the delay & dark days have not done any great harm" (to Mary Mapes Dodge, 5 March [1880], New-York Historical Society).
    3. LMA's journal indicates that she finished *Under the Lilacs* in September 1877, just two months before Mrs. Alcott's death (Cheney, p. 299).

To the Woman's Journal

Editors Journal: — As other towns report their first experience of women at the polls, Concord should be heard from, especially as she has distinguished herself by an unusually well conducted and successful town meeting.

Twenty-eight women intended to vote, but owing to the omission of some formality several names could not be put upon the lists. Three or four were detained at home by family cares and did not neglect their domestic duties to rush to the polls as has been predicted. Twenty, however, were there, some few coming alone, but mostly with husbands, fathers or brothers as they should; all in good spirits and not in the least daunted by the awful deed about to be done.

Our town meetings I am told are always orderly and decent, this one certainly was; and we found it very like a lyceum lecture only rather more tedious than most, except when gentlemen disagreed and enlivened the scene with occasional lapses into bad temper or manners, which amused but did not dismay the women-folk, while it initiated them into the forms and courtesies of parliamentary debate.

Voting for school committee did not come till about three, and as the meeting began at one, we had ample time to learn how the mystic rite was performed, so, when at last our tickets were passed to us we were quite prepared to follow our leader without fear.

Mr. Alcott with a fatherly desire to make the new step as easy as possible for us, privately asked the moderator when the women were to vote, and on being told that they could take their chance with the men or come later, proposed that they should come first as a proper token of respect and for the credit of the town. One of the selectmen said "By all means," and proved himself a tower of strength by seconding the philosopher on this momentous occasion.

The moderator (who is also the registrar and has most kindly and faithfully done his duty to the women in spite of his own difference of opinion) then announced that the ladies would prepare their votes and deposit them before the men did. No one objected, we were ready, and filed out in good order, dropping our votes and passing back to our seats as quickly and quietly as possible, while the assembled gentlemen watched us in solemn silence.

No bolt fell on our audacious heads, no earthquake shook the town, but a pleasing surprise created a general outbreak of laughter and applause, for, scarcely were we seated when Judge Hoar rose and proposed that the polls be closed. The motion was carried before the laugh subsided, and the polls were closed without a man's voting; a perfectly fair proceeding we thought since we were allowed no voice on any other question.

The superintendent of schools expressed a hope that the whole town would vote, but was gracefully informed that it made no difference as the women had all voted as the men would.

Not quite a correct statement by the way, as many men would probably have voted for other candidates, as tickets were prepared and some persons looked disturbed at being deprived of their rights. It was too late, however, for the joke became sober earnest, and the women elected the school committee for the coming year, feeling satisfied, with one or two exceptions, that they had secured persons whose past services proved their fitness for the office.

The business of the meeting went on, and the women remained to hear the discussion of ways and means, and see officers elected with neatness and dispatch by the few who appeared to run the town pretty much as they pleased.

At five the housewives retired to get tea for the exhausted gentlemen, some of whom certainly looked as if they would need refreshment of some sort after their labors. It was curious to observe as the women went out how the faces which had regarded them with disapproval, derision or doubt when they went in now smiled affably, while several men hoped the ladies would come again, asked how they liked it, and assured them that there had not been so orderly a meeting for years.

One of the pleasant sights to my eyes was a flock of school-boys watching with great interest their mothers, aunts and sisters, who were showing them how to vote when their own emancipation day came. Another was the spectacle of women sitting beside their husbands, who greatly enjoyed the affair though many of them differed in opinion and had their doubts about the Suffrage question.

Among the new voters were descendents of Major Buttrick of Concord fight renown, two of Hancock and Quincy,[1] and others whose grandfathers or great grandfathers had been among the first settlers of the town. A goodly array of dignified and earnest women, though some of the "first families" of the historic town were conspicuous by their absence.

But the ice is broken, and I predict that next year our ranks will be fuller, for it is the first step that counts, and when the timid or indifferent, several of whom came to look on, see that we still live, they will venture to express publicly the opinions they held or have lately learned to respect and believe.

L. M. A.

Concord, March 30, 1880.[2]

MS: Unlocated. Printed: *Woman's Journal* 11 (3 April 1880): 105; *LAFL*, pp. 443–445.

1. John Buttrick was the first commander to order his men to fire at the British at the skirmish at Old North Bridge in Concord; John Hancock, signer of the Declaration of Independence; Josiah Quincy, Boston lawyer who was the attorney for the defense at the Boston Massacre trial in 1771.

2. The description of this meeting in the 1 April 1880 *Concord Freeman* has a slightly different — and very patronizing — tone. The announcement to begin voting "caused many a feminine heart to palpitate with excitement and many a hand to unconsciously glide to a bow or bonnet string, or some like feminine fancy, in preparation for the trying ordeal of passing up in front of . . . nearly 200 great horrid men & boys to deposit their maiden vote. The look of eager expectancy . . . [was] not unlike that seen upon the face of a person who is about to have a tooth extracted." After the twenty women voted and George Hoar closed the polls, the clerk "created considerable amusement by the remark that it would make no difference, the ladies have all voted just as the gentlemen would vote" ("Town Meeting in Concord," p. 1).

To Mary Mapes Dodge

Concord, May 29th [1880]

Dear Mrs Dodge.

I was away from home so your letter did not reach me till I got back yesterday.

Thanks for your kind thought of me & recollections of the pleasant week when the L. L.'s had a lark.[1] I should like another, but in this work a day world busy folk dont get many as we know.

If I write a Serial you shall have it; but I have my doubts as to the leisure & quiet needed for such tasks being possible with a year old baby. Of course little Lu is a *very* remarkable child, but I fancy I shall feel as full of responsibility as a hen with one chick, & cluck & scratch industriously for the sole benefit of my daughter.

She may, however, have a literary turn & be my assistant by offering hints & giving studies of character for my work. She comes in Sept. if well.

If I do begin a new story how would "an old fashioned boy" & his life do?[2] I meant that for the title of a book, but another woman stole it.[3] You proposed a Revolutionary tale once[4] but I was not up to it; for this I have quaint material in my father's journals, letters & recollections. He was born with the century & had an uncle in the war of 1812, & his life was very pretty & pastoral in the early days.

I think a new sort of story wouldn't be amiss, with fun in it, & the queer old names & habits. I began it long ago, & if I have a chance will finish off a few chapters & send them to you if you like. I shall be at home through June & at York Harbor in July.[5]

I enclose a copy of the lines. Glad you like them.

yrs cordially L. M. ALCOTT.

Regards to Mrs Burnett & the Boy.[6] Hope he is quite well again.

ALS: Wilkinson Collection of Mary Mapes Dodge, Princeton University Library. Printed: Cheney, p. 333; *LASC*, p. 372.

    1. Possibly a reference to Lucy Larcom, co-editor of *Our Young Folks*.

    2. LMA never finished *An Old-Fashioned Boy*, which was to be based on the life of her father.

    3. Martha Finley, the author of *Elsie Dinsmore*, who wrote under the name Martha Farquharson, published *An Old-Fashioned Boy* in 1871.

    4. For the "Revolutionary tale," see 21 August [1879].

    5. York Harbor on the Maine coast.

    6. Frances Hodgson Burnett, author of *Little Lord Fauntleroy* (1886), and her son Vivian, who served as the model for the title character. She and LMA had been honored at a meeting of the Papyrus Club in Boston in the spring of 1879; LMA then invited the Burnetts and Dodge to Concord for lunch (Marjorie Worthington, *Miss Alcott of Concord* [Garden City, N.Y.: Doubleday, 1958], pp. 269–270).

To Thomas Niles

York, July 20, 1880.

The drawings are all capital, and we had great fun over them down here this rainy day. . . . Mr. Merrill[1] certainly deserves a good penny for his work. Such a fertile fancy and quick hand as his should be well paid, and I shall not begrudge him his well-earned compensation, nor the praise I am sure these illustrations will earn. It is very pleasant to think that the lucky little story has been of use to a fellow-worker, and I am much obliged to him for so improving on my hasty pen-and-ink sketches. What a dear rowdy boy Teddy is with the felt basin on!

The papers are great gossips, and never get anything quite straight, and I do mean to set up my own establishment in Boston (D.V.). Now I have an excuse for a home of my own, and as the other artistic and literary spinsters have a house, I am going to try the plan, for a winter at least.

Come and see how cosey we are next October at 81 Pinckney Street. Miss N. will receive.[2]

Yours truly, L. M. A.

MS: Unlocated. Printed: Cheney, p. 334.

1. Nearly two hundred illustrations by Frank Merrill appeared in *Little Women* (1880), issued by Roberts Brothers as a holiday book (see Raymond L. Kilgour, *Messrs. Roberts Brothers, Publishers* [Ann Arbor: University of Michigan Press, 1952], p. 176, and *LMA*, p. 291).

2. Lulu Nieriker.

To Kirk Munroe

Boston Oct. 7th [1880]

Mr Munroe.[1]

Dear Sir.

I am aware that the story[2] was shorter than you proposed to have it, but on calculating the length to which 13,000 words would bring it I found it would be 100 pages of the sort I sent you, & that it would be a much longer tale than I write for $100.

I declined to write a serial, & sent you a tale of the length I usually write for magazines at the price named.

There is no second part, so if it does not suit your paper please return it, as several others are waiting to be served & my time will not allow me to answer all requests.

I meant to have sent a line with the Ms. explaining this, but forgot it.

yrs respectfully
L. M. ALCOTT.

P.S. My address for the winter is 81 Pinckney St. Boston.[3]

If you do not care to keep the tale will you kindly hand it to the editor of St. Nicholas, as Mrs Dodge likes short stories when serials are impossible, & this will save the trouble of a trip to & fro, & much oblige a very busy woman.

L. M. A.

ALS: Henry W. and Albert A. Berg Collection, New York Public Library, Astor, Lenox, and Tilden Foundations.

1. Kirk Munroe, first editor of *Harper's Young People.*

2. "How It All Happened" appeared in the 21 December 1880 *Harper's Young People.*

3. LMA rented Elizabeth Sewall Willis Wells's house at 81 Pinckney Street in Boston for the winter.

To Amos Bronson Alcott

All send love.

Nov. 10th [1880]

Dear Father.

I suppose you are in Syracuse now[1] & hope you will have a good time. See Charlotte [Wilkinson] if possible & tell her about Lulu.

Her first birthday was very pretty, for after dinner, when she was fresh from her nap & airing, we took her to the parlor in her new white boots, blue sash & green crown, & there was a table full of gifts. The little queen in her high chair sat & looked with delight at the tiny cake with *one* candle burning in it, picture books, flowers, a doll, silver mug, rattle with bells, & some gay cards from her friends. She seemed quite over powered by her feelings & sung, laughed, called "Up! Bow wow, Mama Da," & all her little words, in great glee. Then she chose the picture book & was absorbed by it like a true artist's baby.

She was weighed & is a twenty pounder, plump & lively & so clever & bright I feel as if with a grown person when she talks to me with her blue eyes & expressive hands. She had a happy day & made a sweet picture sitting on the rug looking up at the portraits of mother & grandmother, both framed in vines in honor of the day. I think *both* were there to bless the little darling. She sends love & kisses to Dranpa.

AL: Houghton Library, Harvard University.
    1. Bronson had set off in October for a seven-month tour of the Northeast and the Midwest that would carry him through thirty-seven cities.

To William Torrey Harris

Jan. 7th [1881]

Dear Mr Harris, [1]

    Father entirely forgot your last arrangement & gave me directions as I wrote. It is of no consequence. I am used to these philosophic "lapses" of memory & manage to pay bills with my unphilosophic wits very often.

    I hope to be in Concord next week & if I can come see you I will. About the biography I have little to say as *I* shall never write it, except perhaps in a story some time.

    His philosophy I have never understood, & biography is not in my line. Sanborn & yourself are the persons to do that, & I can only help a little perhaps about the domestic part. [2]

    I hope a good life will some time be written to set him right with the world. Though after all the living it is the main point. He has seen several of his ideals become facts & that is more than most of us ever do.

    I am glad you are safely at home again, & imagine that the old house under the elms does seem pleasanter than ever after foggy London & the wintry Atlantic. [3]

    Regards to Mrs Harris.

Yours truly

L. M. ALCOTT.

MS: Unlocated; typescript copy at Fruitlands Museums, Harvard, Massachusetts.
    1. William Torrey Harris (see 20 December [1875]) rented Orchard House in 1880 and bought it four years later.
    2. Harris had been Bronson's supporter ever since the two met on one of Bronson's Midwest lecture tours in the middle 1850s. As editor of the *Journal of Speculative Philosophy*, Harris often published Bronson's works. His early interest in writing a biography, expressed here, later developed into a collaboration with Frank Sanborn on the two-volume *A. Bronson Alcott: His Life and Philosophy* (1893).
    3. Harris had gone to Europe in August 1880.

To Thomas Niles

February 12, 1881.

Dear Mr. Niles, — Wendell Phillips wrote me a letter[1] begging me to write a preface for Mrs. Robinson's "History of the Suffrage Movement;"[2] but I refused him, as I did Mrs. R., because I don't write prefaces well, and if I begin to do it there will be no end. . . .

Cannot you do a small edition for her? All the believers will buy the book, and I think the sketches of L. M. Child,[3] Abby May, Alcott, and others will add much to the interest of the book.

Has she seen you about it? Will you look at the manuscripts by and by, or do you scorn the whole thing? Better not; for we are going to win in time, and the friend of literary ladies ought to be also the friend of women generally.

We are going to meet the Governor, council, and legislature at Mrs. Tudor's[4] next Wednesday eve and have a grand set-to. I hope he will come out of the struggle alive.

Do give Mrs. R. a lift if you can, and your petitioners will ever pray.

Yours truly, L. M. A.

MS: Unlocated. Printed: Cheney, pp. 341–342.

1. Phillips's letter asked for "ten or fifteen pages from you (not necessarily commending the book — but just talking about it, or anything else) would make any publisher snatch at it — such an Introduction!" ([1881], Houghton Library, Harvard University).

2. Roberts Brothers published Harriet H. Robinson's *Massachusetts in the Woman's Suffrage Movement* in 1881.

3. Lydia Maria Child, a longtime reformer and author of numerous household works. Her *Philothea* (1836) had been an early favorite of the Alcott children, who had dramatized scenes from it (Cheney, p. 41).

4. Mrs. Fenno Tudor, who was "interested in the further extension of the suffrage to women," had invited every member of the legislature to her house on Beacon Street for an "entertainment" (*Boston Evening Transcript*, 16 February 1881, p. 4).

To Thomas Niles

February 19, 1881.

Dear Mr. Niles, — Thank you very much for so kindly offering to look at Mrs. R.'s book. It is always pleasant to find a person who can conquer his prejudices to oblige a friend, if no more.

I think we shall be glad by and by of every little help we may have been able to give to this reform in its hard times, for those who take the tug now will deserve the praise when the work is done.

I can remember when Anti slavery was in just the same state that Suffrage is now, and take more pride in the very small help we Alcotts could give than in all the books I ever wrote or ever shall write.

"Earth's fanatics often make heaven's saints," you know, and it is as well to try for that sort of promotion in time.

If Mrs. R. does send her manuscripts I will help all I can in reading or in any other way. If it only records the just and wise changes Suffrage has made in the laws for women, it will be worth printing; and it is time to keep account of these first steps, since they count most.

I, for one, don't want to be ranked among idiots, felons, and minors any longer, for I am none of the three, but very gratefully yours,

L. M. A.

MS: Unlocated. Printed: Cheney, p. 342.

To Mary Preston Stearns

Feb. 21st 1881.

Dear Miss Stearnes.

Many thanks for the tender thoughtfulness which sends us the precious little notes from the dear dead hands.

They are so characteristic that they bring both mother & May dearly up before me, alive & full of patient courage & happy hopes. I am resigned to my blessed mother's departure, since life was a burden, & the heroic past made a helpless future very hard to think of.

But May's loss just when life was fullest & sweetest seems very bitter to me still, in spite of the sweet baby who is an unspeakable comfort.

I wish you could see the pretty creature who already shows many of her mother's traits & tastes. Her love of pictures is a passion, but she will not look at the common, gay ones most babies enjoy. She chooses the delicate, well drawn & painted figures of Caldicott & Miss Greenaway,[1] over these she broods with rapture, pointing her little finger at the cows or cats, & kissing the children with funny prattlings to these dumb playmates.

She is a fine, tall girl full of energy intelligence & health. Blonde & blue-eyed like her mother, but with her father's features for which I am glad, as

253

he is a handsome man. Louisa May bids fair to be a noble woman, & I hope I may live to see May's child as brave & bright & talented as she was, & much happier in her fate.

Father is at the West, busy & well.[2] Anna joins with me in thanks & affectionate regards.

Ever yrs   L. M. ALCOTT.

ALS: Collection of American Literature, the Beinecke Rare Book and Manuscript Library, Yale University. Printed: Cheney, p. 343.
    1. Randolph Caldecott and Kate Greenaway, both famous illustrators of children's books.
    2. Bronson had left for Cleveland from upstate New York on 9 December 1880.

To Mary Mapes Dodge

Nonquitt Aug. 6th [1881]

Dear Mrs. Dodge,

I am sorry for the children's disappointment, & dont delay for want of urging as the twenty boys & girls here at the beach clamor for more stories & suggest many plans.

None seem to think that a Revolutionary one would be interesting, & I fear that patriotism is not natural to the youthful soul.

Next Fall I will see what I can do. Meantime I will try to get a little story done if the hot weather will let me work.

As I lead the life of an oyster just now I fear it wont be a very thrilling tale, but it may appease the little people till we can promise something better.

Baby is well, thank you, & has just tumbled down stairs for the first time, frightening me out of my wits but not hurting herself a bit.

She is so fat she rolled down like a ball & had not a bruise to show after the exploit.

Yrs truly
L. M. A.

ALS: Special Collections, Harold B. Lee Library, Brigham Young University. Printed: LASC, pp. 372–373.

To Mary Mapes Dodge

Nonquitt Aug 16th [1881]

Dear Mrs Dodge,

I have been looking at the pictures with all my eyes hoping an idea would start up. As yet ideas not heard from, but I shall continue to stare *hard* & cudgel my brain till something comes.

Pussy & the spinning wheel rather took my fancy & a little tale of an old fashioned Thanksgiving looms vaguely before me.[1]

If I could get at the books I'd try "The First Thanksgiving." But it might be too grim & sad.

I have often written up to pictures & find them very suggestive, especially now when invention is at low water mark.

Twenty eight children last night sat round the big chair I occupied, on the arms & back thereof, & clamored for stories. In the exciting crisis of The Three Pigs in the wall of faces before me I saw one little red ear pushed through a narrow place "listening tight", as a small boy expressed it. On examination a flushed & beaming child appeared, saying contentedly, "I couldn't see but I was 'termined to hear, & I did!"

Such an audience must inspire even my used up wits; so, as it is rainy, they all come to my cottage this evening &, sitting round the open fire, have a storytell. I have an eye to business, & out of thier hints, chat & pretty ways hope for the germ of the "forthcoming work."

Yrs truly L. M. A.

ALS: Wilkinson Collection of Mary Mapes Dodge, Princeton University Library.
1. "An Old-Fashioned Thanksgiving" appeared in the November 1881 *St. Nicholas* and was reprinted in the sixth volume of *Aunt Jo's Scrap-Bag* (Boston: Roberts Brothers, 1882), which took its title from this story.

To Horace P. Chandler

[ca. 7 December 1881]

Dear Mr Chandler.[1]

The corrections are certainly rather peculiar, & I fear my struggles to set them right have only produced greater confusion.[2]

Fortunately punctuation is a free institution & all can pepper to suit the taste. I dont care much, & always leave proof readers to quiddle if they like.

Thanks for the tickets. I fear I cannot come till Thursday, but will try; & wont forget the Office since I am not that much-tried soul the Editor.[3]

Yrs truly
L. M. A.

ALS: Parkman Dexter Howe Library, University of Florida. Printed: Cheney, p. 349.

1. Horace P. Chandler, editor and publisher of the *Sword and the Pen* for the Soldiers' Home Bazaar, later editor of *Every Other Saturday*.

2. "My Red Cap" was serialized in the 7–10 December 1881 *Sword and the Pen*.

3. At this time, LMA was absorbed in learning to take care of Lulu, as she wrote to Chandler: "Babies cannot be set aside even for the poor old boys in blue, & as my small tyrant was confided to me by her poor mother I am more anxious to do my duty by her than if she were my own" (8 November [1881], Parkman Dexter Howe Library, University of Florida).

To the Woman's Journal

Editor Journal: — You ask what we are going to do about Municipal Suffrage for women in Concord? and I regret to be obliged to answer, as before — "Nothing but make a motion asking for it at town meeting, and see it promptly laid upon the table again."

It is always humiliating to have to confess this to outsiders, who look upon Concord as a representative town, and are amazed to learn that it takes no active part in any of the great reforms of the day, but seems to be content with the reflected glory of dead forefathers and imported geniuses, and falls far behind smaller but more wide awake towns with no pretensions to unusual intelligence, culture, or renown.

I know of few places where Municipal Suffrage might more safely be granted to our sex than this, for there is an unusually large proportion of tax-paying, well-to-do and intelligent women, who only need a little training, courage, and good leadership to take a helpful and proper share in town affairs. They would not ask or accept town offices, but would be glad to work in their own efficient and womanly way, as they have proved they could work by the success of their church, charity and social labors for years past.

To those who see what brave and noble parts women elsewhere are taking in the larger and more vital questions of the time, the thought very naturally comes: "What a pity that so much good sense, energy, time, and money could not be used for more pressing needs than church-fairs, tea-parties, or clubs for the study of pottery, Faust, and philosophy!"

While a bar room door stands open between two churches, and men drink themselves to death before our eyes, it seems as if Christian men and women should bestir themselves to try at least to stop it; else the commandment "Thou shalt love thy neighbor as thyself" is written over the altars in vain, and the daily prayer "Lead us not into temptation" is but empty breath.

If the women could vote on the license question I think the bar-room would be closed; but while those who own the place say, "It would lessen the value of the property to make a temperance house of it," and the license matter is left to the decision of those men who always grant it, the women can only wait and hope and pray for the good time when souls are counted of more value than dollars, and law and gospel can go hand in hand.

A forty years acquaintance with the town leads me to believe that as the conservative elders pass away, the new generation will care less for the traditions of the past, more for the work of the present, and taking a brave part in it, will add fresh honors to the fine old town, which should be marching abreast with the foremost, not degenerating into a museum for revolutionary relics, or a happy hunting-ground for celebrity-seekers.

A rumor has just reached me that some of the husbands of our few Suffrage women intend to settle the license question in the right way, and perhaps say a good word for our petition before it is shelved. This is encouraging, for it shows that the power behind the throne is gently working, and though the good women have little to say in public, they do know how to plead, advise, and convince in private. So, even if fewer should vote this year than last, and if nothing seems to come of our effort to secure Municipal Suffrage this time, we shall not be disheartened, but keep stirring our bit of leaven, and wait, as housewives know how to do, for the fermentation which slowly but surely will take place, if our faith hope and charity are only strong, bright, and broad enough.

L. M. ALCOTT.

Concord, Mass., Feb. 4, 1882.

MS: Unlocated. Printed: Woman's Journal 13 (11 February 1882): 41; reprinted LAFL, pp. 445–446.

To Mary Mapes Dodge

Feb. 13th [1882?]

Dear Distracted Editor.

I will try. Can a mortal woman say more? The reason why I have refused before is that since I stopped writing my over taxed nerves have given me little trouble, & the care of Baby has been just the right work for me.

For her sake as well as my own I have held off from the pen, knowing that if I once took it up the old hurry & worry would come on, & I should be as fractious as a teething child.

But, as I am pretty well now & Lulu needs me less & less each month, being an independent, sturdy young woman, I will make a beginning & see how it goes. Sitting long & writing are bad things for my troubles, but I will make the attempt, rash as it is, & if I can get a few chapters done may find I can gently amble along if you dont want very long chapters or millions of em.

About the tale, I have only one idea of any body, several plans are vaguely floating in my mind.

"An old Fashioned Boy,"[1] would have a good back bone of truth to it, & much helpful material lies ready at hand, so I think I had better start off on that & get in as much of the simple life & manners of sixty or seventy years ago as possible. It would be unlike any of my other books, & fun is never old fashioned so that can be tucked in. A New Fashioned Girl, is a good idea & I'll "make note on," but as time presses I'll let that simmer & dive recklessly into the other.

If you will kindly agree to let me off *if* I find health wont bear the work, I will do my best; but after five years of woe & worry I do value bodily comfort more than money, & cant give it up after such a tug to win it back.

A woman stole my title & I think the book O. F. Boy is printed, would that make trouble for us? She wrote & told me she wouldn't use it, but did, & I told her I should use it if I liked.

If you think another name better I will get one. Meantime you can make your plans & announcements without a name. Peace be with you, dear soul, in this & all things.

Affectionately yrs.   L. M. A.

ALS: Wilkinson Collection of Mary Mapes Dodge, Princeton University Library.
    1. For "An Old-Fashioned Boy," see 29 May [1880].

To Laura Hosmer

Tuesday eve.
[25 July 1882]

Dear Laura.

I sent you a mean little postal in return for your nice letter, but I was that "drone" with all sorts of things just then I could do no more.

The Emerson day was a regular scrabble.[1] Dr Bartol, Dr Mc Cosh, Mr Watson & my Tommy to lunch.[2] Eight other people coming in a party. Three men to see Pa, & a garden tea at Miss Ripley's.[3] I still live.

I have folks to tea tomorrow, an Emerson party on Friday, & dine at Mrs Cheney's on Monday.

Mrs E. Hoar[4] has a five o clock tea tomorrow.

Our Temperance meeting today was funny with no President, no Vices & only nine warm but faithful ladies present. Miss Munroe[5] forgot it till nearly five but came all the same.

It is as hot as pepper today & yesterday. No rain for some time & the dust flies well.

You sitting aloft among the clouds can pity us panting worms down here.[6]

Miss Mc Clure & C. E. say they had a splendid time, & Anna reports N[onquitt]. unusually gay. I shall go second week in Aug, I think & maybe you will come down from the heights by that time & come & see me.

May I give Lulu raspberries? She is very well, regular, & all right. No other fruit now & she longs for em, but I dont know.

Love to all. Get as hearty as possible & come home your rosy self to your

L. M. A.

ALS: Louisa May Alcott Collection, Barrett Library, University of Virginia Library.

1. The Concord School of Philosophy had a special session in honor of Emerson on 22 July, which was widely reported in the Boston newspapers. Among the speakers were Bronson Alcott, Frank Sanborn, Julia Ward Howe, William Torrey Harris, and Ednah Dow Cheney. Bronson's account of the meeting, along with clippings of various newspaper accounts, is in his "Diary for 1882," pp. 284–299, Houghton Library, Harvard University.

2. Cyrus A. Bartol; the philosopher James McCosh, president of Princeton University and a frequent attender of the Concord School of Philosophy; Benjamin Marston Watson, a friend of the Emersons and Alcotts from Plymouth, Massachusetts; and Thomas Niles.

3. Either of Emerson's unmarried cousins, Elizabeth Bradford Ripley or Phebe Bliss Ripley. Bronson's account of this occasion is in his "Diary for 1882," p. 295, Houghton Library, Harvard University.

4. Either Elizabeth Prichard (Mrs. Edward) Hoar or Caroline Brooks (Mrs. Ebenezer Rockwood) Hoar.

5. Mary Munroe, active in the Concord Women's Christian Temperance Union.

6. Laura Whiting Hosmer practiced medicine in Concord after her marriage to Henry Joseph Hosmer in December 1874. LMA is writing her at Monadnock Mountain House in Troy, New York.

To Anna Alcott Pratt

[October? 1882]

Dear Nan.

Tell Papa & E. E.[1] that I should either print all C. says of Alcott or leave it all out.[2] The last allusion to him is my own opinion, & as it describes Alcott as he really was at that time I would let the last bit go, if Papa does not object.

R. W. E.s own opinion of later times does A. B. A. justice, & is worth all of C's queer sayings. A. B. A. & T. C. never *could* meet or understand one another, & it was vain to try.[3]

yrs
L. M. A.

ALS: Houghton Library, Harvard University.

1. Either Edward or Ellen Emerson.

2. This is probably a reference to the edition of *The Correspondence of Thomas Carlyle and Ralph Waldo Emerson* (1883) that Charles Eliot Norton was editing and the two letters in which Carlyle describes Bronson's visits to him in England. In Norton's published version of the first letter (19 July 1842), Carlyle's comments on the "genial, innocent, simple-hearted man" are printed, but the remaining half of his long paragraph, quite critical of Bronson (e.g., "his present *sally* into modern existence . . . evidently gives him pain") is deleted. Norton's printing of the second letter (29 August 1842) omits entirely a long paragraph in which Carlyle, having heard incessantly of the "vegetable-diet," concludes that Bronson is "ignorant of the life-methods of civilized men" (the complete texts are printed in *The Correspondence of Emerson and Carlyle*, ed. Joseph Slater [New York: Columbia University Press, 1963], pp. 326–327, 329–330).

3. Carlyle's comment on his relations with Bronson was similar: "We differ . . . from the very centre" (19 July 1842, *Correspondence of Emerson and Carlyle* [1963], p. 326).

To Maria S. Porter

[after 24 October 1882]

My poor dear father lies dumb and helpless.[1] He seems to know us all, and it is so pathetic to see my handsome, hale, active old father changed at one fell blow into this helpless wreck. You know that he wrote those

260

forty remarkable sonnets last winter,[2] and these, with his cares as Dean of the School of Philosophy and his many lectures there, were enough to break down a man of eighty-three years. I continually protested and warned him against overwork and taxation of the brain, but 'twas of no avail. Wasn't I doing the same thing myself? I did not practise what I preached, and indeed I have great cause for fear that I may be some day stricken down as he is. He seems so tired of living; his active mind beats against the prison bars. Did I ever tell you what Mr. Emerson once said of him to me! "Louisa, your father could have talked with Plato." Was not that praise worth having? Since then I have often in writing addressed him as "My dear old Plato."

MS: Unlocated. Printed: Maria S. Porter, "Recollections of Louisa May Alcott," *New England Magazine* n.s. 6 (March 1892): 4; Maria S. Porter, *Recollections of Louisa May Alcott, John Greenleaf Whittier, and Robert Browning* (N.p.: New England Magazine Corp., 1893), p. 7. Porter says this letter was written by LMA "just after her father had been stricken with paralysis."

    1. Bronson suffered a paralytic stroke on 24 October. As this and the following letters make clear, he suffered both physical and mental impairments. He never wrote again; both his journal and letters cease in October 1882.

    2. Bronson's *Sonnets and Canzonets* was published by Roberts Brothers in April 1882.

To Mary Preston Stearns

Nov. 4th [1882]

Dear Mrs. Stearns.

Many thanks for your tender thought of us. Father still remains speechless, the right side paralyzed, and his mind in a very dim & feeble state. I think he knows familiar faces & voices for a little while, then the heavy sleep comes again & he cares for no one.

In the morning he is propped up in an invalid chair for an hour while the bed is airing, & sits looking out contentedly, but with that vacant look which is peculiarly pathetic in eyes once so wise, serene, & sweet.

He likes to hold books & try to read them, & makes letters on a sheet of paper. Sometimes a word is written, but usually only letters without meaning.

At first I hoped he would be himself again, but begin to fear it never will be, & for his sake more than ours I cannot wish him to linger feeble in mind & body.

He takes milk only, as he does not swallow solids yet, with the exception of wine jelly which melts & does not choke him.

The bay-rum will be a comfort to him as he loves the odor, & is rubbed

& bathed a good deal. The wine may come of use later to warm up the dear old veins & cheer the heart. I shall tell him, when he can understand, of your kindness and good wishes.

Anna sends love & thanks. I wish May's blooming girl could give you in a kiss some of the balm she brings me when the old heartache comes.

Yours affectionately,
L. M. A.

ALS: Fruitlands Museums, Harvard, Massachusetts.

To Mary Preston Stearns

Nov. 7th [1882]

Dear Friend.

Your splendid jug arrived last eve, & as I bathed father's head I said, "Mrs Stearns sends this", & he smiled & turned his hot forehead for more, as if both the name & the fragrant refreshment were a comfort to him.

It is delicious, & after filling a smaller bottle I hid the jug that no one might be tempted to steal a drop of the precious stuff.

Father was bathed in it today, & the fresh, clean odor makes the whole room sweet. Many thanks for this prompt & thoughtful kindness.

Dr. Wesselhoeft came up yesterday, and said it was only a question of time, *weeks* perhaps, but *days* he feared. So we make ready, & enjoy each hour in spite of the sad eclipse that already seems to part us in a measure.

Mr. Sanborn saw him last eve in one of his bright moments, & will I fear give an impression that he is better than he really is.

My little May is three tomorrow, & we keep the day with a baby party of dolls & two small friends. A sad house for my poor darling, & a sad month, for her mother lost all knowledge of her baby soon after her birth.

Affectionately yrs
L. M. A.

I will send a line from time to time that you may have *true* tidings of our dear pilgrim on his last progress.

ALS: Fruitlands Museums, Harvard, Massachusetts.

To Ednah Dow Cheney

Dear Mrs Cheney.

Thanks for your kind letter, & tender thought of us in your own heavy
sorrow.[1]

I fear Mr Sanborn gave you too favorable an account of father's condition.
He saw him but twice, & the last time excited him a good deal by reading
& talking of things best avoided in his present feeble state of mind & body.

He talks now, but brokenly, & seems to have difficulty in expressing even
the disconnected thoughts that come & go in his bewildered yet active brain.
He suffers no pain, can make his wants known, eats spoon food easily, &
sleeps more quietly than before. But is very wandering in mind & feeble in
body. We do not hope to see him ever his old self, nor to keep him long.
It is not to be desired, & I shall gladly see the end before life is a burden,
or he recalls too clearly the affliction that has befallen him. He would suffer
in the knowledge of his weakness & the probable fate in store for him, so I
do not ask many days or weeks of this pathetic fumbling after the lost intelligence & vigor. A quick & quiet passage from this darkness to the light he
loved & lived in is far better.

I spoke to him of you & he held your letter, but seemed not to remember
the name just then.

Anna sends love, & I am as ever

Affectionately yrs.

L. M. A.

ALS: Sophia Smith Collection, Smith College.
    1. Upon learning of the death of Cheney's daughter, Margaret, who had died on 23
September, LMA wrote: "It is a hard lesson to understand, or to accept without understanding
why those who seem fittest to live should be taken away so soon, & so many seemingly worth-
less creatures left to cumber the earth. We shall know some day, & meantime can only try to
find the sweet drop in the bitter draught, & get new strength from it for the next lesson" (2
October [1882], Sophia Smith Collection, Smith College).

To Mary Preston Stearns

Nov. 26th [1882]

Dear Mrs. Stearns.

The precious letter is received and in Mr Sanborn's hands to be added
to the new edition of the book.[1]

263

Your wish for some copies shall be attended to.

Father is about the same as when I last wrote, except that some days he seems to be feebler & more irritable.

His limbs swell in spite of rubbing, & he does not gain strength though he eats more.

I dont feel that he will ever get up again or be himself. He may linger for weeks but I think he will slowly wear away, his unusual vitality alone keeping him alive so long.

He is now having his twilight talk while his arm is rubbed, & seems to be scolding his nurse because she cannot find & bring him the *Trinity*. He seems to have fragments of old ideas floating in his mind, & brings out very queer remarks, the sublime & the absurd so mixed that one must laugh even with tears in the eyes to see these "sweet bells jangled out of tune." His voice is changed, and the old Conn. accent has come back. Just now he said, "Where is my mother?" "In Heaven, & you will see her some time," answers pious Nurse. "Yes, I think I shall, & she will know me if I *am* eighty three, & wear a bib when I eat."

He is going back to a happy childhood, & the good old mother will find her boy again soon, as innocent as when he read prayers in the little church on Spindle Hill.

Affectionately yrs.

L. M. A.

ALS: Fruitlands Museums, Harvard, Massachusetts.

1. This must refer to Emerson's 5 July 1865 letter to Mrs. Stearns about receiving Bronson's *Emerson* (1865), a limited edition that she had helped finance. However, Emerson's letter was not printed in the 1882 edition of the book, then in progress, but in the 1888 edition.

To Mary Newbury Adams

Concord Dec. 5th [1882]

Dear Mrs Adams. [1]

Thanks for your very kind letter which I read to Father, & think he understood the drift of it.

He was dimly conscious of his birthday & enjoyed the fruit & flowers sent him, though he was sure his age was *twenty three* instead of eighty three.

He seems better in many ways, but will never be his vigorous self again in body or mind.

May's drawing of Madame Costé's pension (1870)

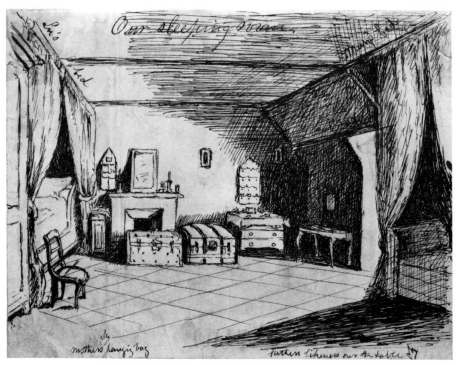

May's drawing of her and Louisa's room at Madame Costé's (1870)

May's drawing of Madame Costé's salon, with Louisa at the fireplace (1870)

Frederick and John Pratt

Engraving of Louisa May
Alcott, with her comments
about it (1870)

Louisa May Alcott,
photographed by
E. L. Allen (1870)

Louisa May Alcott

Louisa May Alcott

Louisa May Alcott writing in her room at Orchard House in the mid-1870s

Abigail May Alcott in the study at Orchard House

Bronson Alcott in his study

Louisa May Alcott's room at Orchard House

The parlor at Orchard House

Engraving of the Boston Fire (1872)

Poster advertising Bronson Alcott's Conversations (1875)

The Thoreau House in Concord, where the Alcotts moved in 1877

April 6th

Dear Mrs Moshier.

The old house is to rent if any one wants it. We none of us care for it now Mother is gone & May married abroad. Annie has her new home & I am to be with her free from the cares always so burdensome to me.

Father still values things & the place he made & does not want to sell it yet. The house is dismantled & looks a very different place from the one you knew, for summer, pictures, books & "Marmee" made it lovely. Now it is a shabby

Letter to Mrs. A. D. Moshier of 6 April [1878]

Orchard House and, at left, the Concord School of Philosophy

*Louisa May Alcott and Lulu
(Louisa May Nieriker)*

Daniel Ricketson's sketch of Louisa May Alcott's cottage at Nonquitt (1885)

Lulu

Louisa May Alcott and the actor James Murdoch

Cover of Lulu's Library (1885)

Louisa May Alcott, photographed
by James Notman (1886?)

John Sewall Pratt Alcott

Dr. Rhoda Lawrence's house in Roxbury

Walton Ricketson's bas-relief of
Louisa May Alcott (1886)

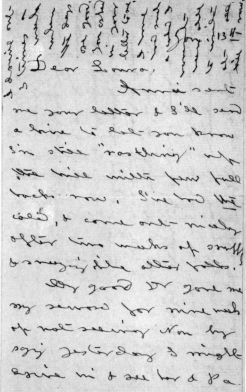

Letter to Laura Hosmer of 13 January
[1888]

Frontispiece to Ednah Dow Cheney's Louisa May Alcott:
The Children's Friend (1888)

He does not leave his bed, eats only spoon food, is still helpless on the right side, & speech is indistinct, though he talks a good deal, & tries to express his thoughts.

He suffers no pain as yet, but I fear the weariness of confinement & debility will soon afflict him, so this brightening of the mind is not without its trials.

He likes the papers in the morning, but soon puts them down & dozes, with piles of books on his table to look at since he cannot read them. The old habits are strong, & at times he likes pencil & paper, trying to write with the feeble left hand since the faithful right is no longer able to stir. This seems to trouble him, & he looks sadly at the swollen, helpless arm which will never serve him again I fear.

Lulu is a little sunbeam in his sickroom, & it is pathetic to see her try to nurse him in her motherly way, while he watches the bright head with smiles as it goes & comes always welcome.

Please thank all the good friends who so kindly remembered the dear old man & kept his memory green.

Anna joins with me in love to yourself.

Cordially yours
L. M. ALCOTT.

ALS: Manuscript Collections, Iowa State Historical Library.

1. Mary Newbury Adams organized numerous literary and philosophical clubs in Dubuque, Iowa, and often hosted Bronson's visits to that city. She maintained an extensive correspondence with him and naturally would have been interested in the state of his health. Her long relationship with Bronson is discussed in Madeleine B. Stern, "Mrs. Alcott of Concord to Mrs. Adams of Dubuque," *New England Quarterly* 50 (June 1977): 331–340, and Richard L. Herrnstadt, "Alcott in Iowa: Two Letters of Mary Newbury Adams and Five Letters of A. Bronson Alcott," *Studies in the American Renaissance 1985*, ed. Joel Myerson (Charlottesville: University Press of Virginia, 1985), pp. 323–331.

To Mary Preston Stearns

Dec. 30th [1882]

Dear Mrs. Stearns.

I have been trying to find a moment to thank you for the wine & tell you about our dear invalid's Xmas.

The two bottles, one with the card tied to it with a gay ribbon & the other holding a nosegay, stood on his bedside table beside a dish of rosy apples, grapes & oranges, flowers & several lovely cards. He enjoyed the little feast, & as the wine was forbidden just now we drank your health in grapes.

"Wine saddening none
Wine gladding all."[1]

I told him who sent the different things, & he said, "Thank them for me."

Through the day we showed him our gifts & he seemed to understand the occasion. I hung a green wreath in his window & he touched it many times, saying, "Xmas, I remember."

Mr Harris with Sanborn called for a few moments, & had their little jokes about the Dean & Faculty of the School of Philosophy. The poor Dean sat up among his pillows & laughed, & tried to talk, but his speech is more indistinct than formerly, & very hard to understand. He says his "brain works and tires him", so we do nothing to excite, even pleasurably.

The arm swells badly, no use of either limb, no solid food, bowels still torpid, & no desire to leave his bed. I think if the spring finds him here, it will only be a shadow of his former self. I hope that he will be gone to the eternal summer, & leave us only a green mound & a green memory of much virture [i.e., virtue], love & beauty.

Affectionately yours,
L. M. A.

ALS: Fruitlands Museums, Harvard, Massachusetts.
    1. From "The Goblet," in Bronson's *Tablets* (Boston: Roberts Brothers, 1868), pp. 93–94.

To Mrs. Leavitt

[ca. 14 January 1883]

Mrs Leavitt
Dear Madam.

Many thanks for the honor done me which I gratefully accept, & will try to be a worthy member of "The Little Women Society."

I have no copy of the dramatized scenes, although they have been acted in many places.

It is very easy to arrange a short play by taking the conversation out of the first chapter, ending with the letter & song.

The Operatic Tragedy for the next act, & any other bit that suits the occasion or actors for the third scene. Beth's illness was once done very prettily; the night when the two girls watch, Laurie & Jo send the telegram, & at the pathetic moment Hannah says Beth is better, & Marmee arrives. Another set of young people had the Pickwick Club & read an original paper, full of local hits which was a great success.

If you care for autographs to sell at your fair I will send you "lots" as the girls say when coolly requesting autographs, photographs & autobiographical sketches of your humble servant.

With best wishes I am

Yrs truly
L. M. ALCOTT.

ALS: Maine Historical Society.

To Louise Chandler Moulton

Jan. 18th / 83

Dear Mrs Moulton.

I have not the least objection to the writing of a sketch of L. M. A. by any one, & should feel quite comfortable in *your* hands.[1]

I have very little material to offer for my journals were all burnt long ago in terror of gossip when I depart & on unwise use of my very frank records of people & events.

F. B. Sanborn wrote a nice little sketch in the Dec. St. Nicholas for 1875 I think. That gives the facts & dates & a too partial estimate of the old lady.

T. Niles can tell you about the books, & in Work, Little Women, Hospital Sketches & Transcendental Wild Oats,[2] you will find the various stages of my career & experience.

I have just recieved a letter from Mr Worthington[3] about the matter, asking me to write a sketch of some one. I have no time for pen work, if I had I would, by your leave, do you, & return the compliment you pay me by choosing your humble servant.

I shall be very glad to give you any particular facts you may want as you go on, after reading F. B. S. & seeing T. N. Dont forget to mention that L. M. A. does n't like lion hunters, does n't send autographs, photographs & autobiographical sketches to the hundreds of boys & girls who ask them, & that she heartily endorses Dr Holmes Atlantic article on the subject.[4] If you want some funny quotations from letters or specimens of what we are expected to do I can give them.

With thanks & best wishes

I am yours truly

L. M. ALCOTT.

ALS: Manuscript Division, Library of Congress.

1. Louise Chandler Moulton's biographical sketch of LMA appeared in *Our Famous Women* (Hartford, Conn.: A. D. Worthington, 1885), pp. 29–52. LMA provided Moulton with biographical information about her mother and herself in two letters (both [n.d.], Houghton Library, Harvard University).

2. "Transcendental Wild Oats," LMA's fictional account of the Fruitlands experiment, appeared in the 18 December 1873 *Independent*.

3. A. D. Worthington, publisher of *Our Famous Women*.

4. Oliver Wendell Holmes, in his "An After-Breakfast Talk," proposed that: no author was "under any obligation" to answer an autograph seeker; no stranger should ask for more than one autograph, ask the author to copy out lines from his writing, nor expect a photograph of the author; each request should include a blank sheet for the autograph and a stamped addressed envelope in which to return it; and sending a stamp "does not constitute a claim on the author for an answer," for he may keep the stamp or give it to "some appropriate charity, as, for instance, the Asylum for Idiots and Feeble-Minded Persons" (*Atlantic Monthly Magazine*, 51 [January 1883]: 73).

To George Gray

Feb. 7th / 83.

Dean Grey.[1]

Dear Sir.

Thanks for your kind letter. My father read it with pleasure & wished me to write at once.

He is much better, but still keeps his bed & is very helpless in body though bright mentally. We hope he will see the Spring again, & be able to enjoy his friends & his study even if work is impossible.

He is as serene & patient as a philosopher should be, & seems to find sweetness & sunshine even in this new experience of pain. He talks still of rounding out his hundred years, & plans work for twenty years to come.

Sanborn & Harris call often & talk *to* him as his own speech is too imperfect to make conversation easy for him.

He reads a little & plays checkers, looks out at the wintry world with tranquil pleasure, & enjoys the pranks of his little grand child who is head-nurse & takes care of "Dranpa" with pretty, maternal tenderness.

It seems to be a beautiful & happy ending to a wise & blameless life, very lovely to watch & very helpful to us who look after the ascending saint to catch a glimpse of Heaven as he enters in.

With regards to Mrs Grey from my father & myself, I am

Yours truly
L. M. ALCOTT.

ALS: Henry W. and Albert A. Berg Collection, New York Public Library, Astor, Lenox, and Tilden Foundations.

1. George Zabriskie Gray, dean of the Episcopal Divinity School in Cambridge, Massachusetts.

To William Warland Clapp, Jr.

Editor Boston Daily Journal.

My attention having been called to the fact that a letter of mine sent to the annual Woman Suffrage meeting, has been entirely misunderstood by the opponents of the cause, I wish to set the matter right, being as anxious as Mrs Howe to have it clearly understood that, though "a well-descended woman" I am heart and soul on the unpopular side of the question.

Those to whom the letter was addressed made no mistake in its meaning, knowing well that while home duties kept me from a festival where I was not needed, nothing but the most pressing care or calamity would prevent me from discharging the duties I owe the cause. I had no time for *pleasure*, but when our Town Meeting comes I shall be there, glad of a chance to help secure good schools for my neighbours' children. Surely this will be as feminine and worthy an act as standing behind a stall at a charity fair, or dancing in a ball-room.

The assertion that suffragists do not care for children and prefer notoriety to the joys of maternity is so fully contradicted by the lives of the women who are trying to make the world a safer and a better place for both sons and daughters, that no defense is needed. Having spent my own life from fifteen to fifty, loving and laboring for children, as teacher, nurse, storyteller and guardian, I know whereof I speak, and value their respect and confidence so highly that for their sakes, if for no other reason, I desire them to know that their old friend never deserts her flag.

So far from losing interest in this question, every year gives me greater faith in it, greater hope of its success, a larger charity for those who cannot see its wisdom, and a more earnest wish to use what influence I possess for its advancement. LOUISA MAY ALCOTT.

Concord.

Mar 6. 1883

MS: Unlocated; manuscript copy in an unidentified hand, which served as printer's copy, at Houghton Library, Harvard University. Printed: "Louisa M. Alcott's Defence of Woman's Suffrage," *Boston Morning Journal,* 8 March 1883, p. 2; *Woman's Journal* 14 (10 March 1883): 1; *LAFL,* p. 447.

To Mary Preston Stearns

May 31st [1883?]

Dear Mrs. Stearns.

The domestic upheaval of spring cleaning has delayed my reply to your very kind note with its offer of wine and sweet waters for my dear old invalid.

He cannot use wine as it heats his head, but the bay rum is his comfort & delight. I have used our generous supply carefully, & the other day when he was warm & worried I put the last on his head, & while I bathed I said, "you are a philosopher & must not be upset by small trials." "Yes, I am. I will do it," he answered with the old, bright look I sometimes get, & from that minute there was no more fretting, & when his nurse came in he put out his hand, & said, like a gentleman, "I was cross, I confess, forgive me. I am so old." It made me think of poor Lear, as he often does at times when the old instincts of a fine & gentle nature show through the weakness & wandering of a troubled brain.

If our good angel likes to fill again the bottle that has not run dry for two years[1] we shall enjoy the refreshment in the warm weather, if it ever comes.

I should much like to bring Lulu (or May) on a little pilgrimage some time to pay her respects to her mother's good friend. Perhaps we may do it yet. We go to the seaside soon, and in the autumn I will show you the healthiest little lass in Mass. D.V.

With many thanks & much love,

Yrs ever

L. M. A.

ALS: Fruitlands Museums, Harvard, Massachusetts.

    1. LMA means that Mrs. Stearns had been sending bay rum for two years, not that a single bottle had lasted that long.

To Thomas Niles

June 23, 1883.

Dear Mr. Niles, — Thanks for the Goethe book.[1] I want everything that comes out about him. "Princess Amelia" is charming, and the surprise at the end well done. Did the author of "My Wife's Sister" write it?[2]

I told L. C. M. she might put "A Modern Mephistopheles" in my list of books.[3] Several people had found it out, and there was no use in trying to keep it secret after that.

Mrs. Dodge begged me to consider myself mortgaged to her for tales, etc., and as I see no prospect of any time for writing books, I may be able to send her some short stories from time to time, and so be getting material for a new set of books like "Scrap-bag," but with a new name.[4] You excel in names, and can be evolving one meantime. . . .

Yours truly, L. M. A.

MS: Unlocated. Printed: Cheney, p. 351; *LASC*, pp. 376–377.
1. Emerson had given LMA Goethe's works when she was fifteen, and they had "been my delight ever since" (n. d., Cheney, p. 398). *A Modern Mephistopheles* reflected LMA's interest in Goethe.
2. Elizabeth W. Latimer's *Princess Amélie* appeared in Roberts Brothers' third No Name Series in 1883. Her *My Wife and My Wife's Sister* appeared in the second No Name Series in 1881.
3. Moulton's article on LMA in *Our Famous Women* (see 18 January 1883).
4. Possibly an early reference to the *Lulu's Library* series, named after May's child, which began in 1886.

To Mary Mapes Dodge

Concord, August 15 [1883].

Dear Mrs. Dodge, — I like the idea of "Spinning-Wheel Stories," and can do several for a series which can come out in a book later.[1] Old-time tales, with a thread running through all from the wheel that enters in the first one.

A Christmas party of children might be at an old farm-house and hunt up the wheel, and grandma spins and tells the first story; and being snow-bound, others amuse the young folks each evening with more tales. Would that do? The mother and child picture would come in nicely for the first tale, — "Grandma and her Mother."[2]

Being at home and quiet for a week or so (as Father is nicely[3] and has a

271

capable nurse), I have begun the serial, and done two chapters; but the spinning-tales come tumbling into my mind so fast I'd better pin a few while "genius burns." Perhaps you would like to start the set Christmas. The picture being ready and the first story can be done in a week, "Sophie's Secret"[4] can come later. Let me know if you would like that, and about how many pages of the paper "S. S." was written on you think would make the required length of tale (or tail?). If you don't want No. 1 yet, I will take my time and do several.

The serial was to be "Mrs. Gay's Summer School,"[5] and have some city girls and boys go to an old farmhouse, and for fun dress and live as in old times, and learn the good, thrifty old ways, with adventures and fun thrown in. That might come in the spring, as it takes me longer to grind out yarns now than of old.

Glad you are better. Thanks for kind wishes for the little house; come and see it, and gladden the eyes of forty young admirers by a sight of M. M. D. next year.

Yours affectionately,

L. M. A.

MS: Unlocated. Printed: Cheney, pp. 374–375; LASC, p. 373.

  1. The stories reprinted in *Spinning-Wheel Stories* (Boston: Roberts Brothers, 1884) appeared in *St. Nicholas* between January 1884 and January 1885.

  2. The first of the *Spinning-Wheel Stories* was "Grandma's Story" in the January 1884 *St. Nicholas*.

  3. The previous week, LMA had written: "The dear old man is having a second birth almost, & slowly growing up from a sad sort of infancy to a happy childhood. I doubt if it is ever anything more, but it is a curious fact that that hair is growing on the blessed head bald for years, & that he uses the same glasses that I do, the first, & hears better than for years. Walks alone with a crutch, but feebly as yet, & begins to use the helpless hand a little. His mind is clear & the vacant look is gone, but the speech is still imperfect & memory also" (to Mrs. Stearns, 9 August [1883?], Fruitlands Museums, Harvard, Massachusetts).

  4. "Sophie's Secret" appeared in the November and December 1883 issues of *St. Nicholas* and was reprinted in Volume 3 of *Lulu's Library* (Boston: Roberts Brothers, 1889).

  5. "Mrs. Gay's Summer School" was never written.

To Mary Preston Stearns

Sunday.

[Fall 1883?]

Dear Mrs. Stearns.

You will be glad to know that father seems brighter in mind, though the body remains helpless & the lips dumb. He reads a little, & understands us better, & seems to enjoy his little comforts.

It is only a temporary change perhaps, but I still hope that it may last & grow still clearer. These painless, peaceful days have a certain sweetness, sad as it is to see the dear hale old man so feeble.

If he can know us & enjoy something of the old life it is worth having though the end may come at any moment.

I think he will speak soon, but trying seems to excite & weary him, so we wait, & now & then a word comes without effort. "Up", was the first one, & seems very characteristic of this beautiful, aspiring soul almost on the wing for Heaven.

He still lives on milk with a little fruit, & beaten eggs. As I write he sits in his chair looking placidly out at the river & the falling leaves. I asked him if he sent his love to you, & he smiled & bowed & moved his hand. He remembers.

Affectionately yours,
L. M. A.

ALS: Fruitlands Museums, Harvard, Massachusetts. Printed: Cheney, p. 360 (partial), where it is placed between letters of 1885 to Stearns and Thomas Niles.

To Elizabeth Wells

Oct. 9th [1883?]

Dear Lizzie.

You & Auntie always remember! Yesterday Annie, Lulu & I went on our pious pilgrimage to give dear Marmee the autumn leaves she loved so much, & while A. & I spread a rosy coverlet over the beloved dust Lulu went like a robin to lay red leaves over little Gladys Hawthorne[1] whom she knew at Nonquit.

Her questions about "Dod" & death were very sweet, & when I told her Gladys & her own dear Marmar were with God, she looked up at the lovely blue sky & pointed a little fat finger, saying with a happy smile,

"Dod lives up there. I like to fink my dear Marmar is there, its so pretty."

She is very good now, & improves rapidly. Changing nurses is bad, but they seem to have no strength, these Yankee girls, though the brains & conscience are there. The Pats[2] are strong but have no principle, & so we rastle along as well as we can with em.

Poor father is more & more care every month, & between my two babies, both looking for me at once, I feel like a nursin ma with twins. Father is jealous of L. & she does n't like me to kiss him before her, & it is funny to see them frown at one another. "Kiss *me*, quick," cries L. "Send her away when you come," orders Pa, & I run to & fro till legs & head are tired out.

Dear old Nan keeps the ten mouths filled & the machinery going in her own sweet way, & is a saint by nature & by grace.

Thanks for the sash. L. will like it much. I was so sorry to miss you for Miss N[ieriker]. seldom goes to B[oston]. & seeing "Tuzzin Lizzie" was to be a great event. We found Mee Mee & that was some comfort. Ruth[3] looked finely, & it was good to see her so plump & rosy. Sorry for your cold. This is a nasty climate, & you must take care after Italy. Come when you can. I shall run over & try to catch you every time I'm down.

Love to R. & much to yourself.   yrs L. M. A.

ALS: Houghton Library, Harvard University.
    1. Julian Hawthorne's daughter, Gladys, had died on 23 September 1882 at fourteen months old while the family was vacationing at Nonquitt.
    2. That is, the Irish.
    3. Ruth Lyman Wells, Lizzie Wells's daughter.

To Portland Cummings

Dear Portland.

I have no bright word to say. I "trudge in harness" & find my burdens heavy & various.

Father is feeble, but has a good nurse, only she is very tired after five months of it & may go.

I care for my baby now, having tried six American girls & found none fit to be a helper to me in the training of my young immortal. Mother is best, & that I must be, leaving pen, pleasure, society & rest to the good time that is so long a coming.

It seems impossible to find strength, refinement, & common-sense combined in a young woman who wants to earn her bread in a decent family. Only one did well, & she was delicate. The strong were stupid, the refined proud & over sensitive, & all lacking in common sense about air, food & practical things.

Do let us teach less French, music & mathematics & fit girls for real work. I am out of patience with the tribe, & want to shake them & thier mothers.

Now I feel better!

I think "Bread Winner" strong but a bit coarse.[1] Crawford tells a pleasant, dramatic story, but writes too fast.

I shall see M. Arnold[2] if I take Lulu [to] visit. I like his books much. "Light & sweetness" are what we need. Have you seen Protap Chundor

Mozoomdor[3] the Hindoo who comes to tell us about thier idea of Christ? He is a most interesting & earnest man. Spoke here, & we afterward met at Mrs Emerson's. I have his book & think you'd like to see it some time. It was most interesting to hear how our faith struck these Hindoos, so new & fresh & romantic. It is old to us, & we dont see its beauty as we ought. They give it a great charm in thier simple, earnest way of treating it.

Wish I had something pretty to send you, but have no time to make, buy or steal a gift. So send love & best wishes.

Affectionately yours
L. M. A.

Oct. 18th [1883]

ALS: Houghton Library, Harvard University.
　　1. John Hay's *The Bread-Winners* (1883), published anonymously, which LMA here believes to be by the historian and novelist F. Marion Crawford.
　　2. In his lectures in Boston in 1883, Matthew Arnold told his audiences that Emerson was neither a first-rate philosopher, poet, or prose writer, and that his real value lay in the inspirational quality of his work. Boston did not take this very well.
　　3. Pratap Chunder Mozoomder lectured at the Unitarian Church in Concord on 2 September, discussing religious reform in India (an account of his lecture is in the 7 September 1883 *Concord Freeman*, p. 1). Ellen Emerson found him a "pure delight," a "superior mind," and a "natural orator" (4 September 1883, *The Letters of Ellen Tucker Emerson*, ed. Edith E. W. Gregg, 2 vols. [Kent, Ohio: Kent State University Press, 1982], 2:515).

To Maggie Lukens

Boston Jan. 14th [1884]

Dear Maggie.

I have *not* forgotten my five sisters, & was glad to hear from them again, though sincerely grieved to learn that one of the dear group had gone.

I know how hard it is to spare these dear sisters, having lost two, & how empty the world seems for a long time. But faith, submission & work sustain, cheer & help so much that after the first sharpness of the loss is over, we often find a very sweet & precious tie still binds us even more tenderly together than when the visible presence was here.

Beth & May are always mine, though twenty five years have passed since we laid the poor shadow of one under the pines at Concord, & the dust of the other sleeps far away in Paris. Both are young, & bright, & live so always in my mind, for the pain & the parting, the years & sea are all as nothing, & I see them safe with Marmee waiting for the rest to come.

May's blooming baby, which she gave me with all her lovely pictures, is a great comfort to me, & promises to be as full of courage, talent & nobility as her gifted mother. I am so busy helping little Louisa May Nieriker live her own sweet story that I find no time to write others, & am settling down to be a cosy old Granny with my specks & knitting.[1]

My dear old father, now 84, is quite helpless & feeble in mind, but serene & happy as a child, suffering little but waiting cheerfully to slip away in God's good time after a long & blameless life.

You speak of "breaking away;" if it can be dutifully & wisely done I think girls *should* see a little of the world, try thier own powers, & keep well & cheerful, mind & body, because life has so much for us to learn, & young people need change. Many ways are open now, & woman can learn, be & do much if they have the will & opportunity.

I hope to see you if you take flight from the nest. With much love & sympathy to all I am, dear Maggie,

Your friend as always
L. M. ALCOTT.

ALS: Boston Public Library. Printed: Bok, 1–2.

    1. In declining an opportunity to contribute to *Every Other Saturday* on 23 March [1884], LMA wrote the editor, Horace Chandler, "I am so busy editing one animated copy of Little Women [Lulu] that I have no time for authorship" (Special Collections, Harold B. Lee Library, Brigham Young University).

To Maggie Lukens

Feb. 5th [1884]

My Dear Maggie.

I hope I never shall be too busy or too old to answer letters like yours as far as I can, for to all of us comes this desire for something to hold by, look up to, & believe in. I will tell you my experience & as it has stood the test of youth & age, health & sickness, joy & sorrow, poverty & wealth I feel that it is genuine, & seem to get more light, warmth & help as I go on learning more of it year by year.

My parents never bound us to any church but taught us that the love of goodness was the love of God, the cheerful doing of duty made life happy, & that the love of one's neighbor in its widest sense was the best help for oneself. Thier lives showed us how lovely this simple faith was, how much honor, gratitude & affection it brought them, & what a sweet memory they left behind for, though father still lives his life is over as far as thought or usefulness are possible.

Theodore Parker & R. W. Emerson did much to help me to see that one can shape life best by trying to build up a strong & noble character through good books, wise people's society, an interest in all reforms that help the world, & a cheerful acceptance of whatever is inevitable. Seeing a beautiful compensation in what often seems a great sacrifice, sorrow or loss, & believing always that a wise, loving & just Father cares for us, sees our weakness & is near to help if we call. Have you read Emerson? He is called a Pantheist or believer in Nature instead of God. He was truly *Christian* & saw God *in* Nature, finding strength & comfort in the sane, sweet influences of the great Mother as well as the Father of all. I too believe this, & when tired, sad, or tempted find my best comfort in the woods, the sky, the healing solitude that lets my poor, weary soul find the rest, the fresh hope, or the patience which only God can give us.

People used to tell me that when sorrow came I should find my faith faulty because it had no name, but they were wrong, for when the heavy loss of my dear, gifted sister found me too feeble to do anything but suffer passively, I still had the sustaining sense of a love that never failed even when I could not see why this lovely life should end when it was happiest.

As a poor, proud, struggling girl I held to the belief that if I *deserved* success it would surely come so long as my ambition was not for selfish ends but for my dear family, & it did come, far more fully than I ever hoped or dreamed tho youth, health & many hopes went to earn it. Now when I might enjoy rest, pleasure & travel I am still tied by new duties to my baby, & give up my dreams sure that something better will be given me in time.

Freedom was always my longing, but I have never had it, so I am still trying to feel that this is the discipline I need & when I am ready the liberty will come.

I think you need not worry about any name for your faith but simply try to be & do good, to love virture [i. e., virtue] in others & study the lives of those who are truely worthy of imitation. Women need a religion of thier own, for they are called upon to lead a quiet self sacrificing life with peculiar trials, needs, & joys, & it seems to me that a very simple one is fitted to us whose hearts are usually more alive than heads, & whose hands are tied in many ways.

Health of body helps health of soul, cheerful views of all things keep up the courage & brace the nerves. Work for the mind *must* be had, or daily duty becomes drudgery & the power to enjoy higher things is lost. Change of scene is sometimes salvation for girls or women who out grow the place they are born in, & it is thier duty to go away even if it is to harder work, for hungrey minds prey on themselves & ladies suffer for escape from a too pale or narrow life.

I have felt this, & often gone away from Concord to teach, (which I never liked) because there was no food for my mind in that small conservative town, especially since Mr Emerson died.

Food, fire & shelter are not *all* that women need, & the noble discontent that asks for more should not be condemned but helped if possible.

At 21 I took my little earnings ($20) & a few clothes, & went to seek my fortune tho I might have sat still & been supported by rich friends. All those hard years were teaching me what I afterward put into the books, & so I made my fortune out of my seeming *mis* fortunes; I speak of myself because what one has *lived* one really knows & so can speak honestly. I wish I had my own house (as I still hope to have) so that I might ask the young women who often write to me as you do, to come & see me, & look about & find what they need, & see the world of wise, good people to whom I could introduce them as others did me thirty years ago. I hope to have it soon, & then you must come & have our talk, & see if any change can be made without neglecting duty.

When one cannot go away one can travel in spirit by means of books. Tell me what you read & like, & perhaps I can send you a key that will at least open a window through which your eyes can wander while the faithful hands & feet are tied by duty at home.

Write freely to me, dear girl, & if I can help in any way be sure I gladly will. A great sorrow often softens & prepares the heart for for a new harvest of good seed, & the sowers God sends are often very humble ones, used only as instruments by him because being very human they come naturally & by every day ways to the help of those who are passing through trials like thier own.

I find one of the compensations for age in the fact that it seems to bring young people nearer to me, & that the experiences so hard to live through now help me to understand others. So I am always glad to do what I can, remembering how I wrote to my father for just such help as you ask, & how he answered as I have tried to answer you.

Let me know if it does comfort you any.

With love to my other girls

I am always your friend
L. M. A.

The simple Buddha religion is very attractive to me, & I believe in it. God is enough for me, & all the prophets are only stepping stones to him. Christ is a great reformer to me not God.

ALS: Boston Public Library. Printed: Bok, 6 (all but last paragraph).

To Maggie Lukens

Dear Maggie.

I am glad that my letter pleased you, & though always busy I at once answer your last because if by word or act one can help a fellow creature in the care or conduct of a soul that is one's first duty.

About the great Hereafter I can only give you my own feeling & belief, for we can *know* nothing, & must wait hopefully & patiently to learn the secret.

Death never seemed terrible to me, the fact I mean, though the ways of going & the sad blow of a sudden end are of course hard to bear & understand.

I feel that in this life we are learning to enjoy a higher, & fitting ourselves to take our place there. If we use well our talents, opportunities, trials & joys here when we pass on it is to the society of nobler souls, as in this world we find our level inevitably.

I think immortality is the passing of a soul thro many lives or experiences, & such as are *truly* lived, used & learned help on to the next, each growing richer higher, happier, carr[y]ing with it only the real memories of what has gone before. If in my present life I love one person truly, no matter who it is, I believe that we meet somewhere again, though where or how I dont know or care, for genuine love is immortal. So is real wisdom, virtue, heroism &c. & these noble attributes lift humble lives into the next experience, & prepare them to go on with greater power & happiness.

I seem to remember former states before this, & feel that in them I have learned some of the lessons that have never been mine here, & in my next step I hope to leave behind many of the trials that I have struggled to bear here & begin to find lightened as I go on.

This accounts for the genius & the great virtue some show here. They have done well in many phases of this great school & bring into our class the virtue or the gifts that make them great & good.

We dont remember the lesser things, they slip away as childish trifles, & we carry on only the real experiences. Some are born sad, some bad, some feeble, mentally & morally I mean, & all thier life here is an effort to get rid of this shadow of grief, sin, weakness in the life before. Others come as Shakespere, Milton Emerson &c. bringing thier lovely reward with them & pass on leaving us the better for thier lives.

This is my idea of immortality. An endless life of helpful change, with the instinct, the longing to rise, to learn, to love, to get nearer the source of all good, & go on from the lowest plane to the highest, rejoicing more & more as we climb into the clearer light, the purer air, the happier life which must exist, for, as Plato said "The soul cannot imagine what does not exist because it is the shadow of God who knows & creates all things."

I dont believe in spiritualism as commonly presented. I dont want to see or feel or hear dead friends except in my own sense of nearness, & as my love & memory paint them. I do believe that they remember us, are with us in a spiritual sense when we need them, & we feel thier presence with joy & comfort, not with fear or curiosity.

My mother is near me sometimes I am sure, for help comes of the sort she alone gave me, & May is about her baby I feel, for out of the innocent blue eyes sometimes come looks so like her mother's that I am startled, for I tended May as a child as I now tend Lulu. This slight tie is enough to hold us still tenderly together, though death drops a veil between us, & I look without doubt or fear toward the time when in some way we shall meet again.

About books. Yes, I've read "Mr Isaacs" & "Dr C." & like them both. The other "To Leeward" is not so good.[1] "Little Pilgrim" was pretty,[2] but why try to paint Heaven? Let it alone, & prepare for it whatever it is, sure that God knows what we need & deserve.

I will send you Emerson's Essays. Read those marked & see what you think of them. They did much for me, & if you like them you shall have more. Ever yr. friend   L. M. A.

Love to the girls & respects to Papa.

ALS: Special Collections, Harold B. Lee Library, Brigham Young University. Printed: Bok, 6.
    1. *Mr. Isaacs* (1882), *Dr. Claudius* (1883), and *To Leeward* (1884), all novels by F. Marion Crawford.
    2. Mrs. Margaret Oliphant's *A Little Pilgrim* (1882).

To Mary Mapes Dodge

Feb. 24th [1884]

Dear Mrs Dodge.

I will send you two tales by Wed. I wanted the old ones to go first, & will send the 6th old one very soon if you will not use the "Girl's Ghost" just yet. "Little Things" can follow "Onawanda" & then the Breton story in which I can use the *pretty girl spinning*.[1] I delayed that because I had to read up a little, & the care of a sick friend upset all my plans, as usual.

If it is not ready in time you can use the "G. G." The modern ones will go faster as I can suit myself about events &c.

T. N. is so very kind & useful that when he decidedly expresses a wish or opinion I like to comply with it.

The prospect of "Jo's Boys" is a very uncertain one,[2] & I have a serial which I think will be done first, if any quiet time *ever* comes.

I am glad if my words, poor as words always are at such times, conveyed a hint of my sympathy. I have felt like an orphan ever since my mother went, & with her the tender, protecting care which had been about me all my life. Nothing takes its place, & if now & then there did not come a blessed sense of her nearness, & the certainty that such love must be immortal, I think it would be much harder than it is to get on in this weary work a day world. Yet work is good & without it life only a selfish thing.

But you know all this better than I can tell it, so I'll stop my bad scribbling with the hope that all will be well with you.

yrs affectionately
L. M. A.

Are the tales the right length? About 45 pages.

ALS: Wilkinson Collection of Mary Mapes Dodge, Princeton University Library.

    1. All these stories, later reprinted in *Spinning-Wheel Stories*, first appeared in *St. Nicholas:* "Jerseys, or, The Girl's Ghost" (July 1884), "Little Things" (May 1884), "Onawandah" (April 1884), and "The Breton Story" and "The Banner of Beaumanoir" (June 1884).

    2. *Jo's Boys*, which LMA had been planning for some time, finally was published by Roberts Brothers in 1886. It did not appear first in *St. Nicholas*, nor did any other of LMA's subsequent works.

To the Woman's Journal

Concord, Mass., May 8, 1884.

Editors Woman's Journal:

There is very little to report about the woman's vote at Concord Town Meeting, as only eight were there in time to do the one thing permitted them.

With the want of forethought and promptness which shows how much our sex have yet to learn in the way of business habits, some dozen delayed coming till the vote for school committee was over. It came third on the warrant, and a little care in discovering this fact would have spared us much disappointment. It probably made no difference in the choice of officers, as there is seldom any trouble about the matter, but it is to be regretted that the women do not give more attention to the duty which they really care for, yet fail, as yet, to realize the importance of, small as it is at present.

Their delay shows, however, that home affairs are *not* neglected, for the good ladies remained doubtless to give the men a comfortable dinner and set their houses in order before going to vote.

Next time I hope they will leave the dishes till they get home, as they do when in a hurry to go to the sewing-society, Bible-class, or picnic. A hasty meal once a year will not harm the digestion of the lords of creation, and the women need all the drill they can get in the new duties that are surely coming to widen their sphere, sharpen their wits, and strengthen their wills, teaching them the courage, intelligence and independence all should have, and many sorely need in a world of vicissitudes. A meeting should be called before the day for action comes, to talk over matters, to get posted as to time, qualifications of persons, and the good of the schools; then the women can act together, know what they are doing, and keep up the proper interest all should feel in so important a matter.

"I come, but I'm lukewarm," said one lady, and that is the spirit of too many.

"We ought to have had a meeting, but you were not here to call it, so no one did," said another, as if it were not a very simple thing to open any parlor and ask the twenty-eight women voters to come and talk an hour.

It was a good lesson, and we hope there will be energy and foresight enough in Concord to register more names, have a quiet little caucus, and send a goodly number of earnest, wide-awake ladies to town-meeting next year.

LOUISA M. ALCOTT.

Concord, May 8, *1884.*

MS: Unlocated. Printed: *Woman's Journal* 15 (17 May 1884): 157; *LAFL,* pp. 447–448.

To Mary Mapes Dodge

June 6th [1884?]

Dear Mrs Dodge.

I have sent the last story to Niles on Monday, & am glad to be done spinning.[1] Wish they were better & brighter, but the old cheeriness is gone, & one cant bring it back however hard one tries.

Now I am off to the rest & coolness of my little cottage by the sea with my baby over "toopin torf."

Thanks for the hint about doves. The story[2] was told me in Brittany & I used it as given, only making the actors boy & girl. I know that doves were used in that way during the French Revolution, & have often read of their doing that sort of work. I said in the tale a *"little file"*, & any stout dove could carry that. They make files of watch-springs strong enough to cut an iron bar, so we will play that was the kind.

I have tried every sort of pen & holder, gold, quill, cork, rubber, glass &c.

The mischief was done using an agate pen & writing on impression paper three copies of "Work" at once.[3] Overstrained some muscle or nerve, & the action of writing, no matter with what, sets the aforesaid nerves to aching. Electricity is helping me I think, & a summer of rest will, I hope, put the old machine in some order for the winter.

yrs ever

L. M. A.

ALS: Wilkinson Collection of Mary Mapes Dodge, Princeton University Library.
 1. Roberts Brothers published *Spinning-Wheel Stories* in November 1884.
 2. "The Banner of Beaumanoir."
 3. In her journal for December 1872, LMA wrote: "Busy with 'Work.' Write three pages at once on impression paper, as Beecher, Roberts, and Low of London all want copy at once." At a later date, LMA added this entry: "This was the cause of the paralysis of my thumb, which disabled me for the rest of my life" (both from Cheney, p. 268).

To Richard Watson Gilder

Aug. 15th [1884]

My Dear Mr Gilder.[1]

In reply to your note I can only say that I very gladly join in congratulating Dr. Holmes on reaching his seventy fifth birthday.

Few can look back on so many useful, cheerful years as he who has made so many hearts merry with the wit & wisdom that lingers in the memory when the laughter is over.

May the smiles he has brought to the faces of his friends always shine upon him, & the warmth of his own genial nature keep the frost of age from chilling the springs of mirth that bubble up so freshly in the heart of our dear & honored Autocrat.

My father would join with me in all good wishes were not mind & memory too feeble to understand the occasion & fitly respond to your letter.

Yrs truly

L. M. ALCOTT.

ALS: Pierpont Morgan Library.
　　1. Richard Watson Gilder, poet and editor of the *Century Magazine*.

To Horace P. Chandler

Dear Mr Chandler.

Thanks for your kindness about the poems.

The eldest of my boys called to see you to day but did not find you.[1]

As he is a modest as well as a clever youth I can perhaps tell you about him better than he can. He is twenty one; was for nearly a year at the Corner book store,[2] salary as a beginner $20 a month with fine prospects which came to nothing.

He has considerable knowledge of short hand, & with a month more of practice will be able to report.

He has literary aspirations & hopes to be on the Advertiser staff if Mr. Bacon[3] (who has seen him) can find an opening for him.

He is steady, intelligent & fond of work. Expects to paddle his own canoe & waits for a launch.

If you can give him a friendly shove in any way his anxious Mamma & Aunt will be grateful.

The words of the immortal Sairy[4] are, "Sech are the consequences of livin in a wale", "a Pilgrin Projis of a wale"[5] she also calls it. I fear you dont know your Dickens as you ought. I am sure I write as well as Sumner & Choate,[6] & printers have no trouble in reading my remarks. What more can be desired?

Love to little Peleg & his proud Mamma.[7]

Yrs truly

L. M. A.

Oct 16th [1884]

Mr E. O. S.[8] may come here for the present, please.

ALS: Parkman Dexter Howe Library, University of Florida.
　　1. LMA's nephew Frederick Alcott Pratt.
　　2. The Old Corner Bookstore, one of the oldest and most famous in Boston.
　　3. Edwin Munroe Bacon had moved from the *Boston Globe* to the *Boston Advertiser*.

4. Sairey Gamp in Dickens's *Martin Chuzzlewit*.

5. These quotes are carefully printed in block letters.

6. Rufus Choate, Massachusetts lawyer and politician.

7. Peleg Whitman Chandler, sixth child of Horace P. Chandler and Grace Webster Chandler, was born on 22 September 1884.

8. *Every Other Saturday*, of which Chandler was editor.

To Mary E. Edie

[11 January 1885]

Miss Alcott does not usually answer any letters from strangers because she has a lame hand & it is impossible for one busy woman to answer the questions of many curious people.

Having a leisure moment she sends the following replies to the inquiries of Mary Edie.

1. My father only is living.

2. *Laurie* was a real boy.

3. Daisy & Demi were both boys & are both alive, one 20 the other 22.

4. Most of the people & things in Little Women are true.

5. I do not sell my pictures.

6. *Amy's* real daughter *Lulu* is not like me. Amy is dead.

7. Amy or May was in Europe three times, an artist, she married a Swiss gentleman & died in Paris five years ago.

8. We do not live in the old house. It is sold. We live in Boston.

9. Meg is alive & Jo, & Teddy[1] who lives in Paris.

L. M. ALCOTT.

ALS: Henry W. and Albert A. Berg Collection, New York Public Library, Astor, Lenox, and Tilden Foundations. The date is taken from the postmark.

1. In *Little Women*, Laurie's real name was Theodore, and Jo often called him Teddy; this reference is to Ladislas Wisniewski.

To Maggie Lukens

Feb. 16th [1885]

My Dear Maggie.

Many thanks for the pretty Valentine. It lies in my book & reminds me of my girl as I read. George Eliot's Life & Letters is wonderfully interesting, & comes in the cheap form so all can enjoy it.[1]

285

What book do you want to see? Let me know & have the pleasure of sending it.[2] What of Emerson have you besides the Essays?

I am glad any advice I have given has been useful or comfortable to you, & I wish I were really "good." I began to try very young & still keep on even more earnestly at fifty than at fifteen, tho I often feel as if I didn't get on at all. But the desire & effort are something, & in the end help us up the long way towards our ideal.

I have not been very ill, only my tired head gave out & I am resting. Thanks for your kind offer. I should love to see you, & hope we may meet sometime.

I shall try to get the book you speak of, for I often have letters from girls, asking me about these classes & what they read or study.

Miss Kill kellys Five Hundred Questions[3] must be very helpful & good, & this method of study is a grand plan for many hungry minds.

I read John Inglesant but dont remember it.[4]

I have been trying the Mind Cure, & find it very wonderful. It is the power of the mind over matter, soul over body, & those who learn it can not only heal themselves but others, & live above the small pains & worries that vex so many of us. Mrs Anna Newman is my teacher, & I enjoy it very much, it is so simple & yet so deep.[5]

We all believe it for it is only the old faith in God & our highest self, but the application of it to pain & care is new. Many wonderful cures I *know* of, & though I cant quite see how it is done done yet, I cannot doubt it since I see the miracles wrought & feel the power myself.

Drs laugh & people call it "humbug" as they do at every new idea, but I am sure a great truth is in it, & am studying it out.

I am in Boston this winter settling my nephews in business, & being very lazy myself.

Glad you enjoy the new house. Let me hear from you whenever the spirit moves, & tell me how to help if I can. That is the sweetest service we can do one another, & it always cheers me up to know I have done even a little for one of my many dear girls.

Love to the sisters.

yrs ever
L. M. A.

I send you a little bunch of forget me nots that wont fade.[6] Wear them for my sake.

ALS: Boston Public Library. Printed: Bok, 2.

1. "George Eliot's new life and letters is well done," LMA wrote Niles, "and we are not sorry we have read them. Mr. Cross has been a wise man, and leaves us all our love and respect

instead of spoiling them as Froude did for Carlyle" ([February? 1885], Cheney, p. 364). LMA is referring to J. W. Cross's edition of *George Eliot's Life as Related in Her Letters and Journals* (1885) and James Anthony Froude's *Thomas Carlyle: A History of the First Forty Years of His Life* (1882) and *Thomas Carlyle: A History of His Life in London* (1884).

2. According to Bok's commentary on the letter, LMA sent Emerson's first series of *Essays* (1841), hoping "it would be as helpful to you as it has been to me." LMA marked those essays she "like[d] best": "Compensation," "Love," "Friendship," "Heroism," and "Self-Reliance." A "little later," she sent the second series of *Essays* (1844), marking with her father's name the passage in "Manners" that begins with a description of "an *individual*, whose manners, though never wholly within the conventions of elegant society, were never learned there, but were original and commanding" (p. 6).

3. The printed text has "Miss Killikelly's Curious Questions."

4. Joseph Henry Shorthouse's novel, *John Inglesant* (1881).

5. The practitioners of the mind cure believed that, since the spirit was superior to the body, cleansing one's mental state would result in a corresponding improvement in one's physical state. LMA's unsuccessful visits to Mrs. Anna B. Newman at 17 Boylston Place in Boston are reported in her "Miss Alcott on Mind-Cure" in the 18 April 1885 *Woman's Journal*.

6. Written on the back of the envelope with this letter is a note by Maggie Lukens Pratt dated 1935: "In one of Louisa M. Alcott's letters to Maggie Lukens she speaks of sending a bunch of 'Forget-me-nots' that 'would not fade.' This little book is what she alluded to. . . . It lived in Pittsburgh quite a while & shows it." The miniature book, *Havergal Forget-Me-Nots from the Writings of Francis Ridley Havergal* (1884), is still with the letter.

To Maggie Lukens

Mar. 15th [1885]

Dear Maggie.

I have had a nice turn of rheumatism in my right arm & hand, so could not use a pen.[1] Now I can scribble a bit & will see about my girl's books. I think the "Conduct of Life"[2] would be good, & you shall [have] my copy. Also the poems, & any other good bits I can find.

I send you a little paper about the Mind Cure, which explains the thing as much as words can.

It is very interesting & I have had some high moments, but they dont last long, & though my mind is cheered up my body does not get over its ails as I hoped.

Mrs Newman says it takes time & long training to get the art of rising above your body & compelling it to be what it ought.

I have my doubts still about the truth of *all* the good enthusiasts say, but they certainly do perform wonderful cures & I know *they* are true as I see the people.

The patient sits quietly with shut eyes, & the Dr the same, for 15 minutes in silence. Some feel nothing & others a good deal.

I feel very still, then very light, & seem floating away on a sea of rest.

Once or twice I seemed to have no body, & to come back from another world. I felt as if I trod on air & was very happy & young for some hours. Yet one does not sleep nor lose consciousness, & there is nothing unpleasant about it. It is not mesmerism.

The power to go into this state of rest is what we want, & many get it. "It is," they say, "simply turning to the Source of all rest & strength &, sitting passive, let it flow into one & heal & cheer body & soul."

A very sweet doctrine if one can only *do it.* I cant yet, but try it out of interest in the new application of the old truth & religion which we all believe, that soul is greater than body, & being so should rule.

This will give you something to think of & as delicate, gentle people often grasp these things more quickly than the positive ones, you may get ahead of me in the new science. Just believe that you will be better & you will, they say. Try it.

Yrs ever
L. M. A.

I'll send the books soon.[3] Must run home to C. & get them. Love to the sisters.

ALS: Boston Public Library. Printed: Bok, 6, where it is incorrectly dated 1884. The year is taken from the postmark.
    1. Concerning her health, LMA wrote Laura Hosmer on the following day: "Mrs N. has gone to Baltimore for a week or two & left me in the care of Miss Adams, the wonderful-care girl. I told N. I didn't seem to get on, for my arm ached again & my head was dizzy & I didn't want another earthquake. She tried to help me, but I still am very lurchy when I walk & dizzy when I stoop. Back of head aches, worse in morning & lying down & a general worried state of body, tho I go on as before, walk, rest, eat carefully & am as lazy as a pig" ([16 March 1885], Louisa May Alcott Collection, Barrett Library, University of Virginia Library).
    2. Emerson's *The Conduct of Life* (1860).
    3. LMA sent both series of Emerson's *Essays* (see 16 February [1885]).

To Ednah Dow Cheney

Mar. 31st [1885?]

Dear Mrs Cheney.

Father desires to thank you "a great deal for the fine book."[1] It pleased him much to be remembered, & with a little help now & then we went back to the early days of the Plato Class when "Ednah Littlehale was my best pupil." "She is always wise & good. Tell her to come & see me. I can walk now, she will like to know it. My words go but *she* knows how to talk, & we always have good times. I want to see her."

These remarks were made earnestly & with a beaming face as he showed me, "my new book," like a happy child.

So you see the long day was cheered by the pleasant memories your gift brought him.

His heart is still as tender & true as ever though the wise old head forgets its high thoughts & the words that clothed them so beautifully.

He is very well otherwise & has great plans for the summer & the School. We shall hope to see you then if not sooner.

Affectionately yrs
L. M. ALCOTT.

ALS: Sophia Smith Collection, Smith College.

    1. Possibly a reference to Cheney's edition of *Selected Poems from Michelangelo Buonarroti* (1885).

To Esther Foord

[early April 1885]

My Dear Miss Ford.[1]

I am forbidden to write, having suffered much from writer's cramp & vertigo this winter, but I will certainly try to pay my grateful tribute of respect to your sister as soon as possible.[2]

I have hoped to come & see her, but in these busy lives of ours many pleasures get pushed aside by the duties that cannot wait. I am very sorry now that it is too late to say good bye if no more.

Father is well for one in his state, but the right arm is useless & he but dimly remembers much of the past. I shall recall Sophia Foord's name to him when I go home & see if he remembers her.

I do, most pleasantly in the old Concord days when she kept school for the Emersons & us. Also during my Dedham experience years later.[3]

I am sorry she was long ill, & glad that eternal health & youth are hers again. I have been much of an invalid since my nursing attempt in war times, so I can sympathize with all who suffer.

My sister Anna desires to be remembered to you, & I am with much sympathy

affectionately yours
L. M. ALCOTT.

31 Chestnut St.

ALS: Louisa May Alcott Collection, Barrett Library, University of Virginia Library.

1. Esther Foord was living with her sister Sophia in Dedham when the latter died on 1 April.

2. "In Memoriam Sophia Foord," discussing LMA's teacher in Concord in the 1840s, appeared in the 11 April 1885 *Woman's Journal.*

3. LMA is referring to her brief stint as a domestic in 1850, a tale she told as "How I Went Out to Service" in the 4 June 1874 *Independent.*

To Thomas Niles

Nonquit, July 13, 1885.

Dear Mr. Niles, — I want to know if it is too late to do it and if it is worth doing; namely, to collect some of the little tales I tell Lulu and put them with the two I shall have printed the last year and the "Mermaid Tale"[1] to match the pictures we bought, and call it "Lulu's Library"? I have several tiny books written down for L.; and as I can do no great work, it occurred to me that I might venture to copy these if it would do for a Christmas book for the younger set.

I ache to fall on some of the ideas that are simmering in my head, but dare not, as my one attempt since the last "Jo's Boys" break-down cost me a week or two of woe and $30 for the doctor. I have lovely long days here, and can copy these and see 'em along if you want them. One has gone to "Harper's Young People,"[2] and one is for "St. Nicholas" when it is done, — about the Kindergarten for the blind.[3] These with Lulu's would make a little book, and might begin a series for small folks.[4] Old ladies come to this twaddle when they can do nothing else. What say you? . . .

Yours truly,

L. M. A.

MS: Unlocated. Printed: Cheney, pp. 360–361; *LASC,* p. 377.

1. The "Mermaid Tale" may be a reference to "Josie Plays Mermaid," which appeared as the eighth chapter of *Jo's Boys.*

2. "Baa! Baa!" appeared in the 15 September and 22 September 1885 issues of *Harper's Young People* and was reprinted in the first volume of *Lulu's Library* (Boston: Roberts Brothers, 1886).

3. "The Blind Lark" appeared in the November 1886 *St. Nicholas* and was reprinted in the third volume of *Lulu's Library.*

4. In September 1885, Alcott wrote in her journal: " 'Lulu's Library' as a 'pot-boiler' will appease the children, and I may be able to work on 'Jo's Boys' " (Cheney, p. 357).

To Lucy Stone

Aug. 31 [1885]

My Dear Mrs Stone.

I should think it was hardly necessary for me to write or to say that it is impossible for me ever to "go back" on Womans Suffrage. I earnestly desire to go forward on that line as far & as fast as the prejudices, selfishness & blindness of the world will let us, & it is a great cross to me that ill health & home duties prevent my devoting heart, pen & time to this most vital question of the age.

After a fifty years acquaintance with the noble men & women of the Anti slavery cause, & the sight of the glorious end to their faithful work, I should be a traitor to all I most love, honor & desire to imitate, if I did not covet a place among those who are giving their lives to the emancipation of the white slaves of America.

If I can do no more let my name stand among those who are willing to bear ridicule & reproach for the truth's sake, & so earn some right to rejoice when the victory is won.

Most *heartily* yours for *Woman's Suffrage* & all other reforms,

LOUISA MAY ALCOTT.

Concord Mass.

ALS: Schlesinger Library, Radcliffe College. This appears to be the printer's copy of the manuscript. Printed: *History of Woman Suffrage*, ed. Elizabeth Cady Stanton et al., 6 vols. (New York and Rochester: Fowler & Wells — S. B. Anthony, 1881–1922), 4:412; *LAFL*, p. 449. There are minor differences between the manuscript and the *History of Woman Suffrage* text.

To Mrs. Jannette E. Sweet

[11 September 1885]

Mrs Sweet,[1]
My Dear Madame.

In reply to your touching letter I am happy to say that I think the outline of a story sent me may be filled up & make an interesting tale for some magazine or paper.[2]

If I may suggest this is what I should do with it.

Rewrite it in the form of a child's story, & let their impressions, words & adventures be the main thread. Give them names, & let them talk as yours did. There is enough in the facts to make a thrilling tale told briefly & dramatically as I am sure you are able to do it. Imagine you are telling it to children & the right words will come, for your language is both picturesque & elegant.

I should open with the father going away, & his good bye, with a hint that it was his last. A few anxious words of the mother's, & happy little plans of the children, with some incident to introduce the Indians & tell a little about their dangerous state just then, in a few words. Then the attack, & the journey & escape, ending with the return to the Fort to find the father dead. A fine bit might be made of the hiding in the reeds, & the brave children, & the sick one, & the mother's hope & heroism. So too the canoe scene, where she goes down the river with her baby on her lap in the leaky boat.

When you have done it send it to me, & I will add a word of introduction & try to dispose of it.[3] Just now the death of "H. H." (Mrs H. Jackson[4] the writer,) gives a special interest to all Indian tales, so it is a good time for yours. We will see.

Thank you for honoring me with your confidence. For what is success given me after years of hard work if I cannot feel tenderly for others in need, & gladly help all I can. There is no more beautiful tribute to my books than the appeals that come to me from strangers who call me "friend." I wish you were nearer me. Write & tell me about the son. How old — does he like books, &c. I am 52, & an invalid but still able to do something thank God.

Hold fast, dear woman, to your faith, else all is lost. God does not forget us, & in time we see *why* the trials come. May He bless your loving effort & let me aid in its success.

yr friend
L. M. ALCOTT.

ALS: Special Collections, Harold B. Lee Library, Brigham Young University. Printed: *LASC*, pp. 355–356. Addressed to Mrs. Sweet at "Marysville, Montana, Lewis & Clarke Co."; the date is taken from the postmark.

1. Jannette De Camp and Joseph Warren De Camp were caught in a massacre in Minnesota in 1862, and she was held captive by the Sioux Indians. In 1866 she married the Reverend J. Sweet.

2. At this period LMA was deeply interested in the American Indians. Her Indian story, "Onawandah," appeared in *St. Nicholas* of April 1884; on 18 September 1885 she wrote to Thomas Niles of Helen Hunt Jackson's *Ramona* as "a noble record of the great wrongs of her chosen people. . . . It recalls the old slavery days, only these victims are red instead of black"

(Cheney, p. 364; she was working on *Jo's Boys*, which included Dan's death while defending "his chosen people," the Indians).

3. "Mrs. J. E. De Camp Sweet's Narrative of Her Captivity in the Sioux Outbreak of 1862" was not published until 1894, when it appeared in the *Minnesota Historical Society Collections*.

4. Helen Hunt Jackson, known for her novel in defense of the Indians, *Ramona* (1884), had died on 12 August 1885.

To Laura Hosmer

Sunday
[8–9 November 1885]

Dear Laura,

I have been hoping to see or hear from you, & began to think you were sick, but in a note from Mrs Vialle[1] she speaks of your being nicely so I feel better about that.

I have been in bed for ten days, ordered there by Conrad,[2] for whom I sent, feeling so poorly I couldn't keep up any longer or go to him. He said it was Bronchial Catarrh & had got deeply seated so it affected stomach & all. I went to him for the dyspepsia but he didn't seem to think it of much consequence & talked about my cough & hoarseness tho at first he said nothing about bronchitis till I gave up & asked "Whats the matter?"

So I kept in bed & coughed & wheezed, & tried to eat, & after ten days got up feeling as if I'd been ill a month. The dyspepsia is better thanks to the toning up of lager beer. I cough less, but have no strength or appetite & sleep poorly, but by lying down a good deal man[a]ge to drag along.

Conrad was lovely, & used to sit & talk delightfully for half an hour. He gave me two of his articles, one on Mind Cure & the other the lecture he delivered to the Harvard medical students. It is fine, & I happened to say I was going to send you mine to read when he said, "I'll give you another & you send it to Dr Hosmer with my regards." So I do.

We wag along pretty well. Our swell cook tumbled down stairs & broke her hand so we have another. Kate & Hatty *must* see their beaux once a week so our dining room is a courting bower & the smell of tobacco is strong in the land.

Anna gets tired running her big family but does it nicely & we fare well. The boys enjoy life heartily, & Lulu is big & bouncing & jolly at her school. She was six yesterday,[3] & is revelling in her sixteen presents. One being a live mouse in a revolving trap.

Pa is rather feeble, but likes his new quarters & old friends, & we *dont* see much of F. B. S[anborn]. for which Oh be joyful!

Now do come & see a body, or drop a line. If its very fine this week I may run up for a day, but its dubersome, I have no pluck now.

Love to F. & the H. Hs. [4] Yrs ever

L. M. A.

Any news besides the deaths of Dowds?[5] Who is married, born, engaged or divorced? Is C[oncord]. as dull as usual?

ALS: Louisa May Alcott Collection, Barrett Library, University of Virginia Library.

1. Mrs. Lucy Rebecca Vialle is listed in the Concord manuscript town records as a housekeeper (Concord Free Public Library).

2. Conrad Wesselhoeft, her physician.

3. Lulu was born on 8 November 1879.

4. Possibly Alfred W. Hosmer, known as Fred, and Laura Hosmer's husband and son, both named Henry Joseph Hosmer.

5. Franklin and Mary Dowd of Concord died on 23 October and 4 November 1885, respectively.

To Amos Bronson Alcott

TO MY FATHER

On His 86th Birthday.

Dear pilgrim, waiting patiently,
    The long, long journey nearly done,
Beside the sacred stream that flows
    Clear shining in the western sun;
Look backward on the varied road
    Your steadfast feet have trod,
From youth to age, through weal and woe,
    Climbing forever nearer God.

Mountain and valley lie behind;
    The slough is crossed, the wicket passed;
Doubt and despair, sorrow and sin,
    Giant and fiend, conquered at last;
Neglect is changed to honor now;
    The heavy cross may be laid down;

The white head wins and wears at length
  The prophet's, not the martyr's crown.

Greatheart and Faithful gone before,
  Brave Christians, Mercy sweet,
Are Shining Ones who stand and wait
  The weary wanderer to greet.
Patience and Love his handmaids are,
  And till time brings release,
Christian may rest in that bright room
  Whose windows open to the east.

The staff set by, the sandals off,
  Still pondering the precious scroll,
Serene and strong, he waits the call
  That frees and wings a happy soul.
Then, beautiful as when it lured
  The boy's aspiring eyes,
Before the pilgrim's longing sight
  Shall the Celestial City rise.

                              L. M. A.

Nov. 29, 1885

MS: Unlocated. Printed: *Woman's Journal* 16 (12 December 1885): 393; Cheney, p. 387; Louisa May Alcott, *Transfiguration. In Memoriam* (N.p.: n.p., 1890?); *LMA*, p. 317.

To Viola Price

                              Boston, Dec. 18th, 1885.
Miss V. V. Price.[1]
Dear Madam,

My replies to your questions are as follows: I write in the morning. Any paper or pen suits me. Quiet is all I require. I work till tired, then rest. Winter is the best time. I enjoy solitude very much. I often have a dozen plots in my head at once and keep them for years. I do not make notes of ideas, etc.

I do not enjoy society, and shirk its duties as much as possible.

I read anything that attracts me. Never study. Have no special method of writing except to use the simplest language, take every day life and make it interesting and try to have my characters alive.

I take many heroes and heroines from real life — much truer than any one can imagine.

My favorite authors are Shakespeare, Dante, . . . Emerson, Carlyle, Thoreau . . . Geo. Eliot and C. Bronte . . . I read no modern fiction. It seems poor stuff when one can have the best of the old writers.

St. Nicholas and Harper are my favorite magazines. I dislike to receive strangers who come out of mere curiosity, as some hundreds do, forgetting that an author has any right to privacy. Autograph letters I do not answer, nor half the requests for money and advice upon every subject from "Who shall I marry" to "Ought I to wear a bustle?" Mss. I have no time to read and "gush" is very distasteful to me.

If you can teach your five hundred pupils to love books but to let authors rest in peace, you will give them a useful lesson and earn the gratitude of the long suffering craft, whose lives are made a burden to them by the modern lion hunter and autograph fiend.

Please give my regards to the young people and thank them for their interest in the little books.

Yrs. truly,
L. M. ALCOTT

P.S. I am an invalid from too much head work, and my right hand is partially paralyzed with writer's cramp, so my writing is, as you see, not a copy for your young people to imitate.

MS: Unlocated. Printed: *Overland Monthly* 91 (August 1933): 106.
    1. Viola Price Franklin, described in the article as a "teacher, writer, librarian and literary critic." The letter is said to be "reprinted exactly as it was written to Mrs. Franklin."

To Maggie Lukens

Feb. 21st [1886]

Dear Maggie.

The book has come & I have read it with much interest, & showed it to my literary nephew. We both think it excellent, & I am glad to have it to refresh my own memory of what I do know as well as to teach me many facts that I do not know.

I am glad you have discovered how much that is lovely as well as useful that word house keeper means. The mere providing of beds, meals &c. is a very small part of the work. The home-making, the comfort, the sympathy, the grace, & atmosphere that a true woman can provide is the noble part, & embraces all that's helpful for soul as well as body.

I wish our girls would see this, & set about being the true house-keepers. Mrs. Ripley[1] used to rock her baby's cradle, shell peas, or sew, & fit a class of young men for college at the same time. One can discuss Greek poetry & chop meat as I saw her doing once with Mr Emerson & Margaret Fuller[2] & the one task ennobled the other because it was duty.

I have been plagued with bronchitis this winter but am better now. Lulu is well & merry. I have no good picture, hope to have some taken soon & will send you one.

With love to the sisters

I am as ever
affectionately yrs
L. M. A.

ALS: Boston Public Library. Printed: Bok, 6 (and partial facsimile).
    1. Sarah Alden Bradford Ripley of Concord, known for both her intellect and happy married life, prepared many young scholars for their entrance to Harvard College.
    2. Margaret Fuller, transcendentalist author best known for her feminist work *Woman in the Nineteenth Century* (1845).

To Mary Mapes Dodge

April 13th [1886]

Dear Mrs. Dodge.

I am glad you are going to have such a fine outing; may it be a very happy one.

I cannot promise anything, but hope to be allowed to write a little, as my doctor has decided that it is as well to let me put on paper the tales "knocking at the sauce pan lid & demanding to be taken out," (like "Mrs Cratchet's" potatoes[1]), as to have them go on worrying me inside. So I'm scribbling at "Jo's Boys" long promised to Mr Niles & clamored for by the children. I may write but one hour a day so cannot get on very fast, but if it is ever done I can think of a serial for St N.

I began one & can easily start it for 88 if head & hand allow.

I will simmer on it this summer & see if it can be done. Hope so, for I dont want to give up work so soon.

I have read "Mrs Null,"[2] but dont like it very well. Too slow & colorless after Tolstoi's "Anna Karanina."[3] I met Mr & Mrs S. at Mrs Aldrich's this winter.[4] Mr Stockton's child's stories I like very much; the older ones are odd but artificial.

Now good by & God be with you, dear woman, & bring you safely home to us all.

Affectionately yrs

L. M. ALCOTT:

ALS: Special Collections, Harold B. Lee Library, Brigham Young University. Printed: Cheney, p. 377, *LASC*, p. 374.

    1. The Cratchits of Dickens's *A Christmas Carol* (1843).

    2. Frank R. Stockton's *The Late Mrs. Null* (1886).

    3. Published in New York in 1886 (see Frank Luther Mott, *Golden Multitudes* [New York: Macmillan, 1947], p. 183).

    4. Stockton and his wife, Marian Edwards Tuttle Stockton; the poet and short-story writer Thomas Bailey Aldrich and his wife, Lilian Woodman Aldrich, then living in Boston.

To Thomas Niles

Sunday, [June?] 1886.

Dear Mr. Niles, — The goodly supply of books was most welcome; for when my two hours pen-work are over I need something to comfort me, and I long to go on and finish "Jo's Boys" by July 1st.

My doctor frowns on that hope,[1] and is so sure it will do mischief to get up the steam that I am afraid to try, and keep Prudence sitting on the valve lest the old engine run away and have another smash-up.

I send you by Fred[2] several chapters, I wish they were neater, as some were written long ago and have knocked about for years; but I can't spare time to copy, so hope the printers won't be in despair.

I planned twenty chapters and am on the fifteenth. Some are long, some short, and as we are pressed for time we had better not try to do too much.

    . . . . I have little doubt it will be done early in July,[3] but things are so contrary with me I can never be sure of carrying out a plan, and I don't want to fail again; so far I feel as if I could, without harm, finish off these dreadful boys.

Why have any illustrations? The book is not a child's book, as the lads are nearly all over twenty, and pretty pictures are not needed. Have the bas-relief[4] if you like, or one good thing for frontispiece.

I can have twenty-one chapters and make it the size of "Little Men."

Sixteen chapters make two hundred and sixteen pages, and I may add a page here and there later, — or if need be, a chapter somewhere to fill up.

I shall be at home in a week or two, much better for the rest and fine air; and during my quiet days in C[oncord]. I can touch up proofs and confer about the book. Sha'n't we be glad when it is done?

Yours truly,
L. M. A.

MS: Unlocated. Printed: Cheney, pp. 372–373; *LASC*, p. 379.
1. LMA wrote this letter in response to Niles's of 19 June inquiring about her health (Houghton Library, Harvard University).
2. Frederick Alcott Pratt, Louisa's nephew, worked for Roberts Brothers.
3. *Jo's Boys* was completed in July 1886 (Cheney, p. 359) and published that October by Roberts Brothers.
4. See [Fall] 1886.

To Thomas Niles

[Fall] 1886.

Dear Mr. Niles, — Sorry you don't like the bas-relief; I do.[1] A portrait, if bright and comely, would n't be me, and if like me would disappoint the children; so we had better let them imagine "Aunt Jo young and beautiful, with her hair in two tails down her back," as the little girl said.

In haste, L. M. A.

MS: Unlocated. Printed: Cheney, p. 376.
1. On 26 December [1885], LMA wrote Florence Phillips about Walton Ricketson's work: "The bas-relief is done, & people like it. Mr R. prefers softness to strength so has missed what I like best, but the old lady looks young & amiable, & as she was some ten or fifteen years ago" (Houghton Library, Harvard University). Ricketson's bas-relief appeared as the frontispiece for *Jo's Boys*.

To Thomas Niles

[September? 1886]

Dear Mr. Niles.

We dont seem to admire either of the pictures.[1] Father's does not look like the original, & mine was always spoiled by the glare, & the hunched up attitude.

Notman[2] wants me to sit again & I will try to get something better.

The fine tone of my picture is very effective, & if the old lady only looked her best it would make a good frontispiece for Alcott's Works.

Some one suggests for Jo's Boys my head among a group of my real boys. I have several of them, handsome Billy Greene & Simmons & Laddie.[3] Could it be done & is it worth the trouble? Fred & John could go in. There is a way of doing it entirely with photographs you know.

I'll ask Notman about it.

yrs truly

L. M. A.

ALS: Louisa May Alcott Collection, Barrett Library, University of Virginia Library. Printed: Carroll A. Wilson, *Thirteen Author Collections of the Nineteenth Century*, eds. Jean C. S. Wilson and David A. Randall, 2 vols. (New York: Scribners, 1950), 1:14 (partial).

    1. LMA was always concerned about how she looked in photographs, as this letter of 17 August [1886?] to Mary Mapes Dodge shows: "If the deed must be done, why then we will try to get the best of the bad pictures. Allen of Temple Place took some just before I last went abroad which were cheerful if nothing more. Warren 465 Washington St Boston did the last. I send a sample of the pensive invalid. In Hearth & Home is a wood cut of the Allen photograph & the only sketch of L. M. A. that is at all worth while. Sanborn did it" (Barrett Library, University of Virginia Library).

    2. James Notman, son of the famous Canadian photographer William Notman, had a studio in Boston; for a portrait of LMA "after" the Notman photograph, see Emma Lazarus, "Louisa May Alcott," *Century Magazine* 42 (May 1891): 65.

    3. Willie Simmons; Laddie is Ladislas Wisniewski.

To Thomas Niles

Oct. 3rd [1886]

Dear Mr Niles.

The first gun fired seems to object to "Jo's Last Scrape" after much twaddle about Thackary &c.[1]

Now you remembe[r] I asked you if it should go in, & you said, "By all means, its very good, & ends Jo, the parasite, off in a natural way."

That was one reason for letting it stand, as the success of L. W. comes from just that same use of real life & one's own experience. Another reason is that in no other way can the rising generation of young autograph fiends be reached so well & pleasantly, & by a little good natured ridicule be taught not to harass the authors whom they honor with thier regard.

If it is not good taste to put this part of Jo's life in print all the rest is a mistake also, for the best liked episodes are the real ones.

I had my doubts, as people are particular about these small matters, but the young folks are the only critics I care for, & if they like it I'm satisfied. So far they enjoy that bit much & find no fault.

If there is much fault found with this bit, you might, later, print my reasons, as I cannot appear. But I fancy there wont be any trouble made except by the old quiddles who expect perfection, & that I never even *try* to attain.

yrs truly

L. M. A.

ALS: Louisa May Alcott Collection, Barrett Library, University of Virginia Library. Printed: *LASC*, p. 380.

1. "Jo's Last Scrape," a chapter in *Jo's Boys*, concerns Jo's (and LMA's) disgust with autograph seekers and curious strangers. LMA's reference is to the review in the 2 October *Boston Daily Advertiser*. The reviewer compares LMA to Thackeray in not having "one single thread of the plot" holding the book together; this mirrors the complexities of life and is a better approach than that of those contemporary writers with a "craze for absolute crystallization of effect and the subordination of every detail to the artistic perfection of the whole." On the other hand, the review continues, "Jo's Last Scrape" is "too much personal gossip" and should have been "omitted" ("Books and Authors," p. 4).

To Louisa Caroline Greenwood Bond

Concord, Tuesday, [12 October] 1886.

Dear Auntie, — I want to find Auntie Gwinn,[1] and don't know whom to ask but you, as your big motherly heart yearns over all the poor babies, and can tell them where to go when the nest is bare. A poor little woman has just died,[2] leaving four children to a drunken father. Two hard-working aunts do all they can, and one will take the oldest girl. We want to put the two small girls and boy into a home till we can see what comes next. Lulu clothes one, and we may be able to put one with a cousin. But since the mother died last Wednesday they are very forlorn, and must be helped. If we were not so full I'd take one; but Lu is all we can manage now.

There is a home at Auburndale, but it is full; and I know of no other but good Auntie Gwinn's. What is her address, please? I shall be in town on Saturday, and can go and see her if I know where.

Don't let it be a bother; but one turns at once in such cases to the saints for direction, and the poor aunts don't know what to do; so this aunt comes to the auntie of all.

I had a pleasant chat with the Papa in the cars, and was very glad to hear that W. is better. My love to both and S.

Thanks for the news of portraits. I'll bear them in mind if G. H. calls. Lulu and Anna send love, and I am as always,

Your LOUISA ALCOTT.

MS: Unlocated. Printed: Cheney, pp. 376–377.
        1. Possibly Mrs. Richard F. Bond, secretary of the Church Home for Orphan and Destitute Children in Boston.
        2. The only "poor little woman" who died in Concord on a Wednesday in 1886 was Mary Ann Connor, age twenty-five, who died on 6 October. This letter dates from the following Tuesday.

To Florence Phillips

Oct. 20th [1886?]

Dear Florence. [1]

I was very glad to hear from you, & learn that all was going well. Keep on, my dear, do your best, & be sure the light will come & the reward though the time may seem long & hard.

Wish to *"believe"* & that will help. Everyone has to come to the faith in his own way, some early some late, some easily, some with much tribulation. Joy teaches this one, sorrow that, & some only catch a glimpse of the comfort near the end of life. But *it is there,* & to those who knock it shall surely be opened. Poverty & pain were my teachers, & sorrow lifted the last veil, so that when I cried for my mother, sick & alone, I found God very near.

It needs no logic, no preaching to make me *sure* of it. The instinct is there & following it as fast as one can brings the fact home at last in a way that cannot be doubted.

If I can help you let me know how, & be sure I shall most gladly do my best, for it is the highest honor to be asked to serve another soul in its groping after the great truth.

I am glad you like Mr Emerson. He was my best help, & even if we dont take in *all* the high, pure atmosphere does us good. Carlyle is stormy, but very genuine, & I used to like him best. Now R. W. E. is my minister & friend.

We are settled at No 10 Louisburg Sq. [2] & hope to be very cosy. All are well except myself & that is an old story. I'm no better than at N[onquitt]. & worry along as best I can. Health & rest will come some day; meantime I hold on to my motto "Hope & keep busy," & get my bits of happiness now & then.

May Chapman wrote for your address as she is [in] N.Y. & wants to see you. She is, or was at No. 166 West 53rd St. so if she does n't get my letter first you can find her, as she is to be there a week longer.

Now good bye, dear, God be with you & help you in all ways.

Yr friend   L. M. ALCOTT.

Lulu sends her love, she has not forgotten the "playing girl" who took such good care of her & strewed Auntie's way with flowers.

ALS: Fales Library, New York University.

    1. Twenty-two-year-old Florence Phillips, who worshiped LMA, met her at Nonquitt in the summer of 1885 (see George Arms, "The Poet as Theme Reader: William Vaughn Moody, a Student, and Louisa May Alcott," *Towards a New Literary History*, ed. Louis J. Budd et al. [Durham, N.C.: Duke University Press, 1980], pp. 140–153).
    2. LMA leased a house at 10 Louisburg Square, Boston, for two years, beginning in October 1885, for Anna, Fred, John, Lulu, and herself.

To Florence Phillips

Dec. 7th [1886]

Dear Florence

I am always glad to hear from you, & to find that you are "creeping on," though I dare say I should think you were learning to walk fast if I saw you.

Being mortal we cannot expect to fly, & must content ourselves with a long slow climb, glad if each year we are one step higher than the last.

Watch, wait, *try* & leave the end to time sure that all will be well if we are patient, trusting & cheerful. It is hard for youn[g] people to believe th[at] *everything* has to wait, & in their hurry they are apt to pull open the buds & so spoil them in stead of letting them bloom as God pleases.

Find some poor people to help, even one girl to cheer up, or a child to clothe, & it will do you good. I'm very poorly with my dyspepsia & I cheer myself up by looking after a very destitute family, & giving them the food I cant eat. Try it.

We are in Boston where we were last winter, & Lulu is blooming & good with an excellent governess.

It *is* a comfort to know that out of any of my own experiences & trials I have extracted help or pleasure for others. I suppose that was why they were sent me. Write when you feel like it. With much hope & all good wishes yr friend [signature cut off]

AL: Houghton Library, Harvard University. Printed: George Arms, "The Poet as Theme Reader: William Vaughn Moody, a Student, and Louisa May Alcott," *Towards a New Literary History*, ed. Louis J. Budd et al. (Durham, N.C.: Duke University Press, 1980), p. 152. The manuscript is torn; missing words or letters are supplied in brackets.

To Lulu Nieriker

Sunday [1886].

My Dearest Dada.

I send you a "tory" to amuse you *after* Miss Hubbard goes. You will see the joke with your sharp little eye, & I hope you will remember the *moral* in your wise little mind.

Pray be Lu Sing,[1] & dont let the "Conscience bird" have to peck at you, but send nice dreams & sing you to sleep every night after a *good* day.

Annah[2] will read the story & laugh over it with you, & help you to be a sweet gentle girl, so Ah Wee will find the best *s'prise* in all the world when she comes home.

We had a concert here the other night & the children sung. Six little girls sang "Send back my Bonny," & I wished *my* girl had been here to sing with them. A boy sang some funny songs, & another played on the violin. The ladies helped, & it was very pretty. Should you like to play on the violin like your papa?

Write & tell me how you like Lu Sing. I hope you wont catch any little birdies. You wouldn't like to have a giant do that to you, would you? Be kind to little creatures & big ones will be kind to you.

Two weeks & I shall have kisses & cuddlings & [undeciphered word]! How lovely! I long to grab my tall girl & feel her arms round me, & her rosy cheek on mine. Good by my darling. X X X X X X R. WEE.

ALS: Houghton Library, Harvard University.
  1. "Lu Sing" was published posthumously (see 11 November [1887]).
  2. Anna Pratt, Lulu's Ah Nah, as LMA was her Ah Wee or R. Wee.

To Thomas Niles

Monday, A.M.
[Spring? 1887?]

Dear Mr. Niles, — My doctor forbids me to begin a long book or anything that will need much thought this summer. So I must give up "Tragedy of To-day,"[1] as it will need a good deal of thinking to be what it ought.

I can give you a girls' book however, and I think that will be better than a novel. I have several stories done, and can easily do more and make a companion volume for "Spinning-Wheel Stories" at Christmas if you want it.

This, with the Lulu stories, will be better than the set of novels I am sure. . . . Wait till I can do a novel, and then get out the set in style, if Alcott is not forgotten by that time.

I was going to send Mrs. Dodge one of the tales for girls, and if there is time she might have more. But nearly all new ones would make a book go well in the holiday season. You can have those already done now if you want them. "Sophie's Secret" is one, "An Ivy Spray: or Cinderella's Slippers"[2] another, and "Mountain Laurel"[3] is partly done. "A Garland for Girls"[4] might do for a title perhaps, as they are all for girls.

Yours truly, L. M. A.

MS: Unlocated. Printed: Cheney, p. 365, where it is incorrectly dated '[1886]'; *LASC*, pp. 378–379. It is dated 1887 here because "An Ivy Spray" is described as "done," and it seems unlikely that publication of the story would have been held up for more than a year.

    1. LMA never finished "Tragedy of To-day."
    2. "An Ivy Spray" appeared in the October 1887 *St. Nicholas* and was reprinted as "An Ivy Spray and Ladies' Slippers" in *A Garland for Girls* (Boston: Roberts Brothers, 1888).
    3. *Mountain-Laurel and Maidenhair* (Boston: Little, Brown, 1903).
    4. *A Garland for Girls* was published in November 1887.

To Laura Hosmer

Sunday Mar. 6th [1887]

Dear Laura.

I am *so* glad to hear good news of you & yours. May peace continue & health soon come.

I dont wonder you are tired, I am amazed that you are not dead after such a winter. Now rest, & enjoy the baby & brood over the little Mamma.

Give her my love & embrace Brown Jr. for me.

I wag along, & suppose I'm slowly mending, though I am a skeleton after ten weeks of spoon-meat. 25 pds gone since Oct. But I gain strength on my gruel & broth & gems, & I chew meat, but don't dare to swallow it because it worries me so.

Conrad says "Eat a good plate of lobster salad, it wont hurt you." Is'nt he crazy; when a mouthful of tender chop upsets me for the day?

I go out twice a day if fair, sleep well, & sew, read, write & mull round a little. But am soon tired & lie down & Dr L[awrence]. reads to me.

The gas & pain in "tummy" are gone, bowels move naturally nearly every day, I'm very hungry, & if my head dont ache I'm in pretty good spirits. But my head does ache a good deal, or feels hot & heavy, & back of neck *wooden*. Dr W. helps it for a time, & the baths will, I hope get it right after a spell. Dr L. is all devotion & tends me like a baby. Several doctors have sent her patients whom they couldn't help, & she is doing well by them. Two dispensarys, & lots of babies so she gets on & is a very busy woman.

Spring is coming, aint you glad?[1] Please send me Mr Bullard's address.[2] I want the rooms for *July* also. Shall you go? Take F. & baby. Dr L. will go with me I hope.

Love to H. yrs ever L.

ALS: Louisa May Alcott Collection, Barrett Library, University of Virginia Library. The date is taken from the postmark.

1. LMA had looked forward all winter to visiting Princeton, Massachusetts: "The omens are good, & my morning verse in one of the little books was 'Lift up thine eyes to the *hills* whence help cometh'. That means Princeton, & off I goes next June D. V." (to Laura Hosmer, 30 November [1886], Barrett Library, University of Virginia Library).

2. Moses Henry Bullard ran a hotel in Princeton.

To Lulu Nieriker

[25 March 1887?]

Dear Lulu.

I was *so* sorry to miss my darling girl yesterday. I hurried to get in before 11 so I could have some kisses & a good look at "teachers rosebud". But she had gone, & I only found the bundle on my table. Did the kitties look all right & play a little?

I suppose tomorrow p.m. you will go off to the theatre as fine as any young lady. Take a fan, & if you get hot & tired go out & walk about between the acts. There is water & a W.C. in the ladies room to the left as you leave the parquette, tell Miss H.[1] Then you will be fresh & "comfy" for the rest. See if the funny, little, fat child runs off alone as she did before. Show Miss H. the white rats as they go over the bridge, I guess she will laugh as we did at the long rows marching to tumble in the water.

You must come & tell me all about it Sunday a.m. with Johnny, & about the *watch secret*. Dont let Fred know till he finds his 'sprises on his plate.[2]

Annah said Lulu was *very good*, & I was very glad. I hope to hear about a *very* good month. You are to give Fred the little pin you know.

Love to Miss H. & lots of kisses for my precious girl from her R. WEE.

ALS: Houghton Library, Harvard University. The date is taken from the postmark.
  1. Mrs. Hall helped Anna Pratt run the Boston house.
  2. Fred Pratt's birthday was on 28 March.

To Frank Carpenter

April 1st [1887]

Mr Carpenter.[1]
Dear Sir.

My methods of work are very simple & soon told. My head is my study, & there I keep the various plans of stories for years some times, letting them grow as they will till I am ready to put them on paper. Then it is quick work, as chapters go down word for word as they stand in my mind & need no alteration. I never copy, since I find by experience that the work I spend the least time upon is best liked by critics & readers.

Any paper, any pen, any place that is quiet suit me, & I used to write from morning till night without fatigue when "the steam was up." Now, however, I am paying the penalty of twenty years of over work, & can write but two hours a day, doing about twenty pages, sometimes more, though my right thumb is useless from writer's cramp.

While a story is under way I live in it, see the people, more plainly than the real ones, round me, hear them talk, & am much interested, surprized, or provoked at their actions, for I seem to have no power to rule them, & can simply record their experiences & performances.

Materials for the children's tales I find in the lives of the little people about me, for no one can invent anything so droll, pretty or pathetic as the sayings & doings of these small actors, poets & martyrs. In the older books the events are mostly from real life, the strongest the truest, & I yet hope to

307

write a few of the novels which have been simmering in my brain while necessity & unexpected success have confined me to juvenile literature.

I gave Mrs Moulton many facts for her article in "Famous Women", & there are many other sketches which will add more if they are wanted. The first edition of "Jo's Boys" was twenty thousand I believe, & over fifty thousand were soon gone.[2] Since January I know little about the sales. People usually ask, "How much have you made?" I am contented with a hundred thousand, & find my best success in the comfort my family enjoy; also a naughty satisfaction in proving that it was better *not* to "stick to teaching" as advised, but to write.

Respectfully yrs.

L. M. ALCOTT.

ALS: Houghton Library, Harvard University. Printed: Jessie Bonstelle and Marian De Forest, *Little Women Letters from the House of Alcott* (Boston: Little, Brown, 1914), pp. 157–160 (partial); *LMA*, pp. 329–330 (partial); *LASC*, p. 357 (partial).

1. Frank George Carpenter, journalist, traveler, and author, was Washington correspondent for the *Cleveland Leader* when this letter was written.

2. The first printing of *Jo's Boys* was 10,000 copies; 47,500 copies were printed by the end of 1886.

To Lulu Nieriker

[4 April 1887]

Dear Lulu.

I send this note to make you laugh over R. Wee's "trials" coming home yesterday, & maybe it will make up for the Foolish candy.

You know we passed lots of West End cars before I got one? Well, I rode nicely along till the man came for the fare, & I found I had only five cents, & not enough for my Warren St. car!

"Oh dear", says I, "how can I fix it?" We were near Lucy Sewall's so I went in & borrowed ten cents, & ran out to meet a car some way down, & felt to see if my money was all safe.

No! I had left my little purse on Lucy's table. So the car had to go by & I went back & got my purse. Then I waited long for a red one, & at last got in all right. "Now my troubles are over," said I, & rumbled along to Northampton St.

Waited long for the "dreen tar" & with my one little five cents held tight I got in. But oh, my goodness me! when I went to pay the man it fell in the straw & I couldn't find it. "No matter," said the man, when I told him I had no more. I was very "mortyfied" & people laughed at R. Wee's empty little purse.

As I went to take off my coat when *at last* I got safely home, down in the bottom of it was a nice quarter of a dollar which had slipped out of that bad "pot book". Wasn't that sad trials? I thought you & Annah would like to laugh over em & stupid Auntie.

The kits got out of the basket today & went tumbling all round & into messes, so the cook made a fence about the basket & the little "rassels" have to kick up thier heels at home now. The Mum tries to lug em out & lay them on the table, in the coal bin, & so on, but Mary wont let her, so she spats & kicks em instead.

I hope you got on nicely & did not fall in any puddles with your high skippings, Miss Grasshopper.

Tell Annah Lucy said there was a carriage at the depot at Melrose, & she hoped we should take the house. I shall come Wed if it is pleasant & buy some nice rugs for the dirty old parlors. Six little dogs are tumbling & playing in the snow opposite. If my blue girl was there I'd like it better.

Love to all & X X X kisses to Lulu from

R. WEE.

I'll try & get some of the funny Fool candy because you *cannot eat* it. Fool John & Fred & Julia[1] with it for me.

ALS: Houghton Library, Harvard University. The date is taken from the postmark.
  1. Julia helped Anna Pratt run the Boston house.

To Mary Mapes Dodge

May 4th [1887]

Dear Mrs Dodge.

The Ms. of the boy's hoax is very funny, & I have no objection to its publication. I enjoy the joke, was taken in by the forgery, & admire the cleverness of "brother Will", but hope he will "never do so any more" or he may come to a bad end. The illustration was delightful, & I trust the persistent goslings were not disappointed in the book when they read it.

About the stories for St N. I am not sure, for, though my first plan was to do several to send you for the coming year, I found Mr Niles so disappointed at my failure to give him another book that I offered the "Garland for Girls" instead, & he was content. It must be ready to issue in Oct. so if you want any of the stories they must appear before that time.[1] One is done & you can have the corrected proofs in a day or two if you want it. Others I shall finish as fast [as] my head will allow; but I cannot do much yet, so go slowly.

The idea is some eight or ten tales for girls, with flowery names as a sort of emblem of the moral or meaning of the stories. Books, travel, charity, home duties, & girlish trials of various sorts are to be illustrated, & make a companion volume for "Spinning Wheel Stories."

I wish there were time to send them all to St N. but you shall have as many as you want, & I will do such as are best for your purpose first. "May-flowers or Girl Charities" would make two parts & is nearly done. "Poppies & Wheat" is the travel tale, & "Pansies" about books.[2]

Which will you have? Or is it too late for any with you fare-handed people? I hope you are well. I am rather better, but a very slow coach still. yrs as ever L. M. A.

ALS: Wilkinson Collection of Mary Mapes Dodge, Princeton University Library.

1. Only two of LMA's stories appeared in *St. Nicholas* between the writing of this letter and the publication of *A Garland for Girls*: "An Ivy Spray" (October 1887) and "Pansies" (November 1887). Both stories were reprinted in *A Garland for Girls*.

2. "May Flowers" and "Poppies and Wheat" both had their first publication in *A Garland for Girls*.

To Thomas Niles

Saturday, A.M., May 7, 1887.

Dear Mr. Niles, — Yours just come. "A Whisper" is rather a lurid tale, but might do if I add a few lines to the preface of "Modern Mephistopheles," saying that this is put in to fill the volume, or to give a sample of Jo March's necessity stories, which many girls have asked for.[1] Would that do?

It seems to me that it would be better to wait till I can add a new novel, and then get out the set. Meantime let "Modern Mephistopheles" go alone, with my name, as a summer book before Irving comes.[2]

I hope to do "A Tragedy of To-day"[3] this summer, and it can come out in the fall or next spring, with "Modern Mephistopheles," "Work," and "Moods."

A spunky new one would make the old ones go. "Hospital Sketches" is not cared for now, and is filled up with other tales you know. . . .

Can that plan be carried out? I have begun my tragedy, and think it will be good; also a shorter thing called "Anna: An Episode," in which I do up Boston in a jolly way, with a nice little surprise at the end. It would do to fill up "Modern Mephistopheles," as it is not long, unless I want it to be.

I will come in next week and see what can be done.

Yours truly,

L. M. A.

MS: Unlocated. Printed: Cheney, pp. 379, 382; LASC, pp. 380–381.

1. "A Whisper in the Dark" was reprinted in A Modern Mephistopheles and A Whisper in the Dark (Boston: Roberts Brothers, 1889). LMA's attitude about her "necessity stories" is expressed in her preface to Proverb Stories (Boston: Roberts Brothers, 1882): "As many girls have asked to see what sort of tales Jo March wrote at the beginning of her career, I have added 'The Baron's Gloves,' as a sample of the romantic rubbish which paid so well once upon a time. If it shows them what not to write, it will not have been rescued from oblivion in vain."

2. Henry Irving played Mephistopheles in William Gorman Wills's version of Faust in New York between December 1886 and April 1887; he toured America with that play and others between November 1887 and March 1888.

3. Like the "Tragedy of To-day," "Anna: An Episode" was not published.

To Laura Hosmer

June 1st [1887]

Dear Laura.

Dr L. met Dr B. at the dinner last eve & heard that you were poorly, so I thought I'd drop a line, though I am in the dumps myself after a three weeks fall down owing to a cold & a "tire." Is n't it discouraging after two months of steady pick up to slump & be flat all upset again? It needs the patience of Job, the courage of Moses & the faith of all the saints to keep one from swear words & general despair of God & man. I'm going with Dr L. to see Dr Henion the magnetic man. A quack I dare say, but he cures people & the regulars dont, so for fun I'm going some day. Dont tell *any one* & I'll report.

So sorry to give up P[rinceton]. but I'm too weak now & Dr L. has babies on hand & cant go yet. So I gave up my rooms & shall stay here till I can sit up a few hours & stand on my legs. No strength left. C. W. comes to see me to day. No special disease *except* no stomach, & for want of that here we are. P. air would set me up if I could only get there & have my food as here. Do drop a line after you go. A good time & lots of health to you all.

Love to F. & H. & the boys.
Was Dan French wrecked? I hear so. [1]

yrs ever
L. M. A.

ALS: Louisa May Alcott Collection, Barrett Library, University of Virginia Library. The date is taken from the postmark.

1. The artist Daniel Chester French was safe studying in Paris at this time, but his stepmother and his cousin and family had been involved (though unharmed) in a ship collision while returning from the Continent in early May. French had written to his aunt in America about this on 9 May, and LMA may be referring to a garbled version of this account (information from the editors of the Daniel Chester French Papers).

To Lulu Nieriker

June 1st [1887]

Darling Lulu. [1]

As it is a rainy day & R. Wee is all alone she thought she would write a little letter to her dear girl & tell her some bits of news.

1st   Kitty hurt his leg & was quite ill for some days. We were afraid the bad old cat had bitten him, but he is well now & very thin. He does n't come to see me any more, but lies on the hearth & warms his toes, or bats his poor old Ma & grabs her tail.

2nd   The Ollins are all gone & the house is nice & still now, though I miss the dear little face that used to come peeping in, & when the children play I often look for a blue hat with long curls under it, & a lively pair of legs flying in the air.

3rd   The great big urn in Mr Stultz's yard fell down & all the flowers were smashed. Monday he had great flags out, & the streets were gay with music & people going to decorate soldier's graves. Kitty & all the family went away to have fun some where. They miss Lulu very much.

I suppose you have nice runs in M. & enjoy your little room. I long to see it. Do you make your bed like Lucy & Harry?[2] Try it. Then when you keep house for Papa you will know how things should be done.

Dr L[awrence]. says you can eat berries for *breakfast* with a *little* sugar & *no* cream. At night they are bad, & give pains in tummy very often. Did you find your boots in Boston or anywhere? Was your new white dress put away

from moths? I wear a bit of it in my breast & love it when I want my girl.
Can you says "joys" now? I hope so.

With lots of kisses & hopes of a little letter some rainy day I am

your loving old
R. WEE.

X X X X X X X X
X X X X X [X X]³
X X X X X [X X X]

ALS: Houghton Library, Harvard University.
  1. Written to Lulu care of Anna Pratt in Melrose, Massachusetts.
  2. Probably a reference to the *Harry and Lucy* books (1801, 1825) by Maria Edgeworth.
  3. The manuscript is torn here.

To Edward Bok

June 16th [1887]

Mr Bok.¹
Dear Sir.

The item about my father is quite incorrect, the following is the truth.

Mr Alcott is entirely incapable of literary work, & merely amuses himself by looking over his old journals. He dictates nothing, being unable to express his thoughts. I have not been at home for six months, & a nurse attends to my father's wants as he is almost helpless, the right side never having recovered from the severe paralytic shock of four years ago.

He is carried to the carriage for a drive once a week, but spends most of his time on a couch sleeping or looking over books. His faculties are still bright, & he enjoys short calls from friends, or the society of his family.

Nothing of his will be published till a Life may appear later, with extracts from his papers & diaries, which will be bequeathed to his daughters for such use as they may think proper.

He remembers perfectly his old friends, & loves to hear about them. Keeps his twelve books near him & often points out how many were written after he was seventy.² Sixty volumes of journals, kept since he was a boy, form a remarkable record of the events of his time, & his intercourse with the best men & women of America.³

He is usually cheerful & serene, but now & then weary in mind & body,

& anxious to "go up", as he expresses the very natural desire for freedom after nearly 88 years of a very changeful life. He still lives on his simple diet, as he has done for half a century, drinks nothing but water, & attributes his good health & present remarkable vigor to his vegetarian fare & temperance in all things.

Of myself there is nothing of public interest to tell, as the life of an invalid is best left to silence.

Mr Alcott desires his regards to the friends who still remember him.

Yrs truly

L. M. ALCOTT.

Dunreath Place, Roxbury Mass.

ALS: Jerome Library, Bowling Green State University.
1. Edward William Bok, writer of a syndicated literary column, in 1889 became editor of the *Ladies' Home Journal.*
2. LMA is including in her count such works as Elizabeth Palmer Peabody's *Record of a School* (1835), *Conversations with Children on the Gospels* (1836–1837), which was written with Peabody's assistance, and the reports of the Concord School Committee, which Bronson wrote. Bronson's actual book-length publications at this time were: *Emerson* (1865), *Tablets* (1868), *Concord Days* (1872), *Table Talk* (1877), *New Connecticut. An Autobiographical Poem* (1881), and *Sonnets and Canzonets* (1882), the last four being published after he was seventy.
3. Bronson kept a journal, or Diary, as he called it, from 1826 until 1882, the year of his stroke. Located today at Harvard's Houghton Library, this work comprises more than fifty manuscript volumes and a number of bound volumes of correspondence and scrapbooks. The Diary, which contains approximately five million words, has been published in a highly selected edition by Odell Shepard (*The Journals of Bronson Alcott,* ed. Odell Shepard [Boston: Little, Brown, 1938]). Individual Diary volumes have been edited in full: Joel Myerson, "Bronson Alcott's 'Journal for 1836,' " *Studies in the American Renaissance 1978,* ed. Joel Myerson (Boston: Twayne, 1978), pp. 17–104, and "Bronson Alcott's 'Scripture for 1840,' " *ESQ: A Journal of the American Renaissance* 20 (4th Quarter 1974): 236–259; and Larry Carlson, "Bronson Alcott's 'Journal for 1837,' " *Studies in the American Renaissance 1981* and *1982,* ed. Joel Myerson (Boston: Twayne, 1981, 1982), pp. 27–132, 53–167. Only six years (including, unfortunately, those of the Fruitlands experiment) are unaccounted for.

To Mary Mapes Dodge

June 23rd [1887]

Dear Mrs Dodge.

Yours just came. Pray cut up the "Ivy Spray" to suit your space. I'll trust you to arrange it prettily even with some of its leaves gone.

"Pansies" is in the hands of the printer, & you shall have the proof as soon as I get it. It is, I think, about fifty pages of note paper like that on which

"Ivy" is written. This also can be cut, & I will do what I can when it comes to me. Writing for a book I let my pen go & so it may be too long for you.

It takes eight of my pages to make one of St N. I think.

"Poppies & Wheat" is not done, & I cannot try to finish it now, as I am just off to Concord & Princeton, & have no time. An hour a day is my limit now, so I accomplish very little, & long to rebel, but dare not.

If Pansies is too long, I have a fairy tale of "Princes & Pansies"[1] ready for Lulu's Library all corrected & illustrated I think. It is *shorter* & I thought of sending it to you but Mr. N. wanted to get the book ready for Xmas so I did not.

Should you want it write to him & he will send you the proofs I am sure. Please mention that I *wished* it as the other failed. That can be shortened by dropping the introduction. It is now called "The Flower's Story," but the "Princes & Pansies" is the tale "Ladies Delight" tells the little girl & can go alone.

My address after July 1st is Mt House Princeton Mass. Till then Concord, as we go thither Sat. for a week. Hope you will enjoy your summer.

yrs as ever   L. M. A.

ALS: Wilkinson Collection of Mary Mapes Dodge, Princeton University Library.
        1. "Princes and Pansies" was incorporated into "The Flower's Story" in the second volume of *Lulu's Library, The Frost King*, published by Roberts Brothers in mid-October 1887.

To John Pratt Alcott

Monday a.m.
[27 June 1887]

Dear John.

As soon as you get this go to Mr Sewall's office or to his house & talk it over, as no time is to be lost. Tell him if I must sign the will before a *justice* I must have it here before *Friday*. If that is not necessary, & I dont think it is, I can do it at P.[1] with two or *three* witnesses? Be sure & let me know as soon as *possible*, & make dear old Sam understand what it all means. Be sure T. N. is right about its being necessary. Also as soon as you are legally mine you must make *your* Will, but what you will do for children to take the copyrights if you die after me I dont see. Ask T. N. They ought to go to F. & Mum. You are to share with them you know & Lulu. Bless you, my son,   yr MUM.

ALS: Louisa May Alcott Collection, Barrett Library, University of Virginia Library. Since LMA was planning to leave Concord for vacation on 1 July, this letter must have been written on the preceding Monday.

    1. LMA spent eight weeks during the summer vacationing in Princeton, Massachusetts.

To Thomas Niles

Tuesday.
[28 June 1887]

Dear Mr. Niles.

    Is it too late to put this Dedication into Lulu's Library? The tales were mostly written for E. E. & I think it would please her to be so remembered.[1]

    Judge Brook has settled the adoption, & John Sewall Pratt is now my "legal son."[2] A very easy process. I think I'll take a few more nice boys as mine. Cant have too much of a good thing.

    Judge B. did not know much about copyrights, but said we had no state law, only a U.S. law, & under that he was not *sure* that an *adopted* child could use the copyrights.

    Who is your lawyer? There are men who are posted on this point, & will know about that & the name. Do let us be sure if we can.

    Has Mrs Dodge sent to you for the "Flower's Story" out of L. L.?[3] She wanted a short one as one of the three months left open in St N. for this year is free, & my other tale too long for a single number. I told her she could use that tale if you liked as it was all ready.

    I have had no proof of "Pansies" yet. After Friday direct M. W. Bullard Mountain House Mt. Wachusett, Mass.

    Till then care B. F. Wheeler Concord Mass.

    If John should die after me & unmarried what can he do about the copyrights? Adopt a child I suppose. Fred may have provided a few by that time. What a funny muddle a little money makes!

    I'm doing nicely & hope to come home almost as good as new.

Yrs truly L. M. A.

ALS: Louisa May Alcott Collection, Barrett Library, University of Virginia Library. Printed: *LASC*, p. 381. Since LMA was planning to leave Concord for vacation on 1 July, this letter must have been written on the preceding Tuesday.

    1. Volume 2 of *Lulu's Library* contained reprints from LMA's first book, *Flower Fables*, originally narrated to Ellen Emerson; hence, the new volume was appropriately dedicated to her.

    2. In June, LMA legally adopted John, who changed his name to John Sewall Pratt

Alcott, and gave $25,000 apiece to John and his brother. On 10 July, she signed her will, which left all her copyrights to John, who was to divide the income among his mother, brother, Lulu, and himself.

3. "The Flower's Story" was included in Volume 2 of *Lulu's Library* but not in *St. Nicholas*.

To Frederick Pratt and John Pratt Alcott

[10 July 1887]

My Dearest Boys: —

I have tried to spare you any probable future trouble which may arise from complications in regard to my money.

If my wishes seem not unwise or impossible, I know you *will* respect and carry them out.

Should conditions now unforeseen arise, I leave it to your judgment to arrange otherwise, believing the living can often judge better than any fore-sight of another "gone before."

And my dearest boys, pray continue to be near each other, and live in harmony and good brotherhood, for the sake of

MOTHER.

MS: Unlocated; typescript copy at Louisa May Alcott Collection, Barrett Library, University of Virginia Library, enclosed with a copy of LMA's will.

To Lulu Nieriker

[13 July 1887]

My Darling. [1]

Now I am better I shall write to my Lulu & tell her some little things she may like to hear.

It is lovely today, & I went out at 7 & laid on a hay rack in the orchard & saw the world wake up. Men were mowing in the great fields, & lots of cows, red & white, feeding all over the great green valley. A wee bird sat on the wall & chirped, he was very small & wore a little grey coat & a white vest. It was a baby bird, & the little Papa & Mama were very busy giving him his "ninny" of flies & worms. He was a greedy little chap & ate & ate, till I counted 18 times that good Mamma had fed him. Then he cuddled

317

down on the warm stone wall & seemed to take a nap while the Papa & Mama sat on a branch close by & sung a soft song to thier baby. It was very pretty.

Then a squirrel without any tail came & peeped at me. He was very funny, & looked rather silly with no fine tail to sit under. I guess the black cat bit it off. We have five pussies round here. A big yellow, & a black, & a white Mama, & two kits one grey & one speckled. Very cunning. The grey one is the pet of a sick old man, & when he lies in his hammock she sits on his breast, & runs up the tree & is very kind to him.

Just now a great barge with six horses came up to the hotel full of children. They all tumbled out & went climbing up the Mt with thier baskets for a picnic on the top. They look very gay & will have a fine time. I wish I saw a little curly girl in a blue dress & hat among them. I should fly out & grab her & give her *hundreds* of kisses. Her picture hangs over my table, & another one of her at the foot of the bed, so I see her all the time & think about her a g[reat] deal. Oh — here come [manuscript torn] more barges, all "bust[manuscript torn] boys & girls singing! Such [manuscript torn]

Annah says you liked your bag. I'm glad. I have another s'prise for by & by. Dont trouble about writing to me. Wait till some rainy day when you cant do anything else. I love to get em, but it is better for my girl to run & play while she can. I love to think of her so well & happy with "dood Annah". Kiss her for me. Yr R. WEE.

ALS: Houghton Library, Harvard University. The manuscript is torn; missing words or letters are supplied in brackets. The date is taken from the postmark.
    1. Written to Lulu care of Anna Pratt in Melrose.

To Thomas Niles

Dear Mr Niles.
    I send two more stories, & hope to bring the rest when I come Sept. 1st.[1]

This makes six. I can have four more if they are needed or stop with eight. I find if I work without my glasses my head is not so soon tired, so I scribble away "going it blind" so to speak, & my Ms. is worse than ever. But the amiable type setters seem to make out so I will continue to scrawl, & get done.

Please let me know how these mss. boil down, as some are longer than my tales usually are.

I am better in this fine air, but still have to live on my prison fare. Hope by another month to be able to look at bread & butter, & nibble at a peach.

John has had a nice quiet time & says he feels quite set up. Wants to come for his other week by & by. Princeton air is a wonderful restorative & all who come revive.

Hope you are alive after the hot weather. I hear it was awful. We know little about it on our cool hill side.

Yrs truly
L. M. A.

Aug. 7th [1887]

ALS: Fruitlands Museums, Harvard, Massachusetts.
    1. Probably for *A Garland for Girls*.

To Lulu Nieriker

[1 September 1887]

Dear Lu.[1]

I have been meaning to write you ever since I saw you, but have been rather poorly & had nothing to tell.

Now I have a sad tale. As I sit at my window I have just seen Johnny, the big boy opposite, torment one of his little sisters so cruelly that I had to open the window & tell him to stop! He took her head between his knees, pulled up her clothes & spanked her, then held her up by her legs & all her "petties" fell over & I could see her legs & "bottie". She screamed & tried to get away, but he dragged her round by the legs & slapped her. Then he & Kitty put her on a board & lugged her about & dropped her with a bang that hurt her very much. Kitty was as bad as the boy, & I was so disgusted with them I said, "Stop hurting that child or I will come over & tell your mother." Then they ran away round the house taking the poor little girl with them & I heard her scream, & just now she went crying into the house all dirty & hurt, & the bad boy threw stones after her. Isn't that a sad tale? When you come to see me I shall not let you play with those rude children,

319

& you can tell them why. You would have been *boiling* with anger to see it,
& when I spoke the boy made faces & said something saucy to me.

All the kits are gone. So many fleas they had to be killed. I am better
today after my baths & meat, & hope to do well. Come & see me some time.
X X X X X.

Love to all AH WEE.

P.S. Tell Ah Nah I sent the *keys to John today*. He may forget em as he
was out when Dr L. left em at the store.

As soon as I am able we will see about the tricycle if you let Susie curl your hair
without any fuss. If not you will have to wait till you do. So be a good dear & look
nice & keep the pretty *Mama* curls.

ALS: Houghton Library, Harvard University. The date is taken from the postmark.
    1. Written to Lulu care of Anna Pratt in Melrose.

To Ellen Emerson

Dear Ellen.

I have ventured to dedicate this little book to you in memory of the
happy old times when the stories were told to you & May & Lizzie & some
other play mates.[1]

We believed in fairies then, & I think we still do though our good &
helpful spirits bear less fanciful names & shapes now.

The earlier tales you will remember in spite of some pruning of too plen-
tiful adjectives; the later ones were told to Lulu who inherits her mother's
love for pen & ink sketches of all kinds.

For the sake of mother & daughter I thought the little book might have
some interest for one who never grows old or forgets those who love her.
Among them is & always will be

her friend
L. M. ALCOTT.

Sept. 24th [1887]

ALS: Houghton Library, Harvard University.
    1. *The Frost King*, Volume 2 of *Lulu's Library* (see 23 June [1887]), was not officially
published until mid-October. This letter accompanied an inscribed copy of the book (Houghton Library, Harvard University).

To Amos Bronson Alcott

Oct. 13th [1887]

Dear Papa.

I have been reading Emerson's Life[1] with great interest & some disappointment, for he did *not* keep his word & tell all the long & strong friendship between himself & you. He said he would, but left it undone, & I am *very* sorry, for he understood you best of all men & valued you highly as the few words he does say prove.

I had no idea he had ever been such an invalid when a young man or so poor. It adds much to the interest of the life to know that he did suffer once like other mortals. I should think it would have made him more tender to sick people. That he *was* charitable to the poor *we* know very well, & how beautifully he helped them.

I am going to write my recollections of him & all I owe him.[2] They may be interesting some day, for though I am no M. Fuller I have loved my Master all my life, & know that he did more for me than any man except my old papa, & Parker in another way.

Pity he could not get a little nearer to people & love them more & let them love him. Like Hawthorne he seems like a beautiful soul in prison trying to reach his fellow beings through the bars, & sad because he cannot.

I feel very rich & proud to have had the honor of knowing him, dont you?

How are you now? I am rather better, but cannot walk yet, & so cannot come & see you in your old corner. I told my good Dr Green[3] to come & see you some day when you wanted a little help. He is a very pleasant & excellent man, & wants to know Mr Alcott. He has cured several people whom Dr Wesselhoeft gave up, & is very successful. I think he will cure me if any one can, for he gives little medicine & believes in plain food, water & sensible things. Now good bye, my dear old father. I long to see you, & as soon as I can ride shall come & have "cuddlings" & talk.

Love to good Mrs Hall.

Affectionately your "Lu Weedy".

ALS: Houghton Library, Harvard University.
   1. James Elliot Cabot's *A Memoir of Ralph Waldo Emerson* was published in September 1887.
   2. LMA's earlier printed accounts of Emerson are "Reminiscences of Ralph Waldo Emerson" in the 25 May 1882 *Youth's Companion* and "R. W. Emerson" in the July 1882 *Demorest's Magazine*.
   3. Dr. Milbrey Green specialized in botanic remedies.

To Louisa Caroline Greenwood Bond

[25?] October, 1887.

Dear Auntie, — I always gave Mother the first author's copy of a new book. As her representative on earth, may I send you, with my love, the little book to come out in November?[1]

The tales were told at sixteen to May and her playmates; then are related to May's daughter at five; and for the sake of these two you may care to have them for the little people.

I am still held by the leg, but seem to gain a little, and hope to be up by and by. Slow work, but part of the discipline I need, doubtless; so I take it as well as I can.

You and I won't be able to go to the golden wedding of S. J. May. I have been alone so long I feel as if I'd like to see any one, and be in the good times again. L[izzie]. W[ells]. reports you as "nicely, and sweet as an angel;" so I rejoice, and wish I could say the same of

Your loving   Lu.

MS: Unlocated. Printed: Cheney, pp. 383–384.
    1. According to Cheney, the book is *The Frost King*.

To Mary Mapes Dodge

1 Dunreath Place
Roxbury, Nov. 11th [1887]

Dear Mrs Dodge.

I have sent you an early copy of "A Garland for Girls"; not for any merit of its own but as a little thank-offering for the kind contribution to my charity fund which the last two stories in St N. brought me.[1]

That $250 has put coal, food & clothes into the home where a good woman, deserted by a drunken husband, was trying to keep her little girls safe under her wing, & nearly starving rather than part from them.

It has also given many comforts to a young girl dying of consumption, & made easy the heart of a woman at the hospital by paying rent during her absence.

These "little chores done for my neighbor," as mother used to call them, are my best medicine & amusement during this long year of exile from home at Saint's Rest, where the victims of over work slowly climb back to health. I have been tied to my sofa for three months with stiff knees, but am able to sew read & write a little, & am much better.

I am now beginning a set of tales for Lulu the scene of each laid in a different country. Chinese Lu Sing, Dutch Trudel, Swiss Anton, & Yankee Polly Rush who is always in a hurry, &c. Do you want any of them?[2] I see my name in the list of St N. writers, & as the book wont come out till next year you can have some if you care for them. I hope you are well & life is kind to you, dear woman.

Affectionately yrs L. M. ALCOTT

ALS: Wilkinson Collection of Mary Mapes Dodge, Princeton University Library.
    1. "An Ivy Spray" and "Pansies."
    2. "Lu Sing" appeared in the December 1902 *St. Nicholas;* "Trudel's Siege" in the April 1888 *St. Nicholas* (and reprinted in the third volume of *Lulu's Library* [1889]). "Swiss Anton" and "Yankee Polly Rush" were probably not finished.

To Anna Ricketson

Sat. 16th.
[12? November 1887]

Dear Anna.

Thanks for your kind letter & advice. The compresses I have used for six months & value very much. Grapes I cant try *yet*, as fruit ferments & wont digest. Have tried em.

I was so discouraged after I got home three weeks ago that I sent Dr W[esselhoeft]. off & am trying Dr Greene on Eclectic.[1] Excellent man, 30 years in practice & very successful with stomach troubles.

I felt nicely at the Mts, & hoped to come home quite set up, but my legs took to lumping up & getting stiff. Poor state of blood, so I told Dr W. to tone me up, & he put me on *solid* food every two hours, meat, eggs onions &c.

In a week I was nearly dead, & one leg drawn up & in a bad way. He was rather scared & so was Dr L. & I rose in my despair & said, "I'll try a new man." Dr L. has known Dr G. for years & we had him. He said liquid food for the poor "tummy" & while it rests tonics for nerves & blood.

So for a week I've lived on peptonized milk thickened with a wheat powder, once in three hours, & peace reigns. No pain, no gas, feel satisfied, & am getting an appetite & a little flesh on my cup full of food that does *digest*

323

& so nursing. Besides this I take a phosphite of lime & soda for blood, & bismuth for stomach. Pack legs in warm lobelia all the time, & they are nearly well.

Warm water packs at night & rubbing. So far all goes well & I begin to hope I may be on the right tack. Its time, heaven knows!

I have too nice rooms at Dr L's & Mrs Garfield is my nurse. All are very kind & I try to be happy, but its hard work.

When my blessed Nan is settled at No 10 & you are near to prop her up I shall be quite at rest & bide my time. She is well, & the Lord takes special care of his *own*, but I long so to help & cant! Oh dear!

Hope Mabel is happy.[2] Glad you are coming home, old dear. Wont take less than 2000 for the cat. Try again next year. Will W. kindly see that all is safe before you come & bring *all* the keys. Mr A. has one.

Love to W. Nan will tell you the news. Ever yrs   L.

Pardon writing, have to do it flat.

Love to M. W. & all I know at N.

ALS: Houghton Library, Harvard University. The date is taken from the postmark of 16 November; the Saturday before the sixteenth was the twelfth in 1887.

    1. LMA liked Dr. Green and his attitude: "As a little sunshine I also send this last word of Dr G. He came yesterday & after lancing my boil & saying all was doing well & giving me a fourth kind of tonic to try as the other troubled me, I said, 'Well, now the oyster will go into her shell again.' " The conversation continued: " 'You mustn't call yourself that when you are doing so nicely. Why some of my patients have to lie in bed in dark rooms for months before I can get them where you are. We are going to have some more fine books in a year or two.' 'Do you *honestly* think so?' 'Certainly, why not?' & he looked as much surprised as if I'd denied that I had a nose on my face. 'Oh, I never expect to be well again, only patched up for a while. At 55 one does n't hope for much' " (to Anna Alcott Pratt, 27 November [1887], Houghton Library, Harvard University).

    2. Mabel Allen (see 12 February [1888]).

To Edward Bok

Nov. 26th [1887]

Mr Bok.

Dear Sir.

So much has already been written about L M Alcott that there is very little left to tell.

I do not think of any literary person who knows any thing of my home life or could make it interesting, as it has been for the last ten years the life of an invalid.

Miss Whiting[1] is a very excellent young journalist but when she writes of women she, like most of her sex, is apt to gush & see these friends in the light of angels, which makes a pleasing but untrue portrait.

Mrs Moulton[2] did fairly well as I gave her most of her material, though she added the praise & fancy touches.

Any one can make a sketch from the many already printed but my *home* life I do not desire to see in print, as it is the last scrap of privacy left me.

My father's history is so well known there is nothing left to tell but the end, which is approaching so slowly & beautifully the words "rest & patience" tell it all.

Yrs truly

L. M. ALCOTT.

ALS: Dreer Collection: American Prose Writers, Historical Society of Pennsylvania.
    1. Lilian Whiting later wrote about LMA in her *Women Who Have Ennobled Life* (1915). She also wrote biographies of Louisa Chandler Moulton and Kate Field.
    2. For Moulton's sketch of LMA, see 18 January 1883.

To Anna Alcott Pratt

Nov. 29th [1887]

My Own Dear Nan.

How shall I thank you for all the steps your dear feet have taken, all the hours spent in planning, all the love that kept your tender heart at work for me? I cant, & I wont try now, but it has touched me very much to find myself so loved, so anxiously cared for & remembered.

Even the busy people here had a surprise table for me this a.m. when I came to my parlor. A cake, a vase of flowers, a pot of blooming white chrysanthemums, a scent bottle & quaint pin cushion, paper poppies very pretty, & many kind messages from my neighbors whom I've never seen. Even the servants washed & sent love. Old Hennill came in to kiss me with tears in her eyes, gentle Mary[1] to say, "God bless you, dear," & my good Dr brooded over me so tenderly I could only lay my head on her fat buzzom & cry. I shall *have* to get well to thank em for it all.

But yesterday was lovely! I kept very quiet, had my nap & only woke up to wait a few minutes before thro the rain came the old "loof" with the dear little face at the window & such a waving of hands, bobbing of heads & mass of bundles that it looked as if a dozen excited babes were bouncing round inside. I never knew dear Anna came till long after, Mrs. G.[2] flew to take the *few* things, & I heard Lulu rush up, then, in the bed room she stopped & came in so quietly, looking so pale & excited I hardly knew her for my tornado. She fell upon me & we had our kisses first, then G. came beaming in with the first load, two great boxes of flowers. I revelled in em till they were taken away to make room for load No 2. Table, cushion, picture, the two first lovely & just what I wanted, the last a *great* & *beautiful* surprise that nearly upset me when I saw the little room where our May was so happy, & her name in the corner. It was a sweet idea, sister, & the dear thing hangs over my mantelpiece with the home faces in the fine case below. John's spirit of a vase was a dream of beauty when filled with white roses, & G's pretty cameo urn of violet & white with red full of buds made a fine mantelpiece, when I had set the old candle sticks between. I looked at it all the p.m. & was so happy I forgot to cry.

Well, it was sweet to see Lulu hand forth with pride the gifts of *others* when the 3rd load came up, & say of her own, "Oh that's only a little thing from me." All were pretty, useful & what I wanted, from bed shoes to tiles, from Jack's dainty book to dear Lu's picture of [manuscript breaks off]

So much to say I fear you cant read it.   L.[3]

ALS: Louisa May Alcott Collection, Barrett Library, University of Virginia Library (partial). The last paragraph and signature are in a postscript at the top of the first page.

1. Mary Joy, Dr. Lawrence's sister, was a housemother at Dunreath Place.
2. Her nurse, Mrs. Gardner.
3. Added as a postscript on the first page.

To Laura Hosmer

Dec. 1st [1887]

Dear Laura.

I had such a jolly birthday that I had to rest after it, or I should have answered your message sooner.

Many thanks for the flowers; they were lovely & *well-chosen*. H. knows what he's about.[1] Your box made 7 that came beside two box trees & 3 plants. I had 40 gifts in all. A real shower fell all day & I lay in a bower of roses. Every one was *very* kind, & all the ladies in the house sent some pretty gift tho I have not seen them. I wish you had happened in that day to see my five little tables full. A cake, a sofa table, pictures books, bags, cushions a blue & gold rose jar roses & no end of pretty little duds. I saw no one but

Dr G. & he was amused to see how my "quiet day" turned out. Said next Nov. his call would *not* be professional. I am *doing well in all ways,* walk a little, am hungry, but dont eat yet, sleep well, & now I see *no one* (not even my Annie), the entire quiet keeps my mind still & I digest & absorb my 2 quarts of milk nicely & my stomach is at peace. Muscles firmer tho no flesh as yet, better color, & brain less congested. One side is worse than the other owing to the blow I had when A. Mc Clure & I smashed up.[2]

So I take heart & hope & keep still, sew read write letters & dawdle. Dull but works well.

Love to the dear boy, glad he is better. Also love to F. & baby & H. H.

Yrs ever L

I told A.[3] to take my new book[4] to you with love for Xmas. Cant go shopping now.

ALS: Louisa May Alcott Collection, Barrett Library, University of Virginia Library. The date is taken from the postmark.
1. Probably Laura's husband, Henry.
2. See *LMA,* pp. 335–336, for more information on this accident, which occurred when LMA's horse ran away with her.
3. Probably Anna Pratt.
4. *A Garland for Girls.*

To Mary Mapes Dodge

Dec. 22ond [1887]

Dear Mrs Dodge.

I send you the story your assistant editor asked for.[1] As it is needed at once I do not delay to copy it, for I can only write an hour a day & do very little.

You are used to my wild Mss. & will be able to read it. I meant to have sent the Chinese tale,[2] but this was nearly done, & so it goes, as it does not matter where we begin.

Do you have the bound volumes of St N. now?

If so will you kindly send me the one for last year. My Lulu adores the dear book, & has worn out the old ones.[3] I want to give it her for New Year if it is to be had. Any time will do, however.

I hope you are well & full of the peace work well done gives the happy doer.

I mend slowly but surely, & my good Dr. says my best work is yet to come. I will be content with health if I can get it.

With all good wishes,

yrs affectionately

L. M. A.

ALS: Special Collections, Harold B. Lee Library, Brigham Young University. Printed: Cheney, p. 384 (partial); *LASC*, pp. 374–375.

    1. "Trudel's Siege."

    2. "Lu Sing."

    3. Lulu's fondness for *St. Nicholas* was long-standing. Two years earlier, LMA had written Dodge: "Lulu crushed me lately by saying decidedly, 'On the whole, Aunty Wee, I like St Nitlus more better than your books. Such lots of pishers in it.' I quite agreed with her" (15 December [1885], Wilkinson Collection of Mary Mapes Dodge, Princeton University Library).

To Anna Ricketson

Happy N. Y. tomorrow!

Dec. 31st [1887]

Dear Anna.

Will you please forward this note to Miss N. as I dont know her address.[1] I've thanked her for the shoes which came at last, & put in a little bit of money as a N. Y. gift to the poor soul.

What does she need most? Do you know that at the Helping Hand Society House[2] Carver St. for girls & women a good room & board can be had for 2 or 3.00 a week & a good chance to look out for work?

If rent troubles Miss N. she'd better try some place of this kind, as people know of her needs then & get interested in her. Ladies who know how to help a lady.

If I had a house of my own I'd have N. come for a visit & see what she *could* do & then fix her, if she would let me. A shove in the right way settles the right pin in the right hole & saves lots of trouble.

When I get on *my* pins I'm going D. V. to devote myself to settling poor souls who need a gentle boost in hard times. I'm going to join the Helping Hands & shall then know all about it. Only a dollar to be a member. Mr Hale started it.

How are you, old dear? I send you a N. Y. joke, cost 10 cents. I've got a lot of em I like em so well. No news for W.[3] yet. Love to him. yrs Lu.

ALS: Houghton Library, Harvard University.

1. Miss Norton was one of LMA's charities. LMA had written Anna Ricketson on 19 January [1887] warning not to "give her *all* the money at once, as it was a good deal to trust to one we dont know much about" (Houghton Library, Harvard University).

2. One of the Lend a Hand clubs, charitable institutions established by Edward Everett Hale after the success of his moralistic tale about the benefits of mutual assistance, "Ten Times Ten Is One" (1870).

3. Anna's brother Walton.

To John Pratt Alcott

Jan. 3rd [1888]

Dear Sonny.[1]

Will you hand the enclosed to T[homas]. N[iles].

Many thanks for the sweet book you sent me. The first thing I read was "Let little worries fall to the ground & keep a quiet soul. Leave all to God, he will conduct your life better than you can, so rest serenely in his care."

Madame Guion.[2]

That was a nice little word from my boy to me on N. Year's day, & I read one each a.m. All good.

Now, dear, as soon as you are *legally* John Alcott get my Will from the vault & let S. E. S. change the name, for if I pop off before its done you lose your copyrights, as you are not my heir till the *Alcott* is tagged on to the string which makes John a kite with a long tail.

Among my papers I've found the Alcott coat of arms with John Alcocke's name &c. Mean to have it cut on a fine seal for the last John. We aint proud but its no harm to have our three cock's crowing as they crowed for the Archbishop of Ely, tutor of one of the Henry's sons, & the founder of Jesus College still standing in England in memory of that good & pious man John Alcocke.[3]

We'll see about it after the great *Event* is over.[4] Love to Ped & all his plans.

X X yrs MUM WEE X X

ALS: Louisa May Alcott Collection, Barrett Library, University of Virginia Library.

1. The adoption plan had been completed the previous summer (see [27 June 1887] and [28 June 1887]).

2. The French mystic Madame Guyon (Jeanne-Marie Bouvier de la Motte).

3. Probably John Alcocke, Lord High Chancellor of England under Henry VII, to whom Bronson thought he was related. The Alcott coat of arms has three crowing cocks and the motto *Semper vigilans* (see Cheney, p. 11).

4. Fred would be married on 8 February 1888.

To Anna Ricketson

[5 January 1888]

Dear Anna.

Glad you liked the bottle. It was got at Houghton's with a lot of others.[1] Guess that lot is gone, but Mrs G. is a great hand to find cheap things & she may get more.[2] In any store you can get em for 50 cts.

About Miss N. I'm uncertain.[3] If I *knew* her I could tell how best to help. But she seems rather a shiftless lot. If sick why not go to a hospital? If she cant pay board why not go to C. U. where board is cheap & food also.[4] The Helping Hands is a good thing but they only give *temporary* help & get places. Miss N. might try for work there. Room & board $2.00 a week. No Irish & a good class of girls. Can help about the house for board, & stands a chance of getting sewing.

I'll ask Nan if she dont want some sheets &c. & N. can do em if she wants to. I'd pay her board for the winter if I was sure about her. How is the man? Did you ever ask about him? I've been so humbugged by such girls I'm rather slow to help em when they want to be *alone* & wont take what they most need.

I cant see any one for another month, Dr G begs I wont as I do so well alone. No more hope of the wedding than of going to the moon. Why, my dear, I have no more strength than a baby, & lie half the time doing nothing. Nan will never know how nearly off I've been. Two years for a cure.

It is to be a long job, but I hope for Nan's sake I may come out fit for something. I look about 70 — grey & wrinkled & bent & lame. A hard year; hope the next will be better or end soon for your loving old L. M. A.

ALS: Houghton Library, Harvard University. The date is taken from the postmark.
1. Houghton and Dutton, dry goods merchants with three stores in Boston.
2. Her nurse, Mrs. Gardner.
3. For Miss Norton, see 31 December [1887].
4. Possibly the Union for Christian Work in Jamaica Plain.

To Laura Hosmer

Jan. 13th [1888]

Dear Laura.

Annie sent me your letter & I'll send a line to let you know I'm still "rastling" up the hill with few fall backs now. I've had *the* cold, & come out nicely after two weeks of snuffling & sneezing like other folks.

My good Dr gave me my reward for nine weeks of not seeing Nan by saying yesterday I might drive in & see her & Pa any fine day for ½ an hour, & try how it went.

I was much pleased for it *has* been hard to be so shut up so long. Lulu comes often & is a blooming posy.

I still live on my milk, as it gives me all I need & all I can manage with *entire* ease as yet. Dr G. says I *can* eat bread & meat & oysters, but they wont *nourish* like milk, & that is what I need, & they *may* upset my cranky stomach if I begin yet. So I hold off & take my milk gruel & cups of warm milk every 3 hours & entire peace reigns. I'm up early & trot round my nice rooms, sew, read & write a little, make things & amuse myself in all sorts of quiet ways. Dr L. sends me to sleep after dinner for an hour or so of rest, & then I go till 8, bath rub & bed, sleep well, & feel all right except a fit of blues now & then, which is naughty as I ought to be good & grateful *all* the time.

So sorry to hear about Mrs B. I do hope she will soon be up & round again. She must wear flannel & look out for the chest in her exposed rides. We *cant* have her ill. Lots of love to her & the dear old mother.

Father is very feeble & Dr G. says may slip away at any moment, heart faint & many signs of failure. So I shall say good bye when I see him.

You must perk up, old dear. I wish you had my Milbrey G. I take homeopathic medicine in homeopathic doses, & here I am doing well. Pepsin & Co. forever! Love to all, L.

I drive out 3 times a week when the days are good. You asked in your letter to me. I have had such a cold I havent been able to visit at all till now.

ALS: Louisa May Alcott Collection, Barrett Library, University of Virginia Library.

To John Pratt Alcott

Wed. a.m.
[18 January 1888]

Dear John.

Next time you go to the Vault for my Oct. money will you take out *Dr L's note for 1000* & send, or bring, it to me.[1] The time is up in Oct. but as she cant pay it we will renew it if you will show me how. I dont want the money, & the interest goes towards my bill so its all right. I shall never ask for it, & if I die I want the note destroyed so she need never be called on for the money. *You make note of that* & se[e] its done. She has been so kind to me it would be the right thing to do.

No great hurry only remember when you go. Look up *all* the dividends this time & keep your old Mum's property in order.

X X X X my dear.

R. W[EE].

ALS: Louisa May Alcott Collection, Barrett Library, University of Virginia Library. The date is taken from the postmark.

1. Probably the note for Dr. Rhoda Lawrence's mortgage on the Dunreath Place house (see 28 September [1875]).

To Louisa Caroline Greenwood Bond

February 7 [1888]

Dear Auntie,— My blessed Anna is so busy, and I can do so little to help her, I feel as if I might take upon me the pleasant duty of writing to you.

Father is better, and we are all so grateful, for just now we want all to be bright for our boy.

The end is not far off, but Father rallies wonderfully from each feeble spell, and keeps serene and happy through everything.

I don't ask to keep him now that life is a burden, and am glad to have him go before it becomes a pain. We shall miss the dear old white head and the feeble saint so long our care; but as Anna says, "He will be with Mother." So we shall be happy in the hope of that meeting.

Sunday he seemed very low, and I was allowed to drive in and say "good-by." He knew me and smiled, and kissed "Weedy," as he calls me, and I thought the drowsiness and difficulty of breathing could not last long. But he revived, got up, and seemed so much as usual, I may be able to see him again. It is a great grief that I am not there as I was with Lizzie and Mother, but though much better, the shattered nerves won't bear much yet, and quiet is my only cure.

I sit alone and bless the little pair like a fond old grandmother. You show me how to do it. With love to all,

Yours ever, LU.

MS: Unlocated. Printed: Cheney, pp. 384–385.

To Louisa Caroline Greenwood Bond

Feb. 8th 1888.

Air
"Haste to the Wedding". [1]

Dear Auntie.

I little knew what a sweet surprise was in store for me when I wrote you yesterday.

As I waked this a.m. my good Dr L. came in with the lovely azalea, her round face beaming through the leaves like a full moon.

It was very dear of you to remember me & cheer up my lonely day with such a beautiful guest.

It stands beside me on Marmee's work-table, & reminds me tenderly of her, for it is one of her favorite flowers, & among those used at her funeral was a spray of this which lasted for two weeks afterwards, opening bud after bud in the glass on her table, where lay the dear old "Jos. May" hymn book, & her diary with the pen shut in as she left it when she last wrote there, three days before the end, "The twilight is closing gently about me, & I am going to my rest in the arms of my children."

So you see I love the delicate flower & enjoy it very much.

I can write now, & soon hope to come out & see you for a few minutes, as I drive every fine day, & go to kiss my people once a week for *fifteen minutes*.

Slow climbing, but I dont slip back, so think of my mercies, & sing cheerfully as dear Marmee used to do, "Thus far the Lord has led me on."

your loving Lu.

ALS: Houghton Library, Harvard University.

1. Frederick Pratt was married on 8 February in Wakefield, Massachusetts; see also 8 February 1888, to Laura Hosmer, and 12 February [1888].

To Laura Hosmer

Feb. 8th 1888.

Dear Laura.

As I cant go to the wedding I console myself by writing about it to several friends who, like me, are shut up.

"Everything is lovely," & two happier babes never lived than F. & his J. [1]

333

We didn't expect many gifts as our best friends are poor, & our rich relations rather "nigh," but presents have poured in on both sides, for Jessie is much beloved & her family respected, while Fred is overpowered by the kindness of his mates, his masters, & all who know him.

Roberts Bros. go to the wedding, & each give a gift. T. Niles a marble clock, very elegant, & Mr R. a large picture. The head man said "No fellow had ever been so well treated in the store as Pratt," & he (the man) had been there 20 years. I rather guess "Pratt" will be a partner before long, as Tommy treats him like a son & pets Jack.[2]

There are two large tables of *solid* silver. So much that Pa Cate[3] is to give them a safe to put it in, & has set up a watchdog to guard the treasure mean time. I have seen none of it but hear of a tall water (not ice) pitcher, tea set, 10 doz spoons, forks knives &c. a watch & chain, bracelets, diamond pendant, & every sort of silver thing from a salver to an olive jar. Lots of bric a brac, tall satin screen, piano lamp, desk, coffee table, easel, chairs, china, glass, dainty things for bridal bower & a chest of real linen sheets & shams, hem stitched & belaced fine to see. Friends in Paris sent lace hdkfs &c, & a sick Aunt just home from Europe brings some swell duds for the little bride.

The dress is heavy corded silk (white of course), with pearl embroidery, tulle viel, lilies of the valley, the pendant on a white velvet, & no other jewel. She will look like a rose, & F. will be a landscape in his white matesed[4] silk vest & new suit.

The four maids are in white silk & lace with blush roses. Marion C. is maid of honor,[5] in cream or pale yellow, being dark, & carries jonquils. John is best man, & four ushers see to the guests. All handsome.

They wanted a quiet *home wedding*, but Mr. C. has bought out his partner, & is to build at W.[6] so it was well to be civil to the town folks, & as the church is large all can come. The reception is informal & only for friends, the house being rather small, but very pretty with two parlors full of fine pictures & books, (best sort of furniture *I* think). Laura's studio is full of gifts, & of course a nice supper will be served.

A special car takes out the guests at 5 & back at 9, *with* Mr P. & wife. "No dodging off in the dark as if ashamed," says F. so they will have rooms at one of the B. hotels till next day when they go to N.Y. for two weeks. J. has relations & F. friends there who are expecting them, & they will have a nice time. Luck & happiness go with em!

Annie has a black lace dress over silk, with duchesse lace. Lulu pink silk, white lace & rose buds. So fine! She was to be a little maid, but we thought the excitement bad for her, so she will only be a guest. Good Susie & Julia go to see Mr Fred married, & see to the guests in the two rooms & parlors at Anna's disposal at a neighbor's house close to church. Helen & her flock are going, & can tell about the fun afterward. It is clearing up & all will be pleasant I hope.

Father is very feeble, but rallies wonderfully under Dr G's care. The cold spell was hard on the ill & old. I stood it nicely, & improve every day. Feel like my old self not like a ghost, go out often, & write, & shop, & am so *much* encouraged I could sing all day. Must still be quiet & careful, for blood poisoning & starvation are no jokes. Glad you are better. Love to Mrs B & all.

yrs L. M. A.

P.S. I find I missed this page, so have numbered them all or you wont get through alive.

I enjoy hearing A's account of the jolly doings that I thought you might. Among F's gifts was a set of furniture, $5000, & a promise of all the china he wanted. The boys know fellows at Mc Duffy & Stratton's,[7] & had pretty glass &c. from them. Concord people also sent remembrances. Hart[?] a fine carved oak chair, Helen the easel, (I think) & the girls glass & silver. All very kind.

ALS: Louisa May Alcott Collection, Barrett Library, University of Virginia Library.

1. Jessica Lilian Cate (b. 1862), Fred's bride, to whom he proposed on 1 January 1887. Anna considered her "a gem among girls, delicate, refined, loving, & true-hearted" (to Alfred Whitman, July [1887], Houghton Library, Harvard University). More information on her is in an obituary in the 16 August 1934 *Concord Herald* (clipping, Concord Free Public Library).

2. Both John and Fred Pratt worked for Thomas Niles and Lewis Roberts at Roberts Brothers. Fred rose to advertising manager, and, after Little, Brown bought Roberts Brothers in 1897, joined with another former employee of the firm to establish Hardy, Pratt, and Company. This new firm, which specialized in Molière and Balzac, failed about 1905. For more information, see Thomas Hollis, "Frederick Alcott Pratt," *Memoirs of Members of the Social Circle in Concord: Fifth Series* (Cambridge, Mass.: University Press, 1940), pp. 59–70.

3. Luther Garland Cate, the bride's father.

4. LMA is probably garbling *matelassé*, a raised or embossed fabric.

5. Marion Wolsey Cate, Jessica's sister.

6. Wakefield, Massachusetts, where the bride's family lived.

7. Jones, McDuffy, and Stratton had two stores in Boston specializing in glassware and china.

To Laura Hosmer

Feb. 12th [1888]

Dear Laura.

Our wedding is well over & the young folks in Washington with friends having a good time. Anna, Mrs Vialle & others tell me it was a pretty show in spite of the ugly church & bad gas. Jessie wouldn't let her father spend a lot of money in trying to decorate the big place for half an hour, so it was very plain but let in all who wanted to come & pleased the towns people.

At the house they had a charming reception & a good supper, to judge by the way *some folks* ate. I dont mean Pa B. Oh no! A man & dog guarded the $500 worth of "siller," & after a general kissing, cutting of the bride cake, (pretty Miss Mulford of Cambridge got the ring) & a great deal of praise to the bride & groom, a car load of jolly people went off to B. Mr & Mrs P. Jr. spent the night at a hotel, (two rooms French style,) & at 10 a.m. were seen off N.Y. & W. by the families who met at the depot with flowers, lunch & good bye cuddlings. J. was very pretty in her blue cloth & blush suit, & F. with "my wife's travelling bag," & a long coat full like a prince of the blood. Dr L. said he & John looked so swell & handsome she didn't know em. J. as happy as if he had been the groom, & F. as calm & easy as if *he* had done it all before. The E. service is much longer than ours, but they got through nicely with the two rings, kneeling &c. Hope J. will go next with lovely Mabel Allen for bride.[1] She is all we want for our very best boy, & he is devoted to her now while she visits A. Ricketson.

Anna was a proud & happy woman, & people say looked very handsome in her lace & roses. Lulu in pink was as sober & dignified as if *she* were the matron Ma.

Father fails fast, but suffers no pain, only weakness. The cold which he used to throw off easily is too much for him now, as any little thing would be in his feeble state, & I hope he will slip away soon.[2] We have two nurses, & Anna lots of good friends to help. I go in often for a little while, but am not needed & keep quiet.

Yes, I *can* eat solid food but dont, as the milk gives me all I need with no fear of troubling me. Never know I have a stomach, & am getting strength & flesh fast now. Warm days will finish me off I hope. Glad you are all mending. Love to Mrs B. Yrs L. M. A.

ALS: Louisa May Alcott Collection, Barrett Library, University of Virginia Library.

1. LMA's hopes were not fulfilled: in 1901 John married Mrs. Eunice Plummer Hunting and adopted her son.

2. When LMA visited her father for the last time, she knelt by his bedside and said,

"Father, here is your Louy, what are you thinking of as you lie here so happily?" He answered, taking her hand and pointing upward, with "I am going *up. Come with me,*" to which she replied, "Oh, I wish I could" (Anna Alcott Pratt to Alfred Whitman, 17 February [1888], Houghton Library, Harvard University).

To Maria S. Porter

[4? March 1888]

Dear Mrs. Porter, — Thanks for the picture. I am very glad to have it. No philosophy is needed for the impending event. I shall be glad when the dear old man falls asleep after his long & innocent life.

Sorrow has no place at such times & death is never terrible when it comes as now in the likeness of a friend.

Yrs truly
L. M. A.

P.S. I have another year to spend in my Saint's Rest, & then I am promised twenty years of health. I dont want so many, & have no idea I shall see them. But as I dont live for myself I hold on for others, & shall find time to die some day, I hope.

MS: Unlocated. Printed (both with partial facsimiles): Maria S. Porter, "Recollections of Louisa May Alcott," *New England Magazine* n.s. 6 (March 1892): 19; Maria S. Porter, *Recollections of Louisa May Alcott, John Greenleaf Whittier, and Robert Browning* (N.p.: New England Magazine Corp., 1893), p. 28. Porter says she wrote LMA on 3 March "enclosing a photograph of her sister May, that I found among the old letters of her own. Referring to my meeting with her the day before, I said: — 'I hope you will be able to bear the impending event [Bronson's death] with the same brave philosophy that was yours when your dear mother died.' She received my note on Saturday morning, together with one from her sister [Anna]. Early in the morning she replied to her sister's note, telling of a dull pain and a weight like iron on her head. Later, she wrote me the last words she ever penned; and in the evening came the fatal stroke of apoplexy, followed by unconsciousness."

We have been unable to determine precisely the years
in which the following two letters were written.

To Mrs. Bowles

Concord May 5th [n.y.]

Dear Mrs Bowles.

We were not living in Concord at the time you speak of, & never
heard anything about the event to which you allude.

I dont believe it amounted to much, for Concord is a conservative old
town & the people slow coaches about reform of any kind.

A few black sheep like the Emersons, Alcotts & Thoreaus are the only
come-outers here.

I cant imagine who the "Female Political Party" was. Not natives I'm sure,
for the good ladies nearly died of horror when my blessed mother, with the
blood of all the Mays & Sewalls "a bilin" in her veins, once said at a Bee that
she hoped to live to vote in the Town Hall with her four daughters at her
back.

It embittered many "dishes of tea" that night & we did not hear the last of
it for a long time.

I hope the stout old lady will yet have her wish, & *one* daughter at least
will be there to give her a "boast" & a cheer.

Sorry I cant throw more light, but we sit in darkness here, & Concord
is a classical humbug as the world will find out some day. yrs in haste
L. M. A.

F. B. Sanborn might know something. If I can catch him I will.

ALS: Richards Collection, Special Collections, Boston University Libraries.

To Mr. Rand

Boston Oct. 23rd [n.y.]

My Dear Mr Rand.

I send you herewith the few facts concerning my short hospital experience; a fuller account of which, if needed, can be found in the little book Hospital Sketches, made from letters written at the time.

I enlisted in Dec. 1862, & was nurse in the Union Hotel temporary hospital at Georgetown. Mrs Ropes[1] of Boston was Matron, & I took Miss Hannah Stevenson's place with Miss Julia Kendal.[2] There were about four hundred patients, as many who were too feeble to go on to Washington were left there to die.

We had men from Fredricksburg & Antietam, as well as some from various skirmishes.

The hospital was badly managed, & all the nurses were ill from bad air & food & overwork, as ten women were all we had.

Mrs Ropes died during my stay, & I narrowly escaped with my life after a fever which left me an invalid for the rest of my days. But I never have regretted that brief yet costly experience, "(only two months,)" for all that is best & bravest in the hearts of man & women comes out in times like those, & the courage, loyalty, fortitude & selfsacrifice I saw & learned to love & admire in both Northern & Southern soldiers can never be forgotten.

I have no picture taken about that time but the likeness of the shadow 3 mos after my illness. The one I send is not very good but it is the nearest to the war-times of any I have.

I wish I had a fuller record to offer, but as one who gladly gave her dearest possession, health, to serve the good cause I may perhaps deserve a humble place among the women who did what they could.

Thanking you for the honor,

I am yrs truly
L. M. ALCOTT.

ALS: Special Collections, Boston University Libraries.

1. Hannah Ropes, matron of the Union Hotel Hospital in Georgetown, died there from typhoid pneumonia in January 1863. Information about her and the Georgetown hospital is in *Civil War Nurse: The Diary and Letters of Hannah Ropes*, ed. John R. Brumgardt (Knoxville: University of Tennessee Press, 1980).

2. Julia C. Kendall had accompanied Hannah Ropes in July 1862 to nurse the soldiers at the Union Hotel Hospital.

INDEX OF NAMES

350